Contents

SPIDERING HACKS™

Other resources from O'Reilly

Related titles   Google Hacks   Wireless Hacks

Amazon Hacks   Mac OS X Hacks

eBay Hacks   Windows XP Hacks

TiVo Hacks   Linux Server Hacks

Hacks Series Home   *hacks.oreilly.com* is a community site for developers and power users of all stripes. Readers learn from each other as they share their favorite tips and tools for Mac OS X, Linux, Google, Windows XP, and more.

oreilly.com   *oreilly.com* is more than a complete catalog of O'Reilly books. You'll also find links to news, events, articles, weblogs, sample chapters, and code examples.

 *oreillynet.com* is the essential portal for developers interested in open and emerging technologies, including new platforms, programming languages, and operating systems.

Conferences   O'Reilly & Associates brings diverse innovators together to nurture the ideas that spark revolutionary industries. We specialize in documenting the latest tools and systems, translating the innovator's knowledge into useful skills for those in the trenches. Visit *conferences.oreilly.com* for our upcoming events.

 Safari Bookshelf (*safari.oreilly.com*) is the premier online reference library for programmers and IT professionals. Conduct searches across more than 1,000 books. Subscribers can zero in on answers to time-critical questions in a matter of seconds. Read the books on your Bookshelf from cover to cover or simply flip to the page you need. Try it today with a free trial.

SPIDERING
HACKS™

Kevin Hemenway
and Tara Calishain

O'REILLY®

Beijing · Cambridge · Farnham · Köln · Paris · Sebastopol · Taipei · Tokyo

Spidering Hacks™

by Kevin Hemenway and Tara Calishain

Copyright © 2004 O'Reilly & Associates, Inc. All rights reserved.
Printed in the United States of America.

Published by O'Reilly & Associates, Inc., 1005 Gravenstein Highway North,
Sebastopol, CA 95472.

O'Reilly & Associates books may be purchased for educational, business, or sales pro-
motional use. Online editions are also available for most titles (*safari.oreilly.com*). For
more information, contact our corporate/institutional sales department: (800) 998-9938
or *corporate@oreilly.com*.

Editor:	Rael Dornfest	**Production Editor:**	G. d'Entremont
Series Editor:	Rael Dornfest	**Cover Designer:**	Emma Colby
Executive Editor:	Dale Dougherty	**Interior Designer:**	David Futato

Printing History:

October 2003:   First Edition.

Nutshell Handbook, the Nutshell Handbook logo, and the O'Reilly logo are registered
trademarks of O'Reilly & Associates, Inc. Many of the designations used by
manufacturers and sellers to distinguish their products are claimed as trademarks.
Where those designations appear in this book, and O'Reilly & Associates, Inc. was
aware of a trademark claim, the designations have been printed in caps or initial caps.
The association between the image of a flex scraper and the topic of spidering is a
trademark of O'Reilly & Associates, Inc.

While every precaution has been taken in the preparation of this book, the publisher and
authors assume no responsibility for errors or omissions, or for damages resulting from
the use of the information contained herein.

The trademarks "Hacks Books" and "The Hacks Series," and related trade dress, are
owned by O'Reilly & Associates, Inc., in the United States and other countries, and may
not be used without written permission. All other trademarks are property of their
respective owners.

ISBN: 0-596-00577-6
[C]

Credits

About the Authors

Kevin Hemenway, coauthor of *Mac OS X Hacks* (O'Reilly), is better known as Morbus Iff, the creator of *disobey.com*, which bills itself as "content for the discontented." Publisher and developer of more home cooking than you could ever imagine (like the popular open source aggregator AmphetaDesk, the best-kept gaming secret *Gamegrene.com*, the popular Ghost Sites and Nonsense Network, giggle-inducing articles at the O'Reilly Network, etc.), he has a fondness for expensive bags of beef jerky. Living in Concord, New Hampshire, he can be reached at *morbus@disobey.com*.

Tara Calishain is the editor of the online newsletter ResearchBuzz (*http://www.researchbuzz.com*) and author or coauthor of several books, including the O'Reilly best seller *Google Hacks*. A search engine enthusiast for many years, she began her foray into the world of Perl when Google released its API in April 2002.

Contributors

The following people contributed their hacks, writing, and inspiration to this book:

- Jacek Artymiak (*http://www.artymiak.com*) is a freelance consultant, developer and writer. He's been programming computers since 1986, starting with Sinclair ZX Spectrum. His interests include network security, computer graphics and animation, and multimedia. Jacek lives in Lublin, Poland, with his wife Gosia and can be reached at *jacek@artymiak.com*.

- Chris Ball (*http://printf.net*) holds a BSc in Computation from UMIST, England, and works on machine learning problems as a researcher in

Cambridge University's Inference Group. In his spare time, he can be found not answering email and hanging rooks at chess tournaments. You can email him at *chris@printf.net*.

- Paul Bausch (*http://www.onfocus.com*) is a web application developer and the cocreator of Blogger (*http://www.blogger.com*), the popular weblog software. His favorite site to spider is Amazon.com, the subject of his book *Amazon Hacks* (O'Reilly). He's also the coauthor of *We Blog: Publishing Online with Weblogs* (John Wiley & Sons), and he posts thoughts and photos almost daily to his personal weblog: onfocus.

- Erik Benson (*http://www.erikbenson.com*) is the Technical Program Manager of Personalized Merchandizing at Amazon.com (*http://www. amazon.com*). He runs All Consuming (*http://www.allconsuming.net*) and has a weblog at *http://www.erikbenson.com*.

- Adam Bregenzer is a programmer in Atlanta, GA. He has been programming for most of his life and is an advocate of Unix-like operating systems. In his free time, he plots to take over the world...and eat Mexican food.

- Daniel Biddle spends far too much time reading abstruse technical documents and solving people's programming problems on IRC at *irc.freenode.net*, where he goes by the nickname `deltab`. He can be contacted at *deltab@osian.net*.

- Sean M. Burke is the author of O'Reilly's *Perl & LWP*, *RTF Pocket Guide*, and many of the articles in the *Best of the Perl Journal* volumes. An active member in the Perl open source community, he is one of CPAN's most prolific module authors and an authority on markup languages. Trained as a linguist, he also develops tools for software internationalization and Native language preservation. He lives in Juneau, Alaska, with his feline overlord, Fang Dynasty.

- Simon Cozens (*http://simon-cozens.org/*) is a Perl programmer and author. He works as a research programmer for Kasei, and has released more than 50 Perl modules. His books include *Beginning Perl*, *Extending and Embedding Perl*, and the forthcoming second edition of *Advanced Perl Programming*. He also maintains the Perl.com (*http://www.perl.com/*) site for O'Reilly. When not stuck in front of a computer, he enjoys making music, playing the Japanese game of Go, and teaching at his local church.

- Rael Dornfest (*http://www.raelity.org*) assesses, experiments, programs, writes, and edits for O'Reilly & Associates. He has edited, coauthored, and contributed to various O'Reilly books. He is program chair for the O'Reilly Emerging Technology Conference. In his copious free time,

Rael develops bits and bobs of freeware, including the Blosxom (*http://www.blosxom.com*) weblog application, and maintains his raelity bytes weblog.

- William Eastler is a freelance web developer and lover of all things Perl. He owns MonkeyMind (*http://www.monkeymind.net*), a decentralized web development company, and he is currently fighting through a mechanical engineering degree after a long absence from school. In his spare time, he enjoys ice dancing, reading, thinking up new inventions, and making offerings of Perl code to the unholy lord Morbus Iff.

- Scott Fallin is a freelance programmer and systems administrator. He is an avid, amateur Artificial Intelligence enthusiast who has thus far failed to achieve the grail of a sentient laptop. Scott believes in nothing if not tomorrow and a tight while loop.

- Ben Hammersley (*http://www.benhammersley.com*) is a writer, journalist, and gentleman adventurer of the most English sort. Living in Florence, Italy, with three hunting dogs and a novelist wife, Ben is failing to develop an opium habit. Nevertheless, his addled rants can be read at *http://www.benhammersley.com*. Or, abandon yourself to his email whims by writing to *ben@benhammersley.com*.

- David Landgren grew up in Australia and moved to France in 1990. He started using Perl 4.019 when awk was no longer sufficient to cope with the things he was trying to accomplish. Since then, he has used, or uses, Perl to do many things, including server and database management, security auditing, document conversion, text processing, typography, reporting, IRC bots, web sites, and more. In 1999, he founded the Paris Perl Mongers, and in 2003 he helped organize the YAPC::Europe conference in Paris. He currently works at a large French human resources firm, where he likes to go by the title of IT Operations Manager. He can be contacted at *david@landgren.net*.

- Andy Lester (*http://petdance.com*) has been a professional programmer for 17 years and a Perl evangelist for a decade. He's the lead developer for *WWW::Mechanize* [Hack #21] and author or maintainer of a dozen other CPAN modules. His latest undertaking is the Phalanx project (*http://qa.perl.org*), devoted to improving the test suites of Perl and CPAN as a stepping stone to Perl 6. By day, he manages programmers for Follett Library Resources (*http://www.titlewave.com*) in McHenry, Illinois, where he lives with his wife Amy and 2-year-old daughter Quinn.

- James Linden (*http://www.kodekrash.com*) has more than 10 years of programming experience, spanning several mainstream languages. He is the chief technology officer of Ticluse Teknologi, a development firm specializing in library and government solutions, as well as the information systems consultant for CMM Concepts, a marketing agency specializing in telecommunications. An aficionado of information-sharing systems, James volunteers quite a bit of time to projects designed to disseminate ebooks and other materials that are part of the public domain.

- Niall Kennedy (*http://niallkennedy.com*) is a Sun Certified Programmer for the Java 2 Platform living and working in San Francisco, California. He has employed spiders since 1995 to gather, relate, and verify large data sets for statistical analysis. He is on a constant search for algorithmic solutions to mundane problems that will help liberate today's information workers. Niall is currently employed at Callan Associates (*http://www.callan.com*) and has helped build both PriceGrabber.com (*http://www.pricegrabber.com*) and the American Express Small Business Network (*http://open.americanexpress.com*).

- l.m.orchard (*http://www.decafbad.com*) wants to be a computer scientist when he grows up, having decided so in second grade before it was cool. His sporadic ramblings and occasionally working code can be found at his 0xDECAFBAD wiki/weblog. Offers for free coffee (fully caffeinated or better, please) can be sent to *deus_x@pobox.com*. l.m.orchard lives in Ann Arbor, Michigan, with two spotted cats and a very cute, very patient girl.

- Sean B. Palmer (*http://infomesh.net/sbp/*) is an interdisciplinary holisticist with a predilection for phenomic words. His homepage has the URI *http://infomesh.net/sbp/* most of the time, and his customary Internet dwelling is *irc://irc.freenode.net/sbp*. Shantung wine can't get him drunk. He wonders if he's the first author ever to use the words *ullage*, *twyndyllyngs*, and *wef* in an autobiography. Since he wasn't allowed to read the other biographies in this book before publication, he couldn't make any funny jokes about the people, which is what he normally does in these things. Pseudorandom quote: "Þe snawe snitered ful snart, þat snayped þe wylde"—Sir Gawain, author or authoress unknown. He feels love in nature, harmony in prose. I'd like to slip out of third person and thank Melissa, Aaron, Morb, Stuart, and my family. Thanks!

- Ron Pacheco is a software engineer and educator who lives in New England with his wife and two boys. His career has been a combination of university teaching, corporate employment, and private consulting. His favorite binary is */usr/bin/perl*; a Perl programmer for over 10 years, he uses it almost daily because *it gets stuff done!* Ron can be contacted via email at *ron@pacheco.net*.

- Dean Peters is a graying code-monkey who by day is a mild-mannered IIS/.NET programmer, but by night becomes a not-so-evil Linux genius as he develops software and articles for his blogs, *http://HealYourChurchWebSite.com* and *http://blogs4God.com*.

- Richard Rose began life at an early age and rapidly started absorbing information, finding that he liked the taste of information relating to computers the best. He has since feasted upon information from the University of Bristol, England, where he earned a BSc with Honors. He lives in Bristol but currently does not work, and he will be returned for store credit as soon as somebody can find the receipt. Richard writes programs for the intellectual challenge. He also turns his hand to system administration and has done the obligatory time in tech support. For fun, he juggles, does close-up magic, and plays the guitar badly. He can also be found on IRC, where he currently is a network operator known as rik on the Open and Free Technology Community (*irc.oftc.net*).

- Mads Toftum is a longtime Perl hacker and Apache abuser who has been working in the ISP business since 1995. He spends way too much of his spare time playing with Unix, Apache, OpenSSL, and other security-related tools. At times, he can be found in the kitchen inventing new dishes or trying out new ideas from his ever-growing collection of cookbooks. He can be reached at *ora@toftum.org*.

- Iain Truskett (*http://iain.truskett.id.au*) created and maintains the Perl Books site (*http://books.perl.org*) and a dozen modules on CPAN, including *WWW::Yahoo::Groups* [Hack #44].

- Eric Vitiello is the owner of Perceive Designs (*http://www.perceive.net*), a web design and programming firm located in Louisville, Kentucky. He likes to write database-driven code in a variety of languages, entertain his children, and make wine from various fruits. Sometimes, he even gets to leave his house. You can contact him at *eric@perceive.net*.

Acknowledgments

Attempting to write a 300+ page book in two months (and failing) is a monumental effort, and if it weren't for a number of spirits (of both the physical and imbibed), we'd be much worse off.

Kevin. Thanks to all the impatient emails encouraging me to finish the book so I could work on AmphetaDesk, to Rich and Ken for being my scapegoats ("well, hey, at least I'm not *that* late"), and to all the folks on IRC who swore not to tell Rael I was goofing off...you're not half as worthless as I made you out to be. To Bruce, for making it easier to serve in heav'n than reign in hell, and to Neil for the days of enjoyment with *The Sandman,* along with a reiteration I knowingly reverse.

Tara. Kevin's been an excellent coauthor to work with on this book. Thanks, Kev. My family has been their usual incredibly patient selves as I worked on this book. Thanks, family. A lot of this book has been the work of some great contributors. They had good ideas, they had fun applications, and they had amusing comments in their code. A big thanks to all of them who took the time and effort to help us.

And thank you for reading.

Preface

When the Web began, it was a pretty small place. It didn't take much to keep abreast of new sites, and with subject indexes like the fledgling Yahoo! and NCSA's "What's New" page, you could actually give keeping up with newly added pages the old college try.

Now, even the biggest search engines—yes, even Google—admit they don't index the entire Web. It's simply not possible. At the same time, the Web is more compelling than ever. More information is being put online at a faster clip—be it up-to-the-minute data or large collections of old materials finding an online home. The Web is more browsable, more searchable, and more useful than it ever was when it was still small. That said, we, its users, can only go so fast when searching, processing, and taking in information.

Thankfully, spidering allows us to bring a bit of sanity to the wealth of information available. *Spidering* is the process of automating the grabbing and sifting of information on the Web, saving us the trouble of having to browse it all manually. Spiders range in complexity from the simplest script to grab the latest weather information from a web page, to the armies of complex spiders working in concert with one another, searching, cataloging, and indexing the Web's more than three billion resources for a search engine like Google.

This book teaches you the methodologies and algorithms behind spiders and the variety of ways that spiders can be used. Hopefully, it will inspire you to come up with some useful spiders of your own.

Why Spidering Hacks?

The term *hacking* has a bad reputation in the press. They use it to refer to someone who breaks into systems or wreaks havoc with computers as their weapon. Among people who write code, though, the term *hack* refers to a "quick-n-dirty" solution to a problem or a clever way to get something done. And the term *hacker* is taken very much as a compliment, referring to someone as being *creative*, having the technical chops to get things done. The Hacks series is an attempt the reclaim the word, document the ways people are hacking (in a good way), and pass the hacker ethic of creative participation on to the uninitiated. Seeing how others approach systems and problems is often the quickest way to learning about a new technology.

Spidering Hacks is about coming up with easier, more automated ways of performing everyday tasks and gathering information. Yes, there are legal issues to consider, and we address them in this book before delving into any code whatsoever. Likewise, there are many right and wrong ways to scrape and compile information; the *best practices* in this book create wholesome spiders, as opposed to harmful or out-of-control automatons.

How This Book Is Organized

There are several facets of spidering: searching for and finding the information, gleaning and gathering, repurposing and repackaging, and sharing it with peers. On the flip side, there's also ensuring that your own site's information is spider-friendly. We've divided this book into six parts:

Chapter 1, *Walking Softly*

Before setting out, it behooves you to make sure you understand all the basics, philosophies, considerations, and issues. This chapter is an overview of all you should know before you build and unleash your spiders on the world.

Chapter 2, *Assembling a Toolbox*

The most useful tools in your spidering toolbox are often those you didn't have to write yourself. There are modules galore, written by prominent members of the programming community and free for borrowing, repurposing, and using as a foundation for your own work. This chapter introduces you to the tools you'll need to program for the Web, spidering and scraping in the most efficient and appropriate manner possible.

Chapter 3, *Collecting Media Files*

Hey, nobody lives by text alone. We'll show you some great resources for media files and some cool ways to go about getting them. From current comic strips to old movies from the Library of Congress, there are some wonderful finds for your media library.

Chapter 4, *Gleaning Data from Databases*

Collections of data are going online at an unbelievable pace. While getting just the data you want isn't as easy as just scraping some words off a web page, we'll show you how to get to just the information you're after, combine it with data from other sites, and repurpose it in just the way you need.

Chapter 5, *Maintaining Your Collections*

Oh, the Web is always a-changin'. We'll show you how to keep your data current, mirror collections to your local hard drive, and schedule your spiders to run on a regular basis.

Chapter 6, *Giving Back to the World*

Maybe you're just as interested in *being spidered* as spidering. Perhaps you have a collection others might find useful. We'll show you how to share your own data in ways that make it easier for those downstream to spider you—avoiding many of the headaches we discuss in this book!

How to Use This Book

You can read the book from cover to cover if you like, but you might be better served by picking an interesting item from the table of contents and just diving in.

If you're relatively new to Perl or spidering, you should consider starting with a few hacks from each progressive chapter. The principles in Chapter 1 give you a firm grounding on what we'll be doing, while Chapter 2 acquaints you with the various network and parsing modules of Perl. Chapter 3 starts off nice and easy by simply downloading files, and Chapter 4, the bulk of the book, moves you into the more complicated realm of repurposing information.

Conventions Used in This Book

The following is a list of the typographical conventions used in this book:

Italic

Used to indicate new terms, URLs, filenames, file extensions, directories, program names, and, of course, for emphasis. For example, a path in the filesystem will appear as */Developer/Applications*.

Constant width

Used to show code examples, anything that might be typed from the keyboard, the contents of files, and the output from commands.

Constant width italic

Used in examples and tables to show text that should be replaced with your own user-supplied values.

Color

The second color is used to indicate a cross-reference within the text, and occasionally to help keep the author awake during late-night writing binges.

You should pay special attention to notes set apart from the text with the following icons:

This is a tip, suggestion, or general note. It contains useful supplementary information about the topic at hand.

This is a warning or note of caution. When you see one of these, your safety, privacy, or money might be in jeopardy.

The thermometer icons, found next to each hack, indicate the relative complexity of the hack:

 beginner   moderate   expert

How to Contact Us

We have tested and verified the information in this book to the best of our ability, but you may find that features have changed (or even that we have made mistakes!). As a reader of this book, you can help us to improve future editions by sending us your feedback. Please let us know about any errors, inaccuracies, bugs, misleading or confusing statements, and typos that you find anywhere in this book.

Please also let us know what we can do to make this book more useful to you. We take your comments seriously and will try to incorporate reasonable suggestions into future editions. You can write to us at:

O'Reilly & Associates, Inc.
1005 Gravenstein Hwy N.
Sebastopol, CA 95472
(800) 998-9938 (in the U.S. or Canada)
(707) 829-0515 (international/local)
(707) 829-0104 (fax)

To ask technical questions or to comment on the book, send email to:

bookquestions@oreilly.com

For more information about this book and others, see the O'Reilly web site:

http://www.oreilly.com

For details about *Spidering Hacks*, including examples, errata, reviews, and plans for future editions, go to:

http://www.oreilly.com/catalog/spiderhks/

Got a Hack?

To explore Hacks books online or to contribute a hack for future titles, visit:

http://hacks.oreilly.com

## CHAPTER ONE

Walking Softly

Hacks #1–7

With over three billion pages on the Web, serious surfers eventually find themselves asking two questions: where's the good stuff and what can I do with it? Everyone has their own idea of what the "good stuff" is, and most people come up with some creative idea of what to do once they find it. In some corners of the Web, repurposing data in interesting ways is encouraged: it inspires those "Eureka!" moments when unusual information combinations bubble forth unimpeded.

From the Web's standpoint, the utility of universally accessible data has only recently been broached. Once Google opened their search listings via an API (see *Google Hacks*), Amazon.com quickly followed (see *Amazon Hacks*), and both have benefited by the creative utilities that have resulted. In this short and sweet chapter, we'll introduce you to the fine art of scraping and spidering: what they are and aren't, what's most likely allowed and what might create risk, finding alternative avenues to your desired data, and how to reassure—and, indeed, educate—webmasters who spot your automation and wonder what you're up to.

HACK #1 A Crash Course in Spidering and Scraping

A few of the whys and wherefores of spidering and scraping.

There is a wide and ever-increasing variety of computer programs gathering and sifting information, aggregating resources, and comparing data. Humans are just one part of a much larger and automated equation. But despite the variety of programs out there, they all have some basic characteristics in common.

Spiders are programs that traverse the Web, gathering information. If you've ever taken a gander at your own web site's logs, you'll see them peppered with User-Agent names like Googlebot, Scooter, and MSNbot. These are all spiders—or *bots*, as some prefer to call them.

Throughout this book, you'll hear us referring to spiders and scrapers. What's the difference? Broadly speaking, they're both programs that go out on the Internet and grab things. For the purposes of this book, however, it's probably best for you to think of *spiders* as programs that grab entire pages, files, or sets of either, while *scrapers* grab very specific bits of information within these files. For example, one of the spiders [Hack #44] in this book grabs entire collections of Yahoo! Group messages to turn into mailbox files for use by your email application, while one of the scrapers [Hack #76] grabs train schedule information. Spiders follow links, gathering up content, while scrapers pull data from web pages. Spiders and scrapers usually work in concert; you might have a program that uses a spider to follow links but then uses a scraper to gather particular information.

Why Spider?

When learning about a technology or way of using technology, it's always good to ask the big question: why? Why bother to spider? Why take the time to write a spider, make sure it works as expected, get permission from the appropriate site's owner to use it, make it available to others, and spend time maintaining it? Trust us; once you've started using spiders, you'll find no end to the ways and places they can be used to make your online life easier:

Gain automated access to resources
> Sure, you can visit every site you want to keep up with in your web browser every day, but wouldn't it be easier to have a program do it for you, passing on only content that should be of interest to you? Having a spider bring you the results of a favorite Google search can save you a lot of time, energy, and repetitive effort. The more you automate, the more time you can spend having fun with and making use of the data.

Gather information and present it in an alternate format
> Gather marketing research in the form of search engine results and import them into Microsoft Excel for use in presentations or tracking over time [Hack #93]. Grab a copy of your favorite Yahoo! Groups archive in a form your mail program can read just like the contents of any other mailbox [Hack #43]. Keep up with the latest on your favorite sites without actually having to pay them a visit one after another [Hack #81]. Once you have raw data at your disposal, it can be repurposed, repackaged, and reformatted to your heart's content.

Aggregate otherwise disparate data sources
> No web site is an island, but you wouldn't know it, given the difficulty of manually integrating data across various sites. Spidering automates this drudgery, providing a 15,000-foot view of otherwise disparate data. Watch Google results change over time [Hack #93] or combine syndicated

content **[Hack #69]** from multiple weblogs into one RSS feed. Spiders can be trained to aggregate data, both across sources and over time.

Combine the functionalities of sites

There might be a search engine you love, but which doesn't do everything you want. Another fills in some of those gaps, but doesn't fill the need on its own. A spider can bridge the gap between two such resources **[Hack #48]**, querying one and providing that information to another.

Find and gather specific kinds of information

Perhaps what you seek needs to be searched for first. A spider can run web queries on your behalf, filling out forms and sifting through the results **[Hack #51]**.

Perform regular webmaster functions

Let a spider take care of the drudgery of daily webmastering. Have it check your HTML to be sure it is standards-compliant and tidy (*http:// tidy.sourceforge.net/*), that your links aren't broken, or that you're not linking to any prurient content.

> For more detail on spiders, robots, crawlers, and scrapers, visit the Web Robot FAQ at *http://www.robotstxt.org/wc/faq.html*.

Best Practices for You and Your Spider

H A C K
#2

Some rules for the road as you're writing your own well-behaved spider.

In order to make your spider as effective, polite, and useful as possible, there are some general things you'll have to keep in mind as you create them.

Be Liberal in What You Accept

To spider, you must pull information from a web site. To pull information from a web site, you must wade your way through some flavor of tag soup, be it HTML, XML, plain text, or something else entirely. This is an inexact science, to put it mildly. If even one tag or bit of file formatting changes, your spider will probably break, leaving you dataless until such time as you retool. Thankfully, most sites aren't doing huge revamps every six months like they used to, but they still change often enough that you'll have to watch out for this.

To minimize the fragility of your scraping, use as little boundary data as you can when gleaning data from the page. *Boundary data* is the fluff around the actual goodness you want: the tags, superfluous verbiage, spaces, newlines, and such. For example, the title of an average web page looks something like this:

```
<title>This is the title</title>
```

If you're after the title, the boundary data is the <title> and </title> tags.

Monitor your spider's output on a regular basis to make sure it's working as expected [Hack #31], make the appropriate adjustments as soon as possible to avoid losing ground with your data gathering, and design your spider to be as adaptive to site redesigns [Hack #32] as possible.

Don't Limit Your Dataset

Just because you're working with the Web doesn't mean you're restricted to spidering HTML documents. If you're considering only web pages, you're potentially narrowing your dataset arbitrarily. There are images, sounds, movies, PDFs, text files—all worthy of spidering for your collection.

Don't Reinvent the Wheel

While it's tempting to think what you're up to is unique, chances are, someone's already spidered and scraped the same or similar sites, leaving clear footprints in the form of code, raw data, or instructions.

CPAN (*http://www.cpan.org*), the Comprehensive Perl Archive Network, is a treasure trove of Perl modules for programming to the Internet, shuffling through text in search of data, manipulating gleaned datasets—all the functionality you're bound to be building into your spider. And these modules are free to take, use, alter, and augment. Who knows, by the time you finish your spider, perhaps you'll end up with a module or three of your own to pass on to the next guy.

Before you even start coding, check the site to make sure you're not spending an awful lot of effort building something the site already offers. If you want a weather forecast delivered to your email inbox every morning, check your local newspaper's site or sites like weather.com (*http://www.weather.com*) to see if they offer such a service; they probably do. If you want the site's content as an RSS feed and they don't appear to sport that orange "XML" button, try a Google search for it (rss site:example.com (filetype:rss | filetype:xml | filetype:rdf)) or check Syndic8 (*http://www.syndic8.com*) for an original or scraped version.

Then, of course, you can always contact the site owner, asking him if he has a particular service or data format available for public consumption. Your query might just be the one that convinces him that an RSS feed of or web service API to his content is a good idea.

See "Going Beyond the Book" [Hack #100] for more pointers on scraping resources and communities.

Best Practices for You

Just as it is important to follow certain rules when programming your spider, it's important to follow certain rules when designing them as well.

Choose the most structured format available. HTML files are fairly unstructured, focusing more on presentation than on the underlying raw data. Often, sites have more than one flavor of their content available; look or ask for the XHTML or XML version, which are cleaner and more structured file formats. RSS, a simple form of XML, is everywhere.

If you must scrape HTML, do so sparingly. If the information you want is available only embedded in an HTML page, try to find a "Text Only" or "Print this Page" variant; these usually have far less complicated HTML and a higher content-to-presentation markup quotient, and they don't tend to change all that much (by comparison) during site redesigns.

Regardless of what you eventually use as your source data, try to scrape as little HTML surrounding the information you want as possible. You want just enough HTML to uniquely identify the information you desire. The less HTML, the less fragile your spider will be. See "Anatomy of an HTML Page" [Hack #3] for more information.

Use the right tool for the job. Should you scrape the page using regular expressions? Or would a more comprehensive tool like WWW::Mechanize [Hack #22] or HTML::TokeParser [Hack #20] fit the bill better? This depends very much on the data you're after and the crafting of the page's HTML. Is it handcrafted and irregular, or is it tool-built and regular as a bran muffin? Choose the simplest and least fragile method for the job at hand—with an emphasis on the latter.

Don't go where you're not wanted. Your script may be the coolest thing ever, but it doesn't matter if the site you want to spider doesn't allow it. Before you go to all that trouble, make sure that the site doesn't mind being spidered and that you're doing it in such a way that you're having the minimal possible impact on site bandwidth and resources [Hack #16]. For more information on this issue, including possible legal risks, see "Keeping Your Spider Out of Sticky Situations" [Hack #6] and "Respecting robots.txt" [Hack #17].

Choose a good identifier. When you're writing an identifier for your spider, choose one that clearly specifies what the spider does: what information it's intended to scrape and what it's used for. There's no need to write a novel; a sentence will do fine. These identifiers are called User-Agents, and you'll learn how to set them in "Adding HTTP Headers to Your Request" [Hack #11].

Whatever you do, do not use an identifier that impersonates an existing spider, such as Googlebot, or an identifier that's confusingly similar to an existing spider. Not only will your spider get iced, you'll also get into trouble with Google or whoever you're imitating. See "Keeping Your Spider Out of Sticky Situations" [Hack #6] for the possible consequences of playing mimicry games.

Make information on your spider readily available. Put up a web page that provides information about your spider and a contact address. Be sure that it's accessible from your friendly neighborhood search engine. See "Registering Your Spider" [Hack #4] for some ways and places to get the word out about its existence.

Don't demand unlimited site access or support. You may have written the greatest application since Google's PageRank, but it's up to the webmaster to decide if that entitles you to more access to site content or restricted areas. Ask nicely, and don't demand. Share what you're doing; consider giving them the code! After all, you're scraping information from their web site. It's only fair that you share the program that makes use of their information.

Best Practices for Your Spider

When you write your spider, there are some good manners you should follow.

Respect robots.txt. *robots.txt* is a file that lives at the root of a site and tells spiders what they can and cannot access on that server. It can even tell particular spiders to leave the site entirely unseen. Many webmasters use your spider's respect—or lack thereof—for *robots.txt* as a benchmark; if you ignore it, you'll likely be banned. See "Respecting robots.txt" [Hack #17] for detailed guidelines.

> Secondary to the *robots.txt* file is the Robots META tag (*http://www.robotstxt.org/wc/exclusion.html#meta*), which gives indexing instructions to spiders on a page-by-page basis. The Robots META tag protocol is not nearly as universal as *robots.txt*, and fewer spiders respect it.

Go light on the bandwidth. You might love a site's content and want to make the most of it for your application, but that's no reason to be greedy. If your spider tries to slurp up too much content in a short stretch of time—dozens or even hundreds of pages per second—you could hurt both the bandwidth allowances of the site you're scraping and the ability of other visitors to access the site. This is often called *hammering* (as in, "That stupid spider is hammering my site and the page delivery has slowed to a crawl!").

There is no agreement on how quickly spiders can politely access pages. One or two requests per page per second has been proposed by contributors to WebmasterWorld.com.

> WebmasterWorld.com (*http://www.webmasterworld.com*) is an online gathering of search engine enthusiasts and webmasters from all over the world. Many good discussions happen there. The best part about WebmasterWorld.com is that representatives from several search engines and sites participate in the discussions.

Unfortunately, it seems that it's easier to define what's unacceptable than to figure out a proper limit. If you're patient, one or two requests a second is probably fine; beyond that, you run the risk of making somebody mad. Anywhere's walking distance if you have the time; in the same manner, if you're in no rush to retrieve the data, impart that to your spider. Refer to "Respecting Your Scrapee's Bandwidth" [Hack #16] for more information on minimizing the amount of bandwidth you consume.

Take just enough, and don't take too often. *Overscraping* is, simply, taking more than you need and thus taking more of the site's bandwidth than necessary. If you need a page, take a page. Don't take the entire directory or (heaven help you) the entire site.

This also applies to time. Don't scrape the site any more often than is necessary. If your program will run with data scraped from the site once a day, stick with that. I wouldn't go more than once an hour, unless I absolutely had to (and had permission from the site owner).

HACK #3 Anatomy of an HTML Page

Getting the knack of scraping is more than just code; it takes knowing HTML and other kinds of web page files.

If you're new to spidering, figuring out what to scrape and why is not easy. Relative scraping newbies might try to take too much information, too little, or information that's too likely to change from what they want. If you know how HTML files are structured, however, you'll find it easier to scrape them and zero in on the information you need.

HTML files are just text files with special formatting. And that's just the kind of file you'll spend most of your time scraping, both in this book and in your own spidering adventures. While we'll also be spidering and grabbing multimedia files—images, movies, and audio files—we won't be scraping and parsing them to glean embedded information.

Anatomy of an HTML Page

That's not to say, however, that there aren't about as many ways to format an HTML page as there are pages on the Web. To understand how your spider might be able to find patterns of information on an HTML page, you'll need to start with the basics—the very basics—of how an HTML web page looks, and then get into how the information within the body can be organized.

The core of an HTML page looks like this:

```
<html>
<head>
  <title>
    Title of the page
  </title>
</head>
<body>
  Body of the page
</body>
</html>
```

That's it. 99% of the HTML pages on the Web start out like this. They can get a lot more elaborate but, in the end, this is the core. What does this mean to your spider? It means that there's only one piece of information that's clearly marked by tags, and that's the page title. If all you need is the title, you're in gravy.

But if you need information from the body of a page—say, a headline or a date—you have some detective work ahead of you. Many times, the body of a page has several tables, JavaScript, and other code that obscures what you're truly looking for—all annoyances that have much more to do with formatting information than truly organizing it. But, at the same time, the HTML language contains several standards for organizing data. Some of these standards make the information larger on the page, representing a heading. Some of the standards organize information into lists within the body. If you understand how the standards work, you'll find it easier to pluck the information you want from the heavily coded confines of a web page body.

Header Information with the H Tags

Important information on a page (headlines, subheads, notices, and so forth) are usually noted with an <Hx> tag, where *x* is a number from 1 to 6. An <H1> tag is normally displayed as the largest, as it is highest in the headline hierarchy.

Depending on how the site is using them, you can sometimes get a good summary of information from a site just by scraping the H tags. For example, if you're scraping a news site and you know they always put headlines in <H2> tags and subheads in <H4> tags, you can scrape for that specific markup and get brief story extractions, without having to figure out the rest of the story's coding. In fact, if you know a site always does that, you can scrape the entire site just for those tags, without having to look at the rest of the site's page structure at all.

List Information with Special HTML Tags

Not all web wranglers use specific HTML tags to organize lists; some of them just start new numbered paragraphs. But, for the more meticulous page-builder, there are specific tags for lists.

Ordered lists (lists of information that are automatically numbered) are bounded with <ol> and </ol> tags, and each item within is bounded by <li> and </li> tags. If you're using regular expressions to scrape for information, you can grab everything between <ol> and </ol>, parse each <li></li> element into an array, and go from there. Here's an ordered list:

```
<ol>
  <li>eggs</li>
  <li>milk</li>
  <li>butter</li>
  <li>sugar</li>
</ol>
```

Unordered lists are just like ordered lists, except that they appear in the browser with bullets instead of numbers, and the list is bounded with <ul> </ul> instead of <ol></ol>.

Non-HTML Files

Some non-HTML files are just as nebulous as HTML files, while some are far better defined. Plain *.txt* files, for example (and there are plenty of them available on the Web), have no formatting at all—not even as basic as "this is the title and this is the body." On the other hand, text files are sometimes easier to parse, because they have no HTML code soup to wade through.

At the other extreme are XML (Extensible Markup Language) files. XML's parts are defined more rigidly than HTML. RSS, a syndication format and a simple form of XML, has clearly defined parts in its files for titles, content, links, and additional information. We often work with RSS files in this book; the precisely defined parts are easy to parse and write using Perl. See "Using XML::RSS to Repurpose Everything" [Hack #94].

The first thing you'll need to do when you decide you want to scrape something is determine what kind of file it is. If it's a plain *.txt* file, you won't be able to pinpoint your scraping. If it's an XML file, you'll be able to zoom in on what you want with regular expressions, or use any number of Perl XML modules (such as *XML::Simple*, *XML::RSS*, or *XML::LibXML*).

XHTML: An XML/HTML Hybrid

From our previous examples, you can see that, while there's plenty of formatting code in HTML, organization code is less apparent and far less common in the average web site. But a standard called XHTML (Extensible Hypertext Markup Language) is on the horizon. The idea is that XHTML will eventually replace HTML. Its coding is stricter than HTML, and the code it produces is cleaner.

Registering Your Spider
HACK #4

If you have a spider you're programming or planning on using even a minimal amount, you need to make sure it can be easily identified. The most low-key of spiders can be the subject of lots of attention.

On the Internet, any number of "arms races" are going on at the same time. You know: spammers versus antispammers, file sharers versus non-file sharers, and so on. A lower-key arms race rages between web spiders and webmasters who don't want the attention.

Who might not want to be spidered? Unfortunately, not all spiders are as benevolent as the Googlebot, Google's own indexer. Many spiders go around searching for email addresses to spam. Still others don't abide by the rules of gentle scraping and data access [Hack #2]. Therefore, spiders have gotten to the point where they're viewed with deep suspicion by experienced webmasters.

In fact, it's gotten to the point where, when in doubt, your spider might be blocked. With that in mind, it's important to name your spider wisely, register it with online databases, and make sure it has a reasonably high profile online.

By the way, you might think that your spider is minimal or low-key enough that nobody's going to notice it. That's probably not the case. In fact, sites like Webmaster World (*http://www.webmasterworld.com*) have entire forums devoted to identifying and discussing spiders. Don't think that your spider is going to get ignored just because you're not using a thousand online servers and spidering millions of pages a day.

Naming Your Spider

The first thing you want to do is name your spider. Choose a name that gives some kind of indication of what your spider's about and what it does. Examplebot isn't a good name. NewsImageScraper is better. If you're planning to do a lot of development, consider including a version number (such as NewsImageScraper/1.03).

If you're running several spiders, you might want to consider giving your spider a common name. For example, if Kevin runs different spiders, he might consider giving them a naming convention starting with disobeycom: disobeycomNewsImageScraper, disobeycomCamSpider, disobeycomRSS-feeds, and so on. If you establish your spiders as polite and well behaved, a webmaster who sees a spider named similarly to yours might give it the benefit of the doubt. On the other hand, if you program rude, bandwidth-sucking spiders, giving them similar names makes it easier for webmasters to ban 'em all (which you deserve).

Considering what you're going to name your spider might give you what, at first glance, looks like a clever idea: why not just name your spider after one that already exists? After all, most corners of the web make their resources available to the Googlebot; why not just name your spider Googlebot?

As we noted earlier, this is a bad idea for many reasons, including the fact that the owner of the spider you imitate is likely to ice your spider. There are web sites, like *http://www.iplists.com*, devoted to tracking IP addresses of legitimate spiders. (For example, there's a whole list associated with the legitimate Googlebot spider.) And second, though there isn't much legal precedent addressing fraudulent spiders, Google has already established that they don't take kindly to anyone misappropriating, or even just using without permission, the Google name.

A Web Page About Your Spider

Once you've created a spider, you'll need to register it. But I also believe you should create a web page for it, so a curious and mindful webmaster has to do no more than a quick search to find information. The page should include:

- Its name, as it would appear in the logs (via User-Agent)
- A brief summary of what the spider was intended for and what it does (as well as a link to the resources it provides, if they're publicly available)
- Contact information for the spider's programmer
- Information on what webmasters can do to block the script or make their information more available and usable to the spider if it's preferred

Places to Register Your Spider

Even if you have a web page that describes your spider, be sure to register your spider at the online database spots. Why? Because webmasters might default to searching databases instead of doing web searches for spider names. Furthermore, webmasters might use databases as a basis for deciding which spiders they'll allow on their site. Here are some databases to get you started:

Web Robots Database (http://www.robotstxt.org/wc/active.html)
> Viewable in several different formats. Adding your spider requires filling out a template and emailing to a submission address.

Search engine robots (http://www.jafsoft.com/searchengines/webbots.html)
> User-Agents and spiders organized into different categories—search engine robots, browsers, link checkers, and so on—with a list of "fakers" at the end, including some webmaster commentary.

List of User-Agents (http://www.psychedelix.com/agents.html)
> Divided over several pages and updated often. There's no clear submission process, though there's an email address at the bottom of each page.

The User Agent Database (http://www.icehousedesigns.com/useragents/)
> Almost 300 agents listed, searchable in several different ways. This site provides an email address to which you can submit your spider.

HACK   Preempting Discovery
#5   Rather than await discovery, introduce yourself!

No matter how gentle and polite your spider is, sooner or later you're going to be noticed. Some webmaster's going to see what your spider is up to, and they're going to want some answers. Rather than wait for that to happen, why not take the initiative and make the first contact yourself? Let's look at the ways you can preempt discovery, make the arguments for your spider, and announce it to the world.

Making Contact

If you've written a great spider, why not tell the site about it? For a small site, this is relatively easy and painless: just look for the Feedback, About, or Contact links. For larger sites, though, figuring out whom to contact is more difficult. Try the technical contacts first, and then web feedback contacts. I've found that public relations contacts are usually best to reach last. Although tempting, because it's usually easy to find their addresses, PR folk like to concentrate on dealing with press people (which you're probably not) and they probably won't know enough programming to understand your request. (PR people, this isn't meant pejoratively. We still love you. Keep helping us promote O'Reilly books. Kiss, kiss.)

If you absolutely can't find anyone to reach out to, try these three steps:

1. Many sites, especially technical ones, have employees with weblogs. See if you can find them via a Google search. For example, if you're looking for Yahoo! employees, the search "work for yahoo" (weblog | blog) does nicely. Sometimes, you can contact these people and let them know what you're doing, and they can either pass your email to some-one who can approve it, or give you some other feedback.

2. 99.9% of the time, an email to *webmaster@* will work (e.g., *webmaster@example.com*). But it's not always guaranteed that anyone reads this email more than once a month, if at all.

3. If you're absolutely desperate, you can't find email addresses or contact information anywhere on the site, and your emails to *webmaster@* have bounced, try looking up the domain registration at *http://www.whois.org* or a similar domain lookup site. Most of the time, you'll find a contact email at this address, but again, there's no guarantee that anyone checks it, or even that it's still active. And remember, this works only for top-level domain information. In other words, you might be able to get the contact information for *www.example.com* but not for *www.example.com/resource/*.

Making the Arguments for Your Spider

Now that you have a contact address, give a line of reasoning for your spi-der. If you can clearly describe what your spider's all about, great. But it may get to the point where you have to code up an example to show to the web-master. If the person you're talking to isn't Perl-savvy, consider making a client-side version of your script with *Perl2Exe* (*http://www.indigostar.com/ perl2exe.htm*) or *PAR* (*http://search.cpan.org/author/AUTRIJUS/PAR*) and sending it to her to test drive.

Offer to show her the code. Explain what it does. Give samples of the output. If she really likes it, offer to let her distribute it from her site! Remember, all the average, nonprogramming webmaster is going to hear is "Hi! I wrote this Program and it Does Stuff to your site! Mind if I use it?" Understand if she wants a complete explanation and a little reassurance.

Making Your Spider Easy to Find and Learn About

Another good way to make sure that someone knows about your spider is to include contact information in the spider's User-Agent **[Hack #11]**. Contact information can be an email or a web address. Whatever it is, be sure to monitor the address and make sure the web site has adequate information.

Considering Legal Issues

Despite making contact, getting permission, and putting plenty of information about your spider on the Web, you may still have questions. Is your spider illegal? Are you going to get in trouble for using it?

There are many open issues with respect to the laws relating to the Web, and cases, experts, and scholars—not to mention members of the Web community—disagree heartily on most of them. Getting permission and operating within its limits probably reduces your risk, particularly if the site's a small one (that is, run by a person or two instead of a corporation). If you don't have permission and the site's terms of service aren't clear, risk is greater. That's probably also true if you've not asked permission and you're spidering a site that makes an API available and has very overt terms of service (like Google).

Legal issues on the Internet are constantly evolving; the medium is just too new to make sweeping statements about fair use and what's going to be okay and what's not. It's not just how your spider does its work, but also what you do with what you collect. In fact, we need to warn you that just because a hack is in the book doesn't mean that we can promise that it won't create risks or that no webmaster will ever consider the hack a violation of the relevant terms of service or some other legal rights.

Use your common sense (don't suck everything off a web site, put it on yours, and think you're okay), keep copyright laws in mind (don't take entire wire service stories and stick them on your site), and ask permission (the worst thing they can say is no, right?). If you're really worried, your best results will come from talking to an experienced lawyer.

Keeping Your Spider Out of Sticky Situations

You see tasty data here, there, and everywhere. Before you dive in, check the site's acceptable use policies.

Because the point of *Spidering Hacks* is to get to data that APIs can't (or haven't been created to) reach, sometimes you might end up in a legal gray area. Here's what you can do to help make sure you don't get anywhere near a "cease and desist" letter or the threat of a lawsuit.

Perhaps, one fine day, you visit a site and find some data you'd simply love to get your hands on. Before you start hacking, it behooves you to spend a little time looking around for an Acceptable Use Policy (AUP) or Terms of Service (TOS)—occasionally you'll see a Terms of Use (TOU)—and familiarize yourself with what you can and can't do with the site itself and its underlying data. Usually, you'll find a link at the bottom of the home page, often along with the site's copyright information. Yahoo! has a Terms of Service link as almost the last entry on its front page, while Google's is at the bottom of their About page. If you can't find it on the front page, look at the corporate information or any About sections. In some cases, sites (mostly smaller ones) won't have them, so you should consider contacting the webmaster—just about always *webmaster@sitename.com*—and ask.

So, you've found the AUP or TOS. Just what is it you're supposed to be looking for? What you're after is anything that has to do with spidering or scraping data. In the case of eBay, their position is made clear with this excerpt from their User Agreement:

> You agree that you will not use any robot, spider, scraper or other automated means to access the Site for any purpose without our express written permission.

Clear enough, isn't it? But sometimes it won't be this obvious. Some usage agreements don't make any reference whatsoever to spidering or scraping. In such cases, look for a contact address for the site itself or technical issues relating to its operation, and ask.

Bad Spider, No Biscuit!

Even with adherence to the terms of service and usage agreements you find on its pages, a web site might simply have a problem with how you're using its data. There are several ways in which a spider might be obeying the letter of a service agreement yet still doing something unacceptable from the perspective of the owners of the content. For example, a site might say that it doesn't want its content republished on a web site. Then, a spider comes along and turns its information into an RSS feed. An RSS feed is not, technically speaking, a web page. But the site owners might still find this use unacceptable. There is nothing stopping a disgruntled site from revising its TOS to deny a spider's access, and then sending you a "cease and desist" letter.

But let's go beyond that for a minute. Of course we don't want you to violate Terms of Service, dance with lawyers, and so on. The Terms of Service are there for a reason. Usually, they're the parameters under which a site needs to operate in order to stay in business. Whatever your spider does, it needs to do it in the spirit of keeping the site from which it draws information healthy. If you write a spider that sucks away all information from advertiser-supported sites, and they can't sell any more advertising, what happens? The site dies. You lose the site, and your program doesn't work any more.

Though it's rarely done in conjunction with spidering, framing data is a long-established legal no-no. Basically, framing data means that you're putting the content of someone else's site under a *frame* of your own design (in effect, *branding* another site's data with your own elements). The frame usually contains ads that are paying you for the privilege. Spidering another site's content and reappropriating it into your own framed pages is bad. Don't do it.

Violating Copyright

I shouldn't even have to say this, but reiteration is a must. If you're spidering for the purpose of using someone else's intellectual property on your web site, you're violating copyright law. I don't care if your spider is scrupulously obeying a site's Terms of Service and is the best-behaved spider in the world, it's still doing something illegal. In this case, you can't fix the spider; it's not the code that's at fault. Instead, you'd better fix the intent of the script you wrote. For more information about copyright and intellectual property on the Web, check out Lawrence Lessig's weblog at *http://www.lessig.org/blog/* (Professor Lessig is a Professor of Law at Stanford Law School); the Electronic Frontier Foundation (*http://www.eff.org*); and Copyfight, the Politics of IP (*http://www.copyfight.org/*).

Aggregating Data

Aggregating data means gathering data from several different places and putting it together in one place. Think of a site that gathers different airline ticket prices in one place, or a site that compares prices from several different online bookstores. These are online aggregators, which represent a gray area in Internet etiquette. Some companies resent their data being aggregated and compared to the data on other sites (like comparison price shopping). Other companies don't care. Some companies actually have agreements with certain sites to have their information aggregated! You won't often find this spelled out in a site's Terms of Service, so when in doubt, ask.

Competitive Intelligence

Some sites complain because their competitors access and spider their data—data that's publicly available to any browser—and use it in their competitive activities. You might agree with them and you might not, but the fact is that such scraping has been the object of legal action in the past. Bidder's Edge was sued by eBay (*http://pub.bna.com/lw/21200.htm*) for such a spider.

Possible Consequences of Misbehaving Spiders

What's going to happen if you write a misbehaving spider and unleash it on the world? There are several possibilities. Often, sites will simply block your IP address. In the past, Google has blocked groups of IP addresses in an attempt to keep a single automated process from violating its TOS. Otherwise, the first course of action is usually a "cease and desist" letter, telling you to knock it off. From there, the conflict could escalate into a lawsuit, depending on your response.

Besides the damages that are assessed against people who lose lawsuits, some of the laws governing content and other web issues—for example, copyright laws—carry criminal penalities, which means fines and imprisonment in really extreme situations.

Writing a misbehaving spider is rarely going to have the police kicking down your door, unless you write something particularly egregious, like something that floods a web site with data or otherwise interferes with that site's ability to operate (referred to as *denial of service*). But considering lawyer's fees, the time it'll take out of your life, and the monetary penalties that might be imposed on you, a lawsuit is bad enough, and it's a good enough reason to make sure that your spiders are behaving and your intent is fair.

Tracking Legal Issues

To keep an eye on ongoing legal and scraping issues, try the Blawg Search (*http://blawgs.detod.com/*) search engine, which indexes only weblogs that cover legal issues and events. Try a search for spider, scraper, or spider lawsuit. If you're really interested, note that Blawg Search's results are also available as an RSS feed for use in popular syndicated news aggregators. You could use one of the hacks in this book and start your own uber-RSS feed for intellectual property concerns.

Other resources for keeping on top of brewing and current legal issues include: Slashdot (*http://slashdot.org/search.pl?topic=123*), popular geek hangout; the Electronic Freedom Foundation (*http://www.eff.org*), keeping tabs on digital rights; and the Berkman Center for Internet & Society at Harvard Law School (*http://cyber.law.harvard.edu/home/*), a research program studying cyberspace and its implications.

Finding the Patterns of Identifiers

#7

If you find that the online database or resource you want uses unique identification numbers, you can stretch what it does by combining it with other sites and identification values.

Some online data collections are just that—huge collections, put together in one place, and relying on a search engine or database program to provide organization. These collections have no unique ID numbers, no rhyme or reason to their organization. But that's not always the case.

As more and more libraries put their collection information online, more and more records and pages have their own unique identification numbers.

So what? Here's what: when a web site uses an identifying method for its information that is recognized by other web sites, you can scrape data across multiple sites using that identifying method. For example, say you want to tour the country playing golf but you're afraid of pollution, so you want to play only in the cleanest areas. You could write a script that searches for golf courses at *http://www.golfcourses.com*, then takes the Zip Codes of the courses returned and checks them against *http://www.scorecard.org* to see which have the most (or least) polluted environment.

This is a silly example, but it shows how two different online data sources (a golf course database and an environmental pollution guide) can be linked together with a unique identifying number (a Zip Code, in this case).

Speaking generally, there are three types of deliberate web data organization:

- Arbitrary classification systems within a collection
- Classification systems that use an established universal taxonomy within a collection
- Classification systems that identify documents across a wide number of collections

Arbitrary Classification Systems Within a Collection

An arbitrary classification system is either not based on an established taxonomy or only loosely based on an established taxonomy. If I give 10 photographs unique codes based on their topics and how much blue they have in them, I have established an arbitrary classification system.

The arbitrary classification system's usefulness is limited. You cannot use its identifying code on other sites. You might be able to detect a pattern in it that allows you to spider large volumes of data, but, on the other hand, you may not. (In other words, files labeled *10A*, *10B*, *10C*, and *10D* might be useful, but files labeled *CMSH113*, *LFFD917*, and *MDFS214* would not.)

Classification Systems that Use an Established Universal Taxonomy Within a Collection

The most overt example of classification systems that use an established universal taxonomy is a library card catalog that follows the Dewey Decimal, Library of Congress, or other established classification.

The benefit of such systems is mixed. Say I look up *Google Hacks* at the University of Tulsa. I'll discover that the LOC number is ZA4251.G66 C3 2003. Now, if I plug that number into Google, I'll find about 13 results. Here's the cool part: the results will be from a variety of libraries. So, if I wanted to, I could plug that search into Google and find other libraries that carry *Google Hacks* and extend that idea into a spidering script **[Hack #65]**.

That's the good thing. The bad thing is that such a search won't list all libraries that carry *Google Hacks*. Other libraries have different classification systems, so if you're looking for a complete list of libraries carrying the book, you're not going to find it solely with this method. But you may find enough libraries to work well enough for your needs.

Classification Systems that Identify Documents Across a Wide Number of Collections

Beyond site classifications that are based on an established taxonomy, there are systems that use an identification number that is universally recognized and applied. Examples of such systems include:

ISBN (International Standard Book Number)
> As you might guess, this number is an identification system for books. There are similar numbers for serials, music, scientific reports, etc. You'll see ISBNs used everywhere from library catalogs to Amazon.com—anywhere books are listed.

EIN (Employer Identification Number)
> Used by the IRS. You'll see this number in tax-filing databases, references to businesses and nonprofits, and so on.

Zip Code
> Allows the U.S. Post Office to identify unique areas.

This list barely scratches the surface. Of course, you can go even further, including unique characteristics such as latitude and longitude, other business identification numbers, or even area codes. The challenge is identifying a unique classification number that requires context that's minimal enough to make it usable by your spider. "918" is a three-number string that has plenty of search results beyond just those related to area codes. So, you might not be able to find a way to eliminate your false positives when building a spider that depends on area codes for results.

On the other hand, an extended classification number, such as an LOC catalog number or ISBN, is going to have few, if any, false positives. The longer or more complicated an identifying number is, the better it serves the purposes of spidering.

Some Large Collections with ID Numbers

There are several places online that use unique classification numbers, which you can use across other sites. Here are a few you might want to play with:

Amazon.com (http://www.amazon.com), Abebooks (http://www.abebooks.com)
    These sites both use ISBN numbers. Combining the two result sets can aggregate seller information to find you the cheapest price on used books.

The International Standard Serial Number Register (http://www.issn.org)
    You need to be a subscriber to use this site, but trials are available. ISSNs are used for both online and offline magazines.

United States Post Office (http://www.usps.com)
    This site allows you to do both standard and nine-digit Zip Code lookups, allowing you to find more specific areas within a Zip Code (and eliminate false positive results from your spider).

GuideStar, a database of nonprofit organizations, has a search page that allows you to search by EIN (*http://www.guidestar.org/search/*). A variety of other business databases also allow you to search by EIN.

Assembling a Toolbox
Hacks #8–32

The idea behind scraping sites often arises out of pure, immediate, and frantic desire: it's late at night, you've forgotten your son's soccer game for the twelfth time in a row, and you're vowing never to let it happen again. Sure, you could place a bookmark to the school calendar in your browser toolbar, but you want something even more insidious, something you couldn't possibly forget or grow accustomed to seeing.

A bit later, you've got a Perl script that automatically emails you every hour of every day that a game is scheduled. You've just made your life less forgetful, your computer more useful, and your son more loving. This is where spidering and scraping shines: when you've got an itch that can best be scratched by getting your computer involved. And if there's one programming language that can quickly scratch an itch better than any other, it's Perl.

Perl is renowned for "making easy things easier and hard things possible," earning the reputation of "Swiss Army chainsaw," "Internet duct tape," or the ultimate "glue language." Since it's a scripting language (as opposed to a compiled one, like C), rapid development is its modus operandi; throw together bits and pieces from code here and there, try it out, tweak, hem, haw, and deploy. Along with its immense repository of existing code (see CPAN, the Comprehensive Perl Archive Network, at *http://www.cpan.org*) and the uncanny ability to "do what you mean," it's a perfect language on which to base a spidering hacks book.

In this book, we're going to assume you have a rudimentary knowledge of Perl. You may not be much more than an acolyte, but we're hoping you can create something a little more advanced then "Hello, World." What we're *not* going to assume, however, is that you've done much, if any, network programming before. We still hear tales of those who have stayed away from Internet programming because they're scared of how difficult it might be.

Trust us, like a lot of things with Perl, it's a lot easier than you think. In this chapter, we'll devote a decent amount of time to getting you up to speed with what you need to know: installing the network access modules for Perl [Hack #8] and then learning how to use them, from the simplest query [Hack #9] on up to progress bars [Hack #18], faking HTTP headers [Hack #11], and so on.

Perl Modules

You may have been tripped up by the word *modules* in the previous paragraph. Don't fret, dear reader. A module is simply an encapsulated bit of Perl code, written by someone else, that you employ in your own application. By leaving the implementation details and much of the dirty work to the module author, using a module rather then writing all the code yourself makes a complicated task far, far easier. When we say we're going to *install* a module, we really mean we're going to get a copy from CPAN (*http://www.cpan.org*), test to make sure it'll work in our environment, ensure it doesn't require other modules that we don't yet have, install it, and then prepare it for general use within our own scripts.

Sounds pretty complicated, right? Repeat ad infinitum: don't fret, dear reader, as CPAN has you covered. One of Perl's greatest accomplishments, CPAN is a large and well-categorized selection of modules created and contributed by hundreds of authors. Mirrored worldwide, there's a good chance your "I wish I had a..." wonderings have been placated, bug-tested, and packaged for your use.

Since CPAN is such a powerful accoutrement to the Perl language, the task of installing a module and ensuring its capabilities has been made far easier than the mumbo jumbo I uttered previously. We cover exactly how to install modules in our first hack of this chapter [Hack #8].

As you browse through this book, you'll see we use a number of noncore modules—where *noncore* is defined as "not already part of your Perl installation." Following are a few of the more popular ones you'll be using in your day-to-day scraping. Again, worry not if you don't understand some of this stuff; we'll cover it in time:

LWP
> A package of modules for web access, also known as *libwww-perl*

LWP::Simple
> Simple functions for getting web documents (*http://search.cpan.org/author/GAAS/libwww-perl/lib/LWP/Simple.pm*)

LWP::UserAgent
> More powerful functions for implementing a spider that looks and acts more like a specialized web browser (*http://search.cpan.org/author/GAAS/libwww-perl/lib/LWP/UserAgent.pm*)

HTTP::Response

A programmatic encapsulation of the response to an HTTP request (*http://search.cpan.org/author/GAAS/libwww-perl/lib/HTTP/Response.pm*)

HTTP::Message and HTTP::Headers

Classes that provide more methods to *HTTP::Response*, such as convenient access to setting and getting HTTP headers (*http://search.cpan.org/author/GAAS/libwww-perl/lib/HTTP/Message.pm, http://search.cpan.org/author/GAAS/libwww-perl/lib/HTTP/Headers.pm*)

URI

Methods to operate on a web address, such as getting the base of a URL, turning a relative URL into an absolute, and returning the individual path segments (*http://search.cpan.org/author/GAAS/URI/URI.pm*)

URI::Escape

Functions for URL-escaping and URL-unescaping strings, such as turning `"this & that"` to `"this%20%26%20that"` and vice versa (*http://search.cpan.org/author/GAAS/URI/URI/Escape.pm*)

HTML::Entities

Functions for HTML-escaping and HTML-unescaping strings, such as turning `"C. & E. Brontë"` to `"C. &amp; E. Bront&euml;"` and vice versa (*http://search.cpan.org/author/GAAS/HTML-Parser/lib/HTML/Entities.pm*)

HTML::TokeParser and HTML::TreeBuilder

Classes for parsing HTML (*http://search.cpan.org/author/GAAS/HTML-Parser/, http://search.cpan.org/author/SBURKE/HTML-Tree/*)

WWW::Mechanize

Automates interaction with sites, including filling out forms, traversing links, sending referrers, accessing a history of URLs visited, and so on (*http://search.cpan.org/author/PETDANCE/WWW-Mechanize/*)

For more information on these modules once they are installed, you can issue a man `Module::Name` command, where `Module::Name` is the name of your desire. Online documentation is also available at CPAN.

Resources You May Find Helpful

If you're new to Perl, or if you would like to brush up on your skills, leaf through the following O'Reilly books, both well-respected additions to any Perl programmer's library:

- *The Perl Cookbook* (*http://www.oreilly.com/catalog/perlckbk2/*) by Tom Christiansen and Nathan Torkington
- *Programming Perl* (*http://www.oreilly.com/catalog/pperl3/*) by Larry Wall, Tom Christiansen, and Jon Orwant

Installing Perl Modules

#8

A fair number of our hacks require modules not included with the standard Perl distribution. Here, we'll show you how to install these modules on Windows, Mac OS X, and Unix-based systems.

As you go through this book, you'll notice that we're constantly mentioning a variety of different Perl modules. Some of them aren't standard installation fare, so it's unlikely that you'll already have them available to your coding.

Why do we mention nonstandard modules? Quite simply, we didn't want to reinvent the wheel. We do some pretty odd toting and lifting in this book, and without the help of many of these modules we'd have to do a lot of extra coding (which means just that many more breakable bits in our scripts).

If you're new to Perl, however, you may be feeling intimidated by the idea of installing modules. Don't worry; it's a snap! If you're running ActiveState Perl for Windows, you'll want to use the Programmer's Package Manager (PPM). Otherwise, you'll use CPAN.

Example: Installing LWP

LWP is used throughout this book, because it's the workhorse for any Perl script with designs on interacting with the Internet. Some Perl installations already have it installed; others don't. We'll use it here as an example of how to install a typical Perl module; the steps apply to almost any available noncore module that we use in our other hacks—and, indeed, that you may encounter in your ongoing programming.

Usually, the easiest way to install a Perl module is via another Perl module. The *CPAN* module, included with just about every modern Perl distribution, automates the installation of Perl modules, fetching components and any prerequisites and building the whole kit and kaboodle for you on the fly.

> *CPAN* installs modules into standard system-wide locations and, therefore, assumes you're running as the root user. If you have no more than regular user access, you'll have to install your module by hand (see "Unix and Mac OS X installation by hand" later in this hack).

Unix and Mac OS X installation via CPAN. Assuming you have the *CPAN* module, have root access, and are connected to the Internet, installation should be no more complicated than this:

```
% su
Password:
# perl -MCPAN -e shell
cpan shell -- CPAN exploration and modules installation (v1.52)
ReadLine support available (try ``install Bundle::CPAN'')
cpan> install libwww-perl
```

Or, if you prefer one-liners:

```
% sudo perl -MCPAN -e 'install libwww-perl'
```

> What's with this *libwww-perl*? I thought we were installing *LWP*! They're actually one and the same, *LWP* being an abbreviation of *libwww-perl*. You'll find more details, should you be interested, at *http://www.linpro.no/lwp/lwpng-paper/*.

In either case, go grab yourself a cup of coffee, meander through the garden, read the paper, and check back once in a while. Your terminal's sure to be riddled with incomprehensible gobbledygook that you can, for the most part, summarily ignore. You may be asked a question or three; in most cases, simply pressing Return to accept the default answer will do the trick.

Unix and Mac OS X installation by hand. If *CPAN* installation didn't quite work as expected, you can of course fall back to installing the module by hand. Download the latest version manually from CPAN (*http://search.cpan.org/author/GAAS/libwww-perl/*, in this case), unpack it, then build it, like so:

```
% tar xvzf libwww-perl-5.69.tar.gz
libwww-perl-5.69/
libwww-perl-5.69/lib/
libwww-perl-5.69/lib/HTTP/
libwww-perl-5.69/lib/HTTP/Cookies.pm
libwww-perl-5.69/lib/HTTP/Status.pm
...
libwww-perl-5.69/Changes
libwww-perl-5.69/README
libwww-perl-5.69/lwpcook.pod
% cd libwww-perl-5.69
% perl Makefile.PL
This package comes with some sample programs that I can try
to install in /usr/local/bin.

    Note that you can avoid these questions by passing
    the '-n' option to 'Makefile.PL'.
...
```

```
% make
mkdir blib
mkdir blib/lib
...
% make test
/usr/bin/perl t/TEST 0
base/common-req.......ok
base/cookies..........ok
base/date............ok
base/headers-auth.....ok
...
% su
Password:
# make install
Installing /Library/Perl/LWP.pm
Installing /Library/Perl/lwptut.pod
...
```

Of course, your output will vary from module to module, version to version, and operating system to operating system.

If, during the perl Makefile.PL phase, you run into any warnings about installing prerequisites, you'll have to install each in turn before attempting to install *LWP* again. A typical prerequisite warning looks something like this:

```
Checking if your kit is complete...
Looks good
Warning: prerequisite HTTP::Daemon failed to load: Can't locate
HTTP/Daemon.pm in @INC (@INC contains: /System/Library/Perl/darwin
/System/Library/Perl /Library/Perl/darwin /Library/Perl /Library/Perl
/Network/Library/Perl/darwin /Network/Library/Perl
/Network/Library/Perl .) at (eval 8) line 3.
```

If you have little more than user access to the system and still insist on installing *LWP* yourself, you'll have to install it and all its prerequisites somewhere in your home directory; *~/lib*, a *lib* directory in your home directory, is as good a place as any. Inform Perl of your preference like so:

```
% perl Makefile.PL LIB=/home/login/lib
```

Replace */home/login/lib* with an appropriate path.

Windows installation via PPM. If you're running Perl under Windows, chances are it's ActiveState's ActivePerl (*http://www.activestate.com/Products/ActivePerl/*). Thankfully, ActivePerl's outfitted with a *CPAN*-like module-installation utility. PPM (*http://aspn.activestate.com/ASPN/Downloads/ActivePerl/PPM/*) grabs nicely packaged module bundles from the

ActiveState archive and drops them into place on your Windows system with little need of help from you.

Simply launch PPM from a DOS window (Start Menu → Run... → *command* → OK) and tell it to install the *LWP* bundle:

```
C:\>ppm
PPM interactive shell (2.1.6) - type 'help' for available commands.
PPM> install libwww-perl
```

If you're running a reasonably recent build, you're in for a pleasant surprise; *libwww-perl* was installed along with ActivePerl itself:

```
Version 5.64 of 'libwww-perl' is already installed.
```

HACK #9   Simply Fetching with LWP::Simple

Suck web content easily using the aptly named LWP::Simple.

LWP (short for "Library for WWW in Perl") is a popular group of Perl modules for accessing data on the Web. Like most Perl module distributions, each of *LWP*'s component modules comes with documentation that is a complete reference to its interface. However, there are so many modules in *LWP* that it's hard to know where to look for information on doing even the simplest things.

> Introducing you to all aspects of using *LWP* would require a whole book—a book that just so happens to exist, mind you (see Sean Burke's *Perl & LWP* at *http://oreilly.com/catalog/ perllwp/*).

If you just want to access a particular URL, the simplest way to do so is to use *LWP::Simple*'s functions. In a Perl program, you can simply call its get($url) routine, where $url is the location of the content you're interested in. *LWP::Simple* will try to fetch the content at the end of the URL. If it's successful, you'll be handed the content; if there's an error of some sort, the get function will return undef, the undefined value. The get represents an aptly named HTTP GET request, which reads as "get me the content at the end of this URL":

```perl
#!/usr/bin/perl -w
use strict;
use LWP::Simple;

# Just an example: the URL for the most recent /Fresh Air/ show
my $url = 'http://freshair.npr.org/dayFA.cfm?todayDate=current';

my $content = get($url);
die "Couldn't get $url" unless defined $content;
```

```
# Do things with $content:
if ($content =~ m/jazz/i) {
    print "They're talking about jazz today on Fresh Air!\n";
} else { print "Fresh Air is apparently jazzless today.\n"; }
```

A handy variant of get is getprint, useful in Perl one-liners. If it can get the page whose URL you provide, it sends it straight to STDOUT; otherwise, it complains to STDERR—both usually are your screen:

```
% perl -MLWP::Simple -e "getprint 'http://cpan.org/RECENT'"
MIRRORED.BY
MIRRORING.FROM
RECENT
RECENT.html
SITES
SITES.html
authors/00whois.html
authors/01mailrc.txt.gz
authors/id/A/AB/ABW/CHECKSUMS
authors/id/A/AB/ABW/Pod-POM-0.17.tar.gz
...
```

The previous command grabs and prints the URL of a plain text file that lists new files added to CPAN in the past two weeks. You can easily make it part of a tidy little shell command, like this one that mails you the list of new *Acme::* modules:

```
% perl -MLWP::Simple -e "getprint 'http://cpan.org/RECENT'" | grep "/by-
module/Acme" | mail -s "New Acme modules! Joy!" $USER
```

There are a few other useful functions in *LWP::Simple*, such as head, which issues an HTTP HEAD request (surprising, eh?). A HEAD returns just the introductory bits of a response, rather than the full content returned by GET. HEAD returns a list of HTTP headers—key/value pairs that tell you more about the content in question (its size, content type, last-modified date, etc.)—like so:

```
% perl -MLWP::Simple -e 'print join "\n", head "http://cpan.org/RECENT"'
text/html
49675
1059640198

Apache/1.3.26 (Unix) PHP/4.2.1 mod_gzip/1.3.19.1a mod_perl/1.27
```

If successful, a HEAD request should return the content type (plain text, in this case), the document length (49675), modification time (1059640198 seconds since the Epoch, or July 31, 2003 at 01:29:58), content expiration date, if any, and a bit about the server itself (Apache under Unix with *PHP*, *gzip*, and *mod_perl* modules onboard).

> If you're going use the *CGI* module with your *LWP::Simple* hacks, be sure to tell *LWP::Simple* not to import the head routine; otherwise, it'll conflict with a similarly named routine from *CGI*. To do this, use:
>
> ```
> use LWP::Simple qw(!head);
> use CGI qw{:standard};
> ```

For anything beyond the basics, you'll want to use *LWP::UserAgent* [Hack #10], the Swiss Army knife of *LWP* and Perl's network libraries.

—*Sean Burke*

H A C K
#10
More Involved Requests with LWP::UserAgent

Knowing how to download web pages is great, but it doesn't help us when we want to submit forms, fake browser settings, or get more information about our request. Here, we'll jump into the more useful LWP::UserAgent.

LWP::Simple's functions [Hack #9] are handy for simple cases, but they don't support cookies or authorization; they don't support setting header lines in the HTTP request; and, generally, they don't support reading header lines in the HTTP response (most notably, the full HTTP error message, in case of problems). To get at all those features, you'll have to use the full *LWP* class model.

While *LWP* consists of dozens of classes, the two that you have to understand are *LWP::UserAgent* and *HTTP::Response*. *LWP::UserAgent* is a class for *virtual browsers*, which you use for performing requests, and *HTTP::Response* is a class for the responses (or error messages) that you get back from those requests.

The basic idiom is $response = $browser->get($url), like so:

```perl
#!/usr/bin/perl -w
use strict;
use LWP 5.64; # Loads all important LWP classes, and makes
              # sure your version is reasonably recent.

my $url = 'http://freshair.npr.org/dayFA.cfm?todayDate=current';

my $browser = LWP::UserAgent->new;
my $response = $browser->get( $url );
die "Can't get $url -- ", $response->status_line
   unless $response->is_success;

die "Hey, I was expecting HTML, not ", $response->content_type
   unless $response->content_type eq 'text/html';
   # or whatever content-type you're dealing with.
```

```
# Otherwise, process the content somehow:
if ($response->content =~ m/jazz/i) {
    print "They're talking about jazz today on Fresh Air!\n";
} else {print "Fresh Air is apparently jazzless today.\n"; }
```

There are two objects involved: $browser, which holds an object of the class *LWP::UserAgent,* and the $response object, which is of the class *HTTP:: Response.* You really need only one browser object per program; but every time you make a request, you get back a new *HTTP::Response* object, which holds some interesting attributes:

- A status code indicating success/failure (test with $response->is_success).

- An HTTP status line, which should be informative if there is a failure. A document not found should return a $response->status_line with something like "404 Not Found."

- A MIME content type, such as text/html, image/gif, image/jpeg, application/xml, and so on, held in $response->content_type.

- The actual content of the response, $response->content. If the response is HTML, that's where the HTML source will be; if it's a GIF or image of some other flavor, then $response->content will be the binary image data.

- Dozens of other convenient and more specific methods, explained in the documentation for *HTTP::Response* and its superclasses, *HTTP:: Message* and *HTTP::Headers.*

—Sean Burke

Adding HTTP Headers to Your Request

Add more functionality to your programs, or mimic common browsers, to circumvent server-side filtering of unknown user agents.

The most commonly used syntax for *LWP::UserAgent* requests is $response = $browser->get($url), but in truth you can add extra HTTP header lines to the request by adding a list of key/value pairs after the URL, like so:

```
$response = $browser->get( $url, $key1, $value1, $key2, $value2, ... );
```

Why is adding HTTP headers sometimes necessary? It really depends on the site that you're pulling data from; some will respond only to actions that appear to come from common end-user browsers, such as Internet Explorer, Netscape, Mozilla, or Safari. Others, in a desperate attempt to minimize bandwidth costs, will send only compressed data [Hack #16], requiring decoding on the client end. All these client necessities can be enabled through the use of HTTP headers. For example, here's how to send more Netscape-like headers:

```
my @ns_headers = (
    'User-Agent' => 'Mozilla/4.76 [en] (Win98; U)',
    'Accept' => 'image/gif, image/x-xbitmap, image/jpeg,
                image/pjpeg, image/png,  */*',
    'Accept-Charset' => 'iso-8859-1,*',
    'Accept-Language' => 'en-US',
);

$response = $browser->get($url, @ns_headers);
```

Or, alternatively, without the interim array:

```
$response = $browser->get($url,
    'User-Agent' => 'Mozilla/4.76 [en] (Win98; U)',
    'Accept' => 'image/gif, image/x-xbitmap, image/jpeg,
                image/pjpeg, image/png, */*',
    'Accept-Charset' => 'iso-8859-1,*',
    'Accept-Language' => 'en-US',
);
```

In these headers, you're telling the remote server which types of data you're willing to Accept and in what order: GIFs, bitmaps, JPEGs, PNGs, and then anything else (you'd rather have a GIF first, but an HTML file is fine if the server can't provide the data in your preferred formats). For servers that cater to international users by offering translated documents, the Accept-Language and Accept-Charset headers give you the ability to choose what sort of native content you get back. For example, if the server offers native French translations of its resources, you can request them with 'Accept-Language'=> 'fr' and 'Accept-Charset'=> 'iso-8859-1'.

If you were only going to change the User-Agent, you could just modify the $browser object's default line from libwww-perl/5.65 (or the like) to whatever you wish, using *LWP::UserAgent*'s agent method (in this case, for Netscape 4.76):

```
$browser->agent('Mozilla/4.76 [en] (Win98; U)');
```

Here's a short list of common User-Agents you might wish to mimic; all perform quite nicely as a replication of a common browser the site in question may be expecting. The first is IE 5.22/Mac, the second is IE 6/Windows, and the third is an example of Mozilla 1.x:

```
Mozilla/4.0 (compatible; MSIE 5.22; Mac_PowerPC)
Mozilla/4.0 (compatible; MSIE 6.0; Windows 98)
Mozilla/5.0 (Windows; U; Windows NT 5.1; en-US; rv:1.3) Gecko/20030312
```

Some sites prefer you arrive from only particular pages on their site or other sites. They do so by requiring a Referer (*sic*) header, the URL of the page you just came from. Faking a Referer is easy; simply set the header, passing it to get as a key/value pair, like so:

```
$response = $browser->get($url, 'Referer' => 'http://site.com/url.html');
```

Just goes to show you that relying upon a certain Referer or specific User-Agent is no security worth considering for your own site and resources.

—Sean Burke and Kevin Hemenway

HACK #12 Posting Form Data with LWP

Automate form submission, whether username and password authentication, supplying your Zip Code for location-based services, or simply filling out a number of customizable fields for search engines.

Say you search Google for three blind mice. Your result URL will vary depending on the preferences you've set, but it will look something like this:

```
http://www.google.com/search?num=100&hl=en&q=%22three+blind+mice%22
```

The query itself turns into an ungodly mess, &q=%22three+blind+mice%22, but why? Whenever you send data through a form submission, that data has to be encoded so that it can safely arrive at its destination, the server, intact. Characters like spaces and quotes—in essence, anything not alphanumeric—must be turned into their encoded equivalents, like + and %22. *LWP* will automatically handle most of this encoding (and decoding) for you, but you can request it at will with *URI::Escape*'s uri_escape and uri_unescape functions.

Let's break down what those other bits in the URL mean.

num=100 refers to the number of search results to a page, 100 in this case. Google accepts any number from 10 to 100. Altering the value of num in the URL and reloading the page is a nice shortcut for altering the preferred size of your result set without having to meander over to the Advanced Search (*http://www.google.com/advanced_search?hl=en*) and rerunning your query.

hl=en means that the language interface—the language in which you use Google, reflected in the home page, messages, and buttons—is in English. Google's Language Tools (*http://www.google.com/language_tools?hl=en*) provide a list of language choices.

The three variables q, num, and hl and their associated values represent a GET form request; you can always tell when you have one by the URL in your browser's address bar, where you'll see the URL, then a question mark (?), followed by key/value pairs separated by an ampersand (&). To run the same search from within *LWP*, you use the *URI* module to assemble a URL with embedded key/value pairs, which is, in turn, passed to an existing *LWP* $browser object. Here's a simple example:

```
#!/usr/bin/perl -w
use strict;
use LWP 5.64;
use URI;

my $browser = LWP::UserAgent->new;
my $url = URI->new( 'http://www.google.com/search' );

# the pairs:
$url->query_form(
    'h1'   => 'en',
    'num' => '100',
    'q' => 'three blind mice',
);

my $response = $browser->get($url);
```

Many HTML forms, however, send data to their server using an HTTP POST request, which is not viewable in the resulting URL. The only way to discern which variables and values will be included in the request is to consult the source code of the form page itself. Here's a basic HTML form example using POST as its submission type:

```
<form method="POST" action="/process">
<input type="hidden" name="formkey1" value="value1">
<input type="hidden" name="formkey2" value="value2">
<input type="submit" name="go" value="Go!">
</form>
```

To simulate a POST from within *LWP*, call the post subroutine, passing it key/value pairs. Simulating a POST from the previous form looks like this:

```
$response = $browser->post( $url,
    [
     formkey1 => value1,
     formkey2 => value2,
     go => "Go!"
     ...
    ],
);
```

Or, if you need to send HTTP headers as well, simply append them like this:

```
$response = $browser->post( $url,
    [
     formkey1 => value1,
     formkey2 => value2,
     go => "Go!"
     ...
    ],
```

```
        headerkey1 => value1,
        headerkey2 => value2,
    );
```

The following program makes a search request to AltaVista (by sending some form data via an HTTP POST request) and extracts from the HTML the report of the number of matches:

```perl
#!/usr/bin/perl -w
use strict;
use LWP 5.64;

my $word = shift;
$word or die "Usage: perl altavista_post.pl [keyword]\n";

my $browser = LWP::UserAgent->new;
my $url = 'http://www.altavista.com/web/results';

my $response = $browser->post( $url,
    [ 'q' => $word,  # the Altavista query string
      'pg' => 'q', 'avkw' => 'tgz', 'kl' => 'XX',
    ]
);

die "$url error: ", $response->status_line unless $response->is_success;
die "Weird content type at $url -- ", $response->content_type
    unless $response->content_type eq 'text/html';

if ( $response->content =~ m{ found ([0-9,]+) results} ) { print "$word: ↵
$1\n"; }
else { print "Couldn't find the match-string in the response\n"; }
```

Save this script as *altavista_post.pl* and invoke it on the command line, passing it a keyword (or quoted set of keywords) you wish to search AltaVista for:

```
% perl altavista_post.pl tarragon
tarragon: 80,349
```

Being able to program form submissions becomes especially handy when you're looking to automate "Keep trying!" contest submissions that require users to manually enter their age, state, Zip Code, or similar bit of ephemera, only to receive "Sorry, try again" repetitively and without remorse.

—*Sean Burke and Tara Calishain*

HACK #13 Authentication, Cookies, and Proxies

Access restricted resources programmatically by supplying proper authentication tokens, cookies, or proxy server information.

Accessing public resources assumes that you have the correct privileges to do so. The vast majority of sites you encounter every day on the Web are usually wide open to any visitor anxious to satisfy his browsing desires. Some sites, however, require password authentication before you're allowed in. Still others will give you a special file called a *cookie*, without which you'll not get any further. And sometimes, your ISP or place of work may require that you use a *proxy server*, a sort of handholding middleman that preprocesses everything you view. All three of these techniques will break any *LWP::UserAgent* [Hack #10] code we've previously written.

Authentication

Many web sites restrict access to documents by using *HTTP Authentication*, a mechanism whereby the web server sends the browser an HTTP code that says "You are entering a protected realm, accessible only by rerequesting it along with some special authorization headers." Your typical web browser deals with this request by presenting you with a username/password prompt, as shown in Figure 2-1, passing whatever you enter back to the web server as the appropriate authentication headers.

Figure 2-1. A typical browser authentication prompt

For example, the Unicode.org administrators stop email-harvesting bots from spidering the contents of their mailing list archives by protecting them with HTTP Authentication and then publicly stating the username and password (at *http://www.unicode.org/mail-arch/*)—namely, username "unicode-ml" and password "unicode".

Consider this URL, part of the protected area of the web site:

```
http://www.unicode.org/mail-arch/unicode-ml/y2002-m08/0067.html
```

If you access this URL with a browser, you'll be prompted to "Enter username and password for 'Unicode-MailList-Archives' at server 'www.unicode.org'".

Attempting to access this URL via *LWP* without providing the proper authentication will not work. Let's give it a whirl:

```
#!/usr/bin/perl -w
use strict;
use LWP 5.64;

my $browser = LWP::UserAgent->new;
my $url = 'http://www.unicode.org/mail-arch/unicode-ml/y2002-m08/0067.html';
my $response = $browser->get($url);

die "Error: ", $response->header('WWW-Authenticate') ||
    'Error accessing', "\n ", $response->status_line,
    "\n at $url\n Aborting" unless $response->is_success;
```

As expected, we didn't get very far:

```
% perl get_protected_resource.pl
Error: Basic realm="Unicode-MailList-Archives"
    401 Authorization Required
    at http://www.unicode.org/mail-arch/unicode-ml/y2002-m08/0067.html
```

You've not told your $browser object about the username and password needed for that realm (Unicode-MailList-Archives) at that host (www.unicode.org). The fix is to provide the proper credentials to the $browser object using the credentials method:

```
$browser->credentials(
    'servername:portnumber',
    'realm-name',
    'username' => 'password'
);
```

In most cases, the port number is 80, the default TCP/IP port for HTTP, and you usually call the credentials method before you make any requests. So, getting access to the Unicode mailing list archives looks like this:

```
$browser->credentials(
    'www.unicode.org:80',
    'Unicode-MailList-Archives',
    'unicode-ml' => 'unicode'
);
```

Enabling Cookies

You know those cards offered by your local carwash, pizza joint, or hairdresser—the ones you pick up the first time you go in and they stamp each time you visit? While the card itself does not identify you in any manner, it does keep track of how many times you've visited and, if you're lucky, when you're owed a free carwash, slice, or haircut for 10, 20, or however many stamps. Now imagine you have one of those cards for each of the popular sites you visit on the Web. That's the idea behind so-called *cookies*—a cookie jar filled with magic cookies slathered with identifiers and information in icing (yes, it is a slightly silly analogy).

Cookies are wodges of text issued by sites to your browser. Your browser keeps track of these and offers them up to the appropriate site upon your next visit. Some cookies simply keep track of your current session and aren't maintained for very long. Others keep track of your preferences from visit to visit. Still others hold identifying information and authentication tokens; you'll usually find these belonging to e-commerce sites like Amazon.com, eBay, E*Trade, your online banking system, library, and so forth.

The magic in these magic cookies is that all this happens behind the scenes; your browser manages the acquisition, offering, and maintenance of all the cookies in your jar. It is careful to pass only the appropriate cookie to the right site, it watches the expiration date and throws out old cookies, and it generally allows for an all-but-seamless experience for you.

Most browsers actually allow you to take a gander at the contents of your cookie jar (Safari on Mac OS X: Safari → Preferences... → Security → Show Cookies; Mozilla on any platform: Tools → Cookie Manager → Manage Stored Cookies; Internet Explorer on Windows: depends on OS/browser version, but generally, a folder called *Temporary Internet Files* or *Cookies* in your home directory). You might even be able to delete cookies, alter your cookie preferences so that you're warned of any incoming cookies, or indeed refuse cookies altogether—the latter two robbing you of some of the seamless experience I was just talking about.

A default *LWP::UserAgent* object acts like a browser with its cookie support turned off. There are various ways of turning cookie support on, by setting the *LWP::UserAgent* object's cookie_jar attribute. A *cookie jar* is an object representing a little database of all the HTTP cookies that a browser can know about. It can correspond to a file on disk (the way Netscape or Mozilla uses its *cookies.txt* file), or it can be just an in-memory object that starts out empty and whose collection of cookies will disappear once the program is finished running.

To use an in-memory empty cookie jar, set the cookie_jar attribute, like so:

```
$browser->cookie_jar({});
```

To give the cookie jar a copy that will be read from a file on disk with any modifications being saved back to the file when the program is finished running, set the cookie_jar attribute like this:

```
use HTTP::Cookies;
$browser->cookie_jar( HTTP::Cookies->new(
    'file' => '/some/where/cookies.lwp',  # where to read/write cookies
    'autosave' => 1,                      # save it to disk when done
));
```

That file will be in an *LWP*-specific format. If you want to access the cookies in your Netscape cookies file, you can use *HTTP::Cookies::Netscape*:

```
use HTTP::Cookies; # yes, loads HTTP::Cookies::Netscape too
$browser->cookie_jar( HTTP::Cookies::Netscape->new(
    'file' => 'c:/Program Files/Netscape/Users/DIR-NAME-HERE/cookies.txt',
));
```

You could add an 'autosave' => 1 line as we did earlier, but it's uncertain whether Netscape will respect or simply discard some of the cookies you write programmatically back to disk.

Using Proxies

In some cases, you have to use proxies to access sites or use certain protocols. This is most commonly the case when your *LWP* program is running (or could be running) on a machine that is behind a firewall or in a business environment. More and more businesses are requiring their employees to use proxies, either to ensure that they're not playing online games during working hours, or to help prevent the accidental display of pornographic or otherwise offensive material.

When a proxy server is installed on a network, a special *environment variable* that points to its location can be defined. This environment variable, HTTP_PROXY, can be automatically understood and processed by programs that know of its existence. To ensure that *LWP* can utilize this information, just call the env_proxy on a User-Agent object before you go making any requests on it:

```
use LWP::UserAgent;
my $browser = LWP::UserAgent->new;
$browser->env_proxy;
```

For more information on proxy parameters, see the *LWP::UserAgent* documentation (type perldoc LWP::UserAgent on the command line), specifically the proxy, env_proxy, and no_proxy methods.

—Sean Burke

Handling Relative and Absolute URLs

Glean the full URL of any relative reference, such as "sample/index.html" or "../../images/flowers.gif", by using the helper functions of URI.

Occasionally, when you're parsing HTML or accepting command-line input, you'll receive a relative URL, something that looks like *images/bob.jpg* instead of the more specific *http://www.example.com/images/bob.jpg*. The longer version, called the *absolute URL*, is more desirable for parsing and display, as it ensures that no confusion can arise over where a resource is located.

The *URI* class provides all sorts of methods for accessing and modifying parts of URLs (such as asking what sort of URL it is with $url->scheme, asking which host it refers to with $url->host, and so on, as described in the docs for the *URI* class). However, the methods of most immediate interest are the query_form method [Hack #12] and the new_abs method for taking a URL string that is most likely relative and getting back an absolute URL, as shown here:

```
use URI; my $abs = URI->new_abs($maybe_relative, $base);
```

For example, consider the following simple program, which scrapes for URLs in the HTML list of new modules available at your local CPAN mirror:

```
#!/usr/bin/perl -w
use strict;
use LWP 5.64;

my $browser = LWP::UserAgent->new;
my $url = 'http://www.cpan.org/RECENT.html';
my $response = $browser->get($url);

die "Can't get $url -- ", $response->status_line
   unless $response->is_success;

my $html = $response->content;
while( $html =~ m/<A HREF=\"(.*?)\"/g ) {
    print "$1\n";
}
```

It returns a list of relative URLs for Perl modules and other assorted files:

```
% perl get_relative.pl
MIRRORING.FROM
RECENT
RECENT.html
authors/00whois.html
authors/01mailrc.txt.gz
authors/id/A/AA/AASSAD/CHECKSUMS
...
```

However, if you actually want to retrieve those URLs, you'll need to convert them from relative (e.g., *authors/00whois.html*) to absolute (e.g., *http://www.cpan.org/authors/00whois.html*). The *URI* module's new_abs method is just the ticket and requires only that you change that while loop at the end of the script, like so:

```
while( $html =~ m/<A HREF=\"(.*?)\"/g ) {
    print URI->new_abs( $1, $response->base ) ,"\n";
}
```

The $response->base method from the *HTTP::Message* module returns the base URL, which, prepended to a relative URL, provides the missing piece of an absolute URL. The base URL is usually the first part (e.g., *http://www.cpan.org*) of the URL you requested.

That minor adjustment in place, the code now returns absolute URLs:

```
http://www.cpan.org/MIRRORING.FROM
http://www.cpan.org/RECENT
http://www.cpan.org/RECENT.html
http://www.cpan.org/authors/00whois.html
http://www.cpan.org/authors/01mailrc.txt.gz
http://www.cpan.org/authors/id/A/AA/AASSAD/CHECKSUMS
...
```

Of course, using a regular expression to match link references is a bit simplistic, and for more robust programs you'll probably want to use an HTML-parsing module like *HTML::LinkExtor*, *HTML::TokeParser* [Hack #20], or *HTML::TreeBuilder*.

—*Sean Burke*

Secured Access and Browser Attributes

#15

If you're planning on accessing secured resources, such as your online banking, intranet, or the like, you'll need to send and receive data over a secured LWP connection.

Some sites are purveyors of such important data that simple password authentication doesn't provide the security necessary. A banking site, for instance, will use a username and password system to ensure you are who you say you are, but they'll also encrypt all the traffic from your computer to theirs. By doing so, they ensure that a malicious user can't "sniff" the data you're transmitting back and forth—credit card information, account histories, and social security numbers. To prevent against this unwanted snooping, using encryption, the server will install an SSL (Secure Sockets Layer) certificate, a contract of sorts between your browser and the web server, agreeing on how to hide the data passed back and forth.

You can tell a secured site by its URL: it will start with *https://*.

When you access an HTTPS URL, it'll work for you just like an HTTP URL, but only if your *LWP* installation has HTTPS support (via an appropriate SSL library). For example:

```
#!/usr/bin/perl -w
use strict;
use LWP 5.64;
```

```
my $url = 'https://www.paypal.com/';   # Yes, HTTPS!
my $browser = LWP::UserAgent->new;
my $response = $browser->get($url);

die "Error at $url\n ", $response->status_line,
    "\n Aborting" unless $response->is_success;

print "Whee, it worked!  I got that ",
    $response->content_type, " document!\n";
```

If your *LWP* installation doesn't yet have HTTPS support installed, the script's response will be unsuccessful and you'll receive this error message:

```
Error at https://www.paypal.com/
    501 Protocol scheme 'https' is not supported
```

If your *LWP* installation does have HTTPS support installed, then the response should be successful and you should be able to consult $response just as you would any normal HTTP response [Hack #10].

For information about installing HTTPS support for your *LWP* installation, see the helpful *README.SSL* file that comes in the *libwww-perl* distribution (either in your local installation or at *http://search.cpan.org/src/GAAS/libwww-perl-5.69/README.SSL/*). In most cases, simply installing the *Crypt::SSLeay* module [Hack #8] will get you up to speed.

Other Browser Attributes

LWP::UserAgent objects have many attributes for controlling how they work. Here are a few notable ones (more are available in the full documentation):

`$browser->timeout(15)`
> Sets this browser to give up when requests don't answer within 15 seconds.

`$browser->protocols_allowed(['http','gopher'])`
> Sets this browser object not to speak any protocols other than HTTP and gopher. If the browser tries accessing any other kind of URL (such as an *ftp:*, *mailto:*, or *news:* URL), then it won't actually try connecting, but instead will immediately return an error code 500, with a message like "Access to ftp URIs has been disabled."

`$browser->conn_cache(LWP::ConnCache->new( ))`
> Tells the browser object to try using the HTTP/1.1 Keep-Alive feature, which speeds up requests by reusing the same socket connection for multiple requests to the same server.

```
$browser->agent('someName/1.23 (more info here)')
```

Changes how the browser object identifies itself in the default User-Agent line of its HTTP requests. By default, it'll send libwww-perl/*versionnumber*, such as libwww-perl/5.65. More information is available in "Adding HTTP Headers to Your Request" [Hack #11].

```
push @{ $ua->requests_redirectable }, 'POST'
```

Tells this browser to obey redirection responses to POST requests (like most modern interactive browsers), even though the HTTP RFC says that should not normally be done.

—Sean Burke

HACK #16 Respecting Your Scrapee's Bandwidth

Be a better Net citizen by reducing load on remote sites, either by ensuring you're downloading only changed content, or by supporting compression.

Everybody has bills, and the more services you partake in, the higher those bills become. It's a blatantly obvious concept, but one that is easily forgotten when you're writing a scraper. See, when you're physically sitting at your computer, clicking through a site's navigation with your browser, you're an active user: sites love you and they want your traffic but, more importantly, your eyeballs.

With a spider, there are no eyeballs; you run a command line, then go watch the latest anime fansub. Behind the scenes, your spider could be making hundreds or thousands of requests. Of course, it depends on what your spider actually purports to solve, but the fact remains: it's an automated process, and one which could be causing the remote site additional bandwidth costs.

It doesn't have to be this way. In this hack, we'll demonstrate three different ways you can save some bandwidth (both for the site, and for your own rehandling of data you've already seen). The first two methods compare metadata you've saved previously with server data; the last covers compression.

If-Modified-Since

In "Adding HTTP Headers to Your Request" [Hack #11], we learned how to fake our User-Agent or add a Referer to get past certain server-side filters. HTTP headers aren't always used for subversion, though, and If-Modified-Since is a perfect example of one that isn't. The following script downloads a web page and returns the Last-Modified HTTP header, as reported by the server:

```
#!/usr/bin/perl -w
use strict;
```

```perl
use LWP 5.64;
use HTTP::Date;

my $url = 'http://disobey.com/amphetadesk/';
my $browser = LWP::UserAgent->new;
my $response = $browser->get( $url );
print "Got: ", $response->status_line;

print "\n". "Epoch: " . $response->last_modified . "\n";
print "English: " . time2str($response->last_modified) . "\n";
```

When run from the command line, it returns the last time the content at that URL was modified, both in seconds since the Epoch and in English:

```
% perl last_modified.pl
Got: 200 OK
Epoch: 1036026316
English: Thu, 31 Oct 2002 01:05:16 GMT
```

Not all sites will report back a Last-Modified header, however; sites whose pages are dynamically generated (by PHP, SSIs, Perl, etc.) simply won't have one. For an example, change the $url to *http://disobey.com/dnn/*, which uses server-side includes to load in sidebars.

But for those that do report Last-Modified and provide a date, what now? The first step to saving bandwidth is to *remember that date*. Save it to disk, database, memory, wherever; just keep track of it. The next time you request the same web page, you now have a way to determine if the page has been modified since that date. If the page hasn't changed (in essence, if the page has the same Last-Modified header), then you'll be downloading duplicate content. Notice the modification date gleaned from the previous script run and fed back to the server:

```perl
#!/usr/bin/perl -w
use strict;
use LWP 5.64;
use HTTP::Date;

my $url = 'http://disobey.com/amphetadesk/';
my $date = "Thu, 31 Oct 2002 01:05:16 GMT";
my %headers = ( 'If-Modified-Since' => $date );

my $browser = LWP::UserAgent->new;
my $response = $browser->get( $url, %headers );
print "Got: ", $response->status_line;
```

Invoked again, the server returns HTTP code 304, indicating that the content has not been modified since the If-Modified-Since date it was provided:

```
% perl last_modified.pl
Got: 304 Not Modified
```

Note that even though we're still using get to request the data from the server, the content was "Not Modified" (represented by the HTTP response code 304), so nothing was actually downloaded. You've saved yourself some processing time, and you've saved the remote site some bandwidth. You're able to check whether you have new data, or whether it's unchanged, like so:

```
if ($response->is_success) { print "process new data"; }
elsif ($response->code == 304) { print "data not modified"; }
```

ETags

An ETag is another HTTP header with a function similar to Last-Modified and If-Modified-Since. Instead of a date, it returns a unique string based on the content you're downloading. If the string has changed, then you can assume the content is different. The chief benefit of supporting ETags is that they are often returned even if the content is dynamically generated—where the modification date is not particularly clear. Our code, assuming we've already saved an ETag from the last download, is similar to what we saw earlier. Here, we combine the getting and sending of the ETag into one script:

```
#!/usr/bin/perl -w
use strict;
use LWP 5.64;

my $url = 'http://www.w3.org/';
my $etag = '"3ef89bc8;3e2eee38"';
my %headers = ( 'If-None-Match' => $etag );

my $browser = LWP::UserAgent->new;
my $response = $browser->get( $url, %headers );
print "ETag from server: " . $response->header("ETag") . "\n";
print "Got: " . $response->status_line . "\n";
```

Compressed Data

What if we could save bandwidth by reducing the size of the new data we're receiving? As with the previous HTTP headers, this is entirely dependent on what's supported by the remote server, but it also requires a little more coding to live up to our end of the bargain.

Most web servers have the ability (either natively or with a module) to take textual data (such as an HTML web page) and reduce its size with the popular gzip compression format. Often, this creates a 50–80% smaller file to be sent across the wires. Think of it as analogous to receiving a ZIP archive by mail instead of receiving the full-sized files. However, the User-Agent (i.e., you) receiving this encoded data needs to know how to decompress it and treat it as the HTML it actually is.

The first thing we need to do is tell the remote server that we can accept gzipped documents. Since these documents are encoded, we add an HTTP header (Accept-Encoding) that states we can *accept* that *encoding*. If the server, in turn, also supports the gzip-encoding scheme for the document we've requested, it'll say as much, as shown by the following script:

```perl
#!/usr/bin/perl -w
use strict;
use LWP 5.64;

my $url = 'http://www.disobey.com/';
my %headers = ( 'Accept-Encoding' => 'gzip; deflate' );
my $browser = LWP::UserAgent->new;
my $response = $browser->get( $url, %headers );

my $data = $response->content;
my $enc = $response->content_encoding;

if ($enc eq "gzip" or $enc eq "deflate") {
    print "Server supports $enc, woo!\n";
}
```

This may look helpful, but it's really not. Simply knowing the server supports gzip doesn't get us very far, as now we have all this compressed junk in $data with no way to actually decode it. *Compress::Zlib* to the rescue!

```perl
#!/usr/bin/perl -w
use strict;
use Compress::Zlib;
use LWP 5.64;

my $url = 'http://www.disobey.com/';
my %headers = ( 'Accept-Encoding' => 'gzip; deflate' );
my $browser = LWP::UserAgent->new;
my $response = $browser->get( $url, %headers );

my $data = $response->content;

if (my $encoding = $response->content_encoding)  ) {
    $data = Compress::Zlib::memGunzip($data) if $encoding =~ /gzip/i;
    $data = Compress::Zlib::uncompress($data) if $encoding =~ /deflate/i;
}
```

Any production-quality spider should consider implementing all the suggestions within this hack; they'll not only make remote sites happier with your scraping, but they'll also ensure that your spider operates faster, by ignoring data you've already processed.

Respecting robots.txt

#17   The robots.txt file is a bastion of fair play, allowing a site to restrict what visiting scrapers are allowed to see and do or, indeed, keep them out entirely. Play fair by respecting their requests.

If you've ever built your own web site, you may have come across something called a *robots.txt* file (*http://www.robotstxt.org*)—a magical bit of text that you, as web developer and site owner, can create to control the capabilities of third-party robots, agents, scrapers, spiders, or what have you. Here is an example of a *robots.txt* file that blocks any robot's access to three specific directories:

```
User-agent: *
Disallow: /cgi-bin/
Disallow: /tmp/
Disallow: /private/
```

Applications that understood your *robots.txt* file will resolutely abstain from indexing those parts of your site, or they'll leave dejectedly if you deny them outright, as per this example:

```
User-agent: *
Disallow: /
```

If you're planning on releasing your scraper or spider into the wild, it's important that you make every possible attempt to support *robots.txt*. Its power comes solely from the number of clients that choose to respect it. Thankfully, with *LWP*, we can rise to the occasion quite simply.

If you want to make sure that your *LWP*-based program respects *robots.txt*, you can use the *LWP::RobotUA* class (*http://search.cpan.org/author/GAAS/libwww-perl/lib/LWP/RobotUA.pm*) instead of *LWP::UserAgent*. Doing so also ensures that your script doesn't make requests too many times a second, saturating the site's bandwidth unnecessarily. *LWP::RobotUA* is just like *LWP::UserAgent*, and you can use it like so:

```
use LWP::RobotUA;

# Your bot's name and your email address
my $browser = LWP::RobotUA->new('SuperBot/1.34', 'you@site.com');
my $response = $browser->get($url);
```

If the *robots.txt* file on $url's server forbids you from accessing $url, then the $browser object (assuming it's of the class *LWP::RobotUA*) won't actually request it, but instead will give you back (in $response) a 403 error with a message "Forbidden by robots.txt." Trap such an eventuality like so:

```
die "$url -- ", $response->status_line, "\nAborted"
    unless $response->is_success;
```

Upon encountering such a resource, your script would die with:

```
http://whatever.site.int/pith/x.html -- 403 Forbidden by robots.txt
```

If this $browser object sees that the last time it talked to $url's server was too recently, it will pause (via sleep) to avoid making too many requests too often. By default, it will pause for one minute, but you can control the length of the pause with the $browser->delay(*minutes*) attribute.

For example, $browser->delay(7/60) means that this browser will pause when it needs to avoid talking to any given server more than once every seven seconds.

—Sean Burke

HACK #18   Adding Progress Bars to Your Scripts
Give a visual indication that a download is progressing smoothly.

With all this downloading, it's often helpful to have some visual representation of its progress. In most of the scripts in this book, there's always a bit of visual information being displayed to the screen: that we're starting this URL here, processing this data there, and so on. These helpful bits usually come before or after the actual data has been downloaded. But what if we want visual feedback while we're in the middle of a large MP3, movie, or database leech?

If you're using a fairly recent vintage of the *LWP* library, you'll be able to interject your own subroutine to run at regular intervals during download. In this hack, we'll show you four different ways of adding various types of progress bars to your current applications. To get the most from this hack, you should have ready a URL that's roughly 500 KB or larger; it'll give you a good chance to see the progress bar in action.

The Code

The first progress bar is the simplest, providing only a visual heartbeat so that you can be sure things are progressing and not just hanging. Save the following code to a file called *progress_bar.pl* and run it from the command line as perl scriptname *URL*, where *URL* is the online location of your appropriately large piece of sample data:

```
#!/usr/bin/perl -w
#
# Progress Bar: Dots - Simple example of an LWP progress bar.
# http://disobey.com/d/code/ or contact morbus@disobey.com.
#
```

```
# This code is free software; you can redistribute it and/or
# modify it under the same terms as Perl itself.
#

use strict; $|++;
my $VERSION = "1.0";

# make sure we have the modules we need, else die peacefully.
eval("use LWP 5.6.9;");  die "[err] LWP 5.6.9 or greater required.\n" if $@;

# now, check for passed URLs for downloading.
die "[err] No URLs were passed for processing.\n" unless @ARGV;

# our downloaded data.
my $final_data = undef;

# loop through each URL.
foreach my $url (@ARGV) {
    print "Downloading URL at ", substr($url, 0, 40), "... ";

    # create a new useragent and download the actual URL.
    # all the data gets thrown into $final_data, which
    # the callback subroutine appends to.
    my $ua = LWP::UserAgent->new( );
    my $response = $ua->get($url, ':content_cb' => \&callback, );
    print "\n"; # after the final dot from downloading.
}

# per chunk.
sub callback {
    my ($data, $response, $protocol) = @_;
    $final_data .= $data;
    print ".";
}
```

None of this code is particularly new, save the addition of our primitive progress bar. We use *LWP*'s standard get method, but add the :content_cb header with a value that is a reference to a subroutine that will be called at regular intervals as our content is downloaded. These intervals can be suggested with an optional :read_size_hint, which is the number of bytes you'd like received before they're passed to the callback.

In this example, we've defined that the data should be sent to a subroutine named callback. You'll notice that the routine receives the actual content, $data, that has been downloaded. Since we're overriding *LWP*'s normal $response->content or :content_file features, we now have to take full control of the data. In this hack, we store all our results in $final_data, but we don't actually do anything with them.

Most relevant, however, is the print statement within the callback routine. This is our first pathetic attempt at visual feedback during the downloading process: every time a chunk of data gets sent our way, we spit out a dot. If the total data size is sufficiently large, our screen will be filled with dots, dots, and more dots:

```
Downloading URL at http://disobey.com/large_file.mov...
..............................................................................
..............................................................................
..............................................................................
..............................................................................
..............................................................................
.....................................................................
```

While useful, it's certainly not very pretty, and it can be especially disruptive for large files (the previous example is the output of downloading just 700 KB). Instead, how about we use a little primitive animation?

If you've worked in the shell or installed various programs (or even a retail version of Linux), you may have seen rotating cursors built from ASCII letters. These cursors could start at \, erase that character, draw a |, erase, /, erase, -, and then \ to restart the loop. Individually, and without the benefit of a flipbook, these look pretty boring. Onscreen, however, they create a decent equivalent to an hourglass or spinning ball.

Modify the previous script, adding the highlighted lines:

```
...
# our downloaded data.
my $final_data = undef;

# your animation and counter.
my $counter; my @animation = qw( \ | / - );

# loop through each URL.
foreach my $url (@ARGV)
...
```

This initializes a counter and creates an array that contains the frames of our animations. As you can see, we use the same frames we discussed earlier. If you don't like 'em, customize your own (perhaps . i l i). The last change we need to make is in our callback routine. Swap out the existing print "." with:

```
print "$animation[$counter++]\b";
$counter = 0 if $counter == scalar(@animation);
```

And that's it. For each chunk of data we receive, the next frame of the animation will play. When our counter is the same as the number of frames, we reset and begin anew. Obviously, we can't show a readily apparent example of what this looks like, so try it at your leisure.

We can still do better, though. We've certainly removed the distracting dot distortion, but we're still left with only simple output; we don't have raw

information on how far we've gone and how far still to go. The following
code provides a progress meter with a visual percentage bar, as well as a
numerical reading:

```perl
#!/usr/bin/perl -w
#
# Progress Bar: Wget - Wget style progress bar with LWP.
# http://disobey.com/d/code/ or contact morbus@disobey.com.
# Original routine by tachyon at http://tachyon.perlmonk.org/
#
# This code is free software; you can redistribute it and/or
# modify it under the same terms as Perl itself.
#

use strict; $|++;
my $VERSION = "1.0";

# make sure we have the modules we need, else die peacefully.
eval("use LWP 5.6.9;");  die "[err] LWP 5.6.9 or greater required.\n" if $@;

# now, check for passed URLs for downloading.
die "[err] No URLs were passed for processing.\n" unless @ARGV;

# happy golucky variables.
my $final_data;  # our downloaded data.
my $total_size;  # total size of the URL.

# loop through each URL.
foreach my $url (@ARGV) {
    print "Downloading URL at ", substr($url, 0, 40), "...\n";

    # create a new useragent and download the actual URL.
    # all the data gets thrown into $final_data, which
    # the callback subroutine appends to. before that,
    # though, get the total size of the URL in question.
    my $ua = LWP::UserAgent->new( );
    my $result = $ua->head($url);
    my $remote_headers = $result->headers;
    $total_size = $remote_headers->content_length;

    # now do the downloading.
    my $response = $ua->get($url, ':content_cb' => \&callback );
}

# per chunk.
sub callback {
    my ($data, $response, $protocol) = @_;
    $final_data .= $data;
    print progress_bar( length($final_data), $total_size, 25, '=' );
}
```

```
# wget-style. routine by tachyon
# at http://tachyon.perlmonk.org/
sub progress_bar {
    my ( $got, $total, $width, $char ) = @_;
    $width ||= 25; $char ||= '=';
    my $num_width = length $total;
    sprintf "|%-${width}s| Got %${num_width}s bytes of %s (%.2f%%)\r",
        $char x (($width-1)*$got/$total). '>',
        $got, $total, 100*$got/+$total;
}
```

You'll notice right off the bat that we've added another subroutine at the bottom of our code. Before we get into that, check out our actual *LWP* request. Instead of just asking for the data, we first check the HTTP headers to see the size of the file we'll be downloading. We store this size in a $total_size variable. It plays an important part in our new subroutine, best demonstrated with a sample:

```
Downloading URL at http://disobey.com/large_file.mov...
|=============>          | Got 422452 bytes of 689368 (61.28%)
```

This is sprintf magic at work, thanks to a little magic from tachyon over at Perl Monks (*http://www.perlmonks.org/index.pl?node_id=80749*). As each chunk of data gets sent to our callback, the display is updated both as a bar and as a byte count and percentage. It's a wonderful piece of work and my preferred progress bar as of this writing. As you can see in the progress_bar line of the callback, you can modify the width as well as the character.

So far, we've rolled our own, but there is a module on CPAN, *Term::ProgressBar* (*http://search.cpan.org/author/FLUFFY/Term-ProgressBar*), that takes care of the lion's share of the work for us. It has a bit more functionality than sprintf, such as titling the progress bar, including an ETA, and growing to the length of the user's terminal width. Here it is in action:

```
#!/usr/bin/perl -w
#
# Progress Bar: Term::ProgressBar - progress bar with LWP.
# http://disobey.com/d/code/ or contact morbus@disobey.com.
# Original routine by tachyon at http://tachyon.perlmonk.org/
#
# This code is free software; you can redistribute it and/or
# modify it under the same terms as Perl itself.
#

use strict; $|++;
my $VERSION = "1.0";

# make sure we have the modules we need, else die peacefully.
eval("use LWP 5.6.9;");
die "[err] LWP is not the required version.\n" if $@;
```

```perl
eval("use Term::ProgressBar;"); # prevent word-wrapping.
die "[err] Term::ProgressBar not installed.\n" if $@;

# now, check for passed URLs for downloading.
die "[err] No URLs were passed for processing.\n" unless @ARGV;

# happy golucky variables.
my $final_data = 0;  # our downloaded data.
my $total_size;      # total size of the URL.
my $progress;        # progress bar object.
my $next_update = 0; # reduce ProgressBar use.

# loop through each URL.
foreach my $url (@ARGV) {
    print "Downloading URL at ", substr($url, 0, 40), "...\n";

    # create a new useragent and download the actual URL.
    # all the data gets thrown into $final_data, which
    # the callback subroutine appends to. before that,
    # though, get the total size of the URL in question.
    my $ua = LWP::UserAgent->new();
    my $result = $ua->head($url);
    my $remote_headers = $result->headers;
    $total_size = $remote_headers->content_length;

    # initialize our progress bar.
    $progress = Term::ProgressBar->new({count => $total_size, ETA => ↵
'linear'});
    $progress->minor(0);            # turns off the floating asterisks.
    $progress->max_update_rate(1); # only relevant when ETA is used.

    # now do the downloading.
    my $response = $ua->get($url, ':content_cb' => \&callback );

    # top off the progress bar.
    $progress->update($total_size);
}

# per chunk.
sub callback {
    my ($data, $response, $protocol) = @_;
    $final_data .= $data;

    # reduce usage, as per example 3 in POD.
    $next_update = $progress->update(length($final_data))
        if length($final_data) >= $next_update;
}
```

And here's its output:

```
Downloading URL at http://disobey.com/large_file.mov...
  13% [========                                          ]9m57s Left
```

More examples are available in the *Term::ProgressBar* documentation.

Scraping with HTML::TreeBuilder

HACK #19

One of many popular HTML parsers available in Perl, HTML::TreeBuilder
approaches the art of HTML parsing as a parent/child relationship.

Sometimes regular expressions [Hack #23] won't get you all the way to the data
you want and you'll need to use a real HTML parser. CPAN has a few of these,
the main two being *HTML::TreeBuilder* and *HTML::TokeParser* [Hack #20], both
of which are friendly façades for *HTML::Parser*. This hack covers the former.

The *Tree* in *TreeBuilder* represents a parsing ideology: trees are a good way
to represent HTML. The <head> tag is a child of the <html> tag. The <title>
and <meta> tags are children of the <head> tag.

TreeBuilder takes a stream of HTML, from a file or from a variable, and
turns it into a tree of *HTML::Element* nodes. Each of these nodes can be
queried for its parent, its siblings, or its children. Each node can also be
asked for a list of children that fulfill certain requirements.

We'll demonstrate this concept by writing a program that extracts a complete list of O'Reilly's books and then does some queries on that data. First,
we have to fetch the page, easily done with *LWP::Simple* [Hack #9]. The script
grabs all the content from O'Reilly's catalog page and constructs a new tree
by feeding the content to the new_from_content method:

```perl
#!/usr/bin/perl -w
use strict;
use LWP::Simple;
use HTML::TreeBuilder;

my $url = 'http://www.oreilly.com/catalog/prdindex.html';
my $page = get( $url ) or die $!;
my $p = HTML::TreeBuilder->new_from_content( $page );
```

The look_down method starts from the top of the tree and then works down-
ward, seeing which nodes match the specified conditions. We specify that
we want anchor tags and the URL has to match a certain regular expression.
This returns a list of matching nodes, which we put in @links:

```perl
my @links = $p->look_down(
    _tag => 'a',
    href => qr{^ \Qhttp://www.oreilly.com/catalog/\E \w+ $}x
);
```

We could happily make a list of titles and URLs, but the page we're fetching
has more: price, ISBN, and whether it's on O'Reilly's subscription-based
Safari online library (*http://safari.online.com/*). This information is contained in a bit of HTML code that looks like this:

```html
<tr bgcolor="#ffffff">
  <td valign="top">
```

```
        <a href="http://oreilly.com/catalog/googlehks">Google Hacks</a><br />
    </td>
    <td valign="top" nowrap="nowrap">0-596-00447-8</td>
    <td valign="top" align="right">$24.95</td>
    <td valign="top" nowrap="nowrap" align="center"> 
        <a href="http://safari.oreilly.com/0596004478">Read it on Safari</a>
    </td>
    <td valign="top" nowrap="nowrap">
        <a href="http://examples.oreilly.com/googlehks/">Get examples</a>
    </td>
</tr>
```

Our previous match with look_down places us at the emphasized code in the
HTML output. To get at the rest of the data, we need to move upward in the
HTML tree until we hit the <tr> element. The parent of our current location is <td>, and the parent of that element is our desired <tr>. Thus, we get
@rows:

```
my @rows = map { $_->parent->parent } @links;
```

We then loop over each of those rows, representing one book at a time. We
find each of the <td> elements, giving us the table cells. The first one is the
title, the second is the ISBN, and the third is price. Since we want only the
text of the table cell, we use as_trimmed_text to return the text, minus any
leading or trailing whitespace:

```
my @books;
for my $row (@rows) {
    my %book;
    my @cells = $row->look_down( _tag => 'td' );
    $book{title}   = $cells[0]->as_trimmed_text;
    $book{isbn}    = $cells[1]->as_trimmed_text;
    $book{price}   = $cells[2]->as_trimmed_text;
    $book{price} =~ s/^\$//;
```

The URLs are slightly trickier. We want the first (only) URL in each of the
cells, but one might not always exist. We add a new routine, get_url, which
is given an *HTML::Element* node and works out the correct thing to do. As
is typical in web scraping, there's a slight bit of cleaning to do. Some URLs
on the page have a trailing carriage return, so we get rid of those:

```
    $book{url}      = get_url( $cells[0] );
    $book{safari}   = get_url( $cells[3] );
    $book{examples} = get_url( $cells[4] );
    push @books, \%book;
}

sub get_url {
    my $node = shift;
    my @hrefs = $node->look_down( _tag => 'a');
    return unless @hrefs;
```

```
    my $url = $hrefs[0]->attr('href');
    $url =~ s/\s+$//;
    return $url;
}
```

Finally, we delete the tree, because it's not needed anymore. Due to the cross-linking of nodes, it has to be deleted explicitly; we can't let Perl try (and fail) to clean it up. Failing to delete your trees will leave unnecessary fragments in Perl's memory, taking up nothing but space (read: memory).

```
$p = $p->delete; # don't need it anymore
```

We now have an array of books with all sorts of information about them. With this array, we can now ask questions, such as how many books are there with "Perl" in the title, which is the cheapest, and how many more Java books can we expect to find:

```
{
    my $count = 1;
    my @perlbooks  = sort { $a->{price} <=> $b->{price} }
                        grep { $_->{title} =~ /perl/i } @books;
    print $count++, "\t", $_->{price}, "\t", $_->{title} for @perlbooks;
}


{
    my @perlbooks = grep { $_->{title} =~ /perl/i } @books;
    my @javabooks = grep { $_->{title} =~ /java/i } @books;
    my $diff = @javabooks - @perlbooks;
    print "There are ".@perlbooks." Perl books and ".@javabooks.
            " Java books. $diff more Java than Perl.";
}
```

Hacking the Hack

Say you want more information on each book. We now have a list of URLs, one for each book. Want to collect author and publication information? First, fetch the individual page for the book in question. As there are 453 titles (at least), it's probably a bad idea to fetch all of them.

From there, we can do this:

```
for my $book ( $books[34] ) {
    my $url = $book->{url};
    my $page = get( $url );
    my $tree = HTML::TreeBuilder->new_from_content( $page );
    my ($pubinfo) = $tree->look_down(
                            _tag => 'span',
                            class => 'secondary2'
    );
    my $html = $pubinfo->as_HTML; print $html;
```

Since as_HTML produces well-formed and regular HTML, you can easily extract the desired information with a set of regular expressions:

```
my ($pages) = $html =~ /(\d+) pages/;
my ($edition) = $html =~ /(\d)(?:st|nd|rd|th) Edition/;
my ($date) = $html =~ /(\w+ (19|20)\d\d)/;

print "\n$pages $edition $date\n";
```

Need the cover?

```
my ($img_node) = $tree->look_down(
                              _tag => 'img',
                              src  => qr{^/catalog/covers/},
);
my $img_url = 'http://www.oreilly.com'.$img_node->attr('src');
my $cover = get( $img_url );
# now save $cover to disk.
}
```

—Iain Truskett

Parsing with HTML::TokeParser

#20

HTML::TokeParser allows you to follow a path through HTML code, storing the contents of tags as you move nearer your desire.

One of the main limitations of HTML as a language for pages on the Web is its lack of separation between content and form. It's not possible for us to look solely at the information an HTML page has to offer; rather, we need to navigate through a mass of tags in order to programmatically split the content of a page from the markup used to specify how it should look.

One way to accomplish this is with the *HTML::TokeParser* module written by Gisle Aas. It allows us to easily model an HTML page as a stream of elements instead of an entire and complete tree, directing the parser to perform actions such as moving to the next tag with a given property and storing the content inside the tag.

For a demonstration, let's write a parser for the Echocloud site (*http://www.echocloud.net/*). Echocloud provides recommendations for music artists, based on the file lists found on popular peer-to-peer networks; if two artists are often found together in the music collections of different people sharing files, Echocloud assumes that people listening to the first artist would enjoy listening to the second, and in this way a list of similar artists is created.

The *HTML::TokeParser* modus operandi is typically something like this:

1. Download the page to be worked on.
2. Determine the structure of the HTML document by looking at the tags present. Is there always a particular tag or group of tags just before the

content we're trying to save? Do tags that contain content have any special modifiers, such as a class attribute?

3. Model the structure in code, storing wanted content as it is found.

By searching for our favorite artist at Echocloud, the snippet of returned HTML for each similar artist looks something like the following mass of code:

```
<TR bgcolor=#F2F2F2><TD class = "cf" nowrap WIDTH='300'><A
HREF='index.php?searchword=Autechre&option=asearch&nrows=40&cur=0
&stype=2&order=0'  class = "cf"> Autechre</A></TD><TD align=center><A
HREF="http://www.amazon.com/exec/obidos/external-search?tag=echocloud-
20&keyword=Autechre&mode=music"><img src="images/M_images/amazon_small.gif"
border=0 align="center"></A>|<a href="http://www.insound.com/search.cfm?
from=52208&searchby=artist&query=Autechre"><img src="images/M_images/
insound.gif" border=0 align="center"></a>   </TD>
<TD><span class = newsflash>8.05 </span></TD><TD><span class
=newsflash>0.50</span> </TD></TR>
```

Thankfully, each of the results helpfully uses a class of cf that is present only for the <A> tags in our search results. Therefore, we use this to discriminate as we travel through the document.

The Code

Save the following code to a file called *echocloud.pl*:

```perl
#!/usr/bin/perl -w
use strict;

use LWP::Simple;
use HTML::TokeParser;
use URI::Escape;

# The artist to search for should be given as an argument.
my $artist = $ARGV[0]; die "No artist specified" unless $artist ne '';

# We use URI::Escape to convert the artist's name
# into a form that can be encoded as part of a URL.
my $search = uri_escape($artist);

# 1.  Download the page to be worked on.
####################################

my $content =
   get('http://www.echocloud.net/index.php?searchword='.
   "$search".'&option=asearch&stype=2&order=0&nrows=6');

# Now that we have our content, initialize a
# new HTML::TokeParser object with it.
my $stream = new HTML::TokeParser(\$content);

print "Artists liked by $artist listeners include:\n";
```

```
# 2.  Determine the structure of the HTML document.
# An HTML result looks like: <a href='index.php?searchword
# =Beck&option=asearch' class="cf"> Beck</a>
#####################################

# 3.  Model the structure in code.
# Given that each <a class="cf"> contains our result, we:
#    - Search for each <a> tag.
#    - If it has a 'class' attribute, and
#      the class attribute is "cf":
#         - Save all the text from <a> to </a>.
#    - Repeat.
#
# Of the methods used below, the two from TokeParser are:
# get_tag:  Move the stream to the next occurence of a tag.
# get_trimmed_text:  Store text from the current location
# of the stream to the tag given.
#####################################

# For each <a> tag
while (my $tag = $stream->get_tag("a")) {

  # Is there a 'class' attribute?  Is it 'cf'?
  if ($tag->[1]{class} and $tag->[1]{class} eq "cf") {

      # Store everything from <a> to </a>.
      my $result = $stream->get_trimmed_text("/a");

      # Remove leading.
      # ' ' character.
      $result =~ s/^.//g;

      # Echocloud sometimes returns the artist we searched
      # for as one of the results.  Skip the current loop
      # if the string given matches one of the results.
      next if $result =~ /$artist/i;

      # And we can print our final result.
      print "  - $result\n";
  }
}
```

Running the Hack

Here, I invoke the script, asking for artists associated with Aimee Mann:

```
% perl echocloud.pl 'Aimee Mann'
Artists liked by Aimee Mann listeners include:
  - Beck
  - Counting Crows
  - Bob Dylan
  - Radiohead
  - Blur
```

While this has been a simple example of the power of *HTML::TokeParser*, modeling more complex pages rarely involves more than increasing the number of get_tag calls and conditional checks on attributes and tags in code. For more complex interactions with sites, your *TokeParser* code can also be combined with *WWW::Mechanize* **[Hack #22]**.

See Also

- For alternative "similar artists" using AudioScrobbler, see "Expanding Your Musical Tastes" **[Hack #60]**.

—Chris Ball

HACK #21 WWW::Mechanize 101

While LWP::UserAgent and the rest of the LWP suite provide powerful tools for accessing and downloading web content, WWW::Mechanize can automate many of the tasks you'd normally have to code.

Perl has great tools for handling web protocols, and *LWP::UserAgent* makes it easy, encapsulating the nitty-gritty details of creating *HTTP::Requests*, sending the requests, parsing the *HTTP::Responses*, and providing the results.

Simple fetching of web pages is, as it should be, simple. For example:

```
#/usr/bin/perl -w
use strict;
use LWP::UserAgent;
my $ua = LWP::UserAgent->new( );

my $response = $ua->get( "http://search.cpan.org" );
die $response->status_line unless $response->is_success;

print $response->title;
my $html = $response->content;
```

Behind the scenes of the get method, all the details of the HTTP protocol are hidden from view, leaving me free to think about the code itself. POSTing requests is almost as simple. To search CPAN by author for my last name, I use this:

```
my %fields = (
    query => 'lester',
    mode => 'author',
);

my $response = $ua->post( "http://search.cpan.org", \%fields );
```

Although *LWP::UserAgent* makes things pretty simple when it comes to grabbing individual pages, it doesn't do much with the page itself. Once I have the results, I need to parse the page myself to handle the content.

For example, let's say I want to go through the search interface to find the CPAN home page for Andy Lester. The POST example does the searching and returns the results page, but that's not where I want to wind up. We still need to find out the address pointed to by the "Andy Lester" link. Once I have the search results, how do I know which Lester author I want? I need to extract the links from the HTML, find the text that matches "Andy Lester" and then find the next page. Maybe I don't know what fields will be on the page and I want to fill them in dynamically. All of this drudgery is taken care of by *WWW::Mechanize*.

Introducing WWW::Mechanize

WWW::Mechanize, or *Mech* for short, is a module that builds on the base of *LWP::UserAgent* and provides an easy interface for your most common web automation tasks (in fact, the first version of Mech was called *WWW::Automate*). While *LWP::UserAgent* is a pure component that makes no assumptions about how you're going to use it, and Mech's intent is to have a miniature web browser in a single object, Mech takes some liberties in the name of simplicity. For example, a Mech object keeps in its memory a history of the pages it's visited and automatically supplies an HTTP Referer header.

My previous example of fetching is even simpler with Mech:

```
#!/usr/bin/perl -w
use strict;
use WWW::Mechanize;

my $mech = WWW::Mechanize->new( );

$mech->get( "http://search.cpan.org" );
die $mech->response->status_line unless $mech->success;

print $mech->title;
my $html = $mech->content; # Big text string of HTML
```

Now that Mech is working for me, I don't even have to deal with any *HTTP::Response* objects unless I specifically want to. The success method checks that the response, carried around by the $mech object, indicates a successful action. The content method returns whatever the content from the page is, and the title method returns the title for the page, if the page is HTML (which we can check with the is_html method).

Using Mech's Navigation Tools

So far, Mech is just a couple of convenience methods. Mech really shines when it's pressed into action as a web client, extracting and following links and filling out and posting forms. Once you've successfully loaded a page, through either a GET or POST, Mech goes to work on the HTML content. It finds all the links on the page, whether they're in an A tag as a link, or in any FRAME or IFRAME tags as page source. Mech also finds and parses the forms on the page.

I'll put together all of Mech's talents into one little program that downloads all of my modules from CPAN. It will have to search for me by name, find my module listings, and then download the file to my current directory. (I could have had it go directly to my module listing, since I know my own CPAN ID, but that wouldn't show off form submission!)

The Code

Save the following code to a file called *mechmod.pl*:

```
#!/usr/bin/perl -w
use strict;
$|++;

use File::Basename;
use WWW::Mechanize 0.48;

my $mech = WWW::Mechanize->new( );

# Get the starting search page
$mech->get( "http://search.cpan.org" );
$mech->success or die $mech->response->status_line;

# Select the form, fill the fields, and submit
$mech->form_number( 1 );
$mech->field( query => "Lester" );
$mech->field( mode => "author" );
$mech->submit( );

$mech->success or die "post failed: ",
    $mech->response->status_line;

# Find the link for "Andy"
$mech->follow_link( text_regex => qr/Andy/ );
$mech->success or die "post failed: ", $mech->response->status_line;

# Get all the tarbulls
my @links = $mech->find_all_links( url_regex => qr/\.tar\.gz$/ );
my @urls = map { $_->[0] } @links;
```

```
    print "Found ", scalar @urls, " tarballs to download\n";

for my $url ( @urls ) {
    my $filename = basename( $url );
    print "$filename --> ";
    $mech->get( $url, ':content_file'=>$filename );
    print -s $filename, " bytes\n";
}
}
```

Running the Hack

Invoke *mechmod.pl* on the command line, like so:

```
% perl mechmod.pl
Found 14 tarballs to download
Acme-Device-Plot-0.01.tar.gz --> 2025 bytes
Apache-Lint-0.02.tar.gz --> 2131 bytes
Apache-Pod-0.02.tar.gz --> 3148 bytes
Carp-Assert-More-0.04.tar.gz --> 4126 bytes
ConfigReader-Simple-1.16.tar.gz --> 7313 bytes
HTML-Lint-1.22.tar.gz --> 58005 bytes
...
```

This short introduction to the world of *WWW::Mechanize* should give you an idea of how simple it is to write spiders and other mechanized robots that extract content from the Web.

—Andy Lester

Scraping with WWW::Mechanize

Never miss another Buffy the Vampire Slayer episode again with this easy-to-learn introduction to WWW::Mechanize and HTML::TokeParser.

Screen scraping is the process of emulating an interaction with a web site—not just downloading pages, but also filling out forms, navigating around, and dealing with the HTML received as a result. As well as for traditional information lookups—like the example we'll be exploring in this hack—you can use screen scraping to enhance a web service into doing something the designers didn't give us the power to do in the first place. Here's a quick example.

I do my banking online, but I quickly get bored with having to go to my bank's site, log in, navigate around to my accounts, and check the balance on each of them. One quick Perl module (*Finance::Bank::HSBC*) later, I can loop through each of my accounts and print their balances, all from a shell prompt. With some more code, I can do something the bank's site doesn't ordinarily let me do: I can treat my accounts as a whole instead of as individual accounts, and find out how much money I have, could possibly spend, and owe, all in total. Another step forward would be to schedule a *cron* entry [Hack #90] every day to use the HSBC option to download a copy of my transactions in Quicken's QIF format, and use Simon Cozens' *Finance::QIF* module to interpret the file and run those transactions against a budget, letting me know whether I'm spending too much lately. This takes a simple web-based system from being merely useful to being automated and bespoke; if you can think of how to write the code, you can do it.

> It's probably wise for me to add the caveat that you should be extremely careful when working with banking information programmatically, and you should be even more careful if you're storing your login details in a Perl script somewhere.

While that's very exciting, there are also more mundane tasks you can take care of with some Perl code and a couple of modules. Andy Lester's *WWW:: Mechanize* [Hack #22] allows you to go to a URL and explore the site, following links by name, taking cookies, filling in forms, and clicking Submit buttons. We're also going to use *HTML::TokeParser* to process the HTML we're given back, which is a process I've written about previously; see *http:// www.perl.com/pub/a/2001/11/15/creatingrss.html*.

The site I've chosen to use for this demonstration is the BBC's Radio Times (*http://www.radiotimes.beeb.com*), which allows users to create a "Diary" for their favorite TV programs and tells them whenever any of the programs are showing on any channel. Being a London Perl M[ou]nger, I have an obsession with *Buffy the Vampire Slayer*. If I tell this to the BBC's site, they'll tell me the time and name of the next episode, so I can check if it's one I've seen previously. I'd have to remember to log into their site every few days to check if there was a new episode coming along, though. Perl to the rescue! Our script will check to see when the next episode is and let us know, along with the name of the episode being shown.

If you're going to run the script yourself, you should register with the Radio Times site (*http://www.radiotimes.beeb.com/jsp/register.jsp*) and create a Diary; the script requires the email you registered with. Figure 2-2 shows an example of the data we'll be scraping, which contains the *Buffy* episodes we'd like to be informed about.

The Code

Save the following code to a file called *radiotimes.pl*:

```perl
#!/usr/bin/perl -w
use strict;

use WWW::Mechanize;
use HTML::TokeParser;
```

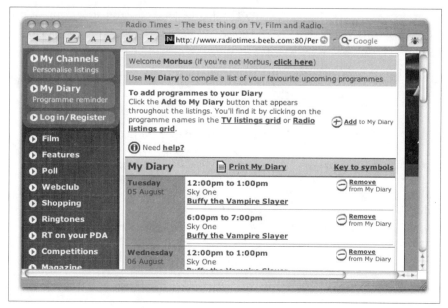

Figure 2-2. Our Diary, configured with Buffy showings

```
# the address you registered
# with Radio Times site here.
my $email = 'your email address';
die "Must provide an email address" unless $email ne '';

# We create a WWW::Mechanize object and tell it the address of the site
# we'll be working from. The Radio Times' front page has an image link
# with an ALT text of "My Diary", so we can use that to get to the right
# section of the site:

my $agent = WWW::Mechanize->new();
$agent->get("http://www.radiotimes.beeb.com/");
$agent->follow("My Diary");

# The returned page contains two forms - one to allow you to choose from a
# list box of program types, and then a login form for the diary
# function. We tell WWW::Mechanize to use the second form for input.
# (Something to remember here is that WWW::Mechanize's list of forms,
# unlike an array in Perl, is indexed starting at 1 rather than 0.
# Therefore, our index is '2'.)

$agent->form(2);

# Now we can fill in our email address for the '<INPUT name="email"
# type="text">' field and click the submit button. Nothing too
# complicated here.

$agent->field("email", $email);
$agent->click();
```

```
# WWW::Mechanize moves us on to our Diary page. This is the page
# we need to process to find the date details. On looking at the
# HTML source for this page, we can see the HTML we need to work
# through is something like:
#
#   <input>
#   <tr><td></td></tr>
#   <tr><td></td><td></td><td class="bluetext">Date of episode</td></tr>
#   <td></td><td></td>
#   <td class="bluetext"><b>Time of episode</b></td></tr>
#   <a href="page_with_episode_info"></a>
#
# This can be modelled with HTML::TokeParser as below. The important
# methods to note are get_tag, which will move the stream on to the
# next start of the tag given, and get_trimmed_text, which will take
# the text between the current tag and a given tag. For example, for the
# HTML code "<b>Bold text here</b>", my $tag = get_trimmed_text("/b")
# would return "Bold text here" to $tag.

# Also note that we're initializing HTML::TokeParser on
# '\$agent->{content}' - this is an internal variable for WWW::Mechanize,
# exposing the HTML content of the current page.

my $stream = HTML::TokeParser->new(\$agent->{content});
my $date; # will hold the current show's datestamp.

# <input>
$stream->get_tag("input");

# <tr><td></td></tr><tr>
$stream->get_tag("tr"); $stream->get_tag("tr");

# <td></td><td></td>
$stream->get_tag("td"); $stream->get_tag("td");

# <td class="bluetext">Date of episode</td></tr>
my $tag = $stream->get_tag("td");
if ($tag->[1]{class} and $tag->[1]{class} eq "bluetext") {
    $date = $stream->get_trimmed_text("/td");
    # The date contains ' ', which we'll translate to a space.
    $date =~ s/\xa0/ /g;
}

# <td></td><td></td>
$stream->get_tag("td");

# <td class="bluetext"><b>Time of episode</b>
$tag = $stream->get_tag("td");
if ($tag->[1]{class} eq "bluetext") {
    $stream->get_tag("b");
    # This concatenates the time of the showing to the date.
    $date .= ", from " . $stream->get_trimmed_text("/b");
}
```

```
# </td></tr><a href="page_with_episode_info"></a>
$tag = $stream->get_tag("a");

# Match the URL to find the page giving episode information.
$tag->[1]{href} =~ m!src=(http://.*?)'!;
my $show = $stream->get_trimmed_text("a");

# We have a scalar, $date, containing a string that looks something like
# "Thursday 23 January, from 6:45pm to 7:30pm.", and we have a URL, in
# $1, that will tell us more about that episode. We tell WWW::Mechanize
# to go to the URL:

$agent->get($1);

# The navigation we want to perform on this page is far less complex than
# on the last page, so we can avoid using a TokeParser for it - a regular
# expression should suffice. The HTML we want to parse looks something
# like this:
#
#   <br><b>Episode</b><br>  The Episode Title<br>
#
# We use a regex delimited with '!' in order to avoid having to escape the
# slashes present in the HTML, and store any number of alphanumeric
# characters after some whitespace, all in between <br> tags after the
# Episode header:

$agent->{content} =~ m!<br><b>Episode</b><br>\s+?(\w+?)<br>!;

# $1 now contains our episode, and all that's
# left to do is print out what we've found:

my $episode = $1;
print "The next Buffy episode ($episode) is on $date.\n";
```

Running the Hack

Invoke the script on the command line and, in our solely configured *Buffy*
example, it'll tell us what the next episode of *Buffy* is and when it's on,
based on the information we've configured in our Diary:

```
% perl radiotimes.pl
The next episode of Buffy(Gone) is on
   Thursday 23 January, from 6:45pm to 7:30pm.
```

Note that even though my favorite show is *Buffy*, yours might be *Farscape*,
and that's just fine; you can configure as many shows as you'd like in your
Radio Times Diary, and the script will always show you what's coming next:

```
% perl radiotimes.pl
The next episode of Farscape (Crackers Don't Matter) is
   on Thursday 23 January, from 10:00am to 11:00am.
```

I hope this gives a light-hearted introduction to the usefulness of these modules; happy screen scraping, and may you never miss your favorite episodes again.

—Chris Ball

In Praise of Regular Expressions

You don't always need to use a module like HTML::TokeParser or HTML::TreeBuilder in order to parse HTML. Sometimes, a few simple regular expressions can save you the effort.

Every so often, someone asks a question about extracting data from the thickets of HTML tag soup. They might have a piece of text like:

```
<p>This is a paragraph</p>
<p>And this is <i>another</i> paragraph</p>
```

and they wonder why they get such strange results when they try to attack it with something like /<p>(.*)<\/ p>/. The standard Perlmonk's reply is to point people to *HTML::Parser*, *HTML::TableExtract*, or even *HTML::TreeBuilder*, depending on the context. The main thrust of the argument is usually that regular expressions lead to fragile code. This is what I term *The Correct Answer*, but alas, in *Real Life*, things are never so simple, as a recent experience just showed me. You can, with minor care and effort, get perfect results with regular expressions, with much better performance.

Using Modules to Parse HTML

I've used *HTML::Parser* in the past to build the Perlmonk Snippets Index (*http://grinder.perlmonk.org/pmsi/*); the main reason is that I wanted to walk down all the pages, in case an old node was reaped. Doing that, I learned it's a real bear to ferry information from one callback to another. I hacked it by using global variables to keep track of state. Later on, someone else told me that *The Right Way* to use *HTML::Parser* is to subclass it and extend the internal hash object to track state that way. Fair enough, but this approach—while theoretically correct—is not a trivial undertaking for a casual user who just wants to chop up some HTML.

More recently, I used *HTML::TreeBuilder* to parse some HTML output from a webified Domino database. Because of the way the HTML was structured in this particular case, it was a snap to just look_down('_tag', 'foo') and get exactly what I wanted. It was easy to write, and the code was straightforward.

Watching the Printers: Score One for Regular Expressions

Then, last week, I got tired of keeping an eye on our farm of HP 4600 color printers to see how their supplies were lasting (they use four cartridges—C, M, Y, and K—and two kits, the transfer and fuser). It turns out that this model has an embedded web server. Point your browser at it, and it will produce a status page that shows you how many pages can be printed, based on what's left in the consumables.

So, I brought *HTML::TreeBuilder* to bear on the task. It wasn't quite as easy. It was no simple matter to find a reliable part in the tree from whence to direct my search. The HTML contains deeply nested tables, with a high degree of repetition for each kit and cartridge. The various pieces of information were scattered in different elements, and collecting and collating it made for some pretty ugly code.

After I'd managed to wrestle the data I wanted out of the web page, I set about stepping through the code in the debugger, to better understand the data structures and see what shortcuts I could figure out by way of method chaining and array slicing in an attempt to tidy up the code. To my surprise, I saw that just building the *HTML::TreeBuilder* object (by calling the parse( ) with the HTML in a scalar) required about a second to execute, and this on some fairly recent high-end hardware.

Until then, I wasn't really concerned about performance, because I figured the parse time would be dwarfed by the time it took to get the request's results back. In the master plan, I intended to use *LWP::Parallel::UserAgent* (*http://search.cpan.org/author/MARCLANG/ParallelUserAgent/*) to probe all of the printers in parallel, rather than loop though them one at a time, and factor out much of the waiting. In a perfect world, it would be as fast as the single slowest printer.

Given the less than stellar performance of the code at this point, however, it was clear that the cost of parsing the HTML would consume the bulk of the overall runtime. Maybe I might be able to traverse a partially fetched page, but at this point, the architecture would start to become unwieldy. Madness!

The Code

So, after trying the orthodox approach, I started again. I broke the rule about parsing HTML with regular expressions and wrote the following code:

```
#!usr/bin/perl -w
use strict;
```

```
my (@s) = m{
        >               # close of previous tag
        ([^<]+)     # text (name of part, e.g., q/BLACK CARTRIDGE/)
        <br>
        ([^<]+)     # part number (e.g., q/HP Part Number: HP C9724A/+)
        (?:<[^>]+>\s*){4} # separated by four tags
        (\d+)           # percent remaining
        |               # --or--
        (?:
            # different text values
            (?:
                Pages\sRemaining
                | Low\sReached
                | Serial\sNumber
                | Pages\sprinted\swith\sthis\ssupply
            ) : (?:\s*<[^>]+>){6}\s* # colon, separated by six tags
        # or just this, within the current element
        | Based\son\shistorical\s\S+\spage\scoverage\sof\s
        )
        (\w+) # and the value we want
    }gx;
```

A single regular expression (albeit with a /g modifier for global matching) pulls out all I want. Actually, it's not quite perfect, since the resulting array also fills up with a pile of undefs, the unfilled parenthesis on the opposite side of the | alternation to the match. This is easily handled with a simple next unless $index addition to any foreach loop on @s.

Is the code fragile? Not really. The HTML has errors in it, such as <td valign= op">, which can trip up some modules that expect perfectly formed HTML, but *HTML::TreeBuilder* coped just fine with this too.

Not Fragile, but Probably Not Permanent Either

The generated HTML is stored in the printer's onboard firmware, so unless I upgrade the BIOS, the HTML isn't going to change; it's written in stone, bugs and all.

Here's the main point: when the HP 4650 or 4700 model is released, it will probably have completely different HTML anyway, perhaps with stylesheets instead of tables. Either way, the HTML will have to be inspected anew, in order to tweak the regular expression or to pull something else out of *TreeBuilder*'s parse tree.

Neither approach, regular expression nor module, is maintenance free. But the regular expression is far less code and 17 times faster. Now, the extraction cost is negligible compared to the page fetch, as it should be. And, as a final bonus, the regular expression approach requires no noncore modules, saving me installation time. Case closed.

—*David Landgren*

Painless RSS with Template::Extract

HACK #24

Wouldn't it be nice if you could simply visualize what data on a page looks like, explain it in template form to Perl, and not bother with the need for parsers, regular expressions, and other programmatic logic? That's exactly what Template::Extract helps you do.

One thing that I'd always wanted to do, but never got around to doing, was produce RSS files for all those news sites I read regularly that don't have their own RSS feeds. Maybe I'd read them more regularly if they notified me when something was new, instead of requiring me to remember to check.

One day, I was fiddling about with the Template Toolkit (*http://www. template-toolkit.com*) and it dawned on me that all these sites were, at some level, generated with some templating engine. The Template Toolkit takes a template and some data and produces HTML output. For instance, if I have the following Perl data structure:

```
@news = (
        { date => "2003-09-02", subject => "Some News!",
          content => "Something interesting happened today." },
        { date => "2003-09-03", subject => "More News!",
          content => "I ran out of imagination today." }
);
```

I can apply a template like so:

```
<ul>
    [% FOREACH item = news %]
        <li> <i> [% item.date %] </i> - <b> [% item.subject %] </b>
            <p> [% item.content %] </p>
        </li>
    [% END %]
</ul>
```

I'll end up with some HTML that looks like this:

```
<ul>
        <li> <i> 2003-09-02 </i> - <b> Some News! </b>
            <p> Something interesting happened today. </p>
        </li>
        <li> <i> 2003-09-03 </i> - <b> More News! </b>
            <p> I  ran out of imagination today. </p>
        </li>
</ul>
```

Okay, you might think, very interesting, but how does this relate to scraping web pages for RSS? Well, we know what the HTML looks like, and we can make a reasonable guess at what the template ought to look like, but we want only the data. If only I could apply the Template Toolkit *backward* somehow. Taking HTML output and a template that could conceivably generate the output, I could retrieve the original data structure and, from then on, generating RSS from the data structure would be a piece of cake.

Like most brilliant ideas, this is hardly original, and an equally brilliant man named Autrijus Tang not only had the idea a long time before me, but—and this is the hard part—actually worked out how to implement it. His *Template::Extract* Perl module (*http://search.cpan.org/author/AUTRIJUS/Template-Extract/*) does precisely this: extract a data structure from its template and output.

I put it to work immediately to turn the blog of one of my favorite singers, Martyn Joseph (*http://www.piperecords.co.uk/news/diary.asp*), into an RSS feed. I'll use his blog for the example in this hack.

First, write a simple bit of Perl to grab the page, and tidy it up to avoid tripping over whitespace issues:

```
#!/usr/bin/perl

my $page = get(" http://www.piperecords.co.uk/news/diary.asp" );
exit unless $page;
$page = join "\n", grep { /\S/ } split /\n/, $page;
$page =~ s/\r//g;
$page =~ s/^\s+//g;
```

This removes blank lines, DOS line feeds, and leading spaces. Once you've done this, take a look at the structure of the page. You'll find that blog posts start with this line:

```
<!--START OF ABSTRACT OF NEWSITEM-->
```

and end with this one:

```
<!--END OF ABSTRACT OF NEWSITEM-->
```

The interesting bit of the diary starts after the close of an HTML comment:

```
-->
```

After a bit more observation, you can glean a template like this:

```
-->
[% FOR records %]
    <!--START OF ABSTRACT OF NEWSITEM-->
    [% ... %]
    <a href="[% url %]"><acronym title="Click here to read this article">
    [% title %]</acronym></a></strong>     ([% date %]) <BR>
    [% ... %]<font size="2">[% content %]</font></font></div>
    [% ... %]
    <!--END OF ABSTRACT OF NEWSITEM-->
[% END %]
```

The special [% ... %] template markup means "stuff" or things that we don't care about; it's the *Template::Extract* equivalent of regular expression's .*. Now, feed your document and this template to *Template::Extract*:

```
my $x = Template::Extract->new( );
my $data = $x->extract($template, $doc);
```

You end up with a data structure that looks like this:

```
$data = { records => [
            { url => "...", title => "...", date => "...", content => "..." },
            { url => "...", title => "...", date => "...", content => "..." },
            ...
         ]};
```

The *XML::RSS* Perl module **[Hack #94]** can painlessly turn this data structure into a well-formed RSS feed:

```
$rss = new XML::RSS;
$rss->channel( title => "Martyn's Diary",
               link => "http://www.piperecords.co.uk/news/diary.asp" ,
               description => "Martyn Joseph's Diary" );

for (@{$data->{records}}) {
      $rss->add_item(
          title => $_->{title},
          link => $_->{url},
          description => $_->{content}
      );
}

print $rss->as_string;
```

Job done—well, nearly.

You see, it's a shame to have solved such a generic problem—scraping a web page into an RSS feed—in such a specific way. Instead, what I really use is the following CGI driver, which allows me to specify all the details of the site and the RSS in a separate file:

```
#!/usr/bin/perl -T
use Template::Extract;
use LWP::Simple qw(get);
use XML::RSS;
use CGI qw(:standard);
print "Content-type: text/xml\n\n";
my $x = Template::Extract->new( );
my %params;

path_info( ) =~ /(\w+)/ or die "No file name given!";
open IN, "rss/$1" or die "Can't open $file: $!";
while (<IN>) { /(\w+): (.*)/ and $params{$1} = $2; last if !/\S/; }
```

```
my $template = do {local $/; <IN>;};
$rss = new XML::RSS;
$rss->channel( title => $params{title}, link => $params{link},
               description => $params{description} );

my $doc = join "\n", grep { /\S/ } split /\n/, get($params{link});
$doc =~ s/\r//g;
$doc =~ s/^\s+//g;

for (@{$x->extract($template, $doc)->{records}}) {
    $rss->add_item(
        title => $_->{title},
        link => $_->{url},
        description => $_->{content}
    );
}

print $rss->as_string;
```

Now I can have a bunch of files that describe how to scrape sites:

```
title: Martyn's Diary
link: http://www.piperecords.co.uk/news/diary.asp
description: Martyn Joseph's diary
-->
[% FOR records %]
    <!--START OF ABSTRACT OF NEWSITEM-->
    [% ... %]
    <a href="[% url %]"><acronym title="Click here to read this article">
    [% title %]</acronym></a></strong>     ([% date %]) <BR>
    [% ... %]<font size="2">[% content %]</font></font></div>
    [% ... %]
    <!--END OF ABSTRACT OF NEWSITEM-->
[% END %]
```

When I point my RSS aggregator at the CGI script (*http://blog.simon-cozens. org/rssify.cgi/martynj*), I have an instant scraper for all those wonderful web sites that haven't made it into the RSS age yet.

Template::Extract is a brilliant new way of doing data-directed screen scraping for structured documents, and it's especially brilliant for anyone who already uses *Template* to turn templates and data into HTML. Also look out for Autrijus's latest crazy idea, *Template::Generate* (*http://search.cpan.org/ author/AUTRIJUS/Template-Generate/*), which provides the third side of the *Template* triangle, turning data and output into a template.

—*Simon Cozens*

A Quick Introduction to XPath

Sure, you've got your traditional HTML parsers of the tree and token variety, and you've got regular expressions that can be as innocent or convoluted as you wish. But if neither are perfect fits to your scraping needs, consider XPath.

XPath is designed to locate and process items within properly formatted XML or HTML documents. At its simplest, XPath works similarly to how a pathname is used to locate a file, but instead of stepping through directories in a filesystem, it steps through elements in a document.

For example, to get the title of an HTML document, you could use /html/head/title to start at the root (/), step into the html element, then into the head, and finally the title. This is similar to tree-based parsers like *HTML:: TreeBuilder* [Hack #19] but has a number of advantages and additional capabilities—most useful of which is that an XPath statement can be a single powerful expression, as opposed to multiple lines of traversal code.

Like filesystems, there's a current location in the tree, and paths that don't start with / are relative to it. . and .. refer to the current node and parent node, respectively, just as they refer to a filesystem's current and parent directories. If the current node is /html/head, then title and ./title mean /html/head/title, and .. means /html.

That's as complex as filesystem paths usually get, but since XPath deals with XML (and HTML), it has to go further—and it goes a *lot* further. Luckily, for both our sanity and page count, we'll only scratch the surface for this introductory hack. If you want to know more, check out the book *XPath and XPointer* (*http://www.oreilly.com/catalog/xpathpointer*).

Directories can contain only one file with a particular name, but an element can contain any number of children with the same type name: paragraphs can contain multiple anchors, lists can contain multiple items, and so on. XPath, unlike filesystems, allows a step, and hence a path, to match any number of nodes; so, ul/li means all the items of all the unordered lists in the current node.

You can distinguish between matched items by adding a number in square brackets, so that a[4] selects the fourth child anchor of a node (note that XPath counts from one, not zero). The fourth cell of each row of the third child table of the body is /html/body/table[3]/tr/td[4].

Attributes are treated similarly to children, except the attribute names are prefixed with @, so that a/@href means the href attributes of the anchors.

XPath allows a path to be abbreviated with //, which matches any number of steps. //a/@href makes a list of every link in a page!

There's much, much more to XPath, but this discussion has given us enough of a background to allow some useful things to be done. When you want to use XPath within a Perl script, the preferred approach is *XML::LibXML*, which depends on the *libxml2* (*http://xmlsoft.org/*) library being installed.

Using LibXML's xmllint

LibXML comes with a tool named *xmllint*, whose most interesting feature is a command-line shell that lets you navigate around a document's object tree using commands named after Unix tools. It's a good way to discover and try out paths interactively.

Let's see it in action on JungleScan (*http://www.junglescan.com/*), which tracks changing Amazon.com ranks for various products. We'll pick out some info from the "top ten winners" list and reformat them for our own purposes:

```
% xmllint --shell --html http://junglescan.com/
```

Utilities with *lint* in the title are referred to as *lint-pickers*: they help clean up and report incorrect and crusty code. In this case, since JungleScan isn't valid HTML (due to unencoded ampersands), the previous command will generate many complaints, similar to this:

```
http://junglescan.com:59: error: htmlParseEntityRef: expecting ';'
```

None of that matters to us, though, as eventually we'll arrive at a prompt:

```
/ >
```

Let's try some navigating:

```
/ > cd //title
title > pwd
/html/head/title
title > cat
<title>JungleScan.com</title>
title > cd ..
head > ls
---         1 style
---         1 title
-a-         5 script
```

That -a- tells us the script element has at least one attribute:

```
head > dir script/@*
ATTRIBUTE language
  TEXT
    content=JavaScript
```

Okay, enough of that—time to find some data. Looking at the page in a browser shows that the first of today's top winners is an exam guide:

```
/ > grep Certification
/html/body/table/tr/td[1]/font/form[2]/table[2]/tr[3]/td[3]/table/tr[1]/td :
-a-        0 img
t--       44     A+ All-In-One Certification Exam Gui...
```

Yep, there it is, and there's one of the paths that leads to it. The tables are nested three deep; I'm glad *xmllint* is keeping track of them for us. We now have the beginnings of our desired data, so let's grab the end (in this case, a camera):

```
/ > grep Camera
/html/body/table/tr/td[1]/font/form[2]/table[2]/tr[12]/td[3]/table/tr[1]/td
:
-a-        0 img
t--       63     Sony DSC-F717 5MP Digital Still Came...
```

Comparing the two paths, we can see that the middle table has a row for each product (the emphasized tr in the previous outputs); inside that is another table containing the product's name. Let's have a closer look at one of these middle table rows:

```
/ > cd /html/body/table/tr/td[1]/font/form[2]/table[2]/tr[4]
```

The other products are named in td[3]/table/tr[1]/td, and so should this one:

```
tr > cat td[3]/table/tr[1]/td
-------
<td>
<img alt="Book" src="/images/book.gif">
    LT's Theory of Pets [UNABRIDGED] </td>
```

Yes, that was the second product in the list. Conveniently, the image's alternate text tells us this is a book. Likewise, the second row of that inner table holds three supplementary links concerning this product (its Amazon.com page, a bulletin board link, and its current JungleScan stats):

```
tr > cat td[3]/table/tr[2]
-------
<tr><td bgcolor="555555">
    ... etc ...
</td></tr>
```

And the percentage this product rose is to the right of that, being the fourth cell:

```
tr > cat td[4]
-------
<td><a href="http://1.junglescan.com/scan/
details.php?asin=0743520041">+677%</a></td>
```

Now we know enough about the page's structure to write a script. In this example, we take a look at the top five products; our code will suck down JungleScan, issue some XPath statements, and spit out the results to the shell.

The Code

Save the following code to a file called *junglescan.pl*:

```perl
#!/usr/bin/perl -w
use strict;
use utf8;
use LWP::Simple;
use XML::LibXML;
use URI;

# Set up the parser, and set it to recover
# from errors so that it can handle broken HTML
my $parser = XML::LibXML->new( ); $parser->recover(1);

# Parse the page into a DOM tree structure
my $url  = 'http://junglescan.com/';
my $data = get($url) or die $!;
my $doc  = $parser->parse_html_string($data);

# Extract the table rows (as an
# array of references to DOM nodes)
my @winners = $doc->findnodes(q{
    /html/body/table/tr/td[1]/font/form[2]/table[2]/tr
});

# The first two rows contain headings,
# and we want only the top five, so slice.
@winners = @winners[2..6];

foreach my $product (@winners) {
    # Get the percentage change and type
    # We use the find method since we only need strings
    my $change = $product->find('td[4]');
    my $type = $product->find('td[3]//img/@alt');

    # Get the title. It has some annoying
    # whitespace, so we trim that off with regexes.
    my $title = $product->find('td[3]//tr[1]');
    $title =~ s/^\s*//; $title =~ s/\xa0$//;

    # Get the first link ("Visit Amazon.com page")
    # This is relative to the page's URL, so we make it absolute
    my $relurl = $product->find('td[3]//a[1]/@href');
    my $absurl = URI->new($relurl)->abs($url);
```

```
                # Output. There isn't always a type, so we ignore it if there isn't.
                print "$change  $title";
                print " [$type]" if $type;
                print "\n          Amazon info: $absurl\n\n";
        }
```

Running the Hack

Invoke the script on the command line:

```
% perl junglescan.pl
+1540%  A+ All-In-One Certification Exam Guide [Book]
        Amazon info: http://junglescan.com/redirect.cfm?asin=0072126795
  +677%  LT's Theory of Pets [UNABRIDGED] [Book]
        Amazon info: http://junglescan.com/redirect.cfm?asin=0743520041
  +476%  The Wellstone [Book]
        Amazon info: http://junglescan.com/redirect.cfm?asin=0553584464
  +465%  Greywolf [DOWNLOAD: MICROSOFT READER] [Book]
        Amazon info: http://junglescan.com/redirect.cfm?asin=B000066U03
  +455%  VirusScan Home Edition 7.0 [Software]
        Amazon info: http://junglescan.com/redirect.cfm?asin=B00006J3FM
```

XPath is a powerful searching technology, and with the explorative capabilities of *xmllint* you can quickly get a direct pointer to the data you're looking for.

—*Daniel Biddle*

HACK #26 Downloading with curl and wget

There are a number of command-line utilities to download files over HTTP and FTP. We'll talk about two of the more popular choices: curl and wget.

There are hundreds of ways to download files located on the Net: FTP, HTTP, NNTP, Gnutella, Hotline, Carracho—the list of possible options goes on and on. There is, however, an odd man out in these protocols, and that's HTTP. Most web browsers are designed to view web pages (as you'd expect); they're not designed to download mass amounts of files from a public web directory. This often leaves users with a few meager choices: should they manually and slowly download each file themselves or go out and find some software that could do it for them?

Oftentimes, you'll have one or more utilities that can answer this question already installed on your machine. We'll first talk about *curl* (*http://curl.sf.net/*), which has an innocent and calming description:

> curl is a client to get documents/files from or send docu-
> ments to a server, using any of the supported protocols
> (HTTP, HTTPS, FTP, GOPHER, DICT, TELNET, LDAP or FILE).
> The command is designed to work without user interaction
> or any kind of interactivity.

Further reading through its manual (accessible by entering man curl as a shell command or a slightly longer version with curl --manual) shows a wide range of features, including the ability to get SSL documents, manipulate authentication credentials, change the user agent, set cookies, and prefill form values with either GET or POST. Sadly, *curl* has some apparent shortcomings, and they all revolve around downloading files that don't have similar names.

Almost immediately, the manual instructs you of *curl*'s range power, so you can download a list of sequentially numbered files with a simple command:

```
% curl -LO http://example.com/file[0-100].txt
```

The -L flag tells *curl* to follow any redirects that may be issued, and the -O flag saves the downloaded files into similarly named copies locally (*./file0.txt*, *./file1.txt*, etc.). Our limitations with the range feature show all too clearly with date-based filenames. Say you want to download a list of files that are in the form of *yymmdd.txt*. You could use this innocent command:

```
% curl -LO http://example.com/[1996-2002]/[000001-999999].txt
```

If you are patient enough, this will work fine. The downside is that *curl* will literally try to grab a million files per year (which would range from 1996 through 2002). While a patient downloader may not care, this will create an insane amount of bandwidth waste, as well as a potentially angry web host. We could split the previous command in two:

```
% curl -LO http://example.com/[1996-1999]/[96-99][01-12][01-31].txt
% curl -LO http://example.com/[2000-2002]/[00-02][01-12][01-31].txt
```

These will also work correctly, at the expense of being lengthy (technically, we could combine the *curl* commands into one, with two URLs), but still cause a large number of "file not found" errors for the web host (albeit not as many as the first one).

Solving this sort of problem is easy with the second of our utilities, *wget* (*http://www.gnu.org/software/wget/wget.html*):

```
% wget -m -A txt -np http://example.com/text/
```

We start off in mirror mode (-m), which allows us to run the command at a later date and grab only content that has changed from what we've previously downloaded. We accept (-A) only files that end in *.txt*, and we don't want to get anything from our parent directory (-np or "no parent"); this stops *wget* from following links that lead us out of the text directory. *wget* (as well as *curl*) will show you a running progress as it's downloading files. More information about *wget* is available by typing man wget on the command line.

More Advanced wget Techniques

wget has a huge number of features that can make downloading data from the web easier than sitting down and rolling your own Perl script. Here, we'll cover some of the more useful configuration options.

wget is capable of fetching files via HTTP, HTTPS, and FTP, and it can even mix all three protocols as needed. Fetching can be optimized for specific uses, including customized HTTP headers, SSL support, and proxy configurations:

```
% wget --referer=http://foo.com/ -U MyAgent/1.0 http://bar.net/
```

In this example, *wget* sends HTTP headers for Referer (--referer) and User-Agent (-U or --user-agent). This is generally considered to be a good practice, as it allows the server administrators to know who and what is getting files from their server. The --referer option is also handy in avoiding some of the more basic antileech/antimirror configurations, which allow only requests with a certain Referer.

It is important to control what *wget* does; otherwise, you could end up attempting to download half the Internet. When mirroring a site, this control starts with setting the depth of the crawl (-l or --level) and whether or not *wget* gets images and other supplementary resources along with text (-p or --page-requisites):

```
% wget -l 2 -p -r http://www.example.com/
```

This recursively retrieves the first two layers of a web site, including all files that the HTML requires. Further control can be attained by setting rate limit (--limit-rate), fetch timeout (-T or --timeout), or using date/time checking (-N or --timestamping). Date/time comparison is highly effective when mirroring is scheduled, because it compares the local file's time and date with the remote file's time and date and fetches only files that are newer than the local version.

Controlling which directories *wget* will recurse into is another means of keeping bandwidth usage (and administrator's tempers) to a minimum. This can be done by telling *wget* either which directories to look in (-I or --include-directories) or which to ignore (-X or --exclude-directories). Similarly, you can control which HTML tags *wget* will follow (--follow-tags) or ignore (--ignore-tags) when dealing with HTML content.

Generally, it isn't necessary to use the HTML tag controls, unless you want to do something specific, such as grab only images, which can be done like this:

```
% wget -m --follow-tags=img http://www.example.com/
```

Many sites require basic HTTP Authentication to view files, and *wget* includes options that make this easy. By appending the username (--http-user) and password (--http-passwd) to the HTTP headers for each request, *wget* will be able to fetch protected content:

```
% wget -r --http-user=me --http-passwd=ssssh http://example.com/
```

One other major consideration is a local matter—keeping your own mirror directories clean and usable. When using *wget*, you can control where it places downloaded files on your own drive:

```
% wget -r -P /home/me http://www.example.com/
```

If the directory is not specified (-P or --directory-prefix), *wget* will simply put the spidered files into the current directory. If you specify the folder, it will create the spidered content in that directory, in this case */home/me*. If you run *cron* jobs to schedule mirroring scripts [Hack #90], this option makes it simple to keep everything straight, without worrying what directory the *cron* job is executing from.

You can also control whether *wget* creates the remote site's directory structure on the local side (-x or --force-directories) or not (-nd or --no-directories). When using the mirror option (-m or --mirror), *wget* automatically creates the directories.

For more advanced spidering applications, *wget* will accept raw HTTP headers (--header) to send with each request, allow you to specify a file with a URL list file (-i or --input-file), save raw server responses (headers and content) to the local files (-s or --save-headers), and log output messages to a file (-o or --output-file).:

```
% wget --header="From: me@sample.com" -i ./urls.txt -s -o ~/wget.log
```

Each file in *./urls.txt* will be requested with the additional HTTP/1.1 header From and saved with raw server responses. A log will also be created as *~/wget.log* and will look something like this:

```
--20:22:39--  http://www.example.com/index.html
      => 'www.example.com/index.html'
Connecting to www.example.com[207.99.3.256]:80... connected.
HTTP request sent, awaiting response... 200 OK
Length: unspecified [text/html]

    OK ........                                   9.74 MB/s
20:22:39 (9.74 MB/s) - 'www.example.com/index.html' saved [10215]

FINISHED --20:22:39--
Downloaded: 10,215 bytes in 1 file
```

These output files are particularly useful when you want to know some specifics about *wget*'s results but don't want to watch it fly by on the screen. It's quite simple to write a script to parse the output file and create graphs based on file sizes, transfer speeds, file types, and status codes.

While some options are exclusive of others, most options can be combined for rather sophisticated spidering uses. The best way to really figure out *wget* is to run variations of the options against your own site.

More information about *wget* is available by typing man wget in your shell.

—James Linden

HACK #28   Using Pipes to Chain Commands

Chaining commands into a one-liner can make for powerful functionality.

If you want to do something only once, writing a full-blown script for it can often be overkill. Part of the design of Unix is to write small applications that do one specific thing. Combining these programs can produce spectacular and powerful results.

In this hack, we'll retrieve a list of files to save locally, then actually download them—all with existing Unix utilities. The logic goes something like this: first, we use *lynx* to grab the list of files; then, we use *grep* to filter the *lynx* data into just the necessary information we desire; finally, we use *wget* [Hack #26] to actually retrieve the final results.

Browsing for Links with lynx

lynx is usually thought of as a console-based web browser. However, as you will see here, it has some powerful command-line uses as well. For example, rather than run an interactive browser session, *lynx* can be told to send its output directly to STDOUT, like so:

```
% lynx -dump "http://google.com/"
```

Not only does *lynx* nicely format the page in glorious plain text, but it also provides a list of links, bibliography style, in the "References" section. Let's give that another spin, this time with the -image_links option:

```
% lynx -dump -image_links "http://google.com/"
```

lynx now includes the URLs of all images in that web page. Thanks to −dump and −image_links, we now have a list of all the links and images related to the URL at hand.

Before moving on, *lynx* has a few more options you might find helpful if you're having trouble accessing a particular page. If the page restricts access using basic authentication (where a dialog box asking for a username and password appears in a visual browser), use the -auth option to pass the appropriate username/password combination to *lynx*:

```
% lynx -dump -auth=user_name:password "http://google.com/"
```

Some sites check for browser type, either to provide a different view depending on the capabilities of the browser, or simply to weed out robots. Thankfully, *lynx* is quite the chameleon and can pretend to be any browser you might need. Use the -useragent option to change the User-Agent variable passed by *lynx* to the web server. For example, pretending to be Internet Explorer 6 on Windows XP with .NET looks like this:

```
% lynx -dump -useragent="Mozilla/4.0 (compatible; MSIE 6.0; ↵
    Windows NT 5.1; .NET CLR 1.0.3705; .NET CLR 1.1.4322)" ↵
    "http://google.com/"
```

Finally, what if the page you are looking for is the result of a form input? This will take some digging into the HTML source of the form (see "Posting Form Data with LWP" [Hack #12] for some examples). Armed with the form's information, you can build a response by placing each input name with its corresponding value, separated by an ampersand, like so:

```
input1=value1&input2=value2
```

If the method is a GET request, the easiest thing to do is append the response value to the end of the destination URL, prefixed with a question mark:

```
% lynx -dump "http://google.com/search?q=unix+pipes"
```

If the method is POST, things are a bit more complicated, as you'll need to use the -post_data option to pass your data to *lynx* via standard input. If the data is a short string, echo the input to *lynx*:

```
% echo "input=value" | lynx -dump -post_data ↵
    "http://www.site.com/put_action"
```

If the data string is long, save it to a file and cat it:

```
% cat data_file | lynx -dump -post_data "http://www.site.com/put_action"
```

By now, you should be able to get almost any page from any source. Next, we will move on to formatting this data to get only the links we want.

grepping for Patterns

The *grep* command is a powerful tool for piping data through and processing using regular expressions. Entire books have been written about regular expressions (e.g., *Mastering Regular Expressions* by Jeffrey E.F. Friedl, O'Reilly & Associates), so I will show only what we need to get the job done. First, we want to grab just the URLs, and no other prose. Since *grep* normally outputs the entire line that matches a search, we will want to use the -o option, which prints only the part of the line that matches what we are searching for. The following invocation searches each line passed on STDIN for http:, followed by the rest of the characters on that line:

```
grep -o "http:.*"
```

Now, let's hook all these commands together into a pipeline, passing a web page in one end and waiting at the other end for a list of URLs. The pipe (|) will serve as glue, sticking the *lynx* and the *grep* commands together so that the output from *lynx* will be fed into *grep*, whose output will then be sent to STDOUT:

```
% lynx -dump "http://google.com/" | grep -o "http:.*"
```

Let's take *grep* a little further, focusing only on links to images. But before we can do that, there is one small hurdle: in its basic form, *grep* understands only a small subset of the regular expression metacharacters, and we'll need more. There are two ways around this. You can pass the -E option to *grep* to force it to understand a more advanced version of regular expressions, or you can use the *egrep* command instead; these approaches are functionally identical. So, our new pipeline, with *egrep* instead of *grep* and a regular expression match for images, looks like this:

```
% lynx -dump -image_links "http://google.com/" | ⏎
    egrep -o "http:.*(gif|png|jpg)"
```

Notice that we're not after all images, only gif, png, or jpg—the three most popular image formats on the Web. This trick can also be used to grab only Java applets (class), Flash files (swf), or any other file format you can think of. Be sure to separate each extension with the | symbol (this time meaning *OR*, not *pipe*), and put them all between the parentheses.

So, now we have our list of files to download, but we still haven't actually retrieved anything. *wget* to the rescue…

wgetting the Files

wget is a popular command-line download tool, usually used to download a single file. However, it can be used for many more interesting purposes. We'll take advantage of its ability to read a list of links and download them one at a time. The first *wget* option we will use is -i, which tells *wget* to read a file and download the links contained within. Combined with the - symbol (short for *standard input*), we can now download a list of dynamically determined links piped to *wget*:

```
% lynx -dump "http://google.com/" | egrep -o "http:.*" | wget -i -
```

There is one little problem, though: all the files are downloaded to the same directory, so multiple files with the same name are suffixed with a number (e.g., *imagename.jpg*, *imagename.jpg.1*, *imagename.jpg.2*, and so forth). *wget* has a yet another command-line solution for us; the -x option creates a directory for each server from which it downloads, recreating the directory structure based on the URL for each file it saves:

```
% lynx -dump "http://google.com/" | egrep -o "http:.*" | wget -xi -
```

So, instead of our initial *wget*, which would create numbered files like this:

```
% ls -l
-rw-r--r--  1 morbus  staff  10690 Aug 13 22:04 advanced_search?hl=en
-rw-r--r--  1 morbus  staff   9688 Aug 13 22:04 dirhp?hl=en&tab=wd&ie=UTF-8
-rw-r--r--  1 morbus  staff   5262 Aug 13 22:04 grphp?hl=en&tab=wg&ie=UTF-8
-rw-r--r--  1 morbus  staff   3259 Aug 13 22:04 imghp?hl=en&tab=wi&ie=UTF-8
-rw-r--r--  1 morbus  staff   3515 Jul  1 18:26 index.html
-rw-r--r--  1 morbus  staff   6393 Jul 16 21:52 index.html.1
-rw-r--r--  1 morbus  staff  13690 Jul 28 19:30 index.html.2
```

our new command will place those duplicate *index.html*'s where they belong:

```
drwxr-xr-x  3 morbus  staff    102 Aug 13 22:06 ads/
-rw-r--r--  1 morbus  staff  10690 Aug 13 22:06 advanced_search?hl=en
-rw-r--r--  1 morbus  staff   9688 Aug 13 22:06 dirhp?hl=en&tab=wd&ie=UTF-8
-rw-r--r--  1 morbus  staff   5262 Aug 13 22:06 grphp?hl=en&tab=wg&ie=UTF-8
-rw-r--r--  1 morbus  staff   3259 Aug 13 22:06 imghp?hl=en&tab=wi&ie=UTF-8
-rw-r--r--  1 morbus  staff  29027 Aug 13 22:06 language_tools?hl=en
drwxr-xr-x  3 morbus  staff    102 Aug 13 22:06 options/
-rw-r--r--  1 morbus  staff  11682 Aug 13 22:06 preferences?hl=en
drwxr-xr-x  3 morbus  staff    102 Aug 13 22:06 services/
```

Voila! With a pipeline of existing Unix command-line applications, you now have a one-liner for grabbing a series of images, Flash animations, or any other set of linked-to files you might want.

Pipes are a powerful tool for completing tasks without writing your own scripts. By combining utilities your system already has onboard, code you may have previously written, and other bits and bobs you might have come across on the Net, you can save yourself the effort of writing a brand-new script for one use only—or, indeed, for aliasing to its own command to be run at any time.

Hacking the Hack

lynx can even deal in any cookies necessary to gain access to the content. Place cookies in a file using the format shared by Netscape and Mozilla or, alternatively, point *lynx* directly to your existing browser cookie file.

 To find your existing Netscape or Mozilla cookie jar, run the following on your command-line : locate cookies.txt.

Here is a sample cookie:

```
.google.com     TRUE    /       FALSE   2147368537      PREF
ID=268a71f72dc9b915:FF=4:LD=en:NR=10:TM=1057718034:
LM=1059678022:S=JxfnsCODMtTmOVen
```

The first column is the domain of the cookie; this is usually the web site of
the page in question. The second column is a flag, TRUE if all subdomains
(e.g., *news.google.com* or *groups.google.com*) should also be passed this
cookie. The third column is a path, signifying the subsections of the site the
cookie should be sent to. For example, a path of *shopping/ties* indicates the
cookie should be sent only to anything deeper than */shopping/ties* in the
URL—*http://servername/shopping/ties/hideous*, for instance. The fourth column should be TRUE if the cookie should be sent only over secure connections, FALSE otherwise. The fifth column is the expiration date of the cookie
in Unix timestamp format; a good browser will usually delete old cookies
from its cookie jar. The sixth column is the cookie's name, and the seventh
and final column is the cookie's value; both are set by the site to something meaningful. Using this format, you can create a cookie jar containing
any cookies you please—they should, of course, be valid—and pass it to
lynx using the -cookie_file option:

```
% lynx -dump -cookie_file=cookies "http://google.com/" | ⏎
  egrep -o "http:.*" | wget -xi -
```

—Adam Bregenzer

Running Multiple Utilities at Once

HACK
#29

You've got scrapers, spiders, and robots aplenty, all to run daily according to
a particular schedule. Should you set up a half-dozen cron jobs, or combine
them into one script?

Finding and collecting information from many sources may involve running
several programs, possibly in conjunction with one another. Combining
multiple utilities into one script has a few benefits: if you're running, heaven
forbid, a dozen different *wget* [Hack #26] commands every night, you can throw
them in a single shell script and worry about only 1 *crontab* entry [Hack #90]
instead of 12. Unlike a dozen separate entries, a single shell script also
allows you to check how each *wget* performed (either by checking the return
code [Hack #34] or by collating and reporting the final results). Likewise, shell
scripts can be used to hold complicated and lengthy pipes [Hack #28], saving
your weary fingers from typing them out each time.

This hack explores doing this kind of combinatorial spidering.

Shell Scripts

A *shell script* is a series of statements that you would otherwise run on the command line, one after another. Perhaps you'd first run a simple Perl script to spit out the Amazon.com PageRank of your book and, if it had lowered, you'd use *curl* to upload a sad face to your web site. If it had risen, you'd upload a happy face, and if it was in the Top 100, you'd automatically email a prepared resignation letter to your day job. A shell script would make these decisions for you, first by checking the output of the Perl script, and then responding appropriately.

Here's a simple shell script, which we'll dissect in a moment. Its purpose is menial: depending on the options passed to it on the command line, we'll use *lynx* to automatically display either an RFC (an Internet "Request for Comments" from *http://www.ietf.org/rfc/*) or a quote from the QDB (a database of humorous IRC quotes at *http://bash.org/*).

```
#!/bin/sh

usage_and_exit() {
    echo "usage: get (rfc|qdb) term" 2>&1
    echo "where term is an rfc number, or a quote number from bash.org" 2>&1
    exit 0
}

if test -z "$1"; then
    usage_and_exit
fi

url=""
case "$1" in
    rfc)
        url="http://www.ietf.org/rfc/rfc$2.txt" ;;
    qdb)
        url="http://bash.org/?$2" ;;
esac

if test -z "$url"; then
    usage_and_exit
fi

lynx -dump $url
```

The first line tells the operating system that the interpreter for the rest of this program is */bin/sh*. Other interpreters run programs written in other languages—for example, Perl (*/usr/bin/perl*) and Python (*/usr/bin/python*).

Next, we define a function called usage_and_exit, which prints our usage message when we don't get the correct number of arguments. Once the message is printed, our shell script will exit.

We then check to see if $1 is empty. $1 is the first argument to a script, $2 is the second, $3 is the third, and so forth, up to $9. Almost all checking of variables in a script will be done with the *test* binary that comes with your system. However, in this script we needed -z only for an "empty string" test.

Note the syntax of the if statement. A full if looks like this:

```
if test -z $some_variable; then
    do_something
elif test $some_variable = $a_different_variable; then
    do_something_else
else
    do_another_thing
fi
```

Next, we check what the contents of $1 actually are. If they match the sites we know how to get quotes from, then we can set the url based on the value of the second argument, $2.

If we still haven't decided on a URL by the time we exit the case statement, then we should show the usage_and_exit. If we have decided on a URL, then we have a whole command line to get the results in *lynx*, so we do so.

That's our complete simple shell script, but it's hardly a large example. We need to know how to combine programs and filter data we want [Hack #28]. Far more information about shell programming, including complete scripts, can be found at the Linux Documentation Project's "Advanced Bash-Scripting Guide" (*http://tldp.org/LDP/abs/html/*).

Perl Equivalence

We can, of course, emulate a shell script using Perl. (Breathe easy, Windows users!) All a shell script is, really, is a series of commands that the shell runs for you. We can run external commands in Perl too, and gather their output as we go. Here's an example of the previous shell script:

```
#!/usr/bin/perl -w
use strict;

my ($db, $num) = (shift, shift);
die "You must specify 'rfc' or 'qdb'!\n" ↵
    unless ($db eq "rfc" || $db eq "qdb");
die "You must specify a numerical search!\n" unless $num =~ /\d+/;

my $url;
if ($db eq "rfc") { $url = "http://www.ietf.org/rfc/rfc$num.txt"; }
elsif ($db eq "qdb") { $url = "http://bash.org/?$num"; }

system("lynx -dump $url");
```

If we want to capture *lynx*'s output and operate on it within Perl, we can do this:

```
open INPUT, "lynx -dump $url |" or die $!;
while (<INPUT>) {
    # process input from lynx.
}
close INPUT;
```

We can use a similar idea to write data to a program that wants input on STDIN:

```
open OUTPUT, "| my_program" or die $!;
foreach my $line (@lines){
    print OUTPUT $line;
}
close OUTPUT;
```

With the knowledge of what a shell script is, the Perl equivalences, and everything else we know about Perl, we can make a powerful set of utilities by combining existing Perl modules with results from other prewritten programs.

—*Richard Rose*

Utilizing the Web Scraping Proxy

With the use of a Perl proxy, you'll be able to browse web sites and have the LWP code written out automatically for you. Although not perfect, it can certainly be a time saver.

In this hack, we're going to use something called a proxy. In essence, a *proxy* is a piece of middleware that sits between you and your Internet connection. When you make a request for a web page, the request goes to the proxy, which downloads the relevant data, optionally preprocesses it, then returns it to the browser as expected.

If you have ever used browsers other than the latest version of Internet Explorer, you've probably had sites complain that your browser isn't supported. When writing code, things can get even more complicated with the inclusion of JavaScript, frames, cookies, and other evil tricks of the trade.

We could use command-line utilities like *tcpdump* to log traffic during a session with particular web sites, and manually copy headers, cookies, and referers to mock up our code as a legitimate browser, but with the Web Scraping Proxy, we can log the data automatically and get a firm basis for our own scripts.

The Web Scraping Proxy (*http://www.research.att.com/~hpk/wsp/*) is a way to automatically generate the Perl code necessary to emulate a real browser within your scripts. The *LWP* code it writes is similar to the various *LWP* hacks we've covered previously in this chapter.

After downloading *wsp.pl* from *http://www.research.att.com/~hpk/wsp/* (be sure to get Version 2), we can set our browser to proxy all requests through *wsp* and get a record of all the transactions. How to set the proxy in our browser really depends on our browser and our OS, but here's a quick sample of starting *wsp.pl* and then requesting, with Mozilla 1.3, an Amazon.com search:

```
% perl wsp.pl
--- Proxy server running on disobey.local. port: 5364

# Request: http://www.amazon.com/exec/obidos/search-handle-form/
# Cookie: [long string here]
# Cookie: 'session-id', '103-3421686-4199019'
# Cookie: 'session-id-time', '1057737600'
# Cookie: 'ubid-main', '430-5587053-7200154'
# Cookie: 'x-main', '?r2eEc7UeYLH@lbaOUWV4wgOoCdCqHdO'
# Referer: http://www.amazon.com/
$req = POST "http://www.amazon.com/exec/obidos/search-handle-form/",
[
        'url' => "index=blended",
        'field-keywords' => "amazon hacks",
        'Go.x' => "0",
        'Go.y' => "0",
] ;
```

As you can see, the last five or six lines spit out the beginnings of some code you'd be able to use in your own Perl scripts, like so:

```
#!/usr/bin/perl
use LWP;
$ua = LWP::UserAgent->new;
$req = $ua->post("http://www.amazon.com/exec/obidos/search-handle-form/",
[
        'url' => "index=blended",
        'field-keywords' => "amazon hacks",
        'Go.x' => "0",
        'Go.y' => "0",
]);
print $req->content;
```

Using this translation, it's simple to make your Perl scripts emulate form submissions, without having to decode the form information yourself. In itself, the Web Scraping Proxy outputs only basic code for use with *LWP*, which is useful only for running the requests, but does not take HTTP headers into account. To emulate a browser fully, you could either copy each header laboriously, as if by using *tcpdump*, or use a bit of additional Perl to generate the ancillary code for you.

The Code

Save the following code to a file called *translate.pl*:

```perl
#!/usr/bin/perl-w
#
# translate.pl - translates the output of wsp.pl -v.
#
# This code is free software; you can redistribute it and/or
# modify it under the same terms as Perl itself.
#

use strict;
my $save_url;
my $count = 1;

# Print the basics
print "#!/usr/bin/perl\n";
print "use warnings;\n";
print "use strict;\n";
print "use LWP::UserAgent;\n";
print "my \$ua = LWP::UserAgent->new;\n\n";

# read through wsp's output.
while (<>) {
    chomp; s/\x0D$//;

    # add our HTTP request headers...
    if (/^INPUT: ([a-zA-Z0-9\-\_]+): (.*)$/) {
        print '$req'.$count.'->header(\''.$1."' => '".$2."');\n";
    }

    # what URL we're actually requesting...
    if (/^Request for URL: (.*)$/) { $save_url=$1; }

    # the HTTP 1.x request line (GET or POST).
    if (/^FIRST LINE: ([A-Z]+) \S+ (.*)$/) {
        print "\n\n### request number $count ###\n";
        print "my \$req$count = HTTP::Request->new($1 => '$save_url');\n";
    }

    # the POST information sent off, if any.
    if (/^POST body: (.*)$/) { print "\$req$count->content('$1');\n"; }

    # and finish up our request.
    if (/^ --- Done sending./) {
        print "print \$ua->request(\$req$count)->as_string;\n";
        $count++; # move on to our next request. yeedawg.
    }
}
```

Running the Hack

The first order of business is to set up your browser to use *wsp.pl* as a proxy. Methods vary from browser to browser, but in most cases you just set HTTP Proxy to localhost and Port to 5364 (see Figure 2-3).

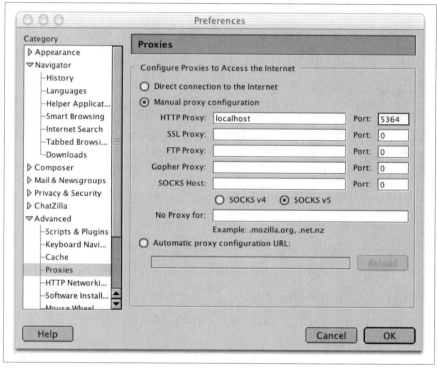

Figure 2-3. Configuring your proxy in the Mozilla browser

Then, in an empty directory, run the following command:

```
% perl wsp.pl -v | translate.pl
```

The output is a stronger version of the previous Amazon.com search script:

```perl
#!/usr/bin/perl -w
use strict;
use LWP::UserAgent;
my $ua = LWP::UserAgent->new;

### request number 1 ###
my $req1 = HTTP::Request->new(POST =>
  'http://amazon.com/exec/obidos/search-handle-form/');
$req1->header('Accept' => '*/*');
$req1->header('Accept-Language' => 'en-us, ja;q=0.33, en;q=0.67');
$req1->header('Cookie' => '[long string here]');
```

```
$req1->header('Referer' => 'http://amazon.com/');
$req1->header('User-Agent' => 'Mozilla/5.0 (Macintosh; U; PPC Mac OS X; ↵
en-us)');
$req1->header('Content-Type' => 'application/x-www-form-urlencoded');
$req1->header('Content-Length' => '61');
$req1->header('Connection' => 'close');
$req1->header('Host' => 'amazon.com');
$req1->content('url=index%3Dblended&field-keywords=amazon+hacks&Go.x=0&Go.↵
y=0');
print $ua->request($req1)->as_string;
```

If you've read through the *transplate.pl* code, you've seen that it simply takes
the output from *wsp.pl* and prints *LWP* code with HTTP headers, as well as
the warnings and strict pragma. The output, as shown in this section, is
Perl code that executes the same requests as your browser did and with the
same settings and headers. Note that in the full output of *translate.pl*, you'd
get another 30 or so requests for each and every image/resource on the
returned Amazon.com page. I've left those out for brevity's sake.

Hacking the Hack

There are many possible improvements for this hack. If you want to use the
output script to simulate real user scenarios in a load test situation, then it
makes sense to add a little timer to *translate.pl* and let it add sleep statements to simulate user inactivity. Another improvement would be to pick up
any Set-Cookie headers and reuse them for the remainder of the session.

—Mads Toftum

HACK Being Warned When Things Go Wrong
#31

When you're writing any script that operates on data you don't control, from
either a database, a text file, or a resource on the Internet, it's always a good
idea to add a healthy dose of error checking.

The minute you decide to operate on somebody else's data, you've opened
up a can of unreliable and constantly changing worms. One day, you may
get one bit of content, while the next day you'll get the same data, only in a
different format, or with a new line in a place you weren't expecting. While
this premise is one of the solutions XML purports to prevent, 90% of this
book is based on HTML: a scourge of "clean" and semantic markup.

Because HTML can change from day to day and is often arbitrary in its format (compare Moby Dick to <book_title>Moby Dick</book_
title>, for instance), and because web sites can be down one second and up
the next, adding error handling to your scripts is an important stopgap to
ensure that you'll get the results you're expecting. Of course, seasoned

programmers of any language will yell "whooptidoo" and move on to the next hack, but for those of you who need a quick brushing up, here are some ways you can make sure your scripts are doing what you expect. Most of them are one- or two-line additions that can save a lot of sanity in the long run.

When you're downloading content from the Web:

```
# using LWP::Simple
my $data = get("http://example.com/");

# using LWP::UserAgent
my $ua = LWP::UserAgent->new( );
my $data = $ua->get("http://example.com/")->content;
```

check to make sure that your content was downloaded successfully:

```
# using LWP::Simple
my $data = get("http://example.com/")
  or die "No content was downloaded!\n";

# using LWP::UserAgent
my $ua = LWP::UserAgent->new( );
my $res = $ua->get("http://example.com/");
die "No content was downloaded\n" unless $res->is_success;
my $data = $res->content;
```

If you're using E-Tags or If-Modified-Since headers, you can check if the content you're requesting has anything newer than what you last saw. You can see some examples of checking the response from the server in "Respecting Your Scrapee's Bandwidth" [Hack #16].

Likewise, check to make sure you have the content you expected to get, instead of just blindly processing your data in hopes that what you want is there. Make some effort to check for data you don't want, to rule out extraneous processing:

```
# instead of blindly assuming:
$data =~ /data we want: (.*)/;
my $victory = $1;

# rule out the negatives first:
die if $data =~ /no matches found/;
die if $data =~ /not authorized to view/;
die if $data =~ /this page has moved/;

# now, if we're this far, we can hope
# that we've ruled out most of the bad
# results that would waste our time.
$data =~ /data we want: (.*)/;
my $victory = $1;
```

Similar checks can be made against the type of content you're receiving:

```
# if you're expecting a URL to be passed
# on the command line, make sure
# a) you got one, and b) it's a URL.
my $url = shift @ARGV;
die unless defined($url);
die unless $url =~ /^http/;

# if you're expecting a number on the command
# line, make sure you have a number and, alternatively,
# check to make sure it's within a certain limit.
my $number = shift @ARGV;
die unless defined($number);
die unless $number =~ /^\d+$/
die if $number <= 0;
die if $number >= 19;

# if you're using matches in a regular expression,
# make sure that you got what you expected:
$data =~ /temp: (\d+) humidity: (\d+) description: (.*)/;
my ($temp, $humidity, $description) = ($1, $2, $3);
unless ($temp && $humidity && $description) {
    die "We didn't get the data we expected!\n";
}
```

Another way of checking that your script has met your expectations is to verify that it has matched all the data you want. Say you're scraping a "top 25 records" list from a popular music site; it's safe to assume that you want 25 results. By adding a simple counter, you can get warned when things have gone awry:

```
# instead of this:
while (/Ranking: (\d+) Title: (.*?) Artist: (.*?)/gism) {
    my ($ranking, $title, $artist) = ($1, $2, $3);
    next unless ($ranking && $title && $artist);
    print "$ranking, $title, $artist\n";
}

# add a counter and check for a total:
my $counter = 1;
while (/Ranking: (\d+) Title: (.*?) Artist: (.*?)/gism) {
    my ($ranking, $title, $artist) = ($1, $2, $3);
    next unless ($ranking && $title && $artist);
    print "$ranking, $title, $artist\n";
    $counter++;
}

if ($counter < 25) { print "Odd, we didn't get 25 records!\n"; }
```

Another change you may want to implement is to decrease the timeout of your network accesses. By default, anytime you request a resource with

LWP::UserAgent, it'll wait for some sort of response for 180 seconds (three minutes). For busy sites, three minutes can seem like an eternity, especially when nothing else is going on. You can reduce the number of seconds in one of two ways:

```
# during the creation of the UserAgent object:
my $ua = LWP::UserAgent->new( timeout => 30 );

# or, after the object has been created:
my $ua = LWP::UserAgent->new( );
$ua->timeout(30);
```

The last, and most important, early-warning system we'll talk about uses the warnings and strict programs. These are the easiest lines to add to your code; simply add the following to start off your scripts:

```
#!/usr/bin/perl -w
use strict;
```

With this simple addition, you'll be forced to write cleaner code, because Perl will resolutely balk and whine at hundreds of additional places where your code could be misunderstood. If you've never written under strict before, it may seem like an unworkable and anal beast, but after a while you'll get used to writing code that passes its quality check. Likewise, you'll scratch your head at all the "errors" and "uninitialized values" from warnings, but again, the more you work with them, the better quality of code you'll produce. All the scripts within this book use both pragmas.

HACK   Being Adaptive to Site Redesigns
#32

It's a typical story: you work all night long to create the perfect script to solve all your woes, and when you wake in the morning ready to run it "for real," you find the site you're scraping has changed its URLs or HTML.

It's a common fact of programming: the minute you get something perfect, someone comes along and messes with the underlying assumptions. This gets even worse when you're downloading data from the Web, because you can't verify that the information is going to be in the same format from day to day, minute to minute, or even second to second. Expecting a web site to break your script eventually is a good way to code proactively: by being prepared for the inevitable downtime, you'll be better equipped to fix it.

One of the easiest things you can do is break the important bits of your code into variables. Take the following example, which, for all intents and purposes, works just fine:

```
#/usr/bin/perl -w
use strict;
use LWP::Simple;
```

```perl
my $data = get("http://example.com")
while ($data =~ /weather: (.*?) horoscope: (.*?)/) {
    my $weather = $1; my $horoscope = $2;
    if ($weather < 56) { &increase_sweat;  }
    if ($horoscope eq "Taurus") { &grow_horns; }
}
```

Obviously, this code exists solely as an illustration for rewriting the important bits into variables. Take a look at the following example, which does
the same thing, only in twice as many lines:

```perl
#/usr/bin/perl
use warnings;
use strict;
use LWP::Simple;

my $url             = "http://example.com";
my $weather_reg     = qr/weather: (.*?)/;
my $horoscope_reg   = qr/horoscope: (.*?)/;
my $weather_limit   = 56;
my $horoscope_sign = "Taurus";

my $data = get($url);
while ($data =~ /$weather_reg $horoscope_reg/) {
    my $weather = $1; my $horoscope = $2;
    if ($weather < $weather_limit) { &increase_sweat; }
    if ($horoscope eq $horoscope_sign) { &grow_horns; }
}
```

Why is code twice as long arguably "better"? Think of it this way: say you
have 600 or more lines of code, and it looks similar to our first example—all
the important bits are spread out amongst comments, subroutines, loops,
and so on. If you want to change your horoscope or your heat tolerance, you
have to search for just the right lines in a haystack of supplementary Perl. If
it's been a couple of months since the last time you opened your script,
there's a good chance it'll take you substantially longer as you try to figure
out what to change and what to leave the same.

By placing all your eggs in the variable basket, there's only one place you
need to go when you wish to modify the script. When a site changes its
design, just modify the regular expression statements at the top, and the rest
of the code will work as you intend. When you've been blessed with a new
baby daughter, tweak the horoscope value at the beginning of the file, and
you're ready to move on. No searching in the script and no spelunking
through code you've forgotten the meaning of. Same with the URL: when
the remote site makes it obsolete, just change the information in the first
dozen lines of code.

Another benefit of segregating your variables from your logic is the ability to easily change where the values come from. Take a look at the following:

```
my $url          = "http://example.com";
my $weather_reg  = qr/weather: (.*?)/;
my $horoscope_reg = qr/horoscope: (.*?)/;
my $weather_limit = shift @ARGV || 56;
my $horoscope_sign = "Taurus";
```

With a simple addition, we now have the ability to get our weather threshold from the command line. Running `perl example.pl` would keep the value as 56, but `perl example.pl 83` would increase it to 83 for that particular run. Likewise, you can add command-line options for all of your variables, and you'll have only one central location to worry about editing: the top of the script.

There are a few scraping utilities that have taken this sort of dynamic configuration to a fault; _dailystrips_ [Hack #37], for instance, is an application for downloading hundreds of comic strips from various sites. Adding new comic strips is a simple matter of defining a new configuration block; there's no code to modify, and, if a comic strip changes URL or format, five minutes can correct it.

## CHAPTER THREE

Collecting Media Files
Hacks #33–42

The easiest data to scrape and spider is entire files, not the specific information within. With one line of download code, you can have the grandeur of a movie, the sound of music, or the beauty of an image. Getting to that one line of power, however, often involves some detective work: finding out exactly where your desired files are stored, and the simplest and laziest way of getting your own copy.

In this chapter, we'll explore the techniques for building your media collection, by archiving freeware clipart, watching old movies from the Library of Congress, or saving historic images from a scenic web cam.

HACK #33 Detective Case Study: Newgrounds

Learn how to gumshoe your way through a site's workflow, regardless of whether there are pop-up windows, JavaScripts, frames, or other bits of obscuring technology.

In this hack, we're going to create a script to suck down the media files of Newgrounds (*http://newgrounds.com*), a site that specializes in odd Flash animations and similar videos. Before we can get to the code, we have to do a little bit of sleuthing to see how Newgrounds handles its operation.

Anytime we prepare to suck data from a site, especially one that isn't just plain old static pages, the first thing we should keep in mind is the URL. Even though we don't have a manual to the coding prowess that went into the design, we really don't need one; we just need to pay attention, make some guesses, and get enough of what we need to script away.

With Newgrounds, the first thing we need to do is find the page from which we'd normally view or download the animation through a regular browser. We'll pick a random item from the main page and check out the

URL: *http://newgrounds.com/portal/view.php?id=66766*. You'll notice immediately the `id=` at the end, which tells us that files are identified as unique
records [Hack #7]. That's a good, if minimal, first step.

But what else can we learn from this? Well, let's start URL hacking. Instead
of clicking anything else on the current web page, let's change the URL. Set
the `id=` to 66767 or 66765, or 1, 2, 3, and so on. Do we get valid responses? In
this case, yes, we do. We've now learned that IDs are sequential. It's time to
return to our original web page and see what else we can find.

The next thing we notice is, regardless of whether the media file is a game or
movie, there's a shiny Go button for every ID. The Go button is our step in
the next direction. Hovering our mouse over it, we can see
`OpenPortalContentWin(66766, 400, 600)` for our destination: the site uses
JavaScript, and passes the ID to the `OpenPortalContentWin` function.

What of those other numbers? Without investigating, we don't yet know
what they are, but we can certainly make a guess: they're probably window
dimensions. 600×400 would fit within the smallest screen resolution (640×
480), so it's a safe bet to expect a window of roughly that size when we click
the link. Do so now. Up pops a new window, a little smaller than we
expected, but well within our guess. Because we are more interested in
downloads than window dimensions, we can ignore those final two numbers; they're not important.

While you were reading the preceding paragraph, the Flash animation was
loading in that 600×400 pop up. Let's use our browser's View Source feature on this new pop-up window. If the file we want is loading, then the
location from which it's loading must be in the HTML code. Remember: if
the browser is showing the page, it has the HTML source; it's just a matter
of finding a way to show it.

In the HTML, we see the following:

```
<EMBED src="http://uploads.newgrounds.com/66000/66766_ganguro.swf"
  quality="high" WIDTH="600" HEIGHT="400" NAME="FlashContent"
  AllowScriptAccess="never" TYPE="application/x-shockwave-flash"
  PLUGINSPAGE="http://www.macromedia.com/go/getflashplayer">
</EMBED>
```

And with barely a whimper, we're done: there's the location of the file we
want to download. We know a few new things as a result of examining the
source:

• All files come from *http://uploads.newgrounds.com/*.

• All files contain their unique ID within the name.

- All filenames contain an underscore and title after the ID.
- All files are stored in directories based on the unique ID.

But the clincher is how many of these things we don't really need to know. If we know that all files must be served from *http://uploads.newgrounds.com/*, then we should be able to write a script that just looks for that string in the pop-up URL's source code, and we'll be ready to download. But how do we find the URL for the pop-up window, especially when it was triggered by a bit of JavaScript, not a normal HTML link? If you're using Mozilla, choose Page Info (see Figure 3-1) from either the View or contextual menus.

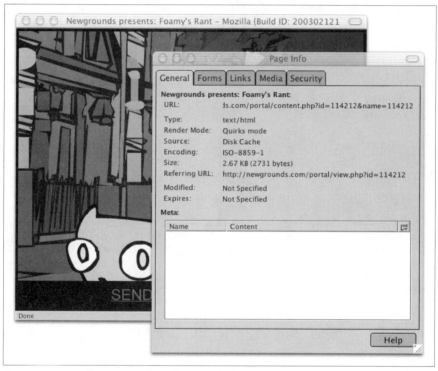

Figure 3-1. Mozilla's Page Info with our pop-up URL

Alternatively, if your browser allows you to turn on toolbars that have been explicitly turned off, turn on the Address Bar (Safari on OS X: View → Address Bar) and take a look. You'll see something similar to:

http://www.newgrounds.com/portal/content. php?id=99362&date=1054526400&quality=b.

Suddenly, things aren't so easy anymore.

The pop-up URL uses the ID, as we expected, but it also requires two more values: date and quality. After experimenting with changing the quality setting on various Newgrounds URLs:

```
http://newgrounds.com/portal/content.php?id=99362&date=1054526400&quality=a
http://newgrounds.com/portal/content.php?id=99362&date=1054526400&quality=c
http://newgrounds.com/portal/content.php?id=99362&date=1054526400&quality=1
```

I've yet to see it make much of a difference, so we'll safely ignore that for now. What's worrisome, however, is the date. Obviously, it's going to change from day to day, and it may even change from second to second. All we know is that if we decrease the date value arbitrarily (to 1054440000, for instance), we don't get the content we want.

In poking around and trying different IDs, we notice the date hasn't changed for the past five minutes. Experimentation-wise, this doesn't help us: making the date larger or smaller has only one effect—more error messages. We're going to have to get the date from the server each time we run our script, and then use that for downloading. It's not that big of a deal, but it's annoying nonetheless.

The Code

Save the following code to a file called *leechgrounds.pl*:

```perl
#!/usr/bin/perl -w
#
# LeechGrounds - saves flash files from Newgrounds.com.
# Part of the Leecharoo suite - for all those hard to leech places.
# http://disobey.com/d/code/ or contact morbus@disobey.com.
#
# This code is free software; you can redistribute it and/or
# modify it under the same terms as Perl itself.
#

use strict; $|++;
my $VERSION = "1.0";
use File::Spec::Functions;

# make sure we have the modules we need, else die peacefully.
eval("use LWP 5.6.9;"); die "[err] LWP 5.6.9 or greater required.\n" if $@;

# our download URLs are found in this URL (which'll
# be tweaked with the date and ID we care about).
my $base_url = "http://newgrounds.com/portal/content.php";
my $dir = "newgrounds";  # save downloads to...?
mkdir $dir;              # make sure that dir exists.
my $date;               # date from newgrounds server.
```

```perl
# create a final hash that contains
# all the IDs we'll be downloading.
my %ids; foreach (@ARGV) {
    next unless /\d/; # numbers only.

    # if it's a range, work through it.
    if (/(\d+)-(\d+)/) {
        my $start = $1; my $end = $2;
        for (my $i = $start; $i <= $end; $i++) {
            $ids{$i} = undef; # alive, alive!
        }
    } else { $ids{$_} = undef; } # normal number.
}

# create a downloader, faking the User-Agent to get past filters.
my $ua = LWP::UserAgent->new(agent => 'Mozilla/4.76 [en] (Win98; U)');

# now that we have a list of IDs we want to
# download, get the date value from first page.
# we'll use this to get the final download URLs.
print "-" x 76, "\n"; # pretty visual seperator.
foreach my $id (sort {$a <=> $b} keys %ids) {

    # get the date first time through.
    unless ($date) {
        print "Trying to grab a date string from $id... ";
        my $response = ↵
            $ua->get("http://newgrounds.com/portal/view.php?id=$id");
        my $data = $response->content; $data =~ /&date=(\d+)&quality=b/;
        unless ($1) { print "bah!\n"; next; } print "yes!\n";
        $date = $1; # store the date for later use.
    }

    # now, we can get the download URL to our Flash file.
    # note that we get ALL the download URLs before we
    # actually download. this saves us from having to
    # error check when we're out-of-date on long downloads.
    print "Determining download URL for $id... ";
    my $response = $ua->get("$base_url?id=$id&date=$date");
    my $data = $response->content; # our content.
    $data =~ /uploads.newgrounds.com\/(.*swf)/;
    $ids{$id} = "http://uploads.newgrounds.com/$1";
    print "done!\n";

} print "-" x 76, "\n"; # pretty!

# if we're here, we have our URLs to download in
# our hash, so we just run through the basics now.
foreach my $id (sort {$a <=> $b} keys %ids) {

    # only work on IDs with URLs.
    next unless defined ($ids{$id});
```

```
# get URL/filename.
my $url = $ids{$id}; $url =~ /([^\/]*.swf)/;
my $filename = $1; print "Downloading $filename... ";

# and use :content_file to autosave to our directory.
$ua->get($url, ':content_file' => "$dir/$filename");
print "done!\n"; # easier said than don... oh, nevermind.

}
```

Running the Hack

Invoke the script on the command line, passing it the IDs of Flash files to download. Specify either a space-separated list of individual IDs (e.g., perl leechgrounds.pl 67355 67354) or space-separated list of ranges (e.g., perl leechgrounds.pl 1-100 67455-67560 615 to download files 1 through 100, 615, and 67455 through 67560). Here, I download four Flash movies:

```
% perl leechgrounds.pl 80376 79461 66767 66765
------------------------------------------------------------------------
Trying to grab a date string from 66765... bah!
Trying to grab a date string from 66767... bah!
Trying to grab a date string from 79461... yes!
Determining download URL for 79461... done!
Determining download URL for 80376... done!
------------------------------------------------------------------------
Downloading 79461_011_Maid_Of_Horror.swf... done!
... etc ...
```

If you read through the code, you'll notice that we get a list of all the download URLs immediately, as opposed to getting one final URL, then downloading, moving on to the next, and so on. By preprocessing the ID list like this, we never have to worry about the date (from the pop-up URLs) expiring, since the *final downloadable* URLs (from *uploads.newgrounds.com*) aren't limited by any date restriction. Likewise, if we can't determine a URL for the final download, we skip it under the assumption that the data has been removed from the server.

Hacking the Hack

We can always do better, of course. For one, we have no pretty progress bar [Hack #18], nor any checks for whether a file has already been downloaded. We also falsely assume that Newgrounds files are always *.swf*, which may not always be the case (though we've yet to find an exception). Finally, we don't capture any information about the file itself, such as the name, author, description, and so on. To get you started, modify the script like this:

```
unless ($date) { # remove this line.
    print "Trying to grab a date string from $id... ";
```

```
my $response = $ua->get("http://newgrounds.com/portal/view.php?id=$id");
my $data = $response->content; $data =~ /&date=(\d+)&quality=b/;
unless ($1) { print "bah!\n"; next; } print "yes!\n";
$date = $1; # store the date for later use.

# new lines for grabbing content.
if ($data =~ /Presents: (.*?)<\/title>/) {
    print " Name: $1\n" if $1; }
if ($data =~ /Email\('.*?', '.*?', '(.*?)'\)/) {
    print " Author: $1\n" if $1; }
} # remove this line.
```

 Detective Case Study: iFilm

Sometimes, the detective work is more complicated than the solution.

iFilm (*http://www.ifilm.com/*) offers a huge selection of worthwhile movies, including special clips and trailers from the latest theater flicks; previews for the newest and coolest games; and odd bits of ephemera from contributors, celebrities, and third-party sites. They also go out of their way to create a true media experience for the end user, with frames here, media markup (like SMIL) there, and convoluted logic that a normal visitor would never worry about.

Of course, we're not your average visitor. In this hack, we'll archive iFilm media, specifically the QuickTime versions (yes, I'm an Apple enthusiast), without wading through ad-heavy windows, pop-up annoyances, or movie-specific recommendations. Similar to the Newgrounds hack [Hack #33], we'd like to pass an ID on the command line and, a few minutes later, have a movie ready for watching.

First, we're going to load a page that has the media we want to download. Picking randomly from the home page, we come across a game trailer located at *http://ifilm.com/filmdetail?ifilmid=2462842&cch=1*. By Jove, there's a unique ID in that URL! We're off to a good start, although we doubt there are two million movies available—a hunch that is confirmed by randomly choosing numbers for the ifilmid and receiving lots of errors. Likewise, that cch gives us no contextual clues; it could stand for just about anything. Removing it from the final URL seems to have no adverse effects, so we'll assume it's not relevant for what we want to do.

 Throwing out ineffectual URL-line arguments both helps you focus on what's actually needed to get the job done and keeps your code clear of seemingly useful, yet utterly unnecessary, variables and values.

Whatever movie page we visit, we see standard links: namely, a button for 56 KB, 200 KB, and 500 KB downloads. Likewise, we notice that, most of the time, the 500 KB download is available only for members—those who have paid for the better quality. Now, if we were viewing this in a browser over a dialup connection, we'd probably always choose the 56 KB version, 'cause we're impatient sleuths. Since we'll be archiving the movies for posterity, however, we'll want the best quality version we can grab, so we'll work our way backward from 500 KB to 56 KB, checking for availability.

Mousing over our three choices, we see they're all using JavaScript links:

```
playVideo(2462842, 56, 'no', '', '1', '');
playVideo(2462842, 200, 'no', '', '1', '');
playVideo(2462842, 500, 'yes', '', '1', '');
```

Exploring such links is always walking a fine line between the information you actually need to know and display and other attributes that need not concern you. By glancing at the links, we've learned three things:

- The ID of the movie is passed to the playVideo function.
- The quality of the movie is passed as the second argument.
- Whether a movie requires pay access is passed as the third argument. We've never investigated the internals of the JavaScript to confirm this assertion, but we've instead relied on the fact that most 500 KB versions were for "members only."

We don't know what the other three arguments are and, honestly, we don't need to: they don't appear to differ from movie to movie, so chances are there's no need to investigate.

Click the best quality link that isn't a pay version (in our example, 200 KB). Up pops a window allowing us to choose (or have autodetected) our media player. As mentioned, my preference is for QuickTime, so I'll select that as my preferred format, arriving eventually at an iFilm Player window with ads, preference settings, navigation, and more.

Viewing the source, we come across the following snippet:

```
<iframe name="mp" id="mp" src='/media/components/mp/if/qt.jsp?pinfo=ipt:
ifilm|gpt:1|fid:2462842|mt:mov|bw:200|refsite:|rcid:|prn:|it:|pop:|lid:|sid:
1|cid:1|cch:100|cr:1|ctxpg:pl|c:true|admt:mov|adid:2471970|adbt:
sponsor|adsn:' style="width:340;height:315;position:absolute;top:60px;left:
340px;z-index:10;overflow : hidden;" frameborder=0 hspace="0" vspace="0"
MARGINWIDTH="0" MARGINHEIGHT="0" SCROLLING="no" class="bg01"></iframe>
```

We'll assume the mp in name="mp" id="mp" means "movie player." The most important portion of this is also the longest: the src. For us to find out more about where the movies are served from, we need to open that URL in a window of its own, instead of that <iframe>. <iframe>, or "inline frames," keeps us from viewing the HTML source the <iframe> refers to. For us to see the actual HTML of our movie player, we'll need to prepend the <iframe>'s URL with *http://ifilm.com/*, load it up, and see what we can see.

In the source, we see yet another URL:

```
QTSRC="http://www.ifilm.com/media/getmetafile.smil?fid=2462842&mt=mov&bw=200
&adid=2471970&admt=mov&refsite=&pinfo=ipt:ifilm|gpt:1|fid:2462842|mt:mov|
bw:200|refsite:|rcid:|prn:|it:|pop:|lid:|sid:1|cid:1|cch:100|cr:1|ctxpg:pl|
c:true|admt:mov|adid:2471970|adbt:sponsor|adsn:"
```

As before, we learn something new. For one, all the URLs are sent around with the movie's unique ID, as well as with our bandwidth choice (&bw). We can also see the format of video the file we chose in various places (mov). All these arguments are handed to something called getmetafile.smil; the .smil extension suggests that at some point we'll be handed a Synchronized Multimedia Integration Language (SMIL) file. SMIL (*http://www.w3.org/AudioVideo/*) is a markup language specifically for integrating media in presentations. You may not have encountered it before, but in the vein of "know only what you need to," it won't prove much of a worry. Load the provided URL in your browser. Depending on your browser, you'll either be asked to download a file, or you'll be shown plain text in the window. That's the SMIL file we were expecting, which is interpreted by the embedded media player in the original pop-up window we opened; on its own and out of the context of that pop-up menu, it provides just the information we're after—the URL of the movie itself:

```
<video src="http://anon.ifilm.speedera.net/anon.ifilm/
qt/portal/2462842_200.mov" title="IFILM.com" region="IFILM" />
```

That URL contains the movie's unique ID (2465042), the format type (qt and .mov), and our preferred quality setting (200). It then becomes a simple matter of passing that off to a downloader like *wget* (see "Downloading with curl and wget" [Hack #26]), and the movie is ours:

```
% wget http://anon.ifilm.speedera.net/anon.ifilm/qt/portal/2462842_200.mov
```

You can do much better than all these manual shenanigans with a little shell scripting. We'll assume *wget* on a Linux system to do the actual downloading and write a simple program to accept a film ID and get the best quality video.

The Code

Save the following code to a file called *leechifilm.sh*:

```
#!/bin/sh
#
# LeechiFilm - saves movies from iFilm.com.
# Part of the Leecharoo suite - for all those hard to leech places.
# http://disobey.com/d/code/ or contact morbus@disobey.com.
#
```

```
# This code is free software; you can redistribute it and/or
# modify it under the same terms as Perl itself.
#

for id in $*; do
    f56="http://anon.ifilm.speedera.net/anon.ifilm/qt/portal/${id}_56.mov"
    f200="http://anon.ifilm.speedera.net/anon.ifilm/qt/portal/${id}_200.mov"
    f500="http://anon.ifilm.speedera.net/anon.ifilm/qt/portal/${id}_500.mov"
    wget -c $f500 || wget -c $f200 || wget -c $f56
done
```

Running the Hack

Invoke the script on the command line, passing it a movie's unique ID. You'll need to do the initial work of gleaning that identifier, as we did previously:

```
% leechifilm.sh 2462842
... etc ...
--21:43:31--  http://anon.ifilm.speedera.net/anon.ifilm/qt/portal/⏎
2462842_200.mov
            => `2462842_200.mov'
Resolving anon.ifilm.speedera.net... done.
Connecting to anon.ifilm.speedera.net[64.15.251.217]:80... connected.
HTTP request sent, awaiting response... 200 OK
Length: 4,231,752 [video/quicktime]
... etc ...
```

You can also pass multiple film IDs, and *wget* will trudge along happily. If you're familiar with *bash*, you can eschew the need for an external script and just define function leechifilm( ) within your *.bash_profile*.

HACK #35 Downloading Movies from the Library of Congress

Often, downloading from the Web is accomplished more easily with a little exploration and a command-line utility or favorite browser than with even the most accomplished programming.

When you're looking at a web site, trying to decipher how best to get at the meaty files or information within, you may already have a preconceived notion that it's going to take more than a little programming to get at it. Often, this is entirely unnecessary.

Directory Indexes

Check to see if the site shows directory indexes, automatically generated lists of the files within a directory. This is easier than it sounds. In most cases, when you create a directory to serve web pages from, you add an *index.html* or *default.html* to signify your default document for that location.

Since these are special filenames, you don't have to specify them in the final URL. For example, the following two addresses are equivalent:

```
http://example.com/directory/index.html
http://example.com/directory/
```

The second, while being smaller and easier to type, also ensures that redesigns (such as from *.html* to *.php*) can happen in the future, without worrying about redirecting nonexistent files to the right place.

In some cases, though, directories are holding tanks for media files, like your typical */images/*, */graphics/*, or */movies/*. Without a user-generated *index.html* file, these directories can often be accessed directly via your browser:

```
http://example.com/directory/images/
http://example.com/directory/movies/
```

One of a few different things will happen, depending on the web server and how it has been configured. You may well get a "Directory Listing Denied" error, which is the web server's way of saying "I've been told not to automatically generate a listing of files within this directory." Sometimes, the web site owner has dropped a snarky comment into an *index.html* file— something to the effect of "These are not the files you seek"—or just a blank page. If you're lucky, you'll be provided with a listing of everything in the directory. Figure 3-2 shows the contents of my images directory, *http://disobey.com/images/*, in my browser.

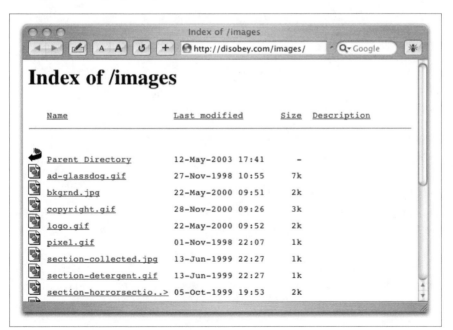

Figure 3-2. An example of a generated file listing

There's no need to scrape those hrefs or srcs from an HTML page; what you see is what's available to you, which can become amazingly handy. Not only can you send this simplified directory listing to a shell utility like *curl* or *wget* [Hack #26], but some web browsers have a Download Manager in which to queue files for local storage. For example, in Internet Explorer on OS X, I can Option-click these images (or any other file) for them to become automatically queued for downloading. (Yes, you could do this on any page, directory listing or not, but an HTML page that's spread out over several pages can make this more trouble than it's worth.) Figure 3-3 shows Internet Explorer's Download Manager.

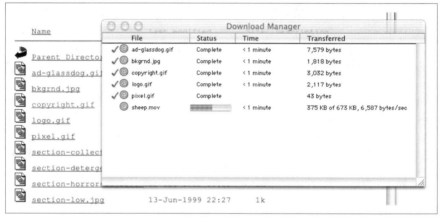

Figure 3-3. Internet Explorer's Download Manager

An Example: Origins of American Animation

The Origins of American Animation site (*http://lcweb2.loc.gov/ammem/ oahtml/oahome.html*) offers 21 animated films and two fragments from the years 1900–1921. If you thought American animation started with Steamboat Willie, get over it. These animations, though mostly very simple, are worth seeing. *He Resolves Not to Smoke* has readable dialog, and it's charming and very, very weird at the same time. It's definitely worth taking the time to archive for your own offline use.

The URL linking to *He Resolves Not To Smoke* is:

```
http://lcweb2.loc.gov/cgi-bin/query/S?ammem/papr:@FILREQ
(@field(TITLE+@od1(He+resolves+not+to+smoke++)
)+@FIELD(COLLID+animat))
```

This is nothing I want to decipher anytime soon. And, in the "hold to heart" repetition of "need to know" basis only, we shouldn't have to. Each movie in the exhibit includes three different file formats, and if we mouse over each of the links for *He Resolves...*, we see:

```
http://memory.loc.gov/mbrs/animp/4067.ram
http://memory.loc.gov/mbrs/animp/4067.mpg
http://memory.loc.gov/mbrs/animp/4067.mov
```

These are much simpler URLs to remember, type, and understand. But what's even better is, as we examine other movie pages, they're all located in the same directory. Taking a calculated chance (*calculated* in the sense that I'm basing a hack on its success), load the following in your browser:

```
http://memory.loc.gov/mbrs/animp/
```

We now have an automated directory listing that provides a complete list of files available to us, without having to follow link after link from page after page just to arrive at the same directory.

If you're using Internet Explorer on Mac OS X, you can Option-click on each of the files in the directory, adding the movies to your download queue. After just a couple of minutes' work, you can go merrily about your day, letting IE do the work of grabbing all those files for you.

Alternatively, now that we have a single listing of all available files, as opposed to multiple pages to worry about, we can use an automated utility like *wget* [Hack #26] to grab them all in a single command:

```
% wget -m --accept=mpg http://memory.loc.gov/mbrs/animp/
```

This instructs *wget* to mirror the entire URL, but to accept (and save) only files that end in *.mpg*. A single command, and that's all there is to it.

Another Example: America at Work, America at Leisure

The same technique can be applied to another find: the Library of Congress's America at Work, America at Leisure project (*http://memory.loc.gov/ammem/awlhtml/*). The site includes more than 100 films made between 1894 and 1915. There are films of firefighters, ice manufacturers, paperboys—you name it—all going about their business. There are lots of Edison films here too.

The directory listing you're after lives at *http://lcweb2.loc.gov/mbrs/awal/*.

Downloading Images from Webshots

#36 Search a large collection of community-contributed images, based on keywords of your choice, and then download the visual finding.

Webshots (*http://www.webshots.com/*) bills itself as "your world of photos." The Community section (*http://www.webshots.com/r/home/community*) has thousands of user-contributed photos available for download, and the Gallery (*http://www.webshots.com/r/home/gallery*) has even more from professional photographers. To access the Gallery, you must be a registered user, but the Community section is prime for automated downloading.

The Code

You'll need the *WWW::Mechanize* Perl module (see "WWW::Mechanize 101" [Hack #21] and "Scraping with WWW::Mechanize" [Hack #22]) installed to run this script.

Save the following code to a file called *webshots.pl*:

```
#!/usr/bin/perl -w
use strict;
use WWW::Mechanize;
use Getopt::Long;

my $max = 10;
GetOptions(
    "max=i" => \$max,
);

my $search = shift or die "Must specify a search term";

my $w = WWW::Mechanize->new;
$w->get( "http://www.webshots.com/explore/" );
$w->success or die "Can't read the search page!\n";

$w->submit_form(
    form_number => 1,
    fields => { words => $search },
);
$w->success or die "Search failed!\n";

# execution of script stops if warning
# about adult content is returned.
if ( $w->content =~ /Adult content/i ) {
    die "Search term probably returns adult content\n";
}

my $ndownloads = 0;
NEXT_PAGE_LOOP: while(1) {
    $w->content =~ /Page (\d+) of (\d+)/
        or warn "Can't find page count\n";
    warn "On page $1 of $2...\n";

    # Pull the "Next" link off before we download pictures
    my $nextlink = $w->find_link( text => "Next >" );
    my $currpage = $w->uri;
```

```
    my @links = $w->find_all_links( url_regex =>
        qr[http://community.webshots.com/photo/] );

for my $link ( @links ) {
    my $url = $link->url;
    my $text = $link->text;
    next if $text eq "[IMG]";

    $w->get( $url );
    $w->success or die "Couldn't fetch $url";

    if ($w->content=~m[(http://community\.webshots\.com/.+?\..↵
(jpg|gif|png))]) {
        my $imgurl = $1; my $type = $2;

        # Make a name based on the webshots title for the pic
        my $filename = lc $text;        # Lowercase everything
        $filename =~ s/\s+/-/g;          # Spaces become dashes
        $filename =~ s/[^0-9a-z-]+//g;  # Strip all nonalphanumeric
        $filename =~ s/(^-|-$)//;        # Strip leading/trailing dashes
        $filename = "$filename.$type";

        # Bring down the image if we don't already have it
        if ( -e $filename ) { warn "Already have $filename\n"; }
        else {
            # use LWP's :content_file to save our
            # image directly to the filesystem,
            # instead of processing it ourselves.
            warn "Saving $filename...\n";
            $w->get( $imgurl, ":content_file"=>$filename );
            ++$ndownloads; last if $ndownloads >= $max;
        }
    } else { warn "Couldn't find an image on $url\n"; }
}

last unless $nextlink && ($ndownloads<$max);

my $nexturl = URI->new_abs( $nextlink->url, $currpage )->as_string;
$w->get( $nexturl ); die "$nexturl failed!\n" unless $w->success;
}
```

Running the Hack

Invoke the script on the command line, passing it a search string, like this:

```
% perl webshots.pl cars
Saving bike02.jpg
Saving escanaba-street-car-bridge.jpg
Saving resort-community-of-playa-car-mexico.jpg
Saving 1969-chevy-camaro.jpg
Saving 1929-ford-roadster.jpg
...
```

If your search string is more than one word, wrap it in double quotes:

```
% perl webshots.pl "chevy camaro"
Already have 1969-chevy-camaro.jpg
Saving 1969-chevy-camaro-z28.jpg
```

Note that the *webshots* script doesn't pull down identically named photos, which saves you time if you're searching for photos with different keywords. By default, the script downloads 10 unique photos and then stops. To download a different number of photos, use the --max switch:

```
% perl webshots.pl --max=40 "german shepherd"
```

Hacking the Hack

There are a few ways you can improve upon this hack.

Starting on a given page. The script will cheerfully skip over photos that it's already seen and move on to more pages. If you're downloading from dozens of pages, this might take some time. The script could, instead, modify the page=x of the URLs to start on a different page number.

Downloading from other areas. The script, as shown, only does keyword searching, but there are two other sections that may be of interest: Most Popular and New Photos. Downloading photos from these sections will be different than downloading from search results, since they're based on albums of photos, not individual photos. You'll need to make the script link to an album, download the photos from there, and then back out to the list of albums. *WWW::Mechanize*'s back( ) method will help here.

Modifying filenames. Sometimes, different photos will have the same name; the script will therefore see them as the same and not download the "duplicate." Maybe a search on cats returns two different photos called *stripes* or, even more likely, *untitled*. If you find this to be the case, you can append an incrementing number to the filename if the file already exists:

```
my $dupe_count = 1;
my $max = 10;
```

And then:

```
# Bring down the image if we don't already have it
if ( -e $filename ) {
    warn "Already have $filename\n";
    $filename = $filename . $dupe_count;
    $dupe_count++;
else {
    warn "Saving $filename\n";
    $w->get( $imgurl, ":content_file"=>$filename );
```

```
        ++$ndownloads; last if $ndownloads >= $max;
    }
```

Note that doing this means you may have duplicate photos with different names.

Bypassing the adult content warning. Currently, the script stops if the search returns a page warning about adult content. You can modify the hack to bypass the warning page automatically. Instead of letting the search end, "click" on the "continue searching" link:

```
    if ( $w->content =~ /adult content/ i ) {
        $w->follow_link( text_regex => qr/Continue with webshots search/i );
        $w->success or die "Couldn't follow warning link";
    }
```

—Andy Lester

Downloading Comics with dailystrips

Love comics but hate visiting multiple sites for your daily dose? Automate your stripping with some easy-to-use open source Perl software.

It's hard to believe that, across all the cultures of the Internet, there's one common denominator of humor. Can you guess what it is? No, no; it's not the "All Your Base Are Belong to Us" videos. It's the comic strip. Whether you're into geek humor, political humor, or unfortunate youngsters forever failing to kick a football, there's a comic strip for you.

In fact, there may be several comic strips for you. There may be so many that it's a pain to visit all the sites containing said comic strips to view them. But there's a great piece of software available to ease your woes: *dailystrips* grabs all the strips for you, presenting them in one HTML file. Combine it with *cron* **[Hack #90]** and you've got a great daily comic strip supplement right in your mailbox or web site. The author, Andrew Medico, makes it clear that if you set this up to run on a web site, you must ensure that you've configured your site to restrict access to you alone or risk some legal consequences.

Getting the Code

dailystrips is available at *http://dailystrips.sourceforge.net/*, and this hack covers Version 1.0.27. There are two components to the program: the program itself and the definitions file, which defines the details of the available comic strips. As of this writing, *dailystrips* supports over 500 different comic strips. Once you've downloaded the program, go back to the download page and grab the latest definitions file, which is updated often. Save it over the *strips.def* file that comes packaged in the ZIP archive with the application.

Running the Hack

After installation (see the *INSTALL* file or installation instructions online at *http://dailystrips.sourceforge.net/1.0.27/install.html*), *dailystrips* runs from the command line with several options. Here are a few of the more important ones:

--list
> Lists available strips

--random
> Downloads a random strip

--defs *filename*
> Uses a user-specified strips definition file

--local
> Saves strips to a local HTML file rather than the default of STDOUT

--help
> Prints a list of available options

To grab the latest "Get Fuzzy" comic and save to a local file, run:

```
% perl dailystrips --local getfuzzy
```

While the program is running, you'll get a count of any errors in retrieving the images of the strips. From my experiments, it looked like the nonsyndicated comics were easier to get and more consistent than the syndicated ones.

Once the program is finished, it'll either spit some HTML to STDOUT or, if you've enacted the --local option, save the strips to an HTML file named using the current date. The file will save into the *dailystrips* directory.

Hacking the Hack

In this hack, we're not hacking the hack so much as hacking the *defs* file. The *defs* file defines from where the strips are retrieved and the code snippets that are used to retrieve them. The *defs* file also includes *groups*, which are shortcuts to retrieving several comics at once. More extensive information on how to define strips is available from the *README.DEFS* file.

Defining strips by URL. The first way to define new strips is by generating a URL based on the current date. Here's an example for James Sharman's "Badtech" comic:

```
strip badtech
    name Badtech
    artist James Sharman
    homepage http://www.badtech.com/
```

```
    type generate
    imageurl http://www.badtech.com/a/%-y/%-m/%-d.jpg
    provides any
end
```

The first line specifies a unique strip name that you'll use to add the strip to a group or get it from the command line. The second line, name, specifies the name of the strip to display in the HTML output. Next, artist includes the name of the illustrator, which will also display in the HTML output. The fourth line determines the home page of the strip, and the fifth line specifies how the strip is found. In this case, we're generating a URL. imageurl specifies the URL of the comic, and %-y, %-m, and %-d specify the year, month, and day, respectively.

The final line, provides, indicates which types of strips the definition can provide: either any for a definition that can provide the strip for any given date, or latest for a definition that can provide only the current strip.

Finding strips with a search. The other type of URL generation, *searching*, is as follows:

```
strip joyoftech
    name The Joy of Tech
    homepage http://www.joyoftech.com/joyoftech/
    type search
    searchpattern <IMG.+?src="(joyimages/\d+\.gif)\"
    matchpart 1
    baseurl http://www.joyoftech.com/joyoftech/
    provides latest
end
```

Notice that the options are similar to the options in the previous example. The strip, name, and homepage options function as they do in the first example, but the type option is now search. With this type, you need to include a searchpattern, which specifies a Perl regular expression that will match the strip's URL. The matchpart line tells the script which paranthetical section to match. In this example, there's only one parenthetical section.

baseurl is necessary only when the searchpattern line does not match a full URL (as in this instance). When specified, it's prepended to whatever the regular expression of searchpattern matches.

Gathering strips into a group. If you want to get a set of the same comic strips every day, it's kind of a pain to type them all in. *dailystrips* lets you specify a group name that gathers several comic strips at the same time. Groups go at the top of the definitions file and look like this:

```
group andrews
    desc Andrew's Favorite Strips
```

```
        include userfriendly dilbert foxtrot
        include pennyarcade joyoftech thefifthwave monty bc
        include wizardofid garfield adamathome
    end
```

group is the name of the group, and desc is its descriptive blurb. On each line after that, use the word include and whatever strips you want gathered into the group. As you can see, there are 11 strips in this group. When you're finished, put end on its own line. You call groups of strips with a @, as in this example:

```
% perl dailystrips -l @andrews
```

HACK #38 Archiving Your Favorite Webcams

Got a number of scenic or strategically placed webcams you watch daily? Or would like to ensure that your coworkers are actually doing the work you've assigned them? Keep on top of your pictorial problems with Python.

Keeping track of a large number of active webcams is a thankless task: half the time the images haven't changed, and the rest of the time it takes just as long to go through refreshing them all or waiting for them to refresh as it does to look at and mentally process the images themselves.

This hack alleviates your grief by automatically downloading images from webcams every 15 seconds—but only if they've been updated, so that we don't waste bandwidth. It's also the only Python script in the entire book and, as such, earns special recognition.

To tell the program which URLs to download, we have to put them in a file, one per line. The program looks for this list by default at *URIs.txt*, but this can be changed both in the source and on the command line.

The program puts each picture in its own file, after producing an index file (which defaults to *webcams.html*) so that we can quickly and easily browse all of the downloaded images in one go.

The Code

Save the following code as *getcams.py*:

```
#!/usr/bin/python
"""

getcams.py - Archiving Your Favorite Web Cams
Sean B. Palmer, <http://purl.org/net/sbp/>, 2003-07.
License: GPL 2; share and enjoy!

Usage:
    python getcams.py [ <filename> ]
```

```
<filename> defaults to URIs.txt
"""

import urllib2, time
from urllib import quote
from email.Utils import parsedate

# # # # # # # # # # # # # # # #
# Configurable stuff
#
# download how often, in seconds
seconds = 15

# what file we should write to
index = 'webcams.html'

# End of configurable stuff!
# # # # # # # # # # # # # # # #

def quoteURI(uri):
    # Turn a URI into a filename.
    return quote(uri, safe='')

def makeHTML(uris):
    # Create an HTML index so that we
    # can look at the archived piccies.
    print "Creating a webcam index at", index

    f = open(index, 'w')
    print >> f, '<html xmlns="http://www.w3.org/1999/xhtml" >'
    print >> f, '<head><title>My Webcams</title></head>'
    print >> f, '<body>'
    for uri in uris:
        # We use the URI of the image for the filename, but we have
        # to hex encode it first so that our operating systems are
        # happy with it. The following code unencodes the URI.
        link = quoteURI(uri).replace('%', '%25')

        # Now we make the image, and provide a link to the original.
        print >> f, '<p><img src="%s" alt=" " /><br />' % link
        print >> f, '-<a href="%s">%s</a></p>' % (uri, uri)
    print >> f, '</body>'
    print >> f, '</html>'
    f.close()
    print "Done creating the index!\n"

metadata = {}

def getURI(uri):
    print "Trying", uri

    # Try to open the URI--we're not downloading it yet.
    try: u = urllib2.urlopen(uri)
```

```
      except Exception, e: print "   ...failed:", e
    else:
        # Get some information about the URI; we do this
        # to find out whether it's been updated yet.
        info = u.info()
        meta = (info.get('last-modified'), info.get('content-size'))
        print "   ...got metadata:", meta

        if metadata.get(uri) == meta:
            print "   ...not downloading: no update yet"
        else:
            # The image has been updated, so let's download it.
            metadata[uri] = meta
            print "   ...downloading; type: %s; size: %s" % \
                (info.get('content-type', '?'), info.get('content-size', '?'))
            data = u.read()
            open(quoteURI(uri), 'wb').write(data)
            print "   ...done! %s bytes" % len(data)

            # Save an archived version for later.
            t = parsedate(info.get('last-modified'))
            archv = quoteURI(uri) + '-' + time.strftime('%Y%m%dT%H%M%S', t) + ↵
'.jpg'
            open(archv, 'wb').write(data)
        u.close()

def doRun(uris):
    for uri in uris:
        startTime = time.time()
        getURI(uri)
        finishTime = time.time()

        timeTaken = finishTime - startTime
        print "This URI took", timeTaken, "seconds\n"
        timeLeft = seconds - timeTaken # time until the next run
        if timeLeft > 0: time.sleep(timeLeft)

def main(argv):
    # We need a list of URIs to download. We require them to be
    # in a file; the next line defaults the filename to URIs.txt
    # if it can't gather one from the command line.
    fn = (argv + [None])[0] or 'URIs.txt'
    data = open(fn).read()
    uris = data.splitlines()

    # Now make an index, and then
    # continuously download the piccies.
    makeHTML(uris)
    while 1: doRun(uris)

if __name__=="__main__":
    import sys
```

```
# If the user asks for help, give it to them!
# Otherwise, just run the program as usual.
if sys.argv[1:] in (['--help', '-h', '-?']):
    print __doc__
else: main(sys.argv[1:])
```

Running the Hack

Here's a typical run, invoked from the command line:

```
% python getcams.py
Creating a webcam index at webcams.html
Done creating the index!

Trying http://example.org/webcams/someplace.jpg
    ...got metadata: ('Thu, 10 Jul 2003 15:50:38 GMT', None)
    ...downloading; type: image/jpeg; size: ?
    ...done! 32594 bytes
This URI took 8.2480000257 seconds

Trying http://example.org/webcams/phenomic.jpg
    ...got metadata: ('Thu, 10 Jul 2003 11:35:51 GMT', None)
    ...not downloading: no update yet
This URI took 1.30099999905 seconds
```

The code, complicated though it looks, consists of only a few stages:

1. Open the list of URLs of each of the webcams.

2. Create an HTML index so that we can view the downloaded webcam images.

3. For each URL in our list, check to see if the image has been updated or not. If it has, download it. In the event that it took under 15 seconds to download, wait for the remainder of the time in an attempt to respect the server resources of others.

Hacking the Hack

The code has a number of limitations:

- We have to know the URL of each picture for downloading. So, if we don't know the URL or if it changes a lot, we have a problem. But really, the biggest problem here is that it's just a bit of an inconvenience to get the actual URL of each picture that we want.

- If a web site goes down, the script hangs. We could get around this problem by using Python's *async* module, but this would add quite a bit of complexity.

- People have been known to fake Last-Modified HTTP headers, so the metadata that we use to ascertain whether a picture has been updated isn't absolutely reliable. However, most Last-Modified headers are faked to force people to use fresh rather than cached versions, so if they're that passionate about it, we may as well let them.

- If you have any files in your directory that have the same names as the quoted versions of the URLs you're trying to download, the program will overwrite them.

Other than these limitations, the code is safe.

—Sean B. Palmer

News Wallpaper for Your Site

#39   Grab today's news images for your web site or as an RSS feed, suitable for viewing in your favorite syndicated news application.

News Wallpaper takes a command-line query and runs it against Yahoo!'s news photo archive, scraping image thumbnails as well as photo information into an RSS feed [Hack #94], which you can then view in an aggregator or add to your own web site [Hack #95]. There are plenty of text RSS feeds available, but this one gives you images to liven up your site and your reader's morning.

The Code

Save the following code as *wallpaper.pl*:

```perl
#!/usr/bin/perl -w
use strict;
use LWP::UserAgent;
use XML::RSS;
use URI;

# how many RSS items?
my $counterlimit = 10;

# prefix for image URLs?
# could be file:// or http://.
my $url_prefix = "file:///Users/morbus/Desktop/";

# get our query, else die miserably.
my $query = shift @ARGV; die unless $query;

# and grab our data.
my $ua  = LWP::UserAgent->new;
my $url = URI->new('http://search.news.yahoo.com/search/news/');
$url->query_form(c => "news_photos", p => $query);
my $photosource = $ua->get($url)->content;
```

```
# if there was no luvin', then no RSS feed.
die "There were no results for this search!\n"
  if $photosource =~ /Sorry, no News Photos Matches/i;

# start the RSS feed.
my $rss = new XML::RSS (version => '0.91');
$rss->channel(
    'link'      => $url_prefix,
    title       => "Yahoo! News Photos Wallpaper",
    description => "News photos matching the keyword '$query'."
);

# our counter.
my $counter = 0;

# get the pictures and descriptions
while ($photosource =~ m!hr width=90%.*?<a href="(.*?)"><img src=(.*?) .↵
*?size=2>(.*?)</font>.*?=timedate>.*?</span>!mgis) {
    last if $counter == $counterlimit; # reached our limit? move on.
    my ($url, $pictureurl, $desc) = ($1, $2, $3);
    unless ($url && $pictureurl && $desc) { next; }

    # download this picture to the current directory.
    $ua->get($pictureurl, ':content_file' => "picture$counter.jpg");

    # add this item
    # to our RSS feed.
    $rss->add_item(
        title       => substr($desc, 0, 75) . "...", 'link' => $url,
        description => "<img src=\"${url_prefix}picture${counter}.jpg\"> ↵
$desc",
    );

    # NexxTXTt!
    $counter++;
}

# and save our RSS.
$rss->save("wallpaper.rdf");
```

Running the Hack

This script goes through three stages:

1. Run a query for the keyword you specify (and die if there's no result).

2. Gather the thumbnails in the results and save them to a local folder.

3. Write an RSS feed, including a reference to the image thumbnails.

You can run this hack as a client-side application—something to fill out your RSS reader—or you can run it as a server application to add some color to your web site. If you run it as a server-side item, you'll want to use something that'll run it regularly; a *cron* job [Hack #90] to run it every day would work well.

Hacking the Hack

There are a few ways you can improve upon this hack.

Picture limits. The most obvious change for this hack would be to change how many pictures the script gathers. To do so, change the $counterlimit to whatever you like:

```
# how many RSS items?
my $counterlimit = 15;
```

Note that, as a best practice, RSS files generally stay under 15 items.

RSS version. RSS wonks will note that the version of RSS used in this script is RSS 0.91. There are two reasons for this. First, it's well-known and supported by all the RSS readers I've ever heard of. Second, for what this script is doing, a version more sophisticated than 0.91 is not required. If you want to use a newer version of RSS, take a look at the *XML::RSS* documentation at *http://search.cpan.org/author/KELLAN/XML-RSS/lib/RSS.pm*.

Image::Size. As they are now, you might decide that the pictures in the feed are too large; you may want them, for example, only half this size. You can do just that, thanks to a Perl module called *Image::Size* (*http://search.cpan.org/author/RJRAY/*). Use it by adding the following line to the top of the program, along with the other use statements:

```
use Image::Size;
```

Now, as you grab picture URLs, you'll want to glean their sizes:

```
$ua->get($pictureurl, ':content_file' => "picture$counter.jpg");
(my $height, $width) = imgsize("picture$counter.jpg");
```

Now that you have the sizes, decide how much smaller you want them. How about half their original size? Calculate the new sizes like so:

```
$ua->get($pictureurl, ':content_file' => "picture$counter.jpg");
(my $height, my $width) = imgsize("picture$counter.jpg");
my $newheight = $height/2; my $newwidth = $width/2;
```

Now, all you have to do is add that height and width to your RSS feed. Change the line that creates an RSS description with no size attributes:

```
description => "<img src=\"${url_prefix}picture${counter}.jpg\"> $desc",
```

to this:

```
description => "<img src=\"${url_prefix}picture${counter}.jpg\" height=\⌐
"$newheight\" width=\"newwidth\"> $desc",
```

This produces the same feed, but with smaller pictures. Note that you're just decreasing the rendered size of the image in your RSS reader, not changing the actual image file itself. If the *Image::Magick* (*http://www.imagemagick.org/www/perl.html*) module is installed, you can actually reduce the size of the image file with the following code:

```
use Image::Magick

open(JPEG, "<picture$counter.jpg ") or die $!;
read(JPEG, my $blob, -s JPEG) or die $!;

my $image = Image::Magick->new( );
$image->BlobToImage($blob);
$magick->Scale(geometry=>"$newheight  x $newwidth");

open(NEW, ">picture$conter.jpg");
print NEW $magick->ImageToBlog( );
close(NEW);
```

Saving Only POP3 Email Attachments

#40 Get oodles of attachments from mailing lists and friends? Learn how to save them to your hard drive automatically with a little Perl voodoo.

Remember those carefree days of yore, when all you got in your email were actual ASCII messages? Nah, me neither. Those days are long gone. Nowadays, your friends are sending you MP3 files of their bands, your aunt Ethel is sending you digital camera shots of her bulldog Zack, and occasionally you get the odd PDF file for work.

This hack pulls down the contents of a POP3 mailbox (which you probably have; most email accounts on the Internet are POP3 accounts) and saves the attachments to a directory. This hack is very customizable, but note that you'll need the Perl modules *Net::POP3* and *MIME::Parser* to use it.

The Code

Save the following code as *leechpop.pl*:

```
#!/usr/bin/perl -w
#
# LeechPOP - save ONLY attachments from a POP3 mailbox, with filtering.
# Part of the Leecharoo suite - for all those hard to leech places.
# http://disobey.com/d/code/ or contact morbus@disobey.com.
#
```

```perl
# This code is free software; you can redistribute it and/or
# modify it under the same terms as Perl itself.

use strict; $|++;
my $VERSION = "1.0";
use Getopt::Long;
my %opts;

# make sure we have the modules we need, else die peacefully.
eval("use Net::POP3;"); die "[err] Net::POP3 not installed.\n" if $@;
eval("use MIME::Parser;"); die "[err] MIME::Parser not installed.\n" if $@;

# define our command line flags (long and short versions).
GetOptions(\%opts, 'server|s=s',      # the POP3 server to use.
                   'username|u=s',    # the POP3 username to use.
                   'password|p=s',    # the POP3 password to use.
                   'begin|b=i',       # what msg number to start at.
);

# at the very least, we need our login information.
die "[err] POP3 server missing, use --server or -s.\n" unless $opts{server};
die "[err] Username missing, use --username or -u.\n"  unless ⌐
$opts{username};
die "[err] Password missing, use --password or -p.\n"  unless ⌐
$opts{password};

# try an initial connection to the server.
print "-" x 76, "\n"; # merely a visual seperator.
my $conn = Net::POP3->new( $opts{server} )
  or die "[err] There was a problem connecting to the server.\n";
print "Connecting to POP3 server at $opts{server}.\n";

# and now the login information.
$conn->login( $opts{username}, $opts{password} )
  or die "[err] There was a problem logging in (.poplock? credentials?).\n";
print "Connected successfully as $opts{username}.\n";

# purdy stats about our mailbox.
my ($msg_total, $mbox_size) = $conn->popstat( );
if ($msg_total eq 0)   { print "No new emails are available.\n"; exit; }
if ($msg_total eq 'OEO')  { print "No new emails are available.\n"; exit; }
print "You have $msg_total messages totalling ", commify($mbox_size), "k.\
n";

# the list of valid file extensions. we do extensions, not
# mime-types, because they're easier to understand from
# an end-user perspective (no research is required).
my $valid_exts = "jpg jpeg png";
my %msg_ids; # used to keep track of seen emails.
my $msg_num = $opts{begin} || 1; # user specified or 1.

# create a subdirectory based on today's date.
my ($d,$m,$y) = (localtime)[3,4,5]; $y += 1900; $m++;
```

```perl
$d = sprintf "%02.0d", $d; $m = sprintf "%02.0d", $m;
print "Using directory '$y-$m-$d' for newly downloaded files.\n";
my $savedir = "$y-$m-$d"; mkdir($savedir, 0777);


# begin looping through each msg.
print "-" x 76, "\n"; # merely a visual seperator.
while ($msg_num <= $msg_total) {

    # the size of the individual email.
    my $msg_size = $conn->list($msg_num);

    # get the header of the message
    # so we can check for duplicates.
    my $headers = $conn->top($msg_num);

    # print/store the good bits.
    my ($msg_subj, $msg_id);
    foreach my $header (@$headers) {

        # print subject line and size.
        if ($header =~ /^Subject: (.*)/) {
            $msg_subj = substr($1, 0, 50); # trim subject down a bit.
            print "Msg $msg_num / ",commify($msg_size),"k / $msg_subj...\n";
        }

        # save Message-ID for duplicate comparison.
        elsif ($header =~ /^Message-ID: <(.*)>/i) {
            $msg_id = $1; $msg_ids{$msg_id}++;
        }

        # move on to the filtering.
        elsif ($msg_subj and $msg_id) { last; }

    }

    # if the message size is too small, then it
    # could be a reply or something of low quality.
    if (defined($msg_size) and $msg_size < 40000) {
        print "  Skipping - message size is smaller than our threshold.\n";
        $msg_num++; next;
    }

    # check for matching Message-ID. If found,
    # skip this message. This will help eliminate
    # crossposting and duplicate downloads.
    if (defined($msg_id) and $msg_ids{$msg_id} >= 2) {
        print "  Skipping - we've already seen this Message-ID.\n";
        $msg_num++; next;
    }

    # get the message to feed to MIME::Parser.
    my $msg = $conn->get($msg_num);
```

```
# create a MIME::Parser object to
# extract any attachments found within.
my $parser = new MIME::Parser;
$parser->output_dir( $savedir );
my $entity = $parser->parse_data($msg);

# extract our mime parts and go through each one.
my @parts = $entity->parts;
foreach my $part (@parts) {

    # determine the path to the file in question.
    my $path = ($part->bodyhandle) ? $part->bodyhandle->path : undef;

    # move on if it's not defined,
    # else figure out the extension.
    next unless $path; $path =~ /\w+\.([^.]+)$/;
    my $ext = $1; next unless $ext;

    # we continue only if our extension is correct.
    my $continue; $continue++ if $valid_exts =~ /$ext/i;

    # delete the blasted thing.
    unless ($valid_exts =~ /$ext/) {
        print "  Removing unwanted filetype ($ext): $path\n";
        unlink $path or print " > Error removing file at $path: $!.";
        next; # move on to the next attachment or message.
    }

    # a valid file type. yummy!
    print "  Keeping valid file: $path.\n";
}

# increase our counter.
$msg_num++;
}

# clean up and close the connection.
$conn->quit;

# now, jump into our savedir and remove all msg-*
# files, which are message bodies saved by MIME::Parser.
chdir ($savedir); opendir(SAVE, "./") or die $!;
my @dir_files = grep !/^\.\.?$/, readdir(SAVE); closedir(SAVE);
foreach (@dir_files) { unlink if $_ =~ /^msg-/; }

# cookbook 2.17.
sub commify {
    my $text = reverse $_[0];
    $text =~ s/(\d\d\d)(?=\d)(?!\d*\.)/$1,/g;
    return scalar reverse $text;
}
```

Running the Hack

To use this hack, you'll need a minimum of three pieces of information: your email account's username, your password, and the name of the POP3 server. If, say, your username is fred, your password is fredpw, and the server is pop.example.com, you'll invoke the script on the command line like this:

```
% perl leechpop.pl -u=fred -p=fredpw -s=pop.example.com
```

Or, if you prefer the wordier version:

```
% perl leechpop.pl --username=fred --password=fredpw ⏎
--server=pop.example.com
```

Assuming you have the proper modules installed and you've provided a correct username, password, and server, your results will look something like this:

```
------------------------------------------------------------------
Connecting to POP3 server at pop.example.com.
Connected successfully as fred.
You have 1040 messages totalling 229,818,136k.
Using directory '2003-06-09' for newly downloaded files.
Beginning downloads, starting at message 1.
------------------------------------------------------------------
...etc...
Msg 20 / 432,827k / [Budding_Rose-Art] The Flame Within.jpg...
    Removing unwanted filetype (txt): 2003-06-09/msg-13522-1.txt
    Keeping valid file: 2003-06-09/The Flame Within-1.jpg.
 Msg 21 / 433,111k / [Graphics_TheAttic] The Flame Within.jpg...
    Skipping - we've already seen this Message-ID.
 Msg 22 / 168,423k / [Budding_Rose-Art] The Sad Clown.jpg...
    Removing unwanted filetype (txt): 2003-06-09/msg-13522-2.txt
    Keeping valid file: 2003-06-09/The Sad Clown.jpg.
 Msg 23 / 558,731k / [Graphics_TheAttic] Sulamith_Wulfing_cal2002_janua...
    Removing unwanted filetype (txt): 2003-06-09/msg-13522-3.txt
    Keeping valid file: 2003-06-09/ma_Sulamith_02_january_white_lilies.jpg.
 Msg 24 / 783,490k / [Graphics_TheAttic] Sulamith_Wulfing_cal2002_febru...
    Removing unwanted filetype (txt): 2003-06-09/msg-13522-4.txt
...etc...
```

The script will attempt to connect to the mailbox, and will report a successful connection if one is made. It'll then report on the number of messages in the mailbox and the total size. For each message, the program will check for any attachments, a valid extension (as specified in the line $valid_exts = "jpg jpeg png";), and total message size.

It is worth noting that my experience with this script has led me to set a threshold of 40,000 bytes for a message to be accepted. Any less than that, and the odds are great that the message is a reply to an earlier message, a brand-new message, or a dual-encoded message that contains both plain text and an HTML equivalent.

If all's well, the file will be saved. If either the extension or message size don't meet the parameters of the program, the file is skipped and we move on.

Hacking the Hack

There are a few ways you can improve upon this hack.

Changing the hardcoded file extensions. One of several ways to hack the script is to change the hardcoded file extensions, which indicate what types of files you want to save. You'll find the list of allowed file extensions in this line:

```
my $valid_exts = "jpg jpeg png";
```

You can add whatever extensions you want to this listing; candidates for additions include *.bmp* and *.gif* (graphics formats) and *.mp3* and *.wav* (audio formats). Adding more extensions looks like this:

```
my $valid_exts = "jpg jpeg png bmp gif mp3 wav";
```

Maybe you want the option to add your own extensions from the command line when you actually run the program. In that case, add an extension option to your GetOptions lines at the top of the script:

```
# define our command line flags (long and short versions).
GetOptions(\%opts, 'server|s=s',      # the POP3 server to use.
                   'username|u=s',     # the POP3 username to use.
                   'password|p=s',     # the POP3 password to use.
                   'begin|b=i',        # what msg number to start at.
                   'extensions|e=s',   # what file extensions to use.
);
```

and then change the line:

```
my $valid_exts = "jpg jpeg png";
```

to:

```
my $valid_exts = $opts{extensions} || "jpg jpeg png";
```

Remember, the extensions to the far right of the line are the defaults; they are used if you don't specify your own. You can make this as elaborate as needed, with several extensions (as in this example), or as minimal as you like, with just one.

Shortening or eliminating the subject line. You might decide that you're not interested in having a long subject line appear while the program is running; by altering the following lines of code, you can shorten the subject line to just a few letters, or remove it completely:

```
if ($header =~ /^Subject: (.*)/) {
    $msg_subj = substr($1, 0, 50); # trim subject down a bit.
    print "Msg $msg_num / ",commify($msg_size),"k / $msg_subj...\n";
```

If you just want to change the length of the subject (defaulting to 50 characters) then focus on substr($1, 0, 50). Change 50 to whatever you like. If
you don't want a subject line to appear at all, remove the line $msg_subj =
substr($1, 0, 50); and the line portion ,"k / $msg_subj...\n".

Saving attachments to the current directory. The way the hack is set up now, a
subdirectory is always created beneath the current one. But if you're in a
hurry, or if you want to keep all your attachments in the same place, you can
remove the directory completely by changing this line:

```
my $savedir = "$y-$m-$d"; mkdir($savedir, 0777);
```

to this:

```
my $savedir = ".";
```

This will save your attachments to the current location. You can also set an
option to define the final resting place from the command line, which means
going back to those GetOptions lines:

```
# define our command-line flags (long and short versions).
GetOptions(\%opts, 'server|s=s',     # the POP3 server to use.
                   'username|u=s',   # the POP3 username to use.
                   'password|p=s',   # the POP3 password to use.
                   'begin|b=i',      # what msg number to start at.
                   'savedir|d=s',    # what directory to save to.
);
```

and changing the $savedir line to this:

```
my $savedir = $opts{savedir} || "$y-$m-$d"; mkdir($savedir, 0777);
```

Specifying the size of saved messages. The hack automatically rejects messages smaller than 40 KB, thinking that a message of 40 KB is not going to
have much in the way of interesting attachments. But you may want to
increase or decrease that number. How? Back to the GetOptions again. Add
this line to the end:

```
'oksize|o=i'      # minimum file size.
```

Then, add these two lines shortly after the GetOptions lines:

```
# what size is okay to download?
my $oksize = $opts{oksize} || 40000;
```

There's one more thing to do. Change this line:

```
if (defined($msg_size) and $msg_size < 40000) {
```

to:

```
if (defined($msg_size) and $msg_size < $oksize) {
```

When you run this hack, you might discover that you are saving tons of small image files: icons, banners, or other detritus. In that case, you might also want to check the width and height of the images before you download them. If that sounds dandy, you'll need to use *Image::Size*, so add the line use Image::Size near the other use lines at the top of the script. Also, insert a few more lines in the code:

```
# check image size. too small? delete.
my ($x, $y) = imgsize($path);
unless (not defined $x or $x > 100) {
    print "  Removing small image size (less than $x pixels tall): $path\n";
    unlink $path or print " > Error removing file at $path: $!.";
    next; # move on to the next attachment or message.
}
```

Image::Size spits out the image height and width, which allows you to capture them into variables. After that, it's simple to compare the size of the variables to see if they're too large or too small. Applied here, it's a simple conditional; it checks to make sure that each graphic file is more than 100 pixels high. If it's not, it's deleted from your directory. You can change the minimum height to whatever you like, base the conditional on both $x and $y, or make the minimum a command-line variable using the GetOptions, as we've done with some of our other tweakeries.

HACK #41 Downloading MP3s from a Playlist

Automatically save the MP3 files that make up an M3U playlist.

Most MP3 players support an *.m3u* file: a plain text file that contains the MP3 filenames and locations that should be played, in a specific order (or randomized from within the player). These M3U files are slightly different from *.pls* files, which are typically used for streaming radio. A sample M3U is shown here:

```
VA-01-Lord_of_the_Rings_OST-The_Prophecy-GREY.mp3
VA-02-Lord_of_the_Rings_OST-Concerning_Hobbits-GREY.mp3
VA-03-Lord_of_the_Rings_OST-The_Shadow_Of_The_Past-GREY.mp3
VA-04-Lord_of_the_Rings_OST-The_Treason_Of_Isengard-GREY.mp3
VA-05-Lord_of_the_Rings_OST-The_Black_Rider-GREY.mp3
VA-06-Lord_of_the_Rings_OST-At_The_Sign_Of_The_Prancing-GREY.mp3
VA-07-Lord_of_the_Rings_OST-A_Knife_In_The_Dark-GREY.mp3
```

This isn't too exciting. However, M3U files can also be filled with MP3 URLs, which is often the case when a user has put her collection online and is streaming them personally or to anyone who'll listen. M3U files have also become the default for listing software, such as Andromeda (*http://www.turnstyle.com/andromeda/*) or *Apache::MP3* (*http://www.apachemp3.com*). Figure 3-4 shows an Andromeda listing from DaylightStation.com.

Figure 3-4. Andromeda listing from DaylightStation.com

Here's a sample M3U with URLs:

```
http://example.com/awesome_album/track1.mp3
http://example.com/awesome_album/track2.mp3
http://example.com/awesome_album/track3.mp3
...
http://example.com/awesome_album/track6.mp3
```

This hack will read M3U files and smartly download the MP3 URLs referenced within—*smartly* in the sense that it will create prettier filenames, as opposed to heavily URL-encoded values like *my%20greatest%20hits*; understand parent folders, which are often the names of the albums; and take care not to download tracks it already has, without skipping tracks that it might have but which are incomplete. It will also give progress readouts [Hack #18] as it's downloading.

A script like this has a major advantage over a utility like *wget*. Since it keeps the same hierarchy represented in the URL, the script has greater control over keeping files well organized, as opposed to *wget*'s input command [Hack #26], which would download the URLs individually.

The Code

Save the following code as a script called *leechm3u.pl*:

```perl
#!/usr/bin/perl -w
#
# LeechM3U - save mp3s listed in an .m3u file, smartly.
# Part of the Leecharoo suite - for all those hard to leech places.
# http://disobey.com/d/code/ or contact morbus@disobey.com.
#
# This code is free software; you can redistribute it and/or
# modify it under the same terms as Perl itself.
#

use strict; $|++;
my $VERSION = "1.0";
use File::Spec::Functions;

# make sure we have the modules we need, else die peacefully.
eval("use LWP 5.6.9;"); die "[err] LWP 5.6.9 or greater required.\n" if $@;
eval("use URI::Escape;"); die "[err] URI::Escape is not installed.\n" if $@;

my $dir = "mp3s";   # save downloads to...?
mkdir $dir;         # make sure that dir exists.
my $mp3_data;       # final holder of our MP3.
my $total_size;     # total size of the MP3.

# loop through each M3U file.
foreach my $file (@ARGV) {

    # open the passed M3U file or move onto the next.
    open(URLS, "<$file") or print "[err] Could not open $file: $!\n";

    # for each line.
    while (<URLS>) {
        next if /^#/;      # skip if it's a comment.
        chomp;             # remove trailing newline.
        my $url = $_;      # more semantic, yes?

        # split the URL into parts, defined by the "/" delimiter
        # in the URL. we'll use this to determine the name of
        # the file, as well as its parent directory. in most
        # cases, the parent directory is the album name.
        my @parts = split(/\//, $url);

        # properly encoded URLs are decimal encoded, with %20
        # representing a space, etc. without conversion, our
        # files would be named like that. we clean these up.
        foreach (@parts) { $_ = uri_unescape($_); }

        # take the second-to-last part, which is the parent
        # directory of our file. we're assuming an album name.
        my $album_dir = $parts[$#parts-1];
```

```
        # create an OS-specific path to our album and file.
        my $album_path = catdir($dir, $album_dir);
        my $file_name = $parts[$#parts]; # prettier.
        my $file_path = catfile($album_path, $file_name);
        mkdir $album_path; # to prepare for dumping.

        # get the size of the MP3 for our progress bar.
        # some sites block Perl User-Agents, so we fakir.
        print "Downloading \"$file_path\"...\n";
        my $ua = LWP::UserAgent->new(agent => ↵
            'Mozilla/4.76 [en] (Win98; U)');
        $total_size = $ua->head($url)->headers->content_length;

        # only download the file if it hasn't been before.
        if (-e $file_path and (stat($file_path))[7] == $total_size) {
            print " Skipping - this file has already been downloaded.\n";
            next;
        }

        # download the file with a callback for progress.
        $ua->get($url, ':content_cb' => \&callback);

        # with the data downloaded into $mp3_data with our
        # callback, save that information to our $file_path.
        # (note: bad grammar so word wrapping won't happen)
        open (MP3, ">$file_path") or die "[err] Can't save: $!\n";
        print MP3 $mp3_data; close(MP3); $mp3_data = undef;
    }

    # next file!
    close(URLS);
}

# per chunk.
sub callback {
    my ($data, $response, $protocol) = @_;
    $mp3_data .= $data; # append to existing data.
    print progress_bar( length($mp3_data), $total_size, 25, '=' );
}

# wget-style. routine by tachyon
# at http://tachyon.perlmonk.org/
sub progress_bar {
    my ( $got, $total, $width, $char ) = @_;
    $width ||= 25; $char ||= '=';
    my $num_width = length $total;
    sprintf "|%-${width}s| Got %${num_width}s bytes of %s (%.2f%%)\r",
        $char x ((($width-1)*$got/$total). '>',
        $got, $total, 100*$got/+$total;
}
```

Running the Hack

To set the script going, invoke it on the command line with a local M3U file:

```
% perl leechm3u.pl m3ufile.m3u
```

This is all fine and dandy, but where are we to find these magical M3U files floating around on the Net? There's the rub: they're not premade; you make them yourself. Utilities like Andromeda and *Apache::MP3*, mentioned earlier in this hack, create an automated list of a user's MP3s. To listen to them, you pick and choose what you want via checkboxes, click the Play button, and whoop, get served an M3U file. Download that M3U playlist to disk instead of letting it queue up in your player, and you now have a local copy to pass to *leechm3u.pl*. You can even pass more than one M3U file at a time to the script.

The next issue is finding sites that run these listing utilities. Oftentimes, if you know the name of the utility, you can find a unique string that will identify it in a Google search. Take Andromeda, for instance. Anytime someone installs it, all the generated files have "Powered by Andromeda" in the footer. By doing a search for that quoted term, you can find a number of entries. Then, it just becomes a matter of queuing up what you want. Since more and more people are releasing their own MP3s this way, you're sure to get a decent number of matches for music you've never heard of, but should.

Here is a collected list of some "software signatures" for your perusal:

Andromeda (http://www.turnstyle.com/andromeda/)
"powered by andromeda" or "search andromeda" "play all"

Apache::MP3 (http://www.apachemp3.com/)
"apache::mp3 was written"

Edna (http://edna.sourceforge.net/)
"powered by edna"

GNUMP3d (http://gnump3d.sourceforge.net/)
intitle:"GNUMP3d" subdirectories

The following signatures aren't applicable to the script in this hack (because they generate either ugly M3U files or something entirely different), but aspiring hackers could probably modify this hack to work with them:

Ampache (http://www.ampache.org)
"welcome to ampache v"

Dynamic MP3 Lister (http://freshmeat.net/projects/dmp3lister/)
"dynamic mp3 lister - listing mp3s in"

Hacking the Hack

This script uses *URI::Escape* to turn an encoded URL into a better-looking filename. However, not everyone will have this module installed or have the time, inclination, or capacity to get it. Those without it (or those who'd like more portability) can replace the following line:

```
foreach (@parts) { $_ = uri_unescape($_); }
```

with a regular expression:

```
foreach (@parts) { $_ =~ s/%([0-9A-Fa-f]{2})/chr(hex($1))/eg; }
```

Likewise, if you're using this script for your own personal purposes, you might not be interested in the remote file's naming scheme. For instance, if you'd rather *artist_name_-_track_name.mp3* be something like *Artist Name-Track Name.mp3*, you can throw in your own renaming filters to clean up $file_name. For example, to replace all those underscores in the filename with spaces, you can use this:

```
# create an OS-specific path to our album and file.
my $album_path = catdir($dir, $album_dir);
my $file_name = $parts[$#parts]; # prettier.
$file_name =~ s/_-_/-/g; $file_name =~ s/_/ /g;
my $file_path = catfile($album_path, $file_name);
mkdir $album_path; # to prepare for dumping.
```

Downloading from Usenet with nget

Even though common wisdom states that porn peddlers and spam pushers have overrun Usenet, there are still a number of groups resolutely producing good content for good folks. In this hack, we'll show how to download files from news groups of your choice.

nget (*http://nget.sourceforge.net/*) is an open source Usenet downloader, available for Linux, FreeBSD, Mac OS X, cygwin32, and mingw32. Much like *wget* [Hack #26] is a downloader for the Web, *nget* excels at a large number of configuration choices for archiving files from Usenet newsgroups.

Once *nget* is installed, you'll need to copy the default *.ngetrc* configuration file into either *~/.ngetrc4/* or *~/_ngetrc/*. The *.ngetrc* is referred to each time you use *nget*, and it contains a hefty dose of sane values to form a basis for your future operations. To get started, we'll have to edit this file to point to our own Usenet server. If your ISP doesn't provide you with one, you can find a list of public access servers at *http://dmoz.org/Computers/Usenet/Public_News_Servers/* (though you might have trouble finding one that

supports *alt.binaries.**, which is what this hack assumes you have access to).
Open the *.ngetrc* file and scroll down until you see this:

```
//hostname aliases
{halias
 {<yourhostalias>
  addr=<yourhostaddress>
  id=1
#optional host config settings:
#  user=<name>
#  pass=<password>
#  fullxover=1
#  shortname=<y>
#  maxstreaming=64
#  idletimeout=300
#  linelenience=0
 }
#Examples:
# {host1
#  addr=news.host1.com
#  fullxover=1
#  id=384845
#  linelenience=0,2
# }
```

For *nget* to know which Usenet server to download from, we'll need to modify the <yourhostalias> and <yourhostaddress> values, like this:

```
//hostname aliases
{halias
 {readfreenews
  addr=biggulp.readfreenews.net
  id=1
... etc ...
```

We can configure as many servers as necessary, simply by creating more hostname alias blocks. What you set for <yourhostalias> can be used on the command line to specify different servers for different downloads (such as nget --host readfreenews or nget --host host1).

Save the file after making those changes. Technically, we're done. With our server configured, we could use the -g flag to pass the group we want to download, and *nget* would resolutely start downloading headers:

```
% nget -g alt.binaries.pictures.comics
make_connection(1,biggulp.readfreenews.net,nntp,0xbfffea20,512)
Connecting to 209.98.153.154:119
r >> 201 NNRP BIGGULP (white) - problems - email news@readfreenews.com
r << GROUP alt.binaries.pictures.comics
r >> 211 7934 2518935 2526868 alt.binaries.pictures.comics
Retrieving headers 2519140-2526868 : 2087/7728/7729  27% 3313B/s 7m44s
...
saving cache: 7932 parts, 5067 files.. done. (7932 sa)
```

```
r << QUIT
OK: 1 group
```

This is all fine and dandy, but no files were actually downloaded, only the message headers. To retrieve files, use the -r flag, which receives a regular expression that defines which files you'd like to download. Regular expressions are a discussion for another time and place, but take a look at the following examples:

```
# this would retrieve every message available.
% nget -g alt.binaries.pictures.comics  -r ".*"

# this would retrieve messages with a subject
# line that contained "jpg" somewhere in it.
% nget -g alt.binaries.pictures.comics -r ".*jpg"

# this would retrieve messages with a subject
# line that matches either "Donald" or "Mickey".
% nget -g alt.binaries.pictures.comics -r "(Donald|Mickey)"

# the exact same command as the above, only
# this time, check for duplicates of files
# we've already downloaded.
% nget -g alt.binaries.pictures.comics -df -r "(Donald|Mickey)"

# download all messages that DO have "jpg" in the
# subject line, but DON'T have the word "unknown".
% nget -g alt.binaries.pictures.comics -r '(?=^(?:(?!unknown).)*$).*jpg'

# same thing as the above, only slightly more readable.
% nget -g alt.binaries.pictures.comics -R "subject jpg == subject unknown != ↵
&&"
```

There's one problem with these examples: we've assumed that you know the name of the group you want to download from. What if you want to find other comic groups to grab files from? Besides investigating on the Net, how are you going to know which groups you want?

Thankfully, there are a few different ways that *nget* can handle this for you. Depending on the server you've configured, you might be able to search the server list directly with nget -XT -r "comics". This may not always work, and the alternative is to download/update the group listing:

```
% nget -a -T -r "comics"
... etc ...
r       alt.alt.comics.jack-chick      ? [r]
r       alt.binaries.pictures.comics    ? [r]
r       alt.binaries.pictures.comics.reposts    ? [r]
r       alt.binaries.pictures.erotica.comics     ? [r]
r       alt.comics.alan-moore   Quis custodiet ipsos custodes. [r]
r       alt.comics.batman       Marketing mania. [r]
...etc...
```

Once you know of other groups to download from, you can include them all at once in the same command, as a comma-spliced list to -g. This next example shows how to download everything from two newsgroups, ignore messages that have no binary attachments, check for file duplicates, and—if file duplicates are found—set a header in the message cache to not check again:

```
% nget --text ignore -dfim -g alt.binaries.pictures.comics, ⏎
        alt.binaries.pictures.comics.reposts -r ".*"
```

nget supports a number of other options, including the ability to filter by author, date, number of lines in the actual message, and so forth. More information about it and the *.netrc* configuration file can be found at *http://nget.sourceforge.net/* or with man nget on your command line.

Gleaning Data from Databases
Hacks #43–89

In Chapter 3, you learned techniques for collecting media files. Now you're going to take those lessons and move in a slightly different direction: gleaning data from databases and information collections.

Information collections can be as large and multifaceted as Google's index of the World Wide Web, or as narrow and precise as King County health collections. You can scrape information as general as archives from Yahoo! Groups, or as targeted as game prices from GameStop.com. In this chapter, we'll look at a variety of ways you can access database information, a variety of sources you might want to try (and a few hints for thinking of your own!), and ways that you can combine the power of programming with already-existing web APIs to make new and powerful tools.

HACK #43 Archiving Yahoo! Groups Messages with yahoo2mbox

Looking to keep a local archive of your favorite mailing list? With yahoo2mbox, you can import the final results into your favorite mailer.

With the popularity of Yahoo! Groups (*http://groups.yahoo.com/*) comes a problem. Sometimes, you want to save the archives of a Yahoo! Group, but you want to be able to access it outside the Yahoo! Groups site. Or you want to move your list somewhere else and be able to take your existing archive with you.

Vadim Zeitlin had these same concerns, which is why he wrote yahoo2mbox (*http://www.lpthe.jussieu.fr/~zeitlin/yahoo2mbox.html*). This hack retrieves all the messages from a mailing list archive at Yahoo! Groups and saves them to a local file in mbox format. Plenty of options make this handy to have when you're trying to transfer information from Yahoo! Groups.

As of this writing, the program is still fairly new, so be sure to visit its URL (cited in the previous paragraph) to download the latest version. Note that you'll need Perl and several additional modules to run this code, including *Getopt::Long, HTML::Entities, HTML::HeadParser, HTML::TokeParser*, and *LWP::UserAgent*.

Running the Hack

Running the code looks like this:

```
perl yahoo2mbox.pl [options] [-o <mbox>] <groupname>
```

The options for running the program are as follows:

```
--help        give the usage message showing the program options
--version     show the program version and exit
--verbose     give verbose informational messages (default)
--quiet       be silent, only error messages are given
-o mbox       save the message to mbox instead of file named groupname
--start=n     start retrieving messages at index n instead of 1
--end=n       stop retrieving messages at index n instead of the last one
--noresume    don't resume, **overwrites** the existing output file if any
--user=name   login to eGroups using this username (default: guest login)
--pass=pass   the password to use for login (default: none)
--cookies=xxx file to use to store cookies (default: none,
              'netscape' uses netscape cookies file).
--proxy=url   use the given proxy; if 'no', don't use proxy
              at all (not even the environment variable http_proxy,
              which is used by default), may use http://username:password\
              @full.host.name/ notation
--country=xx  use the given country code to access localized yahoo
```

So, this command downloads messages from Weird Al Club, starting at message 3258:

```
% perl yahoo2mbox.pl --start=3258 weirdalclub2
Logging in anonymously... ok.
Getting number of messages in group weirdalclub2...
Retrieving messages 3258..3287: ............................ done!
Saved 30 message(s) in weirdalclub2.
```

Here, the messages are saved to a file called *weirdalclub2*. Renaming the file *weirdalclub2.mbx* means that you can immediately open the messages in Eudora, as shown in Figure 4-1. Of course, you can also open the resulting files in any mail program that can import (or natively read) the mbox format.

Hacking the Hack

Because this is someone else's program, there's not too much hacking to be done. On the other hand, you might find that you don't want to end this process with the mbox file; you might want to convert to other formats for

Archiving Yahoo! Groups Messages with WWW::Yahoo::Groups

HACK
#44

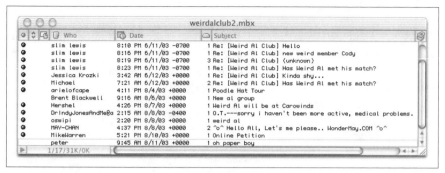

Figure 4-1. A Yahoo! Groups archive in Eudora

use in other projects or archives. In that case, check out these other programs to take that mbox format a little further:

hypermail (http://sourceforge.net/projects/hypermail/)
> Converts mbox format to cross-referenced HTML documents.

mb2md (http://www.gerg.ca/hacks/mb2md/)
> Converts mbox format to Maildir. Requires Python and Procmail.

Mb2md.pl (http://batleth.sapienti-sat.org/projects/mb2md/)
> Converts mbox format to Maildir. Uses Perl.

HACK #44 Archiving Yahoo! Groups Messages with WWW::Yahoo::Groups

Yahoo! Groups makes it easy to run an email discussion group at no cost. Sadly, there's no simple way to download all the messages—until now.

If you've ever wanted to run an email discussion group, but you didn't want to mess around with getting your own server and administering your own software, you should consider looking into Yahoo! Groups (*http://groups.yahoo.com/*). The free (ad-supported) service makes it easy to run a mailing list, and if you or any other group moderator has set a list to support archiving of messages, a handy web interface to browse them is provided. Sadly, the service provides no simple way to download all the messages in one fell swoop, and nobody wants to click and Save As... on hundreds or thousands of links.

Iain Truskett of Canberra, Australia, wanted to keep an offline archive of his Yahoo! Groups mailing lists, so he created the *WWW::Yahoo::Groups* module, available on CPAN (*http://search.cpan.org/dist/WWW-Yahoo-Groups/*). It uses *WWW::Mechanize* to log into Yahoo! Groups, get a count of the messages, and download any given message by number. It even bypasses the pop-up ads and interstitial interruptions!

The Code

You'll need the *WWW::Yahoo::Groups* Perl module installed to use this script. The module requires a number of other modules, but installing from the CPAN shell [Hack #8] should take care of the installation of these prerequisites for you.

Save the following code to a file called *yahoogroups.pl*:

```perl
#!/usr/bin/perl -w

use constant USERNAME => 'your username';
use constant PASSWORD => 'your password';

use strict;
use File::Path;
use Getopt::Long;
use WWW::Yahoo::Groups;
$SIG{PIPE} = 'IGNORE';

# define the command-line options, and
# ensure that a group has been passed.
my ($debug, $group, $last, $first, $stats);
GetOptions(
    "debug"     => \$debug,
    "group=s"   => \$group,
    "stats"     => \$stats,
    "first=i"   => \$first,
    "last=i"    => \$last,
); (defined $group) or die "Must specify a group!\n";

# sign into Yahoo! Groups.
my $w = WWW::Yahoo::Groups->new();
$w->debug( $debug );
$w->login( USERNAME, PASSWORD );
$w->list( $group );
$w->agent->requests_redirectable( [] ); # no redirects now

# first and last IDs of group.
my $first_id = $w->first_msg_id();
my $last_id = $w->last_msg_id();
print "Messages in $group: $first_id to $last_id\n";
exit 0 if $stats; # they just wanted numbers.

# default our IDs to the first and last
# of the $group in question, else use the
# passed command-line options.
$first = $first_id unless $first;
$last  = $last_id  unless $last;
warn "Fetching $first to $last\n";
```

Archiving Yahoo! Groups Messages with WWW::Yahoo::Groups

HACK
#44

```
# get our specified messages.
for my $msgnum ($first..$last) {
    fetch_message( $w, $msgnum );
}

sub fetch_message {
    my $w = shift;
    my $msgnum = shift;

    # Put messages in directories by 100.
    my $dirname = int($msgnum/100)*100;

    # Create the dir if necessary.
    my $dir = "$group/$dirname";
    mkpath( $dir ) unless -d $dir;

    # Don't pull down the message
    # if we already have it...
    my $filename = "$dir/$msgnum";
    return if -f $filename;

    # pull down the content and check for errors.
    my $content = eval { $w->fetch_message($msgnum) };
    if ( $@ ) {
        if ( $@->isa('X::WWW::Yahoo::Groups') ) {
            warn "Could not handle message $msgnum: ",$@->error,"\n";
        } else { warn "Could not get content for message $msgnum\n"; }
    } else {
        open(FH, ">$filename")
            or return warn "Can't create $filename: $!\n";
        print FH $content; close FH; # data has been saved.
        $w->autosleep( 5 ); # so now sleep to prevent saturation.
    }
}
```

Running the Hack

Before you can use the script, you'll need to have a Yahoo! Groups account (*http://edit.yahoo.com/config/eval_register*) and be subscribed to at least one list that has web archives. Remember that we're merely automating the web transactions, not getting at some secret backdoor into Yahoo! Groups. Also, modify the lines at the top of the script that set the USERNAME and PASSWORD constants. If these aren't set, the script can't log in as you and, consequently, you might not have access to the group's messages.

First, find out how many messages there are. In this case, let's check out *milwpm*, the discussion list for the Milwaukee Perl Mongers:

```
% perl yahoogroups.pl --group=milwpm --stats
Messages in milwpm: 1 to 721
```

HACK
#44

Archiving Yahoo! Groups Messages with WWW::Yahoo::Groups

Now, take a look at the last five messages in the archive:

```
% perl yahoogroups.pl --group=milwpm --first=717
Messages in milwpm: 1 to 721
Fetching 717 to 721
```

Behind the scenes, the script has created a directory called *milwpm* and, within that, a directory called *700* for holding all messages between 700 and 799. Each message gets its own file.

```
% ls -al milwpm/700
-rw-r--r--    1 andy      staff        2814 Jul 16 23:04 700
-rw-r--r--    1 andy      staff        4005 Jul 16 23:05 717
-rw-r--r--    1 andy      staff        1511 Jul 16 23:05 718
-rw-r--r--    1 andy      staff        5576 Jul 16 23:05 719
-rw-r--r--    1 andy      staff        5862 Jul 16 23:05 720
-rw-r--r--    1 andy      staff        6632 Jul 16 23:05 721
```

If you want to look at the starting few messages, use the `--last` parameter. You can also use the `--debug` parameter to get running notes of what the script is doing:

```
% perl yahoogroups.pl --group=milwpm --last=5 --debug
Fetching http://groups.yahoo.com/
Fetching http://login.yahoo.com/config/login?.intl=us&.src=ygrp&....
Fetching http://groups.yahoo.com/group/milwpm/messages/1
Messages in milwpm: 1 to 721
Fetching 1 to 5
Fetching http://groups.yahoo.com/group/milwpm/message/1?source=1&unwrap=1
Fetching http://groups.yahoo.com/group/milwpm/message/2?source=1&unwrap=1
Fetching http://groups.yahoo.com/group/milwpm/message/3?source=1&unwrap=1
Fetching http://groups.yahoo.com/group/milwpm/message/4?source=1&unwrap=1
Fetching http://groups.yahoo.com/group/milwpm/interrupt?st=2&m=1&done=%2...
Fetching /group/milwpm/message/4?source=1&unwrap=1
Fetching http://groups.yahoo.com/group/milwpm/message/5?source=1&unwrap=1
```

Hacking the Hack

You can easily extend this hack to manipulate the data before it gets saved to the file. The messages that are returned are in standard Internet mail format, so you can extract just the headers you want, such as To:, From:, and Subject:. The *MailTools* (*http://search.cpan.org/dist/MailTools/MailTools*) distribution has a number of modules that will help.

As a quick example, sans *MailTools*, let's say you want to see the most active threads from the messages you're downloading. This is a rather simple modification to make. Add a hash for our new information before the fetch_ message subroutine (changes are in bold):

```
# Keep track of popular subjects
my %subjects;
```

```
sub fetch_message {
    my $w = shift;
```

Then, add the tracking code for each subject line:

```
    } else { warn "Could not get content for message $msgnum\n"; }
} else {

    # and add one to our subject line counter.
    $content =~ /Subject: (.*)/ig; $subjects{$1}++ if $1;

    open(FH, ">$filename")
        or return warn "Can't create $filename: $!\n";
```

Finally, at the end of the script, display the stats:

```
# now, print our totals.
my @sorted = sort { $subjects{$b} <=> $subjects{$a} } keys %subjects;
foreach (@sorted) { print "$subjects{$_}: $_\n"; }
```

This code can easily be tweaked to save only messages from certain authors—local copies of your own postings, for instance—or subject lines associated with especially thoughtful or useful threads.

Yahoo! Groups also has search capabilities that you can take advantage of with *WWW::Mechanize*. See "Downloading Images from Webshots" [Hack #36] for an example of searching web sites with *WWW::Mechanize*.

—*Andy Lester*

HACK #45 Gleaning Buzz from Yahoo!

Stay hip with the latest Yahoo! Buzz search results.

Google has a Zeitgeist page (*http://www.google.com/press/zeitgeist.html*) that gives you an idea of what people are searching for, but unfortunately it's not updated very often; some parts are updated once a week, while other parts are updated only once a month. Meanwhile, Yahoo! has a Yahoo! Buzz site (*http://buzz.yahoo.com/*) that contains much more annotated information about what people are searching for.

We thought it would be fun to take a Buzz item from the Yahoo! Buzz site (specifically, *http://buzz.yahoo.com/overall/*) and then use it to initiate a search on Google. This hack is part scraping—the Yahoo! Buzz side—and part use of a web API—the Google side. As you'll see, the two work very well together.

The Code

You'll need a Google API developer's key (*http://api.google.com/*) and a lesser-known Perl module (*Time::JulianDay*) to get this hack to work. Save the following code to a file called *ybgoogled.pl*:

```perl
#!/usr/bin/perl -w
# ybgoogled.pl
# Pull the top item from the Yahoo Buzz Index and query
# the last three day's worth of Google's index for it.
# Usage: perl ybgoogled.pl
use strict;
use SOAP::Lite;
use LWP::Simple;
use Time::JulianDay;

# Your Google API developer's key.
my $google_key='insert key here';

# Location of the GoogleSearch WSDL file.
my $google_wdsl = "./GoogleSearch.wsdl";

# Number of days back to
# go in the Google index.
my $days_back = 3;

# Grab a copy of http://buzz.yahoo.com.
my $buzz_content = get("http://buzz.yahoo.com/overall/")
  or die "Couldn't grab the Yahoo Buzz: $!";

# Find the first item on the Buzz Index list.
$buzz_content =~ m!<b>1</b>.*?&cs=bz"><b>(.*?)</b></a> </font>!;
my $buzziest = $1; # assign our match as our search term.
die "Couldn't figure out the Yahoo! buzz\n" unless $buzziest;

# Figure out today's Julian date.
my $today = int local_julian_day(time);

# Build the Google query and say hi.
my $query = "\"$buzziest\" daterange:" . ($today - $days_back) . "-$today";
print "The buzziest item on Yahoo Buzz today is: $buzziest\n",
      "Querying Google for: $query\n", "Results:\n\n";

# Create a new SOAP::Lite instance, feeding it GoogleSearch.wsdl.
my $google_search = SOAP::Lite->service("file:$google_wdsl");

# Query Google.
my $results = $google_search->doGoogleSearch(
              $google_key, $query, 0, 10, "false",
              "", "false", "", "", ""
          );
```

```
# No results?
die "No results" unless @{$results->{resultElements}};

# Loop through the results.
foreach my $result (@{$results->{'resultElements'}}) {
    my $output = join "\n", $result->{title} || "no title",
                 $result->{URL}, $result->{snippet} || 'none',"\n";
    $output =~ s!<.+?>!!g; # drop all HTML tags sloppily.
    print $output; # woo, we're done!
}
```

This code works only as long as Yahoo! formats its Buzz page in the same way; we've had to change it multiple times. If you try this program and it doesn't work, pull out this line:

```
$buzz_content =~ m!<b>1</b>.*?&cs=bz"><b>(.*?)</b></a> </font>!;
```

Take a look at the code pulled out by the variable $buzziest and see if it matches any code in the source code at *http://buzz.yahoo.com/overall/*. If it doesn't, the code's changed. Go to the HTML source view and find the first item on the Buzz list. Look at the source, find that first Buzz listing, and pull the code from around it. You want to pull enough code to get a unique line, but not so much that you can't read it.

Running the Hack

Run this script from the command line, like so:

```
% perl ybgoogled.pl

The buzziest item on Yahoo Buzz today is: Gregory Hines
Querying Google for: "Gregory Hines" daterange:2452861-2452864
Results:

Celebrities @ Hollywood.com-Featuring Gregory Hines. Celebrities ...
http://www.hollywood.com/celebs/detail/celeb/191902
Gregory Hines Vital Stats: Born: February 14, 1946 Birth Place: New York,
New York

Gregory Hines
http://www.rottentomatoes.com/p/GregoryHines-1007016/
 ... Gregory Hines. CELEB QUIK BROWSER &gt; Select A Celebrity. ...

 ...
```

Hacking the Hack

As it stands, this hack returns 10 results. If you want to, you can change the code to return only one result and immediately open it instead of returning a list. This version of the program searches the last three days of indexed pages. Because there's a slight lag in indexing news stories, I would index at least the last two days' worth of pages, but you could extend it to seven days or even a month.

If you want to abandon Google entirely, you can. Instead, you might want to go to Daypop (*http://www.daypop.com*), which also has a news search. Here's a version of the script using the top item on Daypop:

```
#!/usr/bin/perl -w
# ybdaypopped
# Pull the top item from the Yahoo! Buzz Index and query
# Daypop's News search engine for relevant stories
use strict;
use LWP::Simple;

# Grab a copy of http://buzz.yahoo.com.
my $buzz_content = get("http://buzz.yahoo.com/")
  or die "Couldn't grab the Yahoo Buzz: $!";

# Find the first item on the Buzz Index list.
$buzz_content =~ m!<b>1</b>.*?&cs=bz"><b>(.*?)</b></a> </font>!;
my $buzziest = $1; # assign our match as our search term.
die "Couldn't figure out the Yahoo! buzz\n" unless $buzziest;

# Build a Daypop Query.
my $dpquery = "http://www.daypop.com/search?q=$buzziest&t=n";
print "Location: $dpquery\n\n";
```

This version of the program takes the first Buzz item from Yahoo! and opens a Daypop news search for that item (assuming you run this as a CGI script). But hey, maybe we should use that RSS format [Hack #94] all the kids are talking about. In that case, just put &o=rss at the end of $dpquery:

```
my $dpquery = "http://www.daypop.com/search?q=$buzziest&t=n&o=rss";
```

Now you're using Yahoo! Buzz to generate an RSS file with Daypop. From there, you can scrape the RSS file, pass this URL to a routine that puts an RSS file up on a web page [Hack #95], and so on.

—Tara Calishain and Rael Dornfest

Spidering the Yahoo! Catalog
#46

Writing a spider to spider an existing spider's site may seem convoluted, but it can prove useful when you're looking for location-based services. This hack walks through creating a framework for full-site spidering, including additional filters to lessen your load.

In this hack, you'll learn how to write a spider that crawls the Yahoo! group of portals. The choice of Yahoo! was obvious; because it is one of the largest Internet portals in existence, it can serve as an ideal example of how one goes about writing a portal spider.

But before we get to the gory details of code, let's define what exactly a portal spider is. While many may argue with such classification, I maintain that a *portal spider* is a script that automatically downloads all documents from a preselected range of URLs found on the portal's site or a group of sites, as is the case with Yahoo!. A portal spider's main job is to walk from one document to another, extract URLs from downloaded HTML, process said URLs, and go to another document, repeating the cycle until it runs out of URLs to visit. Once you create code that describes such basic behavior, you can add additional functionality, turning your general portal spider into a specialized one.

Although writing a script that walks from one Yahoo! page to another sounds simple, it isn't, because there is no general pattern followed by all Yahoo! sites or sections within those sites. Furthermore, Yahoo! is not a single site with a nice link layout that can be described using a simple algorithm and a classic data structure. Instead, it is a collection of well over 30 thematic sites, each with its own document layout, naming conventions, and peculiarities in page design and URL patterns. For example, if you check links to the same directory section on different Yahoo! sites, you will find that some of them begin with *http://www.yahoo.com/r*, some begin with *http://uk.yahoo.com/r/hp/dr*, and others begin with *http://kr.yahoo.com*.

If you try to look for patterns, you will soon find yourself writing long if/ elsif/else sections that are hard to maintain and need to be rewritten every time Yahoo! makes a small change to one of its sites. If you follow that route, you will soon discover that you need to write hundreds of lines of code to describe every kind of behavior you want to build into your spider.

This is particularly frustrating to programmers who expect to write code that uses elegant algorithms and nicely structured data. The hard truth about portals is that you cannot expect elegance and ease of spidering from them. Instead, prepare yourself for a lot of detective work and writing (and throwing away) chunks of code in a hit-and-miss fashion. Portal spiders are written in an organic, unstructured way, and the only rule you should follow is to keep things simple and add specific functionality only once you have the general behavior working.

Okay, with taxonomy and general advice behind us, we can get to the gist of the matter. The spider in this hack is a relatively simple tool for crawling Yahoo! sites. It makes no assumptions about the layout of the sites; in fact, it makes almost no assumptions whatsoever and can easily be adapted to other portals or even groups of portals. You can use it as a framework for writing specialized spiders.

The Code

Save the following code to a file called *yspider.pl*:

```perl
#!/usr/bin/perl -w
#
# yspider.pl
#
# Yahoo! Spider - crawls Yahoo! sites, collects links from each
# downloaded HTML page, searches each downloaded page, and prints a
# list of results when done.
# http://www.artymiak.com/software/ or contact jacek@artymiak.com
#
# This code is free software; you can redistribute it and/or
# modify it under the same terms as Perl itself.

use strict;
use Getopt::Std;            # parse command-line options.
use LWP::UserAgent;         # download data from the Net.
use HTML::LinkExtor;        # get links inside an HTML document.
use URI::URL;               # turn relative links into absolutes.

my $help = <<"EOH";
---------------------------------------------------------------------------
Yahoo! Spider.

Options: -s    list of sites you want to crawl,
               e.g. -s 'us china denmark'
         -h    print this help

Allowed values of -s are:

    argentina, asia, australia, brazil, canada,
    catalan, china, denmark, france, germany, hongkong,
    india, ireland, italy, japan, korea, mexico,
    newzealand, norway, singapore, spain, sweden, taiwan,
    uk, us, us_chinese, us_spanish

Please, use this code responsibly.  Flooding any site
with excessive queries is bad net citizenship.
---------------------------------------------------------------------------
EOH

# define our arguments and
# show the help if asked.
my %args; getopts("s:h", \%args);
die $help if exists $args{h};

# The list of code names, and
# URLs for various Yahoo! sites.
my %ys = (
    argentina => "http://ar.yahoo.com", asia => "http://asia.yahoo.com",
    australia => "http://au.yahoo.com", newzealand => "http://au.yahoo.com",
```

```
    brazil      => "http://br.yahoo.com", canada   => "http://ca.yahoo.com",
    catalan     => "http://ct.yahoo.com", china    => "http://cn.yahoo.com",
    denmark     => "http://dk.yahoo.com", france   => "http://fr.yahoo.com",
    germany     => "http://de.yahoo.com", hongkong => "http://hk.yahoo.com",
    india       => "http://in.yahoo.com", italy    => "http://it.yahoo.com",
    korea       => "http://kr.yahoo.com", mexico   => "http://mx.yahoo.com",
    norway      => "http://no.yahoo.com", singapore => "http://sg.yahoo.com",
    spain       => "http://es.yahoo.com", sweden   => "http://se.yahoo.com",
    taiwan      => "http://tw.yahoo.com", uk       => "http://uk.yahoo.com",
    ireland     => "http://uk.yahoo.com", us       => "http://www.yahoo.com",
    japan       => "http://www.yahoo.co.jp",
    us_chinese  => "http://chinese.yahoo.com",
    us_spanish  => "http://espanol.yahoo.com"
);

# if the -s option was used, check to make
# sure it matches one of our existing codes
# above. if not, or if no -s was passed, help.
my @sites; # which locales to spider.
if (exists $args{'s'}) {
    @sites = split(/ /, lc($args{'s'}));
    foreach my $site (@sites) {
        die "UNKNOWN: $site\n\n$help" unless $ys{$site};
    }
} else { die $help; }

# Defines global and local profiles for URLs extracted from the
# downloaded pages. These profiles are used to determine if the
# URLs extracted from each new document should be placed on the
# TODO list (%todo) or rejected (%rejects). Profiles are lists
# made of chunks of text, which are matched against found URLs.
# Any special characters, like slash (/) or dot (.), must be properly
# escaped. Remember that globals have precedence over locals.
my %rules = (
    global      => { allow => [], deny => [ 'search', '\*' ] },
    argentina   => { allow => [ 'http:\/\/ar\.' ], deny => [] },
    asia        => { allow => [ 'http:\/\/(aa|asia)\.' ], deny => [] },
    australia   => { allow => [ 'http:\/\/au\.' ], deny => [] },
    brazil      => { allow => [ 'http:\/\/br\.' ], deny => [] },
    canada      => { allow => [ 'http:\/\/ca\.' ], deny => [] },
    catalan     => { allow => [ 'http:\/\/ct\.' ], deny => [] },
    china       => { allow => [ 'http:\/\/cn\.' ], deny => [] },
    denmark     => { allow => [ 'http:\/\/dk\.' ], deny => [] },
    france      => { allow => [ 'http:\/\/fr\.' ], deny => [] },
    germany     => { allow => [ 'http:\/\/de\.' ], deny => [] },
    hongkong    => { allow => [ 'http:\/\/hk\.' ], deny => [] },
    india       => { allow => [ 'http:\/\/in\.' ], deny => [] },
    ireland     => { allow => [ 'http:\/\/uk\.' ], deny => [] },
    italy       => { allow => [ 'http:\/\/it\.' ], deny => [] },
    japan       => { allow => [ 'yahoo\.co\.jp' ], deny => [] },
    korea       => { allow => [ 'http:\/\/kr\.' ], deny => [] },
    mexico      => { allow => [ 'http:\/\/mx\.' ], deny => [] },
```

```
    norway      => { allow => [ 'http:\/\/no\.' ], deny => [] },
    singapore   => { allow => [ 'http:\/\/sg\.' ], deny => [] },
    spain       => { allow => [ 'http:\/\/es\.' ], deny => [] },
    sweden      => { allow => [ 'http:\/\/se\.' ], deny => [] },
    taiwan      => { allow => [ 'http:\/\/tw\.' ], deny => [] },
    uk          => { allow => [ 'http:\/\/uk\.' ], deny => [] },
    us          => { allow => [ 'http:\/\/(dir|www)\.' ], deny => [] },
    us_chinese  => { allow => [ 'http:\/\/chinese\.' ], deny => [] },
    us_spanish  => { allow => [ 'http:\/\/espanol\.' ], deny => [] },
);

my %todo = ( );        # URLs to parse
my %done = ( );        # parsed/finished URLs
my %errors = ( );      # broken URLs with errors
my %rejects = ( );     # URLs rejected by the script

# print out a "we're off!" line, then
# begin walking the site we've been told to.
print "=" x 80 . "\nStarted Yahoo! spider...\n" . "=" x 80 . "\n";
our $site; foreach $site (@sites) {

    # for each of the sites that have been passed on the
    # command line, we make a title for them, add them to
    # the TODO list for downloading, then call walksite( ),
    # which downloads the URL, looks for more URLs, etc.
    my $title = "Yahoo! " . ucfirst($site) . " front page";
    $todo{$ys{$site}} = $title; walksite( ); # process.

}

# once we're all done with all the URLs, we print a
# report about all the information we've gone through.
print "=" x 80 . "\nURLs downloaded and parsed:\n" . "=" x 80 . "\n";
foreach my $url (keys %done) { print "$url => $done{$url}\n"; }
print "=" x 80 . "\nURLs that couldn't be downloaded:\n" . "=" x 80 . "\n";
foreach my $url (keys %errors) { print "$url => $errors{$url}\n"; }
print "=" x 80 . "\nURLs that got rejected:\n" . "=" x 80 . "\n";
foreach my $url (keys %rejects) { print "$url => $rejects{$url}\n"; }

# this routine grabs the first entry in our TODO
# list, downloads the content, and looks for more URLs.
# we stay in walksite until there are no more URLs
# in our TODO list, which could be a good long time.
sub walksite {

    do {
        # get first URL to do.
        my $url = (keys %todo)[0];

        # download this URL.
        print "-> trying $url ...\n";
        my $browser = LWP::UserAgent->new;
```

```
    my $resp = $browser->get( $url, 'User-Agent' => 'Y!SpiderHack/1.0'
);

        # check the results.
        if ($resp->is_success) {
            my $base = $resp->base || '';
            print "-> base URL: $base\n";
            my $data = $resp->content; # get the data.
            print "-> downloaded: " . length($data) . " bytes of $url\n";

            # find URLs using a link extorter. relevant ones
            # will be added to our TODO list of downloadables.
            # this passes all the found links to findurls()
            # below, which determines if we should add the link
            # to our TODO list, or ignore it due to filtering.
            HTML::LinkExtor->new(\&findurls, $base)->parse($data);

            ###########################################################
            # add your own processing here. perhaps you'd like to add #
            # a keyword search for the downloaded content in $data?   #
            ###########################################################

        } else {
            $errors{$url} = $resp->message( );
            print "-> error: couldn't download URL: $url\n";
            delete $todo{$url};
        }

        # we're finished with this URL, so move it from
        # the TODO list to the done list, and print a report.
        $done{$url} = $todo{$url}; delete $todo{$url};
        print "-> processed legal URLs: " . (scalar keys %done) . "\n";
        print "-> remaining URLs: " . (scalar keys %todo) . "\n";
        print "-" x 80 . "\n";
    } until ((scalar keys %todo) == 0);
}

# callback routine for HTML::LinkExtor. For every
# link we find in our downloaded content, we check
# to see if we've processed it before, then run it
# through a bevy of regexp rules (see the top of
# this script) to see if it belongs in the TODO.
sub findurls {
    my($tag, %links) = @_;
    return if $tag ne 'a';
    return unless $links{href};
    print "-> found URL: $links{href}\n";

    # already seen this URL, so move on.
    if (exists $done{$links{href}} ||
        exists $errors{$links{href}} ||
        exists $rejects{$links{href}}) {
```

```
        print "--> I've seen this before: $links{href}\n"; return;
    }

    # now, run through our filters.
    unless (exists($todo{$links{href}})) {
        my ($ga, $gd, $la, $ld); # counters.
        foreach (@{$rules{global}{'allow'}}) {
            $ga++ if $links{href} =~ /$_/i;
        }
        foreach (@{$rules{global}{'deny'}}) {
            $gd++ if $links{href} =~ /$_/i;
        }
        foreach (@{$rules{$site}{'allow'}}) {
            $la++ if $links{href} =~ /$_/i;
        }
        foreach (@{$rules{$site}{'deny'}}) {
            $ld++ if $links{href} =~ /$_/i;
        }

        # if there were denials or NO allowances, we move on.
        if ($gd or $ld) { print "-> rejected: $links{href}\n"; return; }
        unless ($ga or $la) { print "-> rejected: $links{href}\n"; return; }

        # we passed our filters, so add it on the barby.
        print "-> added $links{href} to my TODO list\n";
        $todo{$links{href}} = $links{href};
    }
}
```

Running the Hack

Before sending the spider off, you'll need to make a decision regarding which part of the Yahoo! directory you want to crawl. If you're mainly interested in the United States and United Kingdom, you'll inform the spider using the -s option on the command line, like so:

```
% perl yspider.pl -s "us uk"
===========================================================================
Started Yahoo! spider...
===========================================================================
-> trying http://www.yahoo.com ...
-> base URL: http://www.yahoo.com/
-> downloaded: 28376 bytes of http://www.yahoo.com
-> found URL: http://www.yahoo.com/s/92802
-> added http://www.yahoo.com/s/92802 to my TODO list
-> found URL: http://www.yahoo.com/s/92803
... etc ...
-> added http://www.yahoo.com/r/pv to my TODO list
-> processed legal URLs: 1
-> remaining URLs: 244
---------------------------------------------------------------------------
-> trying http://www.yahoo.com/r/fr ...
-> base URL: http://fr.yahoo.com/r/
```

```
-> downloaded: 32619 bytes of http://www.yahoo.com/r/fr
-> found URL: http://fr.yahoo.com/r/t/mu00
-> rejected URL: http://fr.yahoo.com/r/t/mu00
...
```

You can see a full list of locations available to you by asking for help:

```
% perl yspider.pl -h
```

```
...
Allowed values of -s are:

    argentina, asia, australia, brazil, canada,
    catalan, china, denmark, france, germany, hongkong,
    india, ireland, italy, japan, korea, mexico,
    newzealand, norway, singapore, spain, sweden, taiwan,
    uk, us, us_chinese, us_spanish
```

Hacking the Hack

The section you'll want to modify most contains the filters that determine how far the spider will go; by tweaking the allow and deny rules at the beginning of the script, you'll be able to better grab just the content you're interested in. If you want to make this spider even more generic, consider rewriting the configuration code so that it'll instead read a plain-text list of code names, start URLs, and allow and deny patterns. This can turn a Yahoo! spider into a general Internet spider.

Whenever you want to add code that extends the functionality of this spider (such as searching for keywords in a document, adding the downloaded content to a database, or otherwise repurposing it for your needs), include your own logic where specified by the hashed-out comment block.

See Also

If you're spidering Yahoo! because you want to start your own directory, you might want to consider Google's Open Directory Project (*http://dmoz.org/about.html*). Downloading their freely available directory data, all several hundred megs of it, will give you plenty of information to play with.

—*Jacek Artymiak*

HACK #47 Tracking Additions to Yahoo!

Keep track of the number of sites added to your favorite Yahoo! categories.

Every day, a squad of surfers at Yahoo! adds new sites to the Yahoo! index. These changes are reflected in the Yahoo! What's New page (*http://dir.yahoo.com/new/*), along with the Picks of the Day.

If you're a casual surfer, you might not care about the number of new sites added to Yahoo!. But there are several scenarios when you might have an interest:

You regularly glean information about new sites from Yahoo! Knowing which categories are growing and which categories are stagnant will tell you where to direct your attention.

You want to submit sites to Yahoo! Are you going to spend your hard-earned money adding a site to a category where new sites are added constantly (meaning your submitted site might get quickly buried)? Or will you be paying to add to a category that sees few additions (meaning your site might have a better chance of standing out)?

You're interested in trend tracking. Which categories are consistently busy? Which are all but dead? By watching how Yahoo! adds sites to categories, over time you'll get a sense of their rhythms and trends and detect when unusual activity occurs in a category.

This hack scrapes the recent counts of additions to Yahoo! categories and prints them out, providing an at-a-glance glimpse of additions to various categories. You'll also get a tab-delimited table of how many sites have been added to each category for each day. A tab-delimited file is excellent for importing into Excel, where you can turn the count numbers into a chart.

The Code

Save the following code to a file called *hoocount.pl*:

```perl
#!/usr/bin/perl-w

use strict;
use Date::Manip;
use LWP::Simple;
use Getopt::Long;

$ENV{TZ} = "GMT" if $^O eq "MSWin32";

# the homepage for Yahoo!'s "What's New".
my $new_url = "http://dir.yahoo.com/new/";

# the major categories at Yahoo!. hashed because
# we'll use them to hold our counts string.
my @categories = ("Arts & Humanities",    "Business & Economy",
                  "Computers & Internet", "Education",
                  "Entertainment",        "Government",
                  "Health",               "News & Media",
                  "Recreation & Sports",  "Reference",
                  "Regional",             "Science",
```

```
                    "Social Science",        "Society & Culture");
my %final_counts; # where we save our final readouts.

# load in our options from the command line.
my %opts; GetOptions(\%opts, "c|count=i");
die unless $opts{c}; # count sites from past $i days.

# if we've been told to count the number of new sites,
# then we'll go through each of our main categories
# for the last $i days and collate a result.

# begin the header
# for our import file.
my $header = "Category";

# from today, going backwards, get $i days.
for (my $i=1; $i <= $opts{c}; $i++) {

    # create a Data::Manip time that will
    # be used to construct the last $i days.
    my $day; # query for Yahoo! retrieval.
    if ($i == 1) { $day = "yesterday"; }
    else { $day = "$i days ago"; }
    my $date = UnixDate($day, "%Y%m%d");

    # add this date to
    # our import file.
    $header .= "\t$date";

    # and download the day.
    my $url = "$new_url$date.html";
    my $data = get($url) or die $!;

    # and loop through each of our categories.
    my $day_count; foreach my $category (sort @categories) {
        $data =~ /$category.*?(\d+)/; my $count = $1 || 0;
        $final_counts{$category} .= "\t$count"; # building our string.
    }
}

# with all our counts finished,
# print out our final file.
print $header . "\n";
foreach my $category (@categories) {
    print $category, $final_counts{$category}, "\n";
}
```

Running the Hack

The only argument you need to provide the script is the number of days
back you'd like it to travel in search of new additions. Since Yahoo! doesn't

archive their "new pages added" indefinitely, a safe upper limit is around two weeks. Here, we're looking at the past two days:

```
% perl hoocount.pl --count 2
Category        20030807        20030806
Arts & Humanities       23      23
Business & Economy      88      141
Computers & Internet    2       9
Education       0       4
Entertainment   43      29
Government      3       4
Health  2       7
News & Media    1       1
Recreation & Sports     8       27
Reference       0       0
Regional        142     114
Science 1       2
Social Science  3       0
Society & Culture       7       8
```

Hacking the Hack

If you're not only a researcher but also a Yahoo! observer, you might be interested in how the number of sites added changes over time. To that end, you could run this script under *cron* [Hack #90], and output the results to a file. After three months or so, you'd have a pretty interesting set of counts to manipulate with a spreadsheet program like Excel. Alternatively, you could modify the script to run RRDTOOL [Hack #62] and have real-time graphs.

HACK #48 Scattersearch with Yahoo! and Google

Sometimes, illuminating results can be found when scraping from one site and feeding the results into the API of another. With scattersearching, you can narrow down the most popular related results, as suggested by Yahoo! and Google.

We've combined a scrape of a Yahoo! web page with a Google search [Hack #45], blending scraped data with data generated via a web service API to good effect. In this hack, we're doing something similar, except this time we're taking the results of a Yahoo! search and blending it with a Google search.

Yahoo! has a "Related searches" feature, where you enter a search term and get a list of related terms under the search box, if any are available. This hack scrapes those related terms and performs a Google search for the related terms in the title. It then returns the count for those searches, along with a direct link to the results. Aside from showing how scraped and API-generated data can live together in harmony, this hack is good to use when you're exploring concepts; for example, you might know that something called *Pokemon* exists, but you might not know anything about it. You'll get Yahoo!'s related searches and an idea of how many results each of those searches generates in Google. From there, you can choose the search terms that generate the most results or look the most promising based on your limited knowledge, or you can simply pick a road that appears less traveled.

The Code

Save the following code to a file called *scattersearch.pl*:

```
#!/usr/bin/perl-w
#
# Scattersearch -- Use the search suggestions from
# Yahoo! to build a series of intitle: searches at Google.

use strict;

use LWP;
use SOAP::Lite;
use CGI qw/:standard/;

# get our query, else die miserably.
my $query = shift @ARGV; die unless $query;

# Your Google API developer's key.
my $google_key = 'insert key here';

# Location of the GoogleSearch WSDL file.
my $google_wdsl = "./GoogleSearch.wsdl";

# search Yahoo! for the query.
my $ua  = LWP::UserAgent->new;
my $url = URI->new('http://search.yahoo.com/search');
$url->query_form(rs => "more", p => $query);
my $yahoosearch = $ua->get($url)->content;
$yahoosearch =~ s/[\f\t\n\r]//isg;

# and determine if there were any results.
$yahoosearch =~ m!Related:(.*?)<spacer!migs;
die "Sorry, there were no results!\n" unless $1;
my $recommended = $1;

# now, add all our results into
# an array for Google processing.
my @googlequeries;
while ($recommended =~ m!<a href=".*?">(.*?)</a>!mgis) {
    my $searchitem = $1; $searchitem =~ s/nobr|<|>|\///g;
    push (@googlequeries, $searchitem);
}

# print our header for the results page.
print join "\n",
```

```
start_html("ScatterSearch");
    h1("Your Scattersearch Results"),
    p("Your original search term was '$query'"),
    p("That search had " . scalar(@googlequeries). " recommended terms."),
    p("Here are result numbers from a Google search"),
    CGI::start_ol( );

# create our Google object for API searches.
my $gsrch = SOAP::Lite->service("file:$google_wdsl");

# running the actual Google queries.
foreach my $googlesearch (@googlequeries) {
    my $titlesearch = "allintitle:$googlesearch";
    my $count = $gsrch->doGoogleSearch($google_key, $titlesearch,
                                    0, 1, "false", "",  "false",
                                    "", "", "");
    my $url = $googlesearch; $url =~ s/ /+/g; $url =~ s/\"/%22/g;
    print li("There were $count->{estimatedTotalResultsCount} ".
            "results for the recommended search <a href=\"http://www.".
            "google.com/search?q=$url&num=100\">$googlesearch</a>");
}

print CGI::end_ol( ), end_html;
```

Running the Hack

This script generates an HTML file, ready for you to upload to a publicly accessible web site. If you want to save the output of a search for "siamese" to a file called *scattersearch.html* in your *Sites* directory, run the following command:

```
% perl scattersearch.pl "siamese" > ~/Sites/scattersearch.html
```

Your final results, as rendered by your browser, will look similar to Figure 4-2.

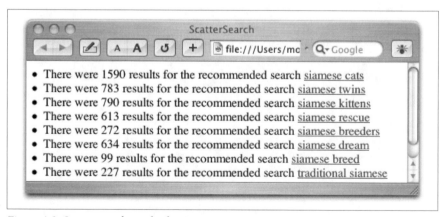

Figure 4-2. Scattersearch results for "siamese"

You'll have to do a little experimenting to find out which terms have related searches. Broadly speaking, very general search terms are bad; it's better to zero in on terms that people would search for and that would be easy to group together. As of this writing, for example, "heart" has no related search terms, but "blood pressure" does.

Hacking the Hack

You have two choices: you can either hack the interaction with Yahoo! or expand it to include something in addition to or instead of Yahoo! itself. Let's look at Yahoo! first. If you take a close look at the code, you'll see we're passing an unusual parameter to our Yahoo! search results page:

```
$url->query_form(rs => "more", p => $query);
```

The rs=>"more" part of the search shows the related search terms. Getting the related search this way will show up to 10 results. If you remove that portion of the code, you'll get roughly four related searches when they're available. That might suit you if you want only a few, but maybe you want dozens and dozens! In that case, replace more with all.

Beware, though: this can generate a lot of related searches, and it can certainly eat up your daily allowance of Google API requests. Tread carefully.

Yahoo! isn't the only search engine that has related search data. If you're looking for related searches that will work with general search terms like "heart", try AltaVista's Prisma (*http://www.altavista.com/prisma/*):

```perl
#!/usr/bin/perl-w
use strict;
use LWP;

# get our query, else die miserably.
my $query = shift @ARGV; die unless $query;

# search Prisma for the query.
my $ua  = LWP::UserAgent->new;
my $url = URI->new('http://www.altavista.com/web/results');
$url->query_form('q' => $query);

my $prismasearch = $ua->get($url)->content;
$prismasearch =~ s/[\f\t\n\r]//isg;

while ($prismasearch =~ m!title="Add.*?to your.*?">(.*?)</a>!mgis) {
    my $searchitem = $1; print "$searchitem\n";
}
```

For clusters of related search results, in addition to similar queries, check out AlltheWeb (*http://www.alltheweb.com*). AlltheWeb's related and clustered results are at the bottom of the search page, instead of at the top:

```perl
#!/usr/bin/perl-w
use strict; use LWP;

# get our query, else die miserably.
my $query = shift @ARGV; die unless $query;

# search Prisma for the query.
my $ua  = LWP::UserAgent->new;
$ua->agent('Mozilla/4.76 [en] (Win98; U)');
my $url = URI->new('http://www.alltheweb.com/search');
$url->query_form('q' => $query, cat => 'web');

my $atwsearch = $ua->get($url)->content;
$atwsearch =~ s/[\f\t\n\r]//isg;

while ($atwsearch =~ m!<li>(.*?)">(.*?)</a>!mgis) {
    my ($searchlink, $searchitem) = ($1, $2);
    next if $searchlink !~ /c=web/;
    print "$searchitem\n";
}
```

HACK
Yahoo! Directory Mindshare in Google
#49
How does link popularity compare in Yahoo!'s searchable subject index versus Google's full-text index? Find out by calculating mindshare!

Yahoo! and Google are two very different animals. Yahoo! indexes only a site's main URL, title, and description, while Google builds full-text indexes of entire sites. Surely there's some interesting cross-pollination when you combine results from the two.

This hack scrapes all the URLs in a specified subcategory of the Yahoo! directory. It then takes each URL and gets its link count from Google. Each link count provides a nice snapshot of how a particular Yahoo! category and its listed sites stack up on the popularity scale.

> What's a link count? It's simply the total number of pages in Google's index that link to a specific URL.

There are a couple of ways you can use your knowledge of a subcategory's link count. If you find a subcategory whose URLs have only a few links each in Google, you may have found a subcategory that isn't getting a lot of attention from Yahoo!'s editors. Consider going elsewhere for your research. If you're a webmaster and you're considering paying to have Yahoo! add you to their directory, run this hack on the category in which you want to be listed. Are most of the links really popular? If they are, are you sure your site will stand out and get clicks? Maybe you should choose a different category.

We got this idea from a similar experiment Jon Udell (*http://weblog. infoworld.com/udell/*) did in 2001. He used AltaVista instead of Google; see *http://udell.roninhouse.com/download/mindshare-script.txt.* We appreciate the inspiration, Jon!

The Code

You will need a Google API account (*http://api.google.com/*), as well as the *SOAP::Lite* (*http://www.soaplite.com/*) and *HTML::LinkExtor* (*http:// search.cpan.org/author/GAAS/HTML-Parser/lib/HTML/LinkExtor.pm*) Perl modules to run the following code:

```perl
#!/usr/bin/perl -w

use strict;
use LWP::Simple;
use HTML::LinkExtor;
use SOAP::Lite;

my $google_key  = "your API key goes here";
my $google_wdsl = "GoogleSearch.wsdl";
my $yahoo_dir   = shift || "/Computers_and_Internet/Data_Formats/XML__".
                  "eXtensible_Markup_Language_/RSS/News_Aggregators/";

# download the Yahoo! directory.
my $data = get("http://dir.yahoo.com" . $yahoo_dir) or die $!;

# create our Google object.
my $google_search = SOAP::Lite->service("file:$google_wdsl");
my %urls; # where we keep our counts and titles.

# extract all the links and parse 'em.
HTML::LinkExtor->new(\&mindshare)->parse($data);
sub mindshare { # for each link we find...

    my ($tag, %attr) = @_;

    # continue on only if the tag was a link,
    # and the URL matches Yahoo!'s redirectory.
    return if $tag ne 'a';
    return unless $attr{href} =~ /srd.yahoo/;
    return unless $attr{href} =~ /\*http/;

    # now get our real URL.
    $attr{href} =~ /\*(http.*)/; my $url = $1;
```

```
        # and process each URL through Google.
        my $results = $google_search->doGoogleSearch(
                        $google_key, "link:$url", 0, 1,
                        "true", "", "false", "", "", ""
                    ); # wheee, that was easy, guvner.
        $urls{$url} = $results->{estimatedTotalResultsCount};
    }

    # now sort and display.
    my @sorted_urls = sort { $urls{$b} <=> $urls{$a} } keys %urls;
    foreach my $url (@sorted_urls) { print "$urls{$url}: $url\n"; }
```

Running The Hack

The hack has its only configuration—the Yahoo! directory you're interested in—passed as a single argument (in quotes) on the command line. If you don't pass one of your own, a default directory will be used instead.

```
% perl mindshare.pl "/Entertainment/Humor/Procrastination/"
```

Your results show the URLs in those directories, sorted by total Google links:

```
340: http://www.p45.net/
246: http://www.ishouldbeworking.com/
81: http://www.india.com/
33: http://www.jlc.net/~useless/
23: http://www.geocities.com/SouthBeach/1915/
18: http://www.eskimo.com/~spban/creed.html
13: http://www.black-schaffer.org/scp/
3: http://www.angelfire.com/mi/psociety
2: http://www.geocities.com/wastingstatetime/
```

Hacking the Hack

Yahoo! isn't the only searchable subject index out there, of course; there's also the Open Directory Project (DMOZ, *http://www.dmoz.org*), which is the product of thousands of volunteers busily cataloging and categorizing sites on the Web—the web community's Yahoo!, if you will. This hack works just as well on DMOZ as it does on Yahoo!; they're very similar in structure.

Replace the default Yahoo! directory with its DMOZ equivalent:

```
my $dmoz_dir = shift || "/Reference/Libraries/Library_and_Information_⏎
Science/Technical_Services/Cataloguing/Metadata/RDF/Applications/RSS/⏎
News_Readers/";
```

You'll also need to change the download instructions:

```
# download the Dmoz.org directory.
my $data = get("http://dmoz.org" . $dmoz_dir) or die $!;
```

Next, replace the lines that check whether a URL should be measured for mindshare. When we were scraping Yahoo! in our original script, all directory entries were always prepended with *http://srd.yahoo.com/* and then the URL itself. Thus, to ensure we received a proper URL, we skipped over the link unless it matched that criteria:

```
return unless $attr{href} =~ /srd.yahoo/;
return unless $attr{href} =~ /\*http/;
```

Since DMOZ is an entirely different site, our checks for validity have to change. DMOZ doesn't modify the outgoing URL, so our previous Yahoo! checks have no relevance here. Instead, we'll make sure it's a full-blooded location (i.e., it starts with *http://*) and it doesn't match any of DMOZ's internal page links. Likewise, we'll ignore searches on other engines:

```
return unless $attr{href} =~ /^http/;
return if $attr{href} =~ /dmoz|google|altavista|lycos|yahoo|alltheweb/;
```

Our last change is to modify the bit of code that gets the real URL from Yahoo!'s modified version. Instead of "finding the URL within the URL":

```
# now get our real URL.
$attr{href} =~ /\*(http.*)/; my $url = $1;
```

we simply assign the URL that *HTML::LinkExtor* has found:

```
# now get our real URL.
my $url = $attr{href};
```

Can you go even further with this? Sure! You might want to search a more specialized directory, such as the FishHoo! fishing search engine (*http://www.fishhoo.com/*).

You might want to return only the most linked-to URL from the directory, which is quite easy, by piping the results [Hack #28] to another common Unix utility:

```
% perl mindshare.pl | head 1
```

Alternatively, you might want to go ahead and grab the top 10 Google matches for the URL that has the most mindshare. To do so, add the following code to the bottom of the script:

```
print "\nMost popular URLs for the strongest mindshare:\n";
my $most_popular = shift @sorted_urls;
my $results = $google_search->doGoogleSearch(
                $google_key, "$most_popular", 0, 10,
                "true", "", "false", "", "", "" );

foreach my $element (@{$results->{resultElements}}) {
    next if $element->{URL} eq $most_popular;
    print " * $element->{URL}\n";
    print "   \"$element->{title}\"\n\n";
}
```

Then, run the script as usual (the output here uses the default hardcoded directory):

```
% perl mindshare.pl
27800: http://radio.userland.com/
6670: http://www.oreillynet.com/meerkat/
5460: http://www.newsisfree.com/
3280: http://ranchero.com/software/netnewswire/
1840: http://www.disobey.com/amphetadesk/
847: http://www.feedreader.com/
797: http://www.serence.com/site.php?page=prod_klipfolio
674: http://bitworking.org/Aggie.html
492: http://www.newzcrawler.com/
387: http://www.sharpreader.net/
112: http://www.awasu.com/
102: http://www.bloglines.com/
67: http://www.blueelephantsoftware.com/
57: http://www.blogtrack.com/
50: http://www.proggle.com/novobot/

Most popular URLs for the strongest mindshare:
 * http://groups.yahoo.com/group/radio-userland/
   "Yahoo! Groups : radio-userland"

 * http://groups.yahoo.com/group/radio-userland-francophone/message/76
   "Yahoo! Groupes : radio-userland-francophone Messages : Message 76 ... "

 * http://www.fuzzygroup.com/writing/radiouserland_faq.htm
   "Fuzzygroup :: Radio UserLand FAQ"
 ...
```

HACK #50   Weblog-Free Google Results

With so many weblogs being indexed by Google, you might worry about too much emphasis on the hot topic of the moment. In this hack, we'll show you how to remove the weblog factor from your Google results.

Weblogs—those frequently updated, link-heavy personal pages—are quite the fashionable thing these days. There are at least 400,000 active weblogs across the Internet, covering almost every possible subject and interest. For humans, they're good reading, but for search engines they are heavenly bundles of fresh content and links galore.

But some people think the search engine's delight in weblogs is slanting their search results and giving too much emphasis to too small a group of recent rather than evergreen content. As I write, for example, I am the third most important Ben on the Internet, according to Google. This rank comes solely from my weblog's popularity.

This hack searches Google, discarding any results coming from weblogs. It uses the Google Web Services API (*http://api.google.com*) and the API of

Technorati (*http://www.technorati.com/members*), an excellent interface to
David Sifry's weblog data-tracking tool [Hack #70]. Both APIs require keys,
available from the URLs mentioned.

Finally, you'll need a simple HTML page with a form that passes a text query
to the parameter q (the query that will run on Google), something like this:

```
<form action="googletech.cgi" method="POST">
Your query: <input type="text" name="q">
<input type="submit" name="Search!" value="Search!">
</form>
```

The Code

You'll need the *XML::Simple* and *SOAP::Lite* Perl modules. Save the following code to a file called *googletech.cgi*:

```perl
#!/usr/bin/perl -w
# googletech.cgi
# Getting Google results
# without getting weblog results.
use strict;
use SOAP::Lite;
use XML::Simple;
use CGI qw(:standard);
use HTML::Entities ();
use LWP::Simple qw(!head);

my $technoratikey = "your technorati key here";
my $googlekey = "your google key here";

# Set up the query term
# from the CGI input.
my $query = param("q");

# Initialize the SOAP interface and run the Google search.
my $google_wdsl = "http://api.google.com/GoogleSearch.wsdl";
my $service = SOAP::Lite->service->($google_wdsl);

# Start returning the results page -
# do this now to prevent timeouts
my $cgi = new CGI;

print $cgi->header();
print $cgi->start_html(-title=>'Blog Free Google Results');
print $cgi->h1('Blog Free Results for '. "$query");
print $cgi->start_ul();

# Go through each of the results
foreach my $element (@{$result->{'resultElements'}}) {

    my $url = HTML::Entities::encode($element->{'URL'});
```

```
        # Request the Technorati information for each result.
        my $technorati_result = get("http://api.technorati.com/bloginfo?".
                                    "url=$url&key=$technoratikey");

        # Parse this information.
        my $parser = new XML::Simple;
        my $parsed_feed = $parser->XMLin($technorati_result);

        # If Technorati considers this site to be a weblog,
        # go onto the next result. If not, display it, and then go on.
        if ($parsed_feed->{document}{result}{weblog}{name}) { next; }
        else {
            print $cgi-> i('<a href="'.$url.'">'.$element->{title}.'</a>');
            print $cgi-> l("$element->{snippet}");
        }
    }
}
print $cgi -> end_ul();
print $cgi->end_html;
```

Let's step through the meaningful bits of this code. First comes pulling in the query from Google. Notice the 10 in the doGoogleSearch; this is the number of search results requested from Google. You should try to set this as high as Google will allow whenever you run the script, or else you might find that searching for terms that are extremely popular in the weblogging world do not return any results at all, having been rejected as originating from a blog.

Since we're about to make a web services call for every one of the returned results, which might take a while, we want to start returning the results page now; this helps prevent connection timeouts. As such, we spit out a header using the *CGI* module, then jump into our loop.

We then get to the final part of our code: actually looping through the search results returned by Google and passing the HTML-encoded URL to the Technorati API as a get request. Technorati will then return its results as an XML document.

> Be careful you do not run out of Technorati requests. As I write this, Technorati is offering 500 free requests a day, which, with this script, is around 50 searches. If you make this script available to your web site's audience, you will soon run out of Technorati requests. One possible workaround is forcing the user to enter her own Technorati key. You can get the user's key from the same form that accepts the query. See the "Hacking the Hack" section for a means of doing this.

Parsing this result is a matter of passing it through *XML::Simple*. Since Technorati returns only an XML construct containing name when the site is thought to be a weblog, we can use the presence of this construct as a marker. If the program sees the construct, it skips to the next result. If it doesn't, the site is not thought to be a weblog by Technorati and we display a link to it, along with the title and snippet (when available) returned by Google.

Hacking the Hack

As mentioned previously, this script can burn through your Technorati allowances rather quickly under heavy use. The simplest way of solving this is to force the end user to supply his own Technorati key. First, add a new input to your HTML form for the user's key:

```
Your query: <input type="text" name="key">
```

Then, suck in the user's key as a replacement to your own:

```
# Set up the query term
# from the CGI input.
my $query = param("q");
$technoratikey = param("key");
```

—*Ben Hammersley*

#51 Spidering, Google, and Multiple Domains

When you want to search a site, you tend to go straight to the site itself and use its native capabilities. But what if you could use Google to search across many similar sites, scraping the pages of most relevance?

If you're searching for the same thing on multiple sites, it's handy to use Google's site: syntax, which allows you to restrict your search to just a particular domain (e.g., *perl.org*) or set of domains (e.g., *org*). For example, if you want to search several domains for the word perl, you might have a query that looks like this:

```
perl ( site:oreilly.com | site:perl.com | site:mit.edu | site:yahoo.com)
```

You can combine this search with a Perl script to do some specific searching that you can't do with just Google and can't do easily with just Perl.

You might wonder why you'd want to involve Google at all in this search. Why not just go ahead and search each domain separately via their search forms and *LWP::Simple* [Hack #9] or *LWP::UserAgent* [Hack #10]? There are a few reasons, the first being that each place you want to search might not have its own search engine. Second, Google might have syntaxes—such as title search, URL search, and full-word wildcard search—that the individual sites aren't providing. Google returns its search results in an array that's easy to manipulate. You don't have to use regular expressions or parsing modules to get what you want. And, of course, you'll also have all your results in one nice, regular format, independent of site-specific idiosyncrasies.

Example: Top 20 Searching on Google

Say you're a publisher, like O'Reilly, that is interested in finding out which universities are using your books as textbooks. You could do the search at Google itself, experimenting with keywords and limiting your search to the top-level domain edu (like syllabus o'reilly site:edu, or syllabus perl "required reading" site:edu), and you'd have some success. But you'd get far more than the maximum number of results (Google returns only 1,000 matches for a given query) and you'd also get a lot of false positives—pages that include mentions about a book but don't provide specific course information, or maybe weblogs discussing a class, or even old news stories! It's difficult to get a list of just class results with keyword searching alone.

So, there are two overall problems to be solved: narrowing your search to edu leaves your pool of potential results too broad, and it's extremely difficult to find just the right keywords for restricting to university course pages.

This hack tries to solve those problems. First, it uses the top 20 computer science grad schools (as ranked by *U.S. News & World Report*) as its site searches and puts those sites into an array. Then, it goes through the array and searches for pages from those schools five at a time using the site: syntax. Each query also searches for O'Reilly * Associates (to match both O'Reilly & Associates and O'Reilly and Associates) and the word syllabus.

The last tweak goes beyond keyword searching and makes use of Perl's regular expressions. As each search result is returned, both the title and the URL are checked for the presence of a three-digit string. A three-digit string? Yup, a course number! This quick regular expression eliminates a lot of the false positives you'd get from a regular Google search. It is not something you can do through Google's interface.

Search results that make it over all these hurdles are saved to a file.

The Code

This hack makes use of the SOAP-based Google Web Services API. You'll need your own Google search key (*http://api.google.com*) and a copy of the *SOAP::Lite* (*http://www.soaplite.com*) Perl module installed.

Save the following code to a file called *textbook.pl*:

```
#!/usr/bin/perl -w
# textbooks.pl
```

```perl
# Generates a list of O'Reilly books used
# as textbooks in the top 20 universities.
# Usage: perl textbooks.pl

use strict;
use SOAP::Lite;

# all the Google information
my $google_key  = "your google key here";
my $google_wdsl = "GoogleSearch.wsdl";
my $gsrch       = SOAP::Lite->service("file:$google_wdsl");

my @toptwenty = ("site:cmu.edu", "site:mit.edu", "site:stanford.edu",
      "site:berkeley.edu", "site:uiuc.edu","site:cornell.edu",
      "site:utexas.edu", "site:washington.edu", "site:caltech.edu",
      "site:princeton.edu", "site:wisc.edu", "site:gatech.edu",
      "site:umd.edu", "site:brown.edu", "site:ucla.edu",
      "site:umich.edu", "site:rice.edu", "site:upenn.edu",
      "site:unc.edu", "site:columbia.edu");

my $twentycount = 0;
open (OUT,'>top20.txt')
 or die "Couldn't open: $!";

while ($twentycount < 20) {

    # our five universities
    my $arrayquery =
      "( $toptwenty[$twentycount] | $toptwenty[$twentycount+1] ".
      "| $toptwenty[$twentycount+2] | $toptwenty[$twentycount+3] ".
      "| $toptwenty[$twentycount+4] )";

    # our search term.
    my $googlequery = "\"o'reilly * associates\" syllabus $arrayquery";
    print "Searching for $googlequery\n";

    # and do it, up to a maximum of 50 results.
    my $counter = 0; while ($counter < 50) {
        my $result = $gsrch->doGoogleSearch($google_key, $googlequery,
                        $counter, 10, "false", "",  "false",
                        "lang_en", "", "");
        # foreach result.
        foreach my $hit (@{$result->{'resultElements'}}){
            my $urlcheck = $hit->{'URL'};
            my $titlecheck = $hit->{'title'};
            my $snip = $hit->{'snippet'};

            # if the URL or title has a three-digit
            # number in it, we clean up the snippet
            # and print it out to our file.
            if ($urlcheck =~/http:.*?\/.*?\d{3}.*?/
                    or $titlecheck =~/\d{3}/) {
```

```
            $snip =~ s/<b>/ /g;
            $snip =~ s/<\/b>/ /g;
            $snip =~ s/&#39;/'/g;
            $snip =~ s/&quot;/"/g;
            $snip =~ s/&amp;/&/g;
            $snip =~ s/<br>/ /g;
            print OUT "$hit->{title}\n";
            print OUT "$hit->{URL}\n";
            print OUT "$snip\n\n";
        }
    }

    # go get 10 more
    # search results.
    $counter += 10;
}

# our next schools.
$twentycount += 5;
}
```

Running the Hack

Running the hack requires no switches or variables:

```
% perl textbooks.pl
```

The output file, *top20.txt*, looks something like this:

```
Programming Languages and Compilers CS 164 - Spring 2002
http://www-inst.eecs.berkeley.edu/~cs164/home.html
... Tentative  Syllabus  & Schedule of Assignments.  ... you might find
useful is "Unix in  a Nutshell (System V Edition)" by Gilly, published by  O
' Reilly  & ...

CS378 (Spring 03): Linux Kernel Programming
http://www.cs.utexas.edu/users/ygz/378-03S/course.html
 ...  Guide, 2nd Edition By Olaf Kirch & Terry Dawson  O ' Reilly   &
Associates, ISBN 1-56592 ...  Please  visit Spring 02 homepage for
information on  syllabus, projects, and  ...

LIS 530: Organizing Information Using the Internet
http://courses.washington.edu/lis541/syllabus-intro.html
Efthimis N. Efthimiadis' Site LIS-541  Syllabus  Main Page Syllabus  - Aims
& Objectives.  ...  Jennifer Niederst.  O'Reilly   and   Associates , 1999.

LIS415B * Spring98 * Class Schedule
http://alexia.lis.uiuc.edu/course/spring1998/415B/lis415.spring98.schedule.
html
LIS415 (section B): Class Schedule. Spring 98.  Syllabus ...  In Connecting
to the Internet:  A buyer's guide. Sebastapol, California:  O ' Reilly   &
Associates .
```

```
Implementation of Information Storage and Retrieval
http://alexia.lis.uiuc.edu/~dubin/429/429.pdf
...  In addition to this  syllabus , this course is governed by the rules
and  ... Advanced  Perl Programming , first edition ( O'Reilly   and
Associates , Inc.,

INET 200: HTML, Dynamic HTML, and Scripting
http://www.outreach.washington.edu/dl/courses/inet200/
...  such as HTML & XHTML: the Definitive Guide, 4 th edition,  O'Reilly
and  Associates   (which I  ... are assigned, and there is one on the course
syllabus  as Appendix B  ...
```

Hacking the Hack

There are plenty of things to change in this hack. Since it uses a very specific array (that is, the top 20 computer science grad schools), tweaking the array to your needs should be the first place you start. You can make that array anything you want: different kinds of schools, your favorite or local schools, and so on. You can even break out schools by athletic conference and check them that way. In addition, you can change the keywords to something more befitting your tastes. Maybe you don't want to search for textbooks, but you'd rather find everything from chemistry labs to vegetarian groups. Change your keywords appropriately (which will probably require a little experimenting in Google before you get them just right) and go to town.

And don't forget, you're also running a regular expression check on each keyword before you save it to a file. Maybe you don't want to do a three-digit check on the title and URL. Maybe you want to check for the string lib, either by itself or as part of the word library:

```
($urlcheck =~/http:.*?\/.*?lib.*?/) or ($titlecheck =~/.*?lib.*?/)
```

This particular search will find materials in a school library's web pages, for the most part, or in web pages that mention the word "library" in the title.

If you've read *Google Hacks* (*http://www.oreilly.com/catalog/googlehks/*), you might remember that Google offers wildcards for full-word searches, but not for stemming. In other words, you can search for three * mice and get three blind mice, three blue mice, three green mice, and so on. But you can't plug the query moon* into Google and get moons, moonlight, moonglow, and so on. When you use Perl to perform these checks, you are expanding the kind of searching possible with Google.

Scraping Amazon.com Product Reviews
#52

While Amazon.com has made some reviews available through their Web
Services API, most are available only at the Amazon.com web site, requiring
a little screen scraping to grab them.

If you've written a book called *Spidering Hacks* and you're interested to hear
what people are saying about it, you could run off to Amazon.com each and
every day to check out the reviews. Well, you certainly could, but you
wouldn't, else you'd deserve every bad comment that came your way. Here's
a way to integrate Amazon.com reviews with your web site. Unlike *linking*
or *monitoring reviews for changes*, this puts the entire text of Amazon.com
reviews into your own pages.

The easiest and most reliable way to access customer reviews programmatically is through Amazon.com's Web Services API. Unfortunately, the API
gives only a small window to the larger number of reviews available. An API
query for the book *Cluetrain Manifesto*, for example, includes only three
user reviews. If you visit the *review page* for that book, though, you'll find
128 reviews. To dig deeper into the reviews available on Amazon.com and
use all of them on your own web site, you'll need to spelunk a bit further
into scripting.

The Code

This Perl script builds a URL to the review page for a given ASIN, uses regular expressions to find the reviews, and breaks the review into its pieces: rating, title, date, reviewer, and the text of the review.

Save the following script to a file called *get_reviews.pl*:

```perl
#!/usr/bin/perl -w
# get_reviews.pl
#
# A script to scrape Amazon, retrieve
# reviews, and write to a file.
# Usage: perl get_reviews.pl <asin>
use strict;
use LWP::Simple;

# Take the ASIN from the command line.
my $asin = shift @ARGV or die "Usage: perl get_reviews.pl <asin>\n";

# Assemble the URL from the passed ASIN.
my $url = "http://amazon.com/o/tg/detail/-/$asin/?vi=customer-reviews";

# Set up unescape-HTML rules. Quicker than URI::Escape.
my %unescape = ('&quot;'=>'"', '&amp;'=>'&', ' '=>' ');
my $unescape_re = join '|' => keys %unescape;
```

```
# Request the URL.
my $content = get($url);
die "Could not retrieve $url" unless $content;

# Loop through the HTML, looking for matches
while ($content =~ m!<img.*?stars-(\d)-0.gif.*?>.*?<b>(.*?)</b>, (.*?)\n.
*?Reviewer:\n<b>\n(.*?)</b>.*?</table>\n(.*?)<br>\n<br>!mgis) {

    my($rating,$title,$date,$reviewer,$review) =
                    ($1||'',$2||'',$3||'',$4||'',$5||'');
    $reviewer =~ s!<.+?>!!g;    # drop all HTML tags
    $reviewer =~ s!\(.+?\)!!g; # remove anything in parenthesis
    $reviewer =~ s!\n!!g;      # remove newlines
    $review =~ s!<.+?>!!g;     # drop all HTML tags
    $review =~ s/($unescape_re)/$unescape{$1}/migs; # unescape.

    # Print the results
    print "$title\n" . "$date\n" . "by $reviewer\n" .
        "$rating stars.\n\n" . "$review\n\n";

}
```

Running the Hack

This script can be run from a command line, and it requires an ASIN—an Amazon.com unique ID that can be found in the Product Details of each and every product, listed as either "ISBN" or "ASIN", as shown in Figure 4-3.

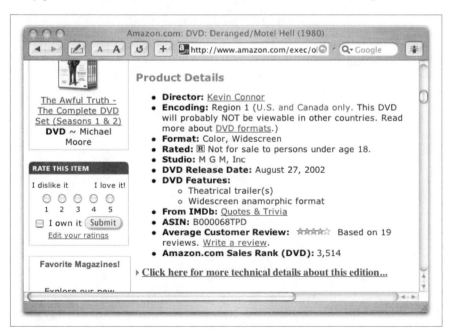

Figure 4-3. Amazon.com's unique ID, listed as an ASIN or ISBN

The reviews are too long to read as they scroll past your screen, so it helps to send the information to a text file (in this case, *reviews.txt*), like so:

```
% perl get_reviews.pl asin > reviews.txt
```

See Also

- *Amazon Hacks* (*http://oreilly.com/catalog/amazonhks/*) by Paul Bausch

—*Paul Bausch*

HACK #53 Receive an Email Alert for Newly Added Amazon.com Reviews

This hack keeps an eye on Amazon.com and notifies you, via email, when a new product review is posted to items you're tracking.

There are obviously some products you care about more than others, and it's good to be aware of how those products are perceived. Reviews give feedback to publishers, authors, and manufacturers; help customers make buying decisions; and help other retailers decide what to stock. If you want to monitor all the reviews for a product or set of products, visiting each Product Details page to see if a new review has been added is a tedious task.

Instead, you can use a script to periodically check the number of reviews for a given item, and have it send you an email when a new review is added.

The Code

This script requires you to have the *XML::Simple* Perl module installed, a Developer's Token (*http://www.amazon.com/gp/aws/landing.html*), and a product's unique ASIN (included in the details of every Amazon.com product).

Save the following script to a file called *review_monitor.pl*:

```perl
#!/usr/bin/perl -w
# review_monitor.pl
#
# Monitors products, sending email when a new review is added.
# Usage: perl review_monitor.pl <asin>
use strict;
use LWP::Simple;
use XML::Simple;

# Your Amazon developer's token.
my $dev_token='insert developer token';

# Your Amazon affiliate code. Optional.
# See http://associates.amazon.com/.
my $af_code='insert affiliate tag';
```

```
# Location of sendmail and your email.
my $sendmailpath = "insert sendmail location";
my $emailAddress = "insert your email address";

# Take the ASIN from the command line.
my $asin = shift @ARGV or die "Usage: perl review_monitor.pl <asin>\n";

# Get the number of reviews the last time this script ran.
open (ReviewCountDB, "<reviewCount_$asin.db");
my $lastReviewCount = <ReviewCountDB> || 0;
close(ReviewCountDB); # errors?! bah!

# Assemble the query URL (RESTian).
my $url = "http://xml.amazon.com/onca/xml2?t=$af_code" .
          "&dev-t=$dev_token&type=heavy&f=xml" .
          "&AsinSearch=$asin";

# Grab the content...
my $content = get($url);
die "Could not retrieve $url" unless $content;

# And parse it with XML::Simple.
my $response = XMLin($content);

# Send email if a review has been added.
my $currentReviewCount = $response->{Details}->{Reviews}->⏎
{TotalCustomerReviews};
my $productName        = $response->{Details}->{ProductName};
if ($currentReviewCount > $lastReviewCount) {
    open (MAIL, "|$sendmailpath -t") || die "Can't open mail program!\n";
    print MAIL "To: $emailAddress\n";
    print MAIL "From: Amazon Review Monitor\n";
    print MAIL "Subject: A Review Has Been Added!\n\n";
    print MAIL "Review count for $productName is $currentReviewCount.\n";
    close (MAIL);

    # Write the current review count to a file.
    open(ReviewCountDB, ">reviewCount_$asin.db");
    print ReviewCountDB $currentReviewCount;
    close(ReviewCountDB);
}
```

This code performs a standard Web Services ASIN query, looking for one bit of data: the total number of customer reviews (TotalCustomerReviews). The script saves the number of reviews in a text file (*ASIN.db*) and, if the number is different than the last time the script was run, sends an email to let you know.

In your local path to *sendmail*, be sure to include a program that sends email from the server. Most ISPs have *sendmail* installed in some form or another (often at */usr/bin/sendmail*). Check with your local administrator or Internet Service Provider (ISP) if you're not sure where it's located.

Running the Hack

Run the script from the command line, passing it an ASIN (to find an ASIN, see Figure 4-3 in "Scraping Amazon.com Product Reviews" [Hack #52] for guidance):

```
% perl review_monitor.pl ASIN
```

Ideally, you want to run this script once every so often in the background, instead of manually executing this query every day. On Linux, you can set it to run as a *cron* job [Hack #90], like so:

```
0 12 * * 1-5 perl review_monitor.pl ASIN
```

This schedules the script to run Monday through Friday at noon on each day. Be sure to replace *ASIN* with a real ASIN, and add jobs as necessary for all the items you want to monitor.

On Windows, you can run the script as a Scheduled Task. From the Control Panel, choose Scheduled Tasks and then Add Scheduled Task. Follow the wizard to set your execution time, and you should be all set for review notifications!

See Also

- *Amazon Hacks* (*http://oreilly.com/catalog/amazonhks/*) by Paul Bausch
- "Scheduling Tasks Without cron" [Hack #91]

—Paul Bausch

HACK #54   Scraping Amazon.com Customer Advice

> Screen scraping can give you access to Amazon.com community features not yet implemented through Amazon.com's public Web Services API. In this hack, we'll implement a script to scrape customer buying advice.

Customer buying advice isn't available through Amazon.com's Web Services API, so if you'd like to include this information on a remote site, you'll have to get it from Amazon.com's site through scraping. The first step to this hack is knowing where to find all the customer advice on one page. The following URL links directly to the advice page for a given ASIN (the unique ID Amazon.com displays for each product [Hack #52]):

```
http://amazon.com/o/tg/detail/-/insert ASIN/?vi=advice
```

For example, here is the advice page for *Mac OS X Hacks*:

```
http://amazon.com/o/tg/detail/-/0596004605/?vi=advice
```

The Code

This Perl script splits the advice page into two variables, based on the headings "in addition to" and "instead of." It then loops through those sections, using regular expressions to match the products' information. The script then formats and prints the information.

Save the following script to a file called *get_advice.pl*:

```perl
#!/usr/bin/perl -w
# get_advice.pl
#
# A script to scrape Amazon to retrieve customer buying advice
# Usage: perl get_advice.pl <asin>
use strict; use LWP::Simple;

# Take the ASIN from the command line.
my $asin = shift @ARGV or die "Usage: perl get_advice.pl <asin>\n";

# Assemble the URL from the passed ASIN.
my $url = "http://amazon.com/o/tg/detail/-/$asin/?vi=advice";

# Set up unescape-HTML rules. Quicker than URI::Escape.
my %unescape = ('&quot;'=>'"', '&amp;'=>'&', ' '=>' ');
my $unescape_re = join '|' => keys %unescape;

# Request the URL.
my $content = get($url);
die "Could not retrieve $url" unless $content;

# Get our matching data.
my ($inAddition) = (join '', $content) ↵
    =~ m!in addition to(.*?)(instead of)?</td></tr>!mis;
my ($instead)    = (join '', $content) ↵
    =~ m!recommendations instead of(.*?)</table>!mis;

# Look for "in addition to" advice.
if ($inAddition) { print "-- In Addition To --\n\n";
    while ($inAddition =~ m!<td width=10>(.*?)</td>\n<td width=90%>.*?ASIN/↵
(.*?)/.*?">(.*?)</a>.*?</td>.*?<td width=10% align=center>(.*?)</td>!mgis) {
        my ($place,$thisAsin,$title,$number) = ($1||'',$2||'',$3||'',$4||'');
        $title =~ s/($unescape_re)/$unescape{$1}/migs; #unescape HTML
        print "$place $title ($thisAsin)\n(Recommendations: $number)\n\n";
    }
}

# Look for "instead of" advice.
if ($instead) { print "-- Instead Of --\n\n";
    while ($instead =~ m!<td width=10>(.*?)</td>\n<td width=90%>.*?ASIN/(..↵
*?)/.*?">(.*?)</a>.*?</td>.*?<td width=10% align=center>(.*?)</td>!mgis) {
```

```
    my ($place,$thisAsin,$title,$number) ↵
      = ($1||'',$2||'',$3||'',$4||'');
    $title =~ s/($unescape_re)/$unescape{$1}/migs; #unescape HTML
    print "$place $title ($thisAsin)\n(Recommendations: $number)\n\n";
  }
}
```

Running the Hack

You can run this script from the command line, passing in any ASIN. Here is the one for *Mac OS X Hacks*:

```
% perl get_advice.pl 0596004605
-- In Addition To --

1. Mac OS X: The Missing Manual, Second Edition (0596004508)
(Recommendations: 1)

2. Mac Upgrade and Repair Bible, Third Edition (0764525948)
(Recommendations: 1)
```

If the book has long lists of alternate products, send the output to a text file. This example sends all alternate product recommendations for *Google Hacks* to a file called *advice.txt*:

```
% perl get_advice.pl 0596004478 > advice.txt
```

See Also

- *Amazon Hacks* (*http://oreilly.com/catalog/amazonhks/*) by Paul Bausch

—Paul Bausch

HACK #55 Publishing Amazon.com Associates Statistics

Share some insider knowledge, such as the most popular item sold, with your site's audience by republishing your Amazon.com Associates sales statistics.

Your web site has a unique audience, and looking at what they purchase through your Amazon.com Associate links can tell you more about them. It can provide insights into other items you might want to sell on your site, and it can help show what's foremost on your visitors' minds (for better or worse). Just as Amazon.com shares its aggregated sales information in the form of purchase circles, you can create your own purchase circle list by publishing your Associates sales information.

Your readers are probably just as curious about sales trends through your site as you are. Publishing the list can build a sense of community and, don't forget, drive more sales through Associate links.

You could save the HTML reports available through your Associates account (*http://associates.amazon.com*) through your browser, but it would be much easier to automate the process and integrate it into your site design with a few lines of Perl.

The Code

To run this code, you'll need to set the email address and password you use to log into your Associates account. This script will then do the logging in for you, and download the appropriate sales report. Once the script has the report, it will reformat it as HTML.

Because this script logs into Amazon.com, it requires the use of a cookie to remind Amazon.com that you're an authenticated user. Since this is a one-time-only request, we use an in-memory cookie (which is forgotten when the script is finished).

 The code listed here intentionally logs you in under an unsecured HTTP connection, to better ensure that the script is portable across systems that don't have the relevant SSL libraries installed. If you know you have them working properly, be sure to change http:// to https:// to gain some added protection for your login information.

Save the following script to a file called *get_earnings_report.pl*:

```perl
#!/usr/bin/perl -w
# get_earnings_report.pl
#
# Logs into Amazon, downloads earning report,
# and writes an HTML version for your site.
# Usage: perl get_earnings_report.pl
use strict;
use URI::Escape;
use HTTP::Cookies;
use LWP::UserAgent;

# Set your Associates account info.
my $email = 'insert email address';
my $pass = 'insert password';
my $aftag = 'insert associates tag';

# Create a user agent object
# and fake the agent string.
my $ua = LWP::UserAgent->new;
$ua->agent("(compatible; MSIE 4.01; MSN 2.5; AOL 4.0; Windows 98)");
$ua->cookie_jar({}); # in-memory cookie jar.
```

```
# Request earning reports, logging in as one pass.
my $rpturl  = "http://associates.amazon.com/exec/panama/login/".
              "attempt/customer/associates/no-customer-id/25/".
              "associates/resources/reporting/earnings/";
my $rptreq  = HTTP::Request->new(POST => $rpturl);
my $rptdata = "report-type=shipments-by-item".   # get individual items
              "&date-selection=qtd".             # all earnings this quarter
              "&login_id=".uri_escape($email).   # our email address.
              "&login_password=".uri_escape($pass).  # and password.
              "&submit.download=Download my report". # get downloadble.
              "&enable-login-post=true"; # log in and post at once.
$rptreq->content_type('application/x-www-form-urlencoded');
$rptreq->content($rptdata); my $report = $ua->request($rptreq);

# Uncomment the following line to see
# the report if you need to debug.
# print $report->content;

# Set the report to array.
my @lines = split(/\n/, $report->content);

# Get the time period.
my @fromdate = split(/\t/, $lines[1]);
my @todate = split(/\t/, $lines[2]);
my $from = $fromdate[1];
my $to = $todate[1];

# Print header...
print "<html><body>";
print "<h2>Items Purchased Through This Site</h2>";
print "from $from to $to <br><br>\n";
print "<ul>";

# Loop through the rest of the report.
splice(@lines,0,5);
foreach my $line (@lines) {
    my @fields  = split(/\t/, $line);
    my $title   = $fields[1];
    my $asin    = $fields[2];
    my $edition = $fields[4];
    my $items   = $fields[8];

    # Format items as HTML for display.
    print "<li><a href=\"http://www.amazon.com/o/ASIN/$asin/ref=nosim/".
          "$aftag\">$title</a> ($items) $edition <br>\n";
}
print "</ul></body></html>";
```

Running the Hack

Run the hack from a command line:

```
% perl get_earnings_report.pl
```

It prints out the formatted HTML results, so you might want to pipe its output to another file, like this:

```
% perl get_earnings_report.pl > amazon_report.html
```

You could also set this to run on a regular schedule [Hack #90] so your community's buying habits stay up-to-date.

See Also

- *Amazon Hacks* (*http://oreilly.com/catalog/amazonhks/*) by Paul Bausch

—Paul Bausch

HACK #56 Sorting Amazon.com Recommendations by Rating

Find the highest-rated items among your Amazon.com product recommendations.

If you've taken the time to fine-tune your Amazon.com recommendations, you know how precise they can be. If you've also looked at the star rating for some of your favorite products, then you know that the rating can be a good indication of quality. The Amazon.com recommendation and the customer rating both add important information to a product, and they can help you make a decision about whether or not to buy one item over another.

To get a feel for the products Amazon.com recommends for you, you can visit your book recommendations at any time at the following URL:

```
http://www.amazon.com/o/tg/stores/recs/instant-recs/-/books/0/
```

In addition to books, you can also find recommendations in other product categories. You can replace books in the URL with any of Amazon.com's catalogs, including music, electronics, dvd, and photo.

When you browse to your recommendations, you'll likely find several pages of items. Wouldn't it be great if you could add the customer review dimension by sorting the entire list by its average star rating? This hack does exactly that with a bit of screen scraping.

The Code

Because Amazon.com doesn't offer sorting by customer rating, this script first gathers all of your Amazon.com book recommendations into one list. By providing your Amazon.com account's email address and password, the script logs in as you and then requests the book recommendations page. It continues to request pages in a loop, picking out the details of your product recommendations with regular expressions. Once all the products and details are stored in an array, they can be sorted by star rating and printed out in any order you want—in this case, the average star rating.

Be sure to replace your email address and password in the proper places in the following code. You'll also need to have write permission in the script's directory so you can store Amazon.com cookies in a text file, *cookies.lwp*.

 The code listed here intentionally logs you in under an unsecured HTTP connection, to better ensure that the script is portable across systems that don't have the relevant SSL libraries installed. If you know you have them working properly, be sure to change http:// to https:// to gain some added protection for your login information.

Save the following script to a file called *get_recommendations.pl*:

```perl
#!/usr/bin/perl  -w
# get_recommendations.pl
#
# A script to log on to Amazon, retrieve
# recommendations, and sort by highest rating.
# Usage: perl get_recommendations.pl

use strict;
use HTTP::Cookies;
use LWP::UserAgent;

# Amazon email and password.
my $email = 'insert email address';
my $password = 'insert password';

# Amazon login URL for normal users.
my $logurl = "http://www.amazon.com/exec/obidos/flex-sign-in-done/";

# Now log into Amazon.
my $ua = LWP::UserAgent->new;
$ua->agent("(compatible; MSIE 4.01; MSN 2.5; AOL 4.0; Windows 98)");
$ua->cookie_jar( HTTP::Cookies->new('file' => 'cookies.lwp','autosave' =>
1));
my %headers = ( 'content-type' => "application/x-www-form-urlencoded" );
$ua->post($logurl,
    [ email       => $email,
      password    => $password,
      method      => 'get', opt => 'oa',
      page        => 'recs/instant-recs-sign-in-standard.html',
      response    => "tg/recs/recs-post-login-dispatch/-/recs/pd_rw_gw_r",
      'next-page' => 'recs/instant-recs-register-standard.html',
      action      => 'sign-in checked' ], %headers);
```

```perl
# Set some variables to hold
# our sorted recommendations.
my (%title_list, %author_list);
my (@asins, @ratings, $done);

# We're logged in, so request the recommendations.
my $recurl = "http://www.amazon.com/exec/obidos/tg/".
             "stores/recs/instant-recs/-/books/0/t";

# Set all Amazon recommendations in
# an array/title and author in hashes.
until ($done) {

    # Send the request for the recommendations.
    my $content = $ua->get($recurl)->content;

    # Loop through the HTML, looking for matches.
    while ($content =~ m!<td colspan=2 width=100%>.*?detail/-/(.*?)/ref.↵
*?<b>(.*?)</b>.*?by (.*?)\n.*?Average Customer Review&#58;.*?(.*?)out of 5 ↵
stars.*?<td colspan=3><hr noshade size=1></td>!mgis) {
        my ($asin,$title,$author,$rating) = ($1||'',$2||'',$3||'',$4||'');
        $title  =~ s!<.+?>!!g; # drop all HTML tags, cheaply.
        $rating =~ s!\n!!g;    # remove newlines from the rating.
        $rating =~ s! !!g;     # remove spaces from the rating.
        $title_list{$asin} = $title;    # store the title.
        $author_list{$asin} = $author;  # and the author.
        push (@asins, $asin);           # and the ASINs.
        push (@ratings, $rating);       # and the ... OK!
    }

    # See if there are more results. If so, continue the loop.
    if ($content =~ m!<a href=(.*?instant-recs.*?)>more results.*?</a>!i) {
        $recurl = "http://www.amazon.com$1"; # reassign the URL.
    } else { $done = 1; } # nope, we're done.
}

# Sort the results by highest star rating and print!
for (sort { $ratings[$b] <=> $ratings[$a] } 0..$#ratings) {
    next unless $asins[$_]; # skip el blancos.
    print "$title_list{$asins[$_]}  ($asins[$_])\n" .
          "by $author_list{$asins[$_]} \n" .
          "$ratings[$_] stars.\n\n";
}
```

Running the Hack

Run the hack from the command line and send the results to another file, like this:

```
% perl get_recommendations.pl > top_rated_recommendations.txt
```

The text file *top_rated_recommendations.txt* should be filled with product recommendations, with the highest-rated items on top. You can tweak the URL in $recurl to look for DVDs, CDs, or other product types, by changing the books URL to the product line you're interested in.

See Also

- *Amazon Hacks (http://oreilly.com/catalog/amazonhks/)* by Paul Bausch

—*Paul Bausch*

HACK #57 Related Amazon.com Products with Alexa

Given any URL, Alexa will return traffic data, user ratings, and even related Amazon.com products. This hack creates a cloud of related product data for any given URL.

Alexa (*http://www.alexa.com*), an Amazon.com property, measures a web site's traffic, then rates it for popularity based on other sites with similar topics. Along with these Related Links, you also have the capability to read, add, and write reviews, as well as find similar products at Amazon.com. Some interesting scripts can be created, simply by following through with the various information Alexa provides via its XML exports. For example, we can create a list of products recommended not only for a given web site, but also for web sites that are related to the original. Following those related web sites and obtaining their related Amazon.com products creates a *cloud* of items related to the original URL. In the following section, we'll walk you through the code for one such cloud creator.

The Code

For this script, you'll need an Amazon.com developer token, which can be obtained from *http://www.amazon.com/webservices/*. Save the following code to a file called *alexa.pl*:

```perl
#!/usr/bin/perl -w
use strict;
use URI;
use LWP::Simple;
use Net::Amazon;
use XML::Simple;
use constant AMAZON_TOKEN => 'your token here';
use constant DEBUG => 0;

# get our arguments. the first argument is the
# URL to fetch, and the second is the output.
my $url = shift || die "$0 <url> [<output>]\n";
my $output = shift || '/www/htdocs/cloud.html';
```

```perl
# we'll need to fetch the Alexa XML at some point, and
# we'll do it a few different times, so we create a
# subroutine for it. Using the URI module, we can
# correctly encode a URL with a query. In fact, you'll
# notice the majority of this function is involved with
# this, and at the end we use LWP::Simple to actually
# download and return the XML.
####################################################
sub fetch_xml {
    my $url = shift;
    $url = "http://$url" unless $url =~ m[^http://];
    warn "Fetching Alexa data for $url\n" if DEBUG;

    my @args = (
        cli => 10,      dat => 'snba',
        ver => '7.0',   url => $url,
    );

    my $base = 'http://data.alexa.com/data';
    my $uri = URI->new( $base );
    $uri->query_form( @args );
    $uri = $uri->as_string;

    return get( $uri );
}


# raw XML is no good for us, though, as we want to extract
# particular items of interest. we use XML::Simple to turn
# the XML into Perl data structures, because it's easier
# than fiddling with event handling (as with XML::Parser
# or XML::SAX), and we know there's only a small amount of
# data. we want the list of related sites and the list of
# related products. we extract and return both.
####################################################
sub handle_xml {
    my $page = shift;
    my $xml = XMLin( $page );
    my @related = map {
        {
            asin => $_->{ASIN},
            title => $_->{TITLE},
            href => $xml->{RLS}{PREFIX}.$_->{HREF},
        }
    } @{ $xml->{RLS}{RL} };

    my @products;
    if (ref $xml->{SD}{AMZN}{PRODUCT} eq 'ARRAY') {
        @products = map { $_->{ASIN} } @{ $xml->{SD}{AMZN}{PRODUCT} };
    } else { @products = $xml->{SD}{AMZN}{PRODUCT}{ASIN}; }

    return ( \@related, \@products );
}
```

```perl
# Functions done; now for the program:
warn "Start URL is $url\n" if DEBUG;
my @products; # running accumulation of product ASINs

{
    my $page = fetch_xml( $url );
    my ($related, $new_products) = handle_xml( $page );
    @products = @$new_products; # running list

    for (@$related) {
        my $xml = fetch_xml( $_->{href} );
        my ($related, $new_products) = handle_xml( $page );
        push @products, @$new_products;
    }
}

# We now have a list of products in @products, so
# we'd best do something with them. Let's look
# them up on Amazon and see what their titles are.
my $amazon = Net::Amazon->new( token => AMAZON_TOKEN );
my %products = map { $_ => undef } @products;

for my $asin ( sort keys %products ) {
    warn "Searching for $asin...\n" if DEBUG;
    my $response = $amazon->search( asin => $asin );
    my @products = $response->properties;
    die "ASIN is not unique!?" unless @products == 1;
    my $product = $products[0];
    $products{$asin} = {
        name => $product->ProductName,
        price => $product->OurPrice,
        asin => $asin,
    };
}

# Right. We now have name, price, and
# ASIN. Let's output an HTML report:
{
    umask 022;
    warn "Writing to $output\n" if DEBUG;
    open my $fh, '>', $output or die $!;
    print $fh "<html><head><title>Cloud around $url</title></head><body>";
    if (keys %products) {
        print $fh "<table>";
        for my $asin (sort keys %products) {
            my $data = $products{$asin};
            printf $fh "<tr><td>".
                       "<a href=\"http://amazon.com/exec/obidos/ASIN/%s\">".
                       "%s</a></td> <td>%s</td></tr>",
                       @{$data}{qw( asin name price )};
        }
        print $fh "</table>";
    }
```

```
    else { print $fh "No related products found.\n"; }
    print $fh "</body></html>\n";
}
```

Running the Hack

Run the script on the command line, passing it the URL you're interested in and a filename to which you'd like the results saved (you can also hardcode a default output location into the script). The following output shows an example of the script's DEBUG output turned on:

```
% perl alexa.pl http://www.gamegrene.com/ testing.html
Start URL is http://www.gamegrene.com/
Fetching Alexa data for http://www.gamegrene.com/
Fetching Alexa data for http://www.elvesontricycles.com/
Fetching Alexa data for http://www.chimeramag.com/
Fetching Alexa data for http://pages.infinit.net/raymondl
Fetching Alexa data for http://www.beyond-adventure.com/
Fetching Alexa data for http://strcat.com/News
Fetching Alexa data for http://members.aol.com/stocdred
Fetching Alexa data for http://lost-souls.hk.st/
Fetching Alexa data for http://www.gamerspulse.com/
Fetching Alexa data for http://www.gignews.com/
Fetching Alexa data for http://www.gamesfirst.com/
Searching for 0070120102...
Searching for 0070213631...
Searching for 0070464081...
Searching for 0070465886...
..etc..
Searching for 1879239027...
Writing to testing.html
```

Figure 4-4 shows an example of the resulting file.

Hacking the Hack

As the script stands, it requires manual running or a *cron* script [Hack #90] to regularly place the latest information on your own pages (if that's your intent, of course). You might want to turn this into a CGI program and let people enter web sites of their own choice. This is pretty easy to do. If you've created an HTML form that accepts the desired web site in an input named url, like this:

```
<form method="GET" action="alexa.pl">
URL: <input type="text" name="url" />
</form>
```

then modifying your script to accept this value means changing this:

```
# get our arguments. the first argument is the
# URL to fetch, and the second is the output.
my $url = shift || die "$0 <url> [<output>]\n";
my $output = shift || '/www/htdocs/cloud.html';
```

Figure 4-4. Amazon.com's related products for Gamegrene.com

to this:

```
use LWP::Simple qw(!head);
use CGI qw/:standard/;
my $url = param('url');
```

and changing the output from a filename from this:

```
warn "Writing to $output\n" if DEBUG;
open my $fh, '>', $output or die $!;
```

to the waiting web browser:

```
my $fh = *STDOUT; # redirect.
print $fh "Content-type: text/html\n\n";
```

Be sure to remove the extraneous use `LWP::Simple`; line at the beginning of the script. Since both *CGI* and *LWP::Simple* have a function named head, you'll get a number of warning messages about redefinitions, unless you change the way *LWP::Simple* has been imported. By telling it not to import its own unnecessary head function, our new code circumvents these warnings.

—*Iain Truskett*

Scraping Alexa's Competitive Data with Java

Alexa tracks the browsing habits of its millions of users daily. This hack allows you to aggregate the traffic statistics of multiple web properties into one RSS file, with subscriptions available daily.

Alexa (*http://www.alexa.com*) recently launched a section of its web site, detailing the observed traffic of its millions of users on a daily basis. Using this freely available data, you can track the traffic of your site, or your competitors' sites, over time. We'll scrape this traffic data into an RSS file [Hack #94] for your consumption.

The Code

The hack consists of five Java classes, each designed to handle different aspects of downloading, parsing, and presenting Alexa's traffic content. The full code can be downloaded from this book's web site (*http://www.oreilly.com/catalog/spiderhks/*).

The primary class of our Java application (*Report*) allows you to pass a URL to Alexa's web site for every domain you're interested in tracking. The appropriate Alexa page is downloaded, and its content is parsed for the key bits of daily data. Once this data is organized, we will need to mark it up for presentation and, finally, write the presentable file to disk.

The first step (*Website*) streams the source into your computer's memory. We eliminate everything but the body of the page, since this is where all of our data lies.

Now that we have the page's source stored in memory, we need to identify the key data components within the myriad lines of HTML. Alexa does not conform to strict XML, and string parse (*Parse*) is our best and quickest route of attack.

We will navigate through the page's source code in serial, pulling the data we need and leaving a marker on our trail to speed up our search. Key phrases of text need to be identified in close vicinity to our key data so that we can consistently pull the correct data, regardless of the size of a web property.

Now that we have all our data, we need somewhere to store our findings for use across multiple classes. We create an entity bean–style data object to store each of the key pieces of data. Our code for doing so is in *TrafficBean*.

Finally, we present our findings to whomever might be interested through an RSS file (*RSSWriter*). By default, the RSS file is saved to the current user's home directory (*C:\Documents And Settings\$user* on Microsoft Windows platforms, or */home/$user* on most versions of Unix). It is assumed that you have sufficient write permissions within your home directory to perform this action.

Running the Hack

The only external library required is Apache's Xerces for Java (*http://xml. apache.org/xerces2-j/*). Web property names should be hardcoded in the *Report* class to allow for consistent scheduled runs. You can pass domain strings in the format of *site.tld* at runtime or, if no parameters are found, the code will iterate through a previously created string array. You might also want to set yourself up with an RSS aggregator if you do not already have one. I use FeedDemon (*http://www.bradsoft.com/feeddemon/index.asp*) for Windows.

Hacking the Hack

Possibilities abound:

- Set up a *cron* script [Hack #90] or Scheduled Tasks [Hack #91] on your machine to generate a new report every evening.
- Using the percentage numbers from the returned subdomains, calculate the total reach and views for each of the domains within the web property.
- Hook your findings into a database for larger comparison sets over time.
- Using the RSS file as your data source, create a time series graph [Hack #62]. Use views or ranges as your y-axis and time as your x-axis. Overlay all of your sites using different colors and save for use in reports.

—Niall Kennedy

HACK #59 Finding Album Information with FreeDB and Amazon.com

By combining identifying information from one database with related information from another, you can create powerful applications with little effort.

Although using an MP3 collection to turn your computer into a jukebox might be all the rage these days, some of us are still listening to audio CDs. And, thanks to the FreeDB project (*http://www.freedb.org*) and the original CDDB before it, we can identify CDs based on their contents and look up information such as artist and the names of tracks. Once we have that information, we can try looking up more from other sources.

With the help of the Amazon.com API (*http://www.amazon.com/webservices/*), we can find things like cover art, other albums by the same artist, and release dates of albums. If we put this all together, we can come up with a pretty decent Now Playing display for what we're listening to.

Getting Started

So, this is what we want our script to do:

- Calculate a disc ID for the current CD.
- Perform a search on FreeDB for details on the CD.
- Use the FreeDB record data to perform a search at Amazon.com.
- Get information from the Amazon.com results for the current album.
- Collect details on other albums from the same artist.
- Construct an HTML page to display all the results.

To get this hack started, let's sketch out the overall flow of our script:

```perl
#!/usr/bin/perl -w
use strict;
use LWP::Simple;

# Settings for our Amazon developer account
our $amazon_affilate_id = "your affiliate ID, if any";
our $amazon_api_key     = "your amazon api key";

# Location of a FreeDB mirror web interface
our $freedb_url = 'http://freedb.freedb.org/~cddb/cddb.cgi';

# Get the discid of the current CD
my $discid = get_discid();

# Search for the CD details on FreeDB
my $cd_info = freedb_search($discid);

# Given the artist, look for music on Amazon
my @amazon_rec = amazon_music_search($cd_info->{artist});

# Try to match the FreeDB title up
# with Amazon to find current playing.
my $curr_rec = undef;
my @other_recs = ();
for my $rec (@amazon_rec) {
  if ( !defined $curr_rec && $cd_info->{title} eq $rec->{title} ) {
    $curr_rec = $rec;
  } else {
    push @other_recs, $rec;
  }
}

print html_template({current=>$curr_rec, others=>\@other_recs});
```

Note that we've set up a few overall configuration variables, such as our Amazon.com affiliate ID and a key for use with calls to the API. You'll want to check out the documentation for Amazon.com Web Services and sign up for a developer token. This allows Amazon.com to identify one consumer of their services from another. Now we have the overall flow of the script, so let's work out the implementation of the functions we're calling.

Checking Your Disc ID

The first part of our hack is a little tricky, and it depends a lot on your operating system. To perform a search on FreeDB, we first need to identify the current CD, and that requires access to the CD device itself. This is fairly easy to do under Linux and Mac OS X; other environments will require more homework.

For Linux and Mac OS X, we can use a small program called *cd-discid* (*http:// lly.org/~rcw/cd-discid/*). If you happen to be using Debian Linux, you can install the *cd-discid* package using *apt-get*. If you're on Mac OS X and have Fink (*http://fink.sourceforge.net*) installed, use fink install cd-discid. If neither of these things apply to you, don't worry, we can skip this step and use a hardcoded disc ID to see how the script works, at least.

Once the program is installed, we can use this function under Linux:

```
sub get_discid {
  # For Linux
  my $cd_discid = '/usr/local/bin/cd-discid';
  my $cd_dev    = '/dev/cdrom';
  return `$cd_discid $cd_dev`;
}
```

Basically, this calls the disc ID program using */dev/cdrom* as the device containing the audio CD to be identified. You might need to adjust the path to both the program and the CD device in this function.

If you're using Mac OS X, then this implementation should work for you:

```
sub get_discid {
  # For Mac OS X
  my $cd_discid = '/sw/bin/cd-discid';
  my ($cd_dev)  = '/dev/'.
    join '', map { /= "(.*?)"$/ }
      grep { /"BSD Name"/ }
        split(/\n/, `ioreg -w 0 -c IOCDMedia`);
  return `$cd_discid $cd_dev`;
}
```

This looks kind of tricky, but it uses a utility called *ioreg*, which lists I/O devices registered with the system. We check for devices in which CD media is currently inserted and do some filtering and scraping to discover the BSD Unix device name for the appropriate device. It's dirty, but it works well.

However, if none of this works for you (either because you're using a Windows machine, or else had installation problems with the source code), you can opt to use a canned disc ID in order to explore the rest of this hack:

```
sub get_discid {
    # If all else fails... use Weird Al's "Alapalooza"
    return "a60a840c+12 150 17795 37657 54225 72617 87907 106037 ".
        "125857 141985 164055 165660 185605 2694";
}
```

Digging Up the FreeDB Details

Once we have a disc ID, we can make a query against the FreeDB web service. From there, we should be able to get the name of the artist, as well as the album title and a list of track titles. Usage of the FreeDB web service is described at:

> *http://www.freedb.org/modules.
> php?name=Sections&sop=viewarticle&artid=28*

under Addendum B, "CDDBP under HTTP."

Let's start implementing the FreeDB search by making a call to the web service:

```
sub freedb_search {
    my $discid = shift;

    # Get the discid for the current
    # CD and make a FreeDB query with it.
    $discid =~ s/ /\+/;
    my $disc_query = get("$freedb_url?cmd=cddb+query+$discid&".
                        "hello=joe_random+www.asdf.com+freebot+2.1&proto=1");
    my ($code, $cat, $id, @rest) = split(/ /, $disc_query);
```

The first thing we do is escape the spaces in the disc ID for use in the URL used to request a query on the FreeDB web service. Then, we request the URL. In response to the request, we get a status code, along with a category and record ID. We can use this category and record ID to look up the details for our audio CD:

```
    # Using the results of the discid query, look up the CD's details.
    # Create a hash from the name/value pairs in the detail response.
    # (Note that we clean up EOF characters in the data.)
    my %freedb_data =
        map { s/\r//; /(.*)=(.*)/ }
            split(/\n/,
                get("$freedb_url?cmd=cddb+read+$cat+$id&".
                    "hello=deusx+www.decafbad.com+freebot+2.1&proto=1"));
```

The result of the FreeDB read request gives us a set of name/value pairs, one per line. So, we can split the result of the query by lines and use a regular expression on each to extract the name/value pairs and place them directly into a hash. However, as we receive it, the data is not quite as convenient to handle as it could be, so we can rearrange and restructure things before returning the results:

```perl
    # Rework the FreeDB result data into
    # a more easily handled structure.
    my %disc_info = ( );

    # Artist and title are separated by ' / ' in DTITLE.
    ($disc_info{artist}, $disc_info{title}) =
    split(/ \/ /, $freedb_data{DTITLE});

    # Extract series of tracks from
    # TTITLE0..TTITLEn; stop at
    # first empty title.
    my @tracks = ( );
    my $track_no = 0;
    while ($freedb_data{"TTITLE$track_no"}) {
      push @tracks, $freedb_data{"TTITLE$track_no"};
      $track_no++;
    }
    $disc_info{tracks} = \@tracks;

    return \%disc_info;
  }
```

With this, we convert a flat set of cumbersome name/value pairs into a more flexible Perl data structure. Artist name and album title are accessible via artist and title keys in the structure, respectively, and track names are available as an array reference under the tracks key.

Rocking with Amazon.com

The next thing our script needs is the ability to search Amazon.com for products by a given artist. Luckily, Amazon.com's Web Services produce clean XML, so it won't be too hard to extract what we need from the data, even without using a full XML parser.

But first, we'll need a couple of convenience functions added to our script:

```perl
    sub trim_space {
      my $val = shift;
      $val=~s/^\s+//;
      $val=~s/\s+$//g;
      return $val;
    }
```

```
sub clean_name {
  my $name = shift;
  $name=lc($name);
  $name=trim_space($name);
  $name=~s/[^a-z0-9 ]//g;
  $name=~s/ /_/g;
  return $name;
}
```

The first function trims whitespace from the ends of a string, and the second cleans up a string to ensure that it contains only lowercase alphanumeric characters and underscores. This last function is used to make fairly uniform hash keys in data structures.

Next, we can implement our Amazon.com Web Services (*http://www. amazon.com/gp/aws/landing.html*) searching code:

```
# Search for authors via the Amazon search API.
sub amazon_music_search {
  my ($artist) = @_;
  $artist =~ s/[^A-Za-z0-9 ]/ /;

  # Construct the base URL for Amazon author searches.
  my $base_url = "http://xml.amazon.com/onca/xml3?t=$amazon_affilate_id&".
    "dev-t=$amazon_api_key&mode=music&type=lite&f=xml".
      "&ArtistSearch=$artist";
```

The first thing we do is take the artist name as a parameter and try to clean up all characters that aren't alphanumeric or spaces. Then, we construct the URL to query the web service, as described in the documentation from the Amazon.com software development kit.

Next, we start to get the results of our search. Queries on Amazon.com's Web Services return results a handful at a time across several pages; so, if we want to gather all the results, we'll first need to figure out how many total pages there are. Luckily, this is a part of every page of results, so we can grab the first page and extract this information with a simple regular expression:

```
# Get the first page of search results.
my $content = get($base_url."&page=1");

# Find the total number of search results pages to be processed.
$content =~ m{<totalpages>(.*?)</totalpages>}mgis;
my ($totalpages) = ($1||'1');
```

After getting the total number of pages, we can start gathering the rest of the pages into an array, starting with the first page we have already downloaded. We can do this with a quick Perl expression that maps the page numbers to page requests, the results of which are added to the array.

Notice that we also sleep for a second in between requests, as per the instructions in the Amazon.com Web Services license:

```
# Grab all pages of search results.
my @search_pages = ($content);
if ($totalpages > 1) {
  push @search_pages,
      map { sleep(1); get($base_url."&page=$_") } (2..$totalpages);
}
```

Now that we have all the pages of the results, we can process them all and extract data for each album found. Details for each item are, appropriately enough, found as children of a tag named details. We can extract these children from each occurrence of the details tag using a regular expression. We can also grab the URL to the item detail page from an attribute named url:

```
# Extract data for all the records
# found in the search results.
my @records;
for my $content (@search_pages) {

  # Grab the content of all <details> tags
  while ($content ↵
      =~ m{<details(?!s) url="(.*?)".*?>(.*?)</details>}mgis) {
    # Extract the URL attribute and tag body content.
    my($url, $details_content) = ($1||'', $2||'');
```

After extracting the child tags for a detail record, we can build a Perl hash from child tag names and their content values, using another relatively simple regular expression and our convenience functions:

```
# Extract all the tags from the detail record, using
# tag name as hash key and tag contents as value.
my %record = (_type=>'amazon', url=>$url);
while ($details_content =~ m{<(.*?)>(.*?)</\1>}mgis) {
  my ($name, $val) = ($1||'', $2||'');
  $record{clean_name($name)} = $val;
}
```

However, not all of the child tags of details are flat tags. In particular, the names of artists for an album are child tags. So, with one more regular expression and a map function, we can further process these child tags into a list. We can also rename productname to title, for more intuitive use later:

```
# Further process the artists list to extract author
# names, and standardize on product name as title.
my $artists = $record{artists} || '';
$record{artists} =
   [ map { $_ } ( $artists =~ m{<artist>(.*?)</artist>}mgis ) ];
$record{title} = $record{productname};
```

```
    push @records, \%record;
  }
}
return @records;
}
```

So, with a few web requests and less than a handful of regular expressions, we can search for and harvest a pile of records on albums found at Amazon.com for a given artist.

Presenting the Results

At this point, we can identify a CD, look up its details in FreeDB, and search for albums at Amazon.com. The last thing our main program does is combine all these functions, determine which Amazon.com product is the current album, and feed it and the rest of the albums to a function to prepare an HTML page with the results.

Now, we can implement the construction of that page:

```
sub html_template {
  my $vars = shift;

  my $out = '';

  $out .= qq^
    <html>
      <head><title>Now Playing</title></head>
      <body>
        <div align="center">
          <h1>Now playing:</h1>
^;
  $out .= format_album($vars->{current}, 1);
  $out .= qq^
          <h1>Also by this artist:</h1>\n";
          <table border="1" cellspacing="0" cellpadding="8">
^;
```

This code begins an HTML page, using a function we'll implement in a minute, which produces a display of an album with title and cover art. Next, we can put together a table that shows the rest of the related albums from this artist. We create a table showing smaller cover art, with three columns per row:

```
my $col = 0;
my $row = '';
for my $rec (@{$vars->{others}}) {
  $row .= '<td align="center" width="33%">';
  $row .= format_album($rec, 0);
  $row .= "</td>\n";
  $col++;
```

```
    if (($col % 3) == 0) {
        $out .= "<tr>\n$row\n</tr>\n";
        $row = '';
    }
}
```

Finally, we close up the table and finish off the page:

```
$out .= qq^
        </table>
    </div>
  </body></html>
^;

    return $out;
}
```

The last thing we need is a function to prepare HTML to display an album:

```
sub format_album {
  my ($rec, $large) = @_;

  my $out = '';

  my $img = ($large) ? 'imageurllarge' : 'imageurlmedium';

  $out .= qq^<a href="$rec->{url}"><img src="$rec->{$img}"/></a><br/>^;
  $out .= qq^<b><a href="$rec->{url}">$rec->{title}</a></b><br />^;

  if (defined $rec->{releasedate}) {
    $out .= qq^Released: $rec->{releasedate}^;
  }

  if (ref($rec->{artists}) eq 'ARRAY') {
    $out .= '<br />by <b>'.join(', ', @{$rec->{artists}}).'</b>';
  }
}
```

This function produces several lines of HTML. The first line displays an album's cover art in one of two sizes, based on the second parameter. The second line displays the album's title, linked to its detail page at Amazon.com. The third line shows when the album was released, if we have this information, and the final line lists the artist who created the album.

Hacking the Hack

With this script and the help of FreeDB and Amazon.com, we can go from a CD in the tray to an HTML Now Playing display. This could be integrated into a CD player application and improved in any number of ways:

- The handful of regular expressions used to parse Amazon.com's XML are mostly adequate, but a proper XML parser, like *XML::Simple*, would be better.

- Errors and unidentified CDs are not handled very well.

- Other web services could be pulled in to further use the harvested CD data.

Maybe someday, something like this could be enhanced with the ability to automatically purchase and download music from an online store, to grab albums you don't yet have in order to expand your jukebox even further. Powerful things happen when one simple tool can be easily chained to another.

—l.m.orchard

Expanding Your Musical Tastes

#60 Looking for new music to complement your stale collection? With this script, you'll be able to pass some names of your favorite artists, and get Audioscrobbler recommendations.

You've downloaded every album by your favorite artist, even the B-sides. Maybe your playlist of 3,000 songs is starting to get stale. For whatever reason, you've decided it is time to find new music to fall in love with. Downloading songs off Limewire (*http://www.limewire.com*) with "GET THIS" in the filename, only to find out it's the ramblings of a broken bagpipe, is hit or miss at best. Wouldn't it be great to see what other people, who tend to like the same music you do, are listening to?

Audioscrobbler (*http://www.audioscrobbler.com*) has a great solution: it accepts playlist information from its users about what they listen to and how often. From there, Audioscrobbler associates artists with each other based on how often users listen to them. We are going to use a script to access the Audioscrobbler web site and retrieve a list of artists with a correlation factor—how closely related that artist is to the artists you submit.

First of all, we need to find the traditional way this is done at the Audioscrobbler web site. A quick check of the site reveals a Related Artists link that takes you to a form where you can type in three artists and get a listing of matches. Since this is exactly what we need, let's take a look at the code that runs the form. Looking at the HTML source, you can see the HTML code for the form at the bottom of the code. It's a GET request with some predefined variables and our three input boxes, named a1, a2, and a3. If you go back to the page, fill in some artists, and click Do It, you'll get a page with the results. Take a second to look at the URL for the page. The first thing to notice is that it is quite long; this is where the GET request parameter for the form comes in, because a GET request means that all the information for the page will be submitted within the URL. Using this knowledge, we can now construct our own URLs with the artists' names in them to retrieve the results.

Once we have the results, we need to figure out how to get the data we need. Back to the HTML source. This time, again near the bottom, we find a single, extremely long line of HTML. Searching through it, you can see there is a simple format: a link for the artist's name, td tags, and two img tags. We'll use the width attribute for the second img tag to find the correlation. It just so happens that the width value is always a number between 1 and 300; this value determines the length of the pretty image on the page to the right of each artist.

The Code

Save the following code to a file called *audioscrobble.pl*:

```perl
#!/usr/bin/perl -w
#
# AudioScrobble - Finds artists similar to those you already like.
# Comments, suggestions, contempt? Email adam@bregenzer.net.
#
# This code is free software; you can redistribute it and/or
# modify it under the same terms as Perl itself.
#

use strict; $|++;
my $VERSION = "1.0";

# make sure we have the modules we need, else die peacefully.
eval("use LWP 5.6.9;"); die "[err] LWP 5.6.9 or greater required.\n" if $@;

# base URL for all requests
my $base_url = "http://www.audioscrobbler.com/modules.php?".
               "op=modload&name=top10&file=scrobblersets";

my $counter = 0;          # counter of artists displayed
my $max_count = 10;       # maximum number of artists to display
my ($a1, $a2, $a3) = '';  # artist input variables

# Reminder: this code checks for arguments, therefore if a band
# name has multiple words make sure you put it in quotes.
# Also, Audioscrobbler accepts at most three band names so we
# will only look at the first three arguments.
$a1 = $ARGV[0] || die "No artists passed!\n";
$a2 = $ARGV[1] || ""; $a3 = $ARGV[2] || "";

# create a downloader, faking the User-Agent to get past filters.
print "Retrieving data for your matches... ";
my $ua = LWP::UserAgent->new(agent => 'Mozilla/4.76 [en] (Win98; U)');
my $data = $ua->get("$base_url&a1=$a1&a2=$a2&a3=$a3")->content;
print "done.\n";
```

```
# print up a nice header.
print "Correlation\tArtist\n";
print "-" x 76, "\n";

# match on the URL before the artist's name through to
# the width of the bar image (to determine correlation).
while ($counter < $max_count && $data =~ /href="modules\.php\↵
?op=modload&name=top10&file=artistinfo&artist=[^"]+">([^<]+)<\/a>[^<]+<\↵
/td><td[^>]+><img[^>]+\/><img[^>]+width="([0-9]+)">(.*)/) {

    # print the correlation factor and the artist's name.
    printf "%1.2f", ($2 / 300); print "\t\t" . $1 . "\n";

    # continue with the
    # data that is left.
    $data = $3; $counter++;
}

if ($counter == 0) {print "No matches.\n";}
print "-" x 76, "\n";
```

Running the Hack

Invoke the script on the command line, passing it up to three artists you like. Make sure you put their names in quotes; you do not need to worry about capitalization. Audioscrobbler cannot handle more than three artists at a time; in fact, you might find that three artists is too many for it (i.e., you might not get any results). In such cases, try removing the last artist and running it again. It is also important to keep in mind that you will get better results if you list artists that are similar to each other. This is a proximity search, so listing a heavy metal, country, and classical artist in the same search is unlikely to return any results.

Appropriately prepared, venture forth into the world of new music and find your next favorite artists. Here is an example in which I find artists similar to Aphex Twin and Autechre:

```
% perl audioscrobble.pl "Aphex Twin" "Autechre"
Retrieving data for your matches... done.
Correlation    Artist
-------------------------------------------------------------------------
1.00           Boards Of Canada
1.00           Plaid
0.83           Underworld
0.83           Radiohead
0.83           Chemical Brothers
0.83           Orbital
0.67           Mu-Ziq
0.67           Led Zeppelin
0.67           AFX
0.67           Squarepusher
```

Hacking the Hack

There are a few ways you can improve upon this hack.

Changing the number of results returned. You can easily change the number of results by changing the hardcoded $max_count value to a different number. However, we are looking for something more elegant. If you add the following code above the comment that starts with #Reminder, you will be able to pass an argument to the script specifying the number of results to return:

```
# Check for a '-c' argument first
# specifying the number of
# results to return.
if ($ARGV[0] =~ /-c/) {
    shift @ARGV;
    $max_count = shift @ARGV;
}
```

And here is the requisite sample output:

```
% perl audioscrobble.pl -c 5 "Aphex Twin" "Autechre"
Retrieving data...done.
Correlation     Artist
--------------------------------------------------------------------
1.00            Boards Of Canada
1.00            Plaid
0.83            Underworld
0.83            Radiohead
0.83            Chemical Brothers
```

If you plan on adding a number of command-line arguments, you might want to use a Perl module designed for the job: *Getopt::Long*. You can find various examples of its use within other hacks in this book.

Looking up artists. Now that you have a list of new artists, the next step is to have the script research these new artists and download sample songs, customer ratings, and so on. Code away, young grasshopper.

See Also

- There are other sites available that aggregate and associate artist playlists, the most promising of late being EchoCloud [Hack #20]. As opposed to Audioscrobbler, which is an opt-in service, EchoCloud works by spidering P2P networks, such as Soulseek, for relevant information.

—Adam Bregenzer

Saving Daily Horoscopes to Your iPod

You've got a zillion songs on your new iPod, and you're traveling around town oblivious to the sounds of the city. Worried about getting hit by a car, finding that special someone, or knowing when to ask for that raise? Take your horoscope along with you by running this hack daily.

With Apple's newest iPods, the functionality you can bring along with you has greatly improved. Not only can you sync up your iCal calendars or Address Book entries, you can also include little snippets of text in the new Notes feature. Limited to 4 KB per note and 1,000 notes, there's certainly room for improvement, but the ability to add your own navigational elements (either to other Notes or to songs and playlists) and paragraph styling (via HTML's <P> and <BR> tags) is a good start for some interesting applications.

This isn't to say that this hack is particularly interesting or useful, but it does give an example of programmatically determining the path to the currently mounted iPod via Perl. It's not foolproof, though; if you're rich enough to have more than one iPod mounted at the same time, then one will be chosen at random. Dealing with more than one iPod is an exercise you can pay someone else to do.

The Code

Save the following code to a file called *horopod.pl*:

```perl
#!/usr/bin/perl -w
#
# HoroPod - save your daily horoscope to the iPod.
# http://disobey.com/d/code/ or contact morbus@disobey.com.
#
# This code is free software; you can redistribute it and/or
# modify it under the same terms as Perl itself.
#

use strict; $|++;
my $VERSION = "1.0";
use File::Spec::Functions;

# make sure we have the modules we need, else die peacefully.
eval("use LWP;"); die "[err] LWP is not installed.\n" if $@;

# really cheap Perl-only way of finding the path to
# the currently mounted iPod. searches the mounted
# Volumes for an iPod_Control folder and uses that.
my $ipod = glob("/Volumes/*/iPod_Control");
unless ($ipod) { die "[err] Could not find an iPod: $!\n"; }
```

```perl
$ipod =~ s/iPod_Control//g;  # we want one directory higher.
my $ipod_dir = catdir($ipod, "Notes", "Horoscopes");
mkdir $ipod_dir;  # no error checking by intention.

# create a downloader, faking the User-Agent to get past filters.
my $ua = LWP::UserAgent->new(agent => 'Mozilla/4.76 [en] (Win98; U)');

# now, load up our horoscopes. first, define all the
# signs - these are used throughout the forloop.
my @signs = qw( aries taurus gemini cancer leo virgo libra
                scorpio sagittarius capricorn aquarius pisces );

# loop through each sign.
foreach my $sign (@signs) {

    # make it purdier for humans.
    my $display_sign = ucfirst($sign);

    # the Yahoo! URL, specific to the current sign.
    print "Grabbing horoscope for $display_sign...\n";
    my $url = "http://astrology.yahoo.com/us/astrology/".
              "today/$sign"."dailyhoroscope.html";

    # suck down the data or die.
    my $data = $ua->get($url)->content
      or die "[err] Could not download any data: $!\n";

    # snag the date by signature, not design.
    $data =~ /(\w{3} \w{3}\.? \d{1,2}, \d{4})/; my $date = $1;

    # and get the relevance. we could use an
    # HTML parser, but this is mindlessly easier.
    my $preface = '<font face="Arial" size="-1" color=black>';
    my $anteface = '</font></TD></TR></table>'; # ante up!
    $data =~ /$preface(.*)$anteface/i; my $proverb = $1;

    # save this proverb to our file.
    my $ipod_file = catfile($ipod_dir, $display_sign);
    open(IPOD_FILE, ">$ipod_file") or die "[err] Could not open file: $!\n";
    print IPOD_FILE "$display_sign\n$date\n\n";
    print IPOD_FILE "$proverb\n"; close(IPOD_FILE);

}
```

Running the Hack

To run the hack, make sure your iPod is mounted as a FireWire HD (i.e., you can see it on your Desktop when it's plugged into your Mac or docking bay), launch the Terminal application (Applications → Utilities → Terminal), and type perl horopod.pl on the command line. After a few lines of output, your newly scraped horoscopes should be on your iPod as a *Horoscopes* folder under the Notes feature. They'll be one file—or note—per sign.

Hacking the Hack

There are a few ways you can tweak the script, all mindlessly simple. For one, you might not want your horoscopes under a directory called *Horoscopes*; to change that behavior, merely tweak my `$ipod_dir = catdir($ipod, "Notes", "Horoscopes");` to your desired path.

Concerning the source data itself, Yahoo! Horoscopes has a number of different sorts of predictions available; you can get them tweaked to Music, Movies, Romance, and what have you. Be sure to check out *http://astrology.yahoo.com/* to find your desired version. When tweaking the script to support another type, you'll want to tweak the URL being used, making sure to place $sign where appropriate:

```
my $url = "http://astrology.yahoo.com/us/astrology/".
          "today/$sign"."dailyhoroscope.html";
```

Also, tweak the $preface and $anteface of the code surrounding the actual fortune:

```
my $preface = '<font face="Arial" size="-1" color=black>';
my $anteface = '</font></TD></TR></table>'; # ante up!
```

Alternatively, you could scrap the entire horoscope feature and combine in another of the data scrubbers within this book, utilizing only the iPod-related code in this hack.

See Also

- VersionTracker (*http://www.versiontracker.com*) for other iPod utilities, including Pod2Go (for weather, stocks, and more); PodNotes (for the latest news and driving directions); and VoodooPad (for Wiki-like Notes editing).

H A C K

#62

Graphing Data with RRDTOOL

Graphing data over time, either by itself or in comparison with another dataset, is the Holy Grail of analytical research. With the use of RRDTOOL, you'll be able to store and display time-series data.

In this hack, we're going to get some example data from Amazon.com and use the Round Robin Database Tool (RRDTOOL, *http://people.ee.ethz.ch/~oetiker/webtools/rrdtool/*) to graph changes in Amazon.com Sales Rank over time.

Round robin is a way of storing a fixed amount of data and a pointer to the current element. This is much like a cyclic buffer with a fixed number of slots for data, where adding a new element pushes out the oldest to make space. This is a nice feature, because you never have to worry about using all your disk space or clearing out old data. The downside is that you have to decide the time period up front. This hack assumes you have RRDTOOL installed as per the online instructions.

First, let's create a database to log an Amazon.com Sales Rank for a month:

```
% rrdtool create salesrank.rrd --start 1057241523  --step 86400
  DS:rank:GAUGE:86400:1:U  RRA:AVERAGE:0.5:1:31  RRA:AVERAGE:0.5:7:10
```

We have now created a database called *salesrank.rrd*, starting when this was written, adding new data every 24 hours, and keeping two round robin datasets. There are numerous settings when creating a database, many more than we can hope to explain here. To give you a feel for it, we'll just briefly explain the settings we used in this hack:

--start 1057241523 --step 86400

> Defines when the time series starts, using Unix timestamps. Executing date +%s gives you the current time in the necessary format (number of seconds since the Epoch). Setting the number to 86400 for step defines the time in seconds between our data points. We arrive at that number with the following equation: $24 \times 60 \times 60 = 86400$—or, 24 hours of 60 minutes each and each minute containing 60 seconds. In this case, we're graphing one bit of data per day, every day, starting now.

DS:rank:GAUGE:86400:1:U

> DS defines a dataset, rank is the name, and GAUGE is used when we're more interested in the absolute number than a percentage change. We set the scale to begin with 1, because we know that the highest Sales Rank is 1. We set the upper limit of the scale to unlimited (U), because we don't know how many products Amazon.com has; therefore, we can't know how badly ranked our book will be, and thus the need for unlimited.

RRA:AVERAGE:0.5:1:31
RRA:AVERAGE:0.5:7:10

> Here, we define our two round robin databases, the first keeping daily numbers and running for a total of 31 days, the second running weekly numbers (7 days) for a total of 10 weeks.

Now that we have the database created, it is time to start filling in some numbers by using the *rrdtool* update command:

```
% rrdtool update salesrank.rrd 1057241524:3689
% rrdtool update salesrank.rrd 1057327924:3629
...etc...
% rrdtool update salesrank.rrd 1059833523:2900
```

The numbers are in the format of *timestamp:value*, which, in this case, indicates a Sales Rank of 3689 for the first entry and 3629 for the next entry 24 hours later. The rule is that every update should be at least one second after the previous entry. With a total of 31 data points (not all are shown in the example), we now have something to display. To get textual results, we can use the fetch feature of *rrdtool*:

```
% rrdtool fetch salesrank.rrd AVERAGE --start 1057241524 --end 1059833524
1057190400: nan
1057276800: 3.6290017008e+03
1057363200: 3.6094016667e+03
...etc...
```

It's not very pretty to look at, but it's essentially the same as when we entered the data with *timestamp:value*. These are calculated numbers, so they are not exactly the same as those we entered. But (finally!) on to where this whole hack started: drawing graphs based on time-series data:

```
% rrdtool graph osxhacks.png --start 1057241524 --end 1059833524
  --imgformat PNG --units-exponent 0 DEF:myrank=salesrank.rrd:rank:AVERAGE
  LINE1:myrank#FF0000:"Mac OS X Hacks"
```

This code produces the graph shown in Figure 4-5.

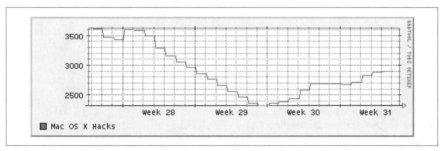

Figure 4-5. Graph of the Amazon.com Sales Rank for Mac OS X Hacks

There's an almost never-ending list of settings when displaying the graphs, which would be impossible to cover here. Most notable in our previous command is that we get the rank parameter out of our database and graph it in red with the legend "Mac OS X Hacks." Other than that, we ask for files in PNG format and tell the graph not to do any scaling on the y-axis.

Doing this by hand on a regular basis would be incredibly tedious at best. *cron* and Perl to the rescue! First, we'll create a Perl script that sucks down the Amazon.com product we're interested in, and then we'll capture the Sales Rank with a simple regular expression. This captured data, as well as the current timestamp, will be used to update our RRDTOOL database, and a new graph will be created.

The Code

Save the following code in a file called *grabrank.pl*:

```perl
#!/usr/bin/perl -w
#
# grabrank.pl
#
# This code is free software; you can redistribute it and/or
# modify it under the same terms as perl
#

use strict;
use LWP::Simple;
my $time=time();

# path to our local RRDTOOL.
my $rrd = '/usr/local/bin/rrdtool';

# Get the Amazon.com page for Mac OS X Hacks
my $data = get("http://www.amazon.com/exec/obidos/ASIN/0596004605/");
$data =~ /Amazon.com Sales Rank: <\/b> (.*) <\/span><br>/;
my $salesrank=$1; # and now the sales rank is ours! Muahh!

# Get rid of commas.
$salesrank =~ s/,//g;

# Update our rrdtool database.
`$rrd update salesrank.rrd $time:$salesrank`;

# Update our graph.
my $cmd= "$rrd graph osxhacks.png --imgformat PNG --units-exponent ".
        "0 DEF:myrank=salesrank.rrd:rank:AVERAGE LINE1:myrank#FF0000:".
        "'Mac OS X Hacks' --start ".($time-31*86400)." --end $time";
`$cmd`; # bazam! we're done.
```

Running the Hack

First, we need a *cron* job [Hack #90] to run this script once every day. On some systems, you can simply place the script in */etc/cron.daily*. If you don't have that option, then add something like this to your *crontab* file, which will tell *cron* to run our script every night at five minutes after midnight:

```
5 0 * * *       /path/to/your/grabrank.pl
```

Hacking the Hack

The graphs are not exactly pretty, so there are many possible improvements to be made, playing with intervals, colors, and so forth. If you look at the graph, you'll see that the way it is displayed is somewhat counterintuitive, because a low figure is a sign of a higher ranking. If we knew the exact Sales

Rank of the worst-selling item at Amazon.com in advance, then we could simply subtract the rank of the day from that and create a graph that rose with a higher ranking. Not having the right numbers, it's going to take a few more calculations.

If you want to graph more than one Sales Rank, there's not much to change, other than defining an extra data source when creating the database:

```
DS:otherrank:GAUGE:86400:1:U
```

And remember to add an extra `DEF` and `LINE1` to the *rrdtool* graph command:

```
DEF:myotherrank=salesrank.rrd:rank:AVERAGE
LINE1:myotherrank#11EE11:"My other book"
```

Grabbing the extra data from Amazon.com is left as an exercise for the reader.

—*Mads Toftum*

HACK #63 Stocking Up on Financial Quotes

Keeping track of multiple stocks can be a cumbersome task, but using the Finance::Quote Perl module can greatly simplify it. And, while we're at it, we'll generate pretty graphs with RRDTOOL.

Collecting stock prices can be done using *LWP* [Hack #9] to download a financial site and regular expressions [Hack #23] to scrape the data, as well as always keeping a watchful eye for site design changes that could break things. But why go to the trouble when *Finance::Quote* (*http://search.cpan.org/author/ PJF/Finance-Quote/*) provides a simple interface with numerous sources, such as Fidelity Investments, Trustnet, The Motley Fool, or Yahoo!?

Here's a typical bit of code that uses *Finance::Quote* to fetch stock prices:

```
#!/usr/bin/perl
use Finance::Quote;
my $q = Finance::Quote->new;
my $quotes = $q->fetch("nasdaq","IBM");
print "Price range: $quotes->{'IBM','year_range'}\n";
```

We create a new *Finance::Quote* object and fetch data with `$q-> fetch($market,@stocks)`. In this case, we let the market point to `nasdaq`. Though `@stocks` is normally a list of desired stocks, we use just one (`IBM`). To get at the information that the module has grabbed for us, we use `$quotes-> {'IBM','year_range'}`, which will get us the price range for the last 52 weeks:

```
% perl finance.pl
Price range: 54.01 - 90.404
```

There is much more information in addition to year_range; consult the
Finance::Quote documentation for further explanation and details on which
information is available from which sources. When in doubt, you can get a
complete list of the available values by printing the returned $quotes
structure:

```
use Data::Dumper;
print Dumper($quotes);
```

Adding these two lines to the previous code produces the following output:

```
$VAR1 = {
            'IBM{avg_vol' => 7264727,
            'IBM{div' => '0.64',
            'IBM{ask' => undef,
            'IBM{date' => '7/22/2003',
            'IBM{method' => 'yahoo',
            'IBM{div_yield' => '0.78',
            'IBM{low' => '81.65',
            'IBM{symbol' => 'IBM',
            'IBM{cap' => '141.2B',
            'IBM{day_range' => '81.65 - 83.06',
            'IBM{open' => '82.50',
            'IBM{bid' => undef,
            'IBM{eps' => '3.86',
            'IBM{time' => '1:40pm',
            'IBM{currency' => 'USD',
            'IBM{success' => 1,
            'IBM{volume' => 6055000,
            'IBM{last' => '81.70',
            'IBM{year_range' => '54.01 - 90.404',
            'IBM{close' => '82.50',
            'IBM{high' => '83.06',
            'IBM{net' => '-0.80',
            'IBM{p_change' => '-0.97',
            'IBM{ex_div' => 'May  7',
            'IBM{price' => '81.70',
            'IBM{pe' => '21.37',
            'IBM{name' => 'INTL BUS MACHINE',
            'IBM{div_date' => 'Jun 10'
        };
```

The first part of the variable name (IBM, in this case) is the stock symbol, the
second part is a delimiter of some kind, and the third is the name of the data
being referred to. The information we printed in our first code sample is
emphasized in the preceding output as a guide.

We have the data; now it's time to start plotting it into a graph. As in
"Graphing Data with RRDTOOL" [Hack #62] we use RRDTOOL (*http://people.
ee.ethz.ch/~oetiker/webtools/rrdtool/*) to plot our data, but this time we will
use a Perl interface. RRDTOOL has two Perl interfaces, but we will use the

"Shared RRD module" only, as it is the most flexible of the two. The Perl interface will be very familiar to those who know the command-line interface.

To add data to *stocks.rrd*, for example, we would normally run this command:

```
% rrdtool update stocks.rrd N:12345
```

Using the Perl interface, all we have to do is call RRDs::update, like this:

```
use RRDs;
RRDs::update ("stocks.rrd","N:12345");
```

Similarly, RRDs::create, RRD::graph, and others all work like their command-line counterparts. More information on the Perl bindings are available within the supplied RRDTOOL documentation.

Putting it all together in a Perl script, we use a "does this database exist?" check to see whether we should create a new database or update an existing one. Then, we get new stock figures using *Finance::Quote* and add them to our database using RRDs::update. To create graphs, we run once with RRDs::graph and --start -1w to create a graph for the last week, and once with -1m to graph the entire last month.

The Code

Save the following code in a file called *grabstocks.pl*:

```perl
#!/usr/bin/perl -w
use strict; use RRDs;
use Finance::Quote qw/asx/;

# Declare basic variables.
my @stocks       = ('IBM','MSFT','LNUX');
my @stock_prices = (0,0,0);
my $workdir      = "./stocks";
my $db           = "$workdir/stocks.rrd";
my $now          = time();

# if the database hasn't been created,
# do so now, or die with an error.
if (!-f $db) {
    RRDs::create ($db, "--start", $now-1,
            "DS:IBM:ABSOLUTE:900:0:U",
            "DS:MSFT:ABSOLUTE:900:0:U",
            "DS:LNUX:ABSOLUTE:900:0:U",
            "RRA:AVERAGE:0.5:1:4800",
            "RRA:AVERAGE:0.5:4:4800",
            "RRA:AVERAGE:0.5:24:3000",
    );
```

```
        if (my $ERROR = RRDs::error) { die "$ERROR\n"; }
    }

    # now, get the quote information
    # for IBM, Microsoft, and Linux.
    my $q       = Finance::Quote->new( );
    my %quotes = $q->fetch("usa",@stocks);

    # for each of our stocks, check to
    # see if we got data, and if so,
    # add it to our stock prices.
    foreach my $code (@stocks) {
        my $count = 0; # array index.
        unless ($quote{$code, "success"}) {
            warn "$code lookup failed: ".$quote{$code,"errormsg"}."\n";
            $count++; next; # well, that's not a good sign.
        }

        # update the stock price, and move to the next.
        $stock_prices[$count] = $quote{$code,'last'}; $count++;
    }

    # we have our stock prices; update our database.
    RRDs::update($db, "--template=" . join(':',@stocks),
                      "$now:" . join(':',@stock_prices));
    if (my $ERROR = RRDs::error) { die "$ERROR\n"; }

    # Generate weekly graph.
    RRDs::graph("$workdir/stocks-weekly.png",
      "--title",      'Finance::Quote example',
      "--start",      "-1w",
      "--end",        $now+60,
      "--imgformat", "PNG",
      "--interlace", "--width=450",
      "DEF:ibm=$db:IBM:AVERAGE",
      "DEF:msft=$db:MSFT:AVERAGE",
      "DEF:lnux=$db:LNUX:AVERAGE",
      "LINE1:ibm#ff4400:ibm\\c",
      "LINE1:msft#11EE11:msft\\c",
      "LINE1:lnux#FF0000:lnux\\c"
    ); if (my $ERROR = RRDs::error) { die "$ERROR\n"; }

    # Generate monthly graph.
    RRDs::graph ("$workdir/stocks-weekly.png",
      "--title",      'Finance::Quote example',
      "--start",      "-1m",
      "--end",        $now+60,
      "--imgformat", "PNG",
      "--interlace", "--width=450",
      "DEF:ibm=$db:IBM:AVERAGE",
      "DEF:msft=$db:MSFT:AVERAGE",
      "DEF:lnux=$db:LNUX:AVERAGE",
      "LINE1:ibm#ff4400:ibm\\c",
```

```
    "LINE1:msft#11EE11:msft\\c",
    "LINE1:lnux#FF0000:lnux\\c"
); if (my $ERROR = RRDs::error) { die "$ERROR\n"; }
```

Running the Hack

First, we need a *cron* job [Hack #90] to run this script once every 15 minutes. To do that, add something like this to your *crontab*, telling *cron* to run our script four times every hour:

```
*/4 * * * Mon-Fri /path/to/your/grabstocks.pl
```

With that in place, new graphs will be generated every time the script runs.

Hacking the Hack

The first and most obvious thing is to change the code to get more data for more interesting stocks. The periods chosen in this hack might also need some updating, since getting data every 15 minutes gives a much higher resolution than we need if we're interested in only monthly graphs. Likewise, running the script 24 hours a day doesn't make much sense if there will be stock changes only during business hours.

—*Mads Toftum*

<h2>HACK
#64 Super Author Searching</h2>

By combining multiple sites into one powerful script, you can get aggregated data results that are more complete than just one site could give.

Have you ever obsessively tried to find everything written by a favorite author? Have you ever wanted to, but never found the time? Or have you never really wanted to, but think it would be neat to search across several web sites at once? Well, here's your chance.

To search for authors, let's pick a few book-related sites, such as the Library of Congress (*http://www.loc.gov*), Project Gutenberg (*http://promo.net/pg/*), and Amazon.com (*http://www.amazon.com*). Between these three web sites, we should be able to get a wide range of works by an author. Some will be for sale, some will be available for free download, and others will be available at a library (or the Library of Congress, at least).

Gathering Tools

Before we do anything else, let's get some tools together. We're going to use Perl for this hack, with the following modules: *LWP::Simple* [Hack #9], *WWW::RobotRules*, *WWW::Mechanize* [Hack #21], and *HTML::Tree*. These modules give us the means to navigate sites and grab content to find and extract data

from, all while trying to be a good little robot that follows the rules
("Respecting robots.txt" [Hack #17] offers guidance on using *LWP::RobotsUA*
to accomplish the same thing). It might seem like unnecessary effort, but
taking a few extra steps to obey the Robots Exclusion Protocol (*http://www.
robotstxt.org*) can go a long way in keeping us from trouble or losing access
to the resources we want to gather.

Our script starts like so:

```perl
#!/usr/bin/perl-w
use strict;
use Data::Dumper qw(Dumper);

use LWP::Simple;
use WWW::RobotRules;
use WWW::Mechanize;
use HTML::Tree;

our $rules = WWW::RobotRules->new('AuthorSearchSpider/1.0');
our $amazon_affilate_id = "your affiliate ID here";
our $amazon_api_key     = "your key here";

my $author = $ARGV[0] || 'dumas, alexandre';

my @book_records = sort {$a->{title} cmp $b->{title}}
  (amazon_search($author), loc_gov_search($author), pg_search($author));

our %item_formats =
  (
   default => \&default_format,
   amazon  => \&amazon_format,
   loc     => \&loc_format,
   pg      => \&pg_format
  );

print html_wrapper($author,
                   join("\n", map { format_item($_) } @book_records));
```

So, here's the basic structure of our script. We set up a few global resources,
such as a way to mind rules of robot spiders and a way to access Amazon.com
Web Services. Next, we attempt to get aggregate results of searches on several web sites and sort the records by title. Once we have those, we set up formatting for each type of result and produce an HTML page of the results.

Whew! Now, let's implement all the subroutines that enable all these steps.
First, in order to make a few things easier later on, we're going to set up our
robot rules handler and write a few convenience functions to use the handler and clean up bits of data we'll be extracting:

```perl
# Get web content,
# obeying robots.txt
```

```
sub get_content {
  my $url = shift;
  return ($rules->allowed($url)) ? get($url) : undef;
}

# Get web content via WWW::
# Mechanize, obeying robots.txt
sub get_mech {
  my $url = shift;
  if ($rules->allowed($url)) {
    my $a = WWW::Mechanize->new( );
    $a->get($url);
    return $a;
  } else { return undef }
}

# Remove whitespace from
# both ends of a string
sub trim_space {
  my $val = shift;
  $val=~s/^\s+//;
  $val=~s/\s+$//g;
  return $val;
}

# Clean up a string to be used
# as a field name of alphanumeric
# characters and underscores.
sub clean_name {
  my $name = shift;
  $name=lc($name);
  $name=trim_space($name);
  $name=~s/[^a-z0-9 ]//g;
  $name=~s/ /_/g;
  return $name;
}
```

Now that we have a start on a toolbox, let's work on searching. The idea is to build a list of results from each of our sources that can be mixed together and presented as a unified whole.

Hacking the Library of Congress

Now, let's visit the library. Right on the front page, we see a link inviting visitors to Search Our Catalogs, which leads us to a choice between a Basic Search and a Guided Search. For simplicity's sake, we'll follow the basic route.

This brings us to a simple-looking form (*http://catalog.loc.gov/cgi-bin/ Pwebrecon.cgi?DB=local&PAGE=First*), with options for the search text, the type of search we want, and the number of records per page. Using *WWW::Mechanize*, we can start our subroutine to use this form like this:

```
sub loc_gov_search {
  my $author = shift;

  # Submit search for author's name
  my $url = 'http://catalog.loc.gov/cgi-bin/Pwebrecon.
cgi?DB=local&PAGE=First';
  my $a = get_mech($url);
  $a->submit_form
    (
      form_number => 1,
      fields => { Search_Arg=>$author, Search_Code=>'NAME_', CNT=>70}
    );
```

The first result of this search is a list of links with which to further refine our author search. So, let's try looking for links that contain the closest match to our author name:

```
  # Data structure for book data records
  my @hit_links = grep { $_->text() =~ /$author/i } $a->links();
  my @book_records = ();
  for my $hit_link (@hit_links) {
    my $a = get_mech
      ('http://catalog.loc.gov/cgi-bin/Pwebrecon.cgi?DB=local&PAGE=First');
    $a->submit_form
      (
        form_number => 1,
        fields => { Search_Arg=>$author, Search_Code=>'NAME_', CNT=>70}
      );
    $a->follow_link(text=>$hit_link->text());
```

This particular bit of code uses the link-extraction feature of *WWW::Mechanize* to grab link tags from the initial search results page to which we just navigated. Due to some quirk in session management in the Library of Congress search, we need to start over from the search results page, rather than simply use the back function.

Once we have each secondary author page of the search, we can extract links to publications from these pages:

```
    # Build a tree from the HTML
    my $tree = HTML::TreeBuilder->new();
    $tree->parse($a->content());

    # Find the search results table: first, look for a header
    # cell containing "#", then look for the parent table tag.
    my $curr;
    ($curr) = $tree->look_down
      (_tag => 'th', sub { $_[0]->as_text() eq '#' } );
    next if !$curr;
    ($curr) = $curr->look_up(_tag => 'table');
```

```
my ($head, @rows) = $curr->look_down
    (_tag => 'tr', sub { $_[0]->parent() == $curr } );
```

This code uses the *HTML::Tree* package to navigate the structure of the HTML content that makes up the search hits page. Looking at this page, we see that the actual table listing the search hits starts with a table header containing the text "#". If we look for this text, then walk back up to the containing parent, we can then extract the table's rows to get the search hits.

Once we have the rows that contain links to details pages, let's process them:

```
# Extract and process the search
# results from the results table.
my @book_records = ( );
while (@rows) {

    # Take the results in row pairs; extract
    # the title and year cells from the first row.
    my ($r1, $r2) = (shift @rows, shift @rows);
    my (undef, undef, undef, undef, $td_title, $td_year, undef) =
        $r1->look_down(_tag => 'td', sub { $_[0]->parent() == $r1 });

    # Get title link from the results; extract the detail URL.
    my ($a_title) = $td_title->look_down(_tag=>'a');
    my $title_url = "http://catalog.loc.gov".$a_title->attr("href");

    # Get the book detail page; follow the link to the Full record.
    $a->follow_link(url => $title_url);
    $a->follow_link(text => "Full");
```

Looking at this page, we see that each publication is listed as a pair of rows. The first row in each pair lists a few details of the publication, and the second row tells where to find the publication in the library. For our purposes, we're interested only in the title link in the first row, so we extract the cells of the first row of each pair and then extract the URL to the publication detail page from that.

From there, we follow the details link, which brings us to a brief description of the publication. But we're interested in more details than that, so on that details page we follow a link named "Full" to a more detailed list of information on a publication.

Finally, then, we've reached the full details page for a publication by our author. So, let's figure out how to extract the fields that describe this publication. Looking at the table, we see that the table starts with a header containing the string "LC Control Number". So, we look for that header, then backtrack to the table that contains it:

```
# Find table containing book detail data by looking
# for table containing a header with text "LC Control Number".
```

```
my $t2 = HTML::TreeBuilder->new( );
$t2->parse($a->content( ));
my ($c1) = $t2->look_down
  (_tag=>'th', sub { $_[0]->as_text( ) =~ /LC Control Number/ }) ||
    next;
$c1 = $c1->look_up(_tag=>"table");
```

After finding the table that contains the details of our publication, we can walk through the rows of the table and extract name/value pairs. First, we start building a record for this book by noting the type of the search, as well as the URL of the publication details page:

```
# Now that we have the table, look
# for the rows and extract book data.
my %book_record = (_type => 'loc', url=>$title_url);
my @trs = $c1->look_down(_tag=>"tr");
for my $tr (@trs[1..$#trs]) {

    # Grab the item name and value table
    # cells; skip to next if empty.
    my ($th_name)  = $tr->look_down(_tag=>"th");
    my ($td_value) = $tr->look_down(_tag=>"td");
    next if (!$th_name) || (!$td_value);

    # Get and clean up the item name and value
    # table data; skip to next if the name is empty.
    my $name  = clean_name($th_name->as_text( ));
    my $value = trim_space($td_value->as_text( ));
    next if ($name eq '');

    $book_record{$name} = $value;
}
```

Luckily, the table that contains information about our publication is fairly clean, with every name contained in a header cell and every value contained in a corresponding data cell in the same row. So, we walk through the rows of the details table, collecting data fields by using the convenience methods we wrote earlier.

Now, we can finish up our subroutine, doing a little cleanup on the publication title and adding the finished record to a list that we return when all our wandering through the library is done:

```
($book_record{title}, undef)
    = split(/ \//, $book_record{main_title});

push @book_records, \%book_record;

# Back up to the search results page.
$a->back( ); $a->back( );
```

```
    }
  }
  return @book_records;
}
```

To summarize, this subroutine does the following:

1. Performs an author search on the Library of Congress web site
2. Follows links to author search results pages
3. Follows publication details links on author search results pages
4. Digs further down to full-detail records on publications
5. Harvests data fields that describe a publication

In the end, by drilling down through several layers of search hits and details pages, we have collected a slew of records that describe publications by our author. These records are stored as a list of Perl hashes, each containing name/value pairs.

Each record also contains a value that indicates which source it was harvested from (i.e., _type=>'loc'). This will become important shortly, when we mix the results of other searches together.

Perusing Project Gutenberg

Next, let's take a look at Project Gutenberg (*http://promo.net/pg/*). In case you've never heard of it, this is an effort to make public-domain books and publications available to the public in formats usable by practically all personal computers available. In the Project Gutenberg library, you can find an amazing array of materials, so our author search could benefit from a stroll through their stacks.

Wandering around the project's site, we uncover a search form (*http://www.ibiblio.org/gutenberg/cgi-bin/sdb/t9.cgi/*). One of the fields in this form is Author, just what we need. Our search subroutine for this site begins like this:

```
# Search Project Gutenberg
# for books by an author
sub pg_search {
  my $author = shift;

  my $pg_base = 'http://www.ibiblio.org/gutenberg/cgi-bin/sdb';
  my @book_records = ( );

  # Submit an author search at Project Gutenberg
  my $a1 = get_mech("$pg_base/t9.cgi/");
  $a1->submit_form
```

```
(
  form_number => 1,
  fields => { author => $author }
);
```

As it turns out, this search results page is quite simple, with a link to every result contained in a list bullet tag. So, we can write a quick set of map expressions to find the bullets and the links within them, and extract the link URLs into a list:

```
# Extract all the book details
# pages from the search results
my $t1 = HTML::TreeBuilder->new( );
$t1->parse($a1->content( ));
my (@hit_urls) =
  map { "$pg_base/".$_->attr('href') }
    map { $_->look_down(_tag=>'a') }
      $t1->look_down(_tag=>'li');
```

Now that we have a list of links to publication details pages, let's chase each one down and collect the information for each book:

```
# Process each book detail
# page to extract book info
for my $url (@hit_urls) {
  my $t2 = HTML::TreeBuilder->new( );
  $t2->parse(get_content($url));
```

Luckily, these details pages also have a fairly simple and regular structure. So, we can quickly locate the table that contains the details by finding a table cell with the word download and backtrack to its parent table.

```
# Find the table of book data: look for a table
# cell containing 'download' and find its parent table.
my ($curr) = $t2->look_down
  (_tag=>"td",
    sub { $_[0]->as_text( ) =~ /download/i });
($curr) = $curr->look_up(_tag=>"table");
```

Most rows of this table contain name/value pairs in data cells, with the name of the pair surrounded by <tt> tags. The names also end in a colon, so we can add that for good measure:

```
# Find the names of book data items: look for
# all the <tt> tags in the table that contain ':'
my (@hdrs) = $curr->look_down
  (_tag=>'tt',
    sub { $_[0]->as_text( ) =~ /\:/});
```

After finding all the book details field names, we can visit each of them to dig out the values. For each tag that contains a name, we find its parent table row and grab the row's second column, which contains the value of the pair. So, we can start constructing a record for this book. Again, notice that we start out by identifying which source this search result was harvested from (i.e., _type=>'pg'):

```
# Extract name/value data from book details page.
my %book_record = (_type=>'pg', url=>$url);
for my $hdr (@hdrs) {

    # Name is text of <tt> tag.
    my $name = clean_name($hdr->as_text());
    next if ($name eq '');

    # Find the field value by finding the parent
    # table row, then the child table data cell.
    my ($c2) = $hdr->look_up(_tag=>'tr');
    (undef, $c2) = $c2->look_down(_tag=>'td');
```

Most values are simple strings, with the exception of the publication's download links. When we encounter this value, we go a step further and extract the URLs from those links. Otherwise, we just extract the text of the table data cell. Using what we've extracted, we build up the book record:

```
    # Extract the value. For most fields, simply use the text of the
    # table cell. For the download field, find the URLs of all links.
    my $value;
    if ($name eq 'download') {
      my (@links) = $c2->look_down
        (_tag=>"a",
         sub { $_[0]->as_text() =~ /(txt|zip)/} );
      $value = [ map { $_->attr('href') } @links ];
    } else {
      $value = $c2->as_text();
    }

    # Store the field name and value in the record.
    $book_record{$name} = $value;
  }
```

Finally, we store each book record in a list and return it from our subroutine:

```
    push @book_records, \%book_record;
  }
  return @book_records;
}
```

Although simpler, this search is similar to searching the Library of Congress:

1. Perform an author search on the Project Gutenberg web site.

2. Follow links in the search results to find publication details pages.

3. Harvest data fields that describe a publication.

And, like the Library of Congress search, we collect a list of Perl hashes that contain book details. Also, each record is tagged with the source of the search.

Navigating the Amazon

Our final search involves the online catalog at Amazon.com, via its Web Services API (*http://www.amazon.com/webservices*). This API allows developers and webmasters to integrate a wide range of the features of their sites into their own applications and content. But before we can do anything with Amazon.com's Web Services API, we need to sign up for a developer token. This allows Amazon.com to identify one consumer of its services from another. Once we have a token, we can get started using the API. First, we download the software development kit (SDK). In the documentation, we find that, among other services, the API offers simple XML-based author searches. So, we can use this service to build a search subroutine. Based on the SDK's instructions, we can start like this:

```
# Search for authors via
# the Amazon search API.
sub amazon_search {
  my $author = shift;

  # Construct the base URL for Amazon author searches.
  my $base_url = "http://xml.amazon.com/onca/xml3?t=$amazon_affilate_id&".
    "dev-t=$amazon_api_key&AuthorSearch=$author&".
      "mode=books&type=lite&f=xml";
```

The first step is to use the XML service to submit a search query for our author. One quirk in the otherwise simple service is that results are served up only a few at a time, across a number of pages. So, we'll grab the first page and extract the total number of pages that make up our search results:

```
# Get the first page of search results.
my $content = get_content($base_url."&page=1");

# Find the total number of search results pages to be processed.
$content =~ m{<totalpages>(.*?)</totalpages>}mgis;
my ($totalpages) = ($1||'1');
```

Note that, in this hack, we're going for a quick-and-dirty regular expression method for extracting information from XML. Normally, we'd want to use a proper XML parser, but this approach will work well enough to get this job done for now.

The next step, after getting the first page of search results and extracting the total number of pages, is to grab the rest of the pages for our search query. We can do this with another quick map expression in Perl to step through all the pages and store the content in a list.

One thing to note, however, is that we wait at least one second between grabbing results pages. The company may or may not enforce this restriction, but the license for using the Amazon.com Web Services API specifies that an application should make only one request per second. So, just as we make an effort to obey the Robots Exclusion Protocol, we should try to honor this as well.

Here's how we do it:

```
# Grab all pages of search results.
my @search_pages = ($content);
if ($totalpages > 1) {
  push @search_pages,
    map { sleep(1); get_content($base_url."&page=$_") } (2..$totalpages);
}
```

Now that we have the content of all the search pages, we can extract records on the publications, just as we have in the previous two search subroutines. The biggest difference in this case, however, is that XML content is so much easier to handle than HTML tag soup. In fact, we can use some relatively simple regular expressions to process this data:

```
# Extract data for all the books
# found in the search results.
my @book_records;
for my $content (@search_pages) {

  # Grab the content of all <details> tags.
  while ($content=~ m{<details(?!s) url="(.*?)".*?>(.*?)</details>}mgis) {

    # Extract the URL attribute and tag body content.
    my($url, $details_content) = ($1||'', $2||'');

    # Extract all the tags from the detail record, using
    # tag name as hash key and tag contents as value.
    my %book_record = (_type=>'amazon', url=>$url);
    while ($details_content =~ m{<(.*?)>(.*?)</\1>}mgis) {
      my ($name, $val) = ($1||'', $2||'');
      $book_record{clean_name($name)} = $val;
    }
```

This code uses regular expressions to extract the contents of XML tags, starting with the details tag. The search results pages contain sets of these tags, and each set contains tags that describe a publication. We use a regular expression that matches on opening and closing tags, extracting the tag name and tag data as the name and value for each field. The names of these tags are described in the SDK, but we'll just stuff them away in a book record for now.

Notice that this process is much simpler than walking through a tree built up from parsed HTML, looking for tag patterns. Things like this are usually simpler when an explicit service is provided for our use. So, we can apply a little last-minute processing—extracting lists of author subtags—finish up our book record, and wrap up our Amazon.com search subroutine:

```
# Further process the authors list to extract author
# names, and standardize on product name as title.
my $authors = $book_record{authors} || '';
$book_record{authors} =
    [ map { $_ } ( $authors =~ m{<author>(.*?)</author>}mgis ) ];
$book_record{title} = $book_record{productname};

push @book_records, \%book_record;
        }
    }

    return @book_records;
}
```

Compared to the previous two searches, this is the simplest of all. Since the XML provided by the Amazon.com search API is a well-defined and easily processed document, we don't have to do any of the searching and navigation that is needed to extract records from HTML.

And, like the Library of Congress search, we collect a list of Perl hashes that contain book details. Also, each record is tagged with the source of the search.

Presenting the Results

We now have three subroutines with which to search for an author's works. Each of them produces a similar set of results, as a list of Perl hashes that contain book details in name/value pairs. Although each site's result records contain different sets of data, there are a few fields common to all three subroutines: _type, title, and url.

We can use these common fields to sort by title and format the results differently for each type of record. Now, we can build the parts to make the aggregate search and result formatting that we put together toward the beginning of the script. Let's start with the wrapper HTML template:

```
sub html_wrapper {
  my ($author, $content) = @_;

  return qq^
    <html>
      <head><title>Search results for $author</title></head>
      <body>
        <h1>Search results for $author</h1>
        <ul>$content</ul>
      </body>
    </html>
    ^;
}
```

This is a simple subroutine that wraps a given bit of content with the makings of an HTML page. Next, let's check out the basics of item formatting:

```
sub format_item {
  my $item = shift;
  return "<li>".((defined $item_formats{$item->{_type}})
    ? $item_formats{$item->{_type}}->($item)
    : $item_formats{default}->($item))."</li>";
}

sub default_format {
  my $rec = shift;
  return qq^<a href="$rec->{url}">$rec->{title}</a>^;
}
```

The first subroutine, format_item, uses the hash table of routines built earlier to apply formatting to items. The second subroutine, default_format, provides a simple implementation of an item format. Before we fill out implementations for the other record types, let's build a quick convenience function:

```
sub field_layout {
  my ($rec, $fields) = @_;
  my $out = '';
  for (my $i=0; $i<scalar(@$fields); $i+=2) {
    my ($name, $val) = ($fields->[$i+1], $rec->{$fields->[$i]});
    next if !defined $val;
    $out .= qq^<tr><th align="right">$name:</th><td>$val</td></tr>^;
  }
  return $out;
}
```

This function takes a record and a list of fields and descriptions in order. It returns a string that contains a set of table rows, with descriptions paired with values. We'll use this in the rest of the formatters to build tables quickly.

First, we build a formatter for the Library of Congress search records. Basically, this is an incremental improvement over the default formatter. It identifies the source of this result and uses the field-layout function we just built to display a small set of common fields found in Library of Congress publication records:

```
sub loc_format {
  my $rec = shift;
  my $out = qq^[LoC] <a href="$rec->{url}">$rec->{title}</a><br /><br />^;
  $out .= qq^<table border="1" cellpadding="4" cellspacing="0" ↵
      width="50%">^;
  $out .= field_layout
    ($rec,
      [
        'publishedcreated'  => 'Published',
        'type_of_material'  => 'Type of material',
```

```
                'description'        => 'Description',
                'dewey_class_no'     => 'Dewey class no.',
                'call_number'        => 'Call number',
                'lc_classification'  => 'LoC classification',
                'lc_control_number'  => 'LoC control number',
                'isbn'               => 'ISBN',
            ]
        );
    $out .= "</table><br />";
    return $out;
  }
```

Next, we build a formatter for the Project Gutenberg records. This implementation doesn't display as many fields, but it has a special treatment of the download field in order to present the URLs as links:

```
sub pg_format {
  my $rec = shift;
  my $out = qq^[PG] <a href="$rec->{url}">$rec->{title}</a><br /><br />^;
  $out .= qq^<table border="1" cellpadding="4" cellspacing="0" ⏎
      width="50%">^;
  $out .= field_layout($rec, ['language' => 'Language']);
  $out .= qq^
    <tr><th align="right">Download:</th>
      <td>
  ^;
  for my $link (@{$rec->{download}}) {
    $out .= qq^<a href="$link">$link</a><br />^;
  }
  $out .= qq^</td></tr></table><br />^;
  return $out;
}
```

Finally, we build a formatter for the Amazon.com records, which has much in common with the Library of Congress record formatter. The biggest difference is that we've added the display of the publication's cover image that is available at Amazon.com:

```
sub amazon_format {
  my $rec = shift;
  my $out = qq^[Amazon] <a href="$rec->{url}">$rec->{title}</a>⏎
<br /><br />^;
  $out .= qq^
    <table border="1" cellpadding="4" cellspacing="0" width="50%">
      <tr><th align="center" colspan="2">
        <img src="$rec->{imageurlmedium}" />
      </th></tr>
  ^;
  $out .= field_layout
    ($rec,
      [
        'releasedate'  => 'Date',
        'manufacturer' => 'Manufacturer',
```

```
            'availability' => 'Availability',
            'listprice'    => 'List price',
            'ourprice'     => "Amazon's price",
            'usedprice'    => 'Used price',
            'asin'         => 'ASIN'
        ]
    );
    $out .= "</table><br />";
    return $out;
}
```

Running the Hack

Now our script is complete. We have code to search for an author across several sites, we have a means of driving these searches and aggregating the results, and we have a flexible means of presenting the results of our search. The design of this script should easily lend itself to adding further sites to be searched, as well as formatters for those results. Figure 4-6 shows the default format.

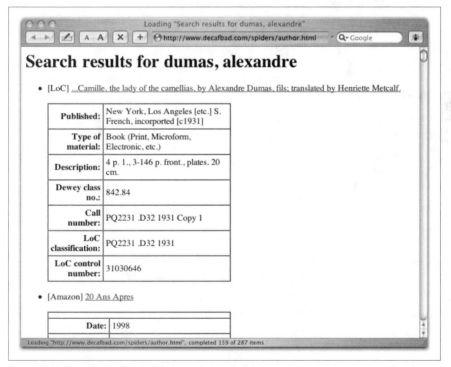

Figure 4-6. Search results for "dumas, alexandre"

This script is best used from the command line, with the results saved to a file for viewing when the process is complete. Since this is a robot that spiders across quite a few pages from several sites, it won't be unusual for this to take quite a bit of time. Also, since it generates quite a bit of traffic on the sites it visits, you'll likely want to refrain from running it very often. In particular, this script is not really a good idea to adapt as a CGI script for a web search form.

Hacking the Hack

Exercises left for the reader include breaking up the search results into pages to make the results friendlier to browse. Also, without too much effort, this script could be modularized and turned into a fairly flexible search robot. In any case, enjoy your new powers of author searching, and good luck in building new search robots.

—l.m.orchard

HACK #65   Mapping O'Reilly Best Sellers to Library Popularity

If you're using Google to look for books in university libraries, you'll get better results using a Library of Congress Number than a plain old ISBN.

Earlier in the book, we looked at the variety of unique identifiers that can be used on a web site [Hack #7]. A number of these unique identifiers deal with books and other media.

You may one day find yourself with one identifier for a set of data but needing another set of data that uses a different identifier. That's where I found myself when I was wondering exactly how many O'Reilly books were in university libraries, compared to their best-selling status (O'Reilly publishes a weekly list of best sellers at *http://www.oreilly.com/catalog/top25.html*).

Now, I could just use the ISBN, which O'Reilly supplies, and try to find library holdings that way. The problem, though, is that searching for ISBNs on Google will lead you to lots of false positives—bookstores or just mentions of books, instead of actual library holdings. But we do have an alternative: searching for a book's Library of Congress (LOC) call number will eliminate most of those false positives.

But how do we get the LOC call number for each book? It's not available from O'Reilly. I found a good search interface at the Rochester Institute of Technology's library. I used the ISBNs from O'Reilly's site to look up the LOC call number at RIT's library. After I had the call number, I used Google's API to count how many times the call number appeared in Google's database.

Since the vast majority of LOC call numbers appear in Google search results from university web sites (and specifically library pages), this is a good way to gauge how popular an O'Reilly book is in university libraries versus how it ranks on O'Reilly's overall best-selling list. Are the results perfect? No; most of the search results find acquisitions lists, not catalog search results. But you can get some idea of which books are popular in libraries and which ones apparently have very little appearance in libraries at all!

There's another issue with this script. LOC call numbers end with the date a book was issued; for example, the call number for *Mac OS X Hacks* is QA76.76.O63 D67 2003. The "2003" is the year the book was published. In the case of *Mac OS X Hacks*, this is not a problem, since there's only one edition of the book. But in cases of books like *Learning Perl*, where there are several editions available, searching for just the call number with the year of publication could miss libraries that simply have older versions of the book on their acquisitions lists.

To that end, this program actually takes two counts in Google using the LOC call number. In the first case, it searches for the entire number. In the second case, it searches for the number without the year at the end, giving two different results.

The Code

Save the following code to a file called *isbn2loc.pl*:

```perl
#!/usr/bin/perl-w
use strict;
use LWP::Simple;
use SOAP::Lite;

# All the Google information.
my $google_key  = "your Google API key";
my $google_wdsl = "GoogleSearch.wsdl";
my $gsrch       = SOAP::Lite->service("file:$google_wdsl");
my $bestsellers = get("http://www.oreilly.com/catalog/top25.html");

# Since we're getting a list of best sellers,
# we don't have to scrape the rank. Instead
# we'll just start a counter and increment
# it every time we move to the next book.
my $rank = 1;
while ($bestsellers =~ m!\[<a href="(.*?)">Read it on Safari!mgis) {
    my $bookurl = $1; $bookurl =~ m!http://safari.oreilly.com/(\w+)!;
    my $oraisbn = $1; next if $oraisbn =~ /^http/;

    # Here we'll search the RIT library for the book's ISBN. Notice
    # the lovely URL that allows us to get the book information.
```

```perl
    my $ritdata = get("http://albert.rit.edu/search/i?SEARCH=$oraisbn");
    $ritdata =~ m!field C --> <A HREF=.*?>(.*?)</a>!mgs;
    my $ritloc = $1; # now we've got the LOC number.

    # Might as well get the title too, eh?
    $ritdata =~ m!<STRONG>\n(.*?)</STRONG>!ms; my $booktitle = $1;

    # Check and see if the LOC code was found for the book.
    # In a few cases it won't be. If it was, keep on going.
    if ($ritloc =~ /^Q/ or $ritloc =~ /^Z/) {

        # The first search we're doing is for the entire LOC call number.
        my $results = $gsrch ->doGoogleSearch($google_key, "\"$ritloc\"",
                             0, 1, "false", "",  "false", "", "", "");
        my $firstcount = $results->{estimatedTotalResultsCount};

        # Now, remove the date and check for all editions.
        $ritloc =~ m!(.*?) 200\d{1}!ms; my $ritlocall = $1;
        $results = $gsrch ->doGoogleSearch($google_key, "\"$ritlocall\"",
                             0, 1, "false", "",  "false", "", "", "");
        my $secondcount = $results->{estimatedTotalResultsCount};

        # Now we print everything out.
        print "The book's title is $booktitle. \n";
        print "The book's O'Reilly bestseller rank is $rank.\n";
        print "The book's LOC number is $ritloc. \n";
        print "Searching for $ritloc on Google gives $firstcount results. \n";
        print "Searching for all editions on Google ($ritlocall) gives ".
              "$secondcount results.\n \n";
    }
    $rank++;
}
```

Running the Hack

Unlike many of the hacks in this book, this hack has no command-line switches or options. You just run it from the command line. It visits the top 25 best-seller list, gets the ISBNs, uses the ISBNs to get the LOC call numbers from the library at RIT, and then searches Google for the LOC call numbers with and without the year of publication. Output looks like this:

```
% perl isbn2loc.pl
The book's title is Learning Perl.
The book's O'Reilly bestseller rank is 8.
The book's LOC number is QA76.73.P33 S34 2001.
Searching for QA76.73.P33 S34 2001 on Google gives 0 results.
Searching for all editions on Google (QA76.73.P33 S34) gives 9 results.

The book's title is Running Linux.
The book's O'Reilly bestseller rank is 13.
The book's LOC number is QA76.76.063 W465 2002.
```

```
Searching for QA76.76.063 W465 2002 on Google gives 1 results.
Searching for all editions on Google (QA76.76.063 W465) gives 20 results.

The book's title is Programming Perl.
The book's O'Reilly bestseller rank is 14.
The book's LOC number is QA76.73.P22 W348 2000.
Searching for QA76.73.P22 W348 2000 on Google gives 1 results.
Searching for all editions on Google (QA76.73.P22 W348) gives 10 results.
```

Hacking the Hack

This is a very closed hack; it has certain sources it uses and that's that. So, the first thing I think of when I think about modifications is using different sources. O'Reilly doesn't have the only best-seller list out there, you know. You could use Amazon.com, Barnes & Noble, or some other online book-store or book list. You could also reference your own text file full of ISBN numbers.

You could also use Google's daterange: syntax to check by month and see when the new acquisitions pages are being indexed. (There are too few search results to try to search on a day-by-day basis.) Another idea is to out-put the results into comma-delimited format, allowing you to put the infor-mation into a spreadsheet and lay it out that way.

Using All Consuming to Get Book Lists

#66 You can retrieve a list of the most-mentioned books in the weblog community, as well as personal book lists and recommendations, through either of All Consuming's two web service APIs.

This hack could represent the future of web applications. It glues together pieces of several web service APIs and then, in turn, offers an API to its fea-tures. If someone were to create a derivative application with this API, it would represent a third layer of abstraction from Amazon.com's service. Entire lightweight services may someday be built layer upon layer like this, with dozens of interconnected applications exchanging data freely behind the scenes.

If this is a book about scraping and spidering, why include instructions on how to use web-based APIs? Quite simply, *they make scraping easier.* Instead of having to worry about ever-changing HTML **[Hack #32]**, you merely have to do some quick research to learn the provided interface. Likewise, using an API makes it easier to combine raw data from scraping with prepared data from sites like Technorati, All Consuming, Alexa, and Amazon.com. For an example, check out "Finding Album Information with FreeDB and Amazon.com" **[Hack #59]**.

All Consuming (*http://www.allconsuming.net*) is a fairly small application, built on top of a mountain of information that has been made freely available through web services. Amazon.com's Web Services API fuels the invaluable book information, Google's API allows us to get related web sites for book titles, and Weblogs.com has an XML file that lets us know which web sites have been updated each hour. Combining these three services, we can create lists of books that are being talked about on the Web. It only makes sense for us to give back to this generous community by opening up SOAP and REST interfaces to All Consuming's information, to be used for free and in any way that can be invented.

The SOAP Code

Here's an example of how you can access All Consuming information on your own, using SOAP and Perl. Create a file called *display_weekly_list_with_soap.cgi*:

```perl
#!/usr/bin/perl -w
# display_weekly_list_with_soap.cgi
use strict;

use SOAP::Lite +autodispatch =>
    uri => 'http://www.allconsuming.net/AllConsumngAPI',
    proxy => 'http://www.allconsuming.net/soap.cgi';

# optional values for the API.
my ($hour,$day,$month,$year) = qw( 12 05 28 2003 );

my $AllConsumingObject =
AllConsumingAPI->new(
                     $hour,  # optional
                     $day,   # optional
                     $month, # optional
                     $year   # optional
                    );
```

This creates a new object, $AllConsumingObject, which you can then use to retrieve a wide variety of data, as explained in the following sections.

Most-mentioned lists. Every hour, All Consuming crawls recently updated weblogs to see if any new books have been mentioned for the first time on any given site. It combines this information with Amazon.com's Web Services API, aggregates frequently mentioned books into hourly and weekly lists, and archives them all the way back to August 2002. GetHourlyList sends you the most recent hour's list information, GetWeeklyList sends you the most recent aggregation of all activity during the last week, and GetArchiveList returns you the hourly or weekly list that corresponds with the date that you specify when creating the object (the $hour, $day, $month, and $year variables). For example:

```
my $HourlyData = $AllConsumingObject->GetHourlyList;
my $WeeklyData = $AllConsumingObject->GetWeeklyList;
my $ArchivedData = $AllConsumingObject->GetArchiveList;
```

Personal book lists. People have created their own book lists directly through All Consuming, assigning them to categories like Currently Reading, Favorite Books, and Completed Books. Although some of these lists are available for use on other sites through methods like JavaScript includes, if someone wants to add a Favorite Books list to their site, they'll have to use the SOAP or REST interfaces to do so:

```
my $CurrentlyReading = $AllConsumingObject->GetCurrentlyReadingList('insert ↵
name');
my $FavoriteBooks = $AllConsumingObject->GetFavoriteBooksList('insert ↵
name');
my $PurchasedBooks = $AllConsumingObject->GetPurchasedBooksList('insert ↵
name');
my $CompletedBooks = $AllConsumingObject->GetCompletedBooksList('insert ↵
name');
```

Book metadata and weblog mentions. Some users have added valuable metadata about books, such as first lines and number of pages. This is mostly for fun, and it allows me to have an hourly "first line trivia" question on my homepage, to see if you can guess the book that the first line comes from. In any case, if you want to retrieve book metadata for a given book, you can do so with the following method:

```
my $Metadata = $AllConsumingObject->GetMetadataForBook('insert ISBN');
```

The argument passed in is the ISBN (International Standard Book Number) for the book you'd like to retrieve metadata from. For a list of metadata that's currently available for use, you can check out the metadata scorecard at All Consuming (*http://www.allconsuming.net/scorecard.html*).

Alternatively, if you'd like to receive a list of all of the weblogs that have mentioned a particular book, you can retrieve that information using the following method:

```
my $WeblogMentions = $AllConsumingObject->GetWeblogMentionsForBook('insert ↵
ISBN');
```

Friends and recommendations. All Consuming also has friend relationships—between people who have marked their favorite web sites so they can keep track of what they're reading—as well as book recommendations based on the sum of all those friend relationships. You can get a list of web sites that you or someone else has marked as a friend, by including your weblog URL:

```
my $Friends = $AllConsumingObject->GetFriends('insert URL');
```

And to get a list of books that all of your friends are currently reading, sorted by those that are mentioned recently and the most times, you can do this:

```
my $Recommendations = $AllConsumingObject->GetRecommendations('insert URL');
```

To iterate through the results these methods return, do something like this:

```
# The array here may differ depending
# on the type of data being returned.
if (ref($WeeklyData->{'asins'}) eq 'ARRAY') {
    foreach my $item (@{$WeeklyData->{'asins'}}) {
        print "TITLE: $item->{'title'}\n",
        "AUTHOR: $item->{'author'}\n\n";
    }
}
```

Of course, in either of these examples, you can change the URL passed to any other URL. For a full list of methods you can invoke on this object, visit the instructions (*http://allconsuming.net/news/000012.html*) and code samples (*http://allconsuming.net/soap-code-example.txt*).

The REST Code

For those who think SOAP is a bit of overkill for simple applications like this, you can get the same information REST-style. Add this code to a file called *display_weekly_list_with_rest.cgi*:

```
#!/usr/bin/perl -w
# display_weekly_list_with_rest.cgi
use strict;
use LWP::Simple;
use XML::Simple;

# Any of the URLs mentioned below can replace this one.
my $URLToGet = 'http://allconsuming.net/rest.cgi?weekly=1';

# Download and parse.
my $XML = get($URLToGet);
my $ParsedXML = XMLin($XML, suppressempty => 1);

# The array here may differ depending
# on the type of data being returned.
if (ref($ParsedXML->{'asins'}) eq 'ARRAY') {
    foreach my $item (@{$ParsedXML->{'asins'}}) {
        print "TITLE: $item->{'title'}\n",
        "AUTHOR: $item->{'author'}\n\n";
    }
}
```

Following are the URL formats you can access via HTTP to return XML data directly.

Most-mentioned lists. Here's the REST interface for requesting the hourly and weekly most-mentioned lists:

```
http://allconsuming.net/rest.cgi?hourly=1
http://allconsuming.net/rest.cgi?weekly=1
```

If you'd like to retrieve an archived list of most-mentioned books, you can specify the date, like so:

```
http://allconsuming.net/rest.cgi?archive=1&hour=12&day=12&month=5&year=2003
```

Personal book lists. To retrieve a list of any of your categorized books in XML format, add your username to any of the following URLs. Note the category name in the URL.

```
http://allconsuming.net/rest.cgi?currently_reading=1&username=insert name
http://allconsuming.net/rest.cgi?favorite_books=1&username=insert name
http://allconsuming.net/rest.cgi?purchased_books=1&username=insert name
http://allconsuming.net/rest.cgi?completed_books=1&username=insert name
```

Book metadata and weblog mentions. To get XML data about a specific item, include the ISBN in these URLs:

```
http://allconsuming.net/rest.cgi?metadata=1&isbn=insert ISBN
http://allconsuming.net/rest.cgi?weblog_mentions_for_book=1&isbn=insert ISBN
```

Friends and recommendations. To find XML data that includes friends or recommendations for a given weblog, you can include the weblog's URL in the appropriate format:

```
http://allconsuming.net/rest.cgi?friends=1&url=insert URL
http://allconsuming.net/rest.cgi?recommendations=1&url=insert URL
```

Running the Hack

Running *display_weekly_list_with_rest.cgi* without modification shows:

```
% perl display_weekly_list_with_rest.cgi
TITLE: Peer-to-Peer : Harnessing the Power of Disruptive Technologies
AUTHOR: Andy Oram

TITLE: Quicksilver : Volume One of The Baroque Cycle
AUTHOR: Neal Stephenson

TITLE: A Pattern Language: Towns, Buildings, Construction
AUTHOR: Christopher Alexander, Sara Ishikawa, Murray Silverstein

TITLE: Designing With Web Standards
AUTHOR: Jeffrey Zeldman
```

TITLE: Slander: Liberal Lies About the American Right
AUTHOR: Ann H. Coulter

TITLE: Bias : A CBS Insider Exposes How the Media Distort the News
AUTHOR: Bernard Goldberg

TITLE: The Adventures of Charmin the Bear
AUTHOR: David McKee, Joanna Quinn

The XML Results

The returned output of both the SOAP and REST interfaces will be XML
that looks something like this:

```
<opt>
  <header
    lastBuildDate="Sat May 28 13:30:02 2003"
    title="All Consuming"
    language="en-us"
    description="Most recent books being talked about by webloggers."
    link="http://allconsuming.net/"
    number_updated="172"
  />
  <asins
    asin="0465045669"
    title="Metamagical Themas"
    author="Douglas R. Hofstadter"
    url="http://www.erikbenson.com/"
    image="http://images.amazon.com/images/P/0465045669.01.THUMBZZZ.jpg"
    excerpt="Douglas Hoftstadter's lesser-known book, Metamagical Themas,
has a great chapter or two on self-referential sentences like 'This sentence
was in the past tense.'."
    amazon_url="http://amazon.com/exec/obidos/ASIN/0465045669/"
    allconsuming_url="http://allconsuming.net/item.cgi?id=0465045669"
  />
</opt>
```

If multiple items are returned, there will be multiple <asins /> elements.

Hacking the Hack

Although All Consuming currently tracks only book trends, it also stores
information about other types of items that are available at Amazon.com,
such as CDs, DVDs, and electronics. You can't find this information anywhere on All Consuming's site, but if you use either of the APIs to retrieve
weblog mentions for an ASIN (Amazon.com Standard Identification Number) that belongs to a product category other than books, it will still faith-
fully return any weblog data that it has for that item.

—Erik Benson

Tracking Packages with FedEx

When you absolutely, positively have to know where your package is right now!

So many times when using the Web, all you need is one bit of information, especially when you're running a specific search. You want to know when your flight is coming in. You want to know how much a book costs. You want to know when your FedEx package is going to arrive.

Spidering is ideal for grabbing this one bit of information without expending a lot of effort. This hack helps you track FedEx packages.

The Code

Save the following code as *fedex_tracker.pl*:

```perl
#!/usr/bin/perl -w
use strict;
use LWP::Simple;
use HTML::TableExtract;

# we use the Canada/English site, because its table
# of package tracking is simpler to parse than the "us".
my $url_base = "http://www.fedex.com/cgi-bin/tracking?action=track".
               "&cntry_code=ca_english&tracknumbers="; # woo hah.

# user wants to add a new tracking number.
my @tracknums; push(@tracknums, shift) if @ARGV;

# user already has some data on disk, so suck it in.
# we could technically add a grep on the readdir, but
# we have to postprocess @files anyway, so...
opendir(CWD, ".") or die $!; my @files = readdir(CWD); closedir(CWD);
foreach (@files) { /fedex_tracker_(\d+).dat/; push(@tracknums, $1) if $1; }
unless (@tracknums) { die "We have no packages to track!\n"; }
my %h; undef (@h{@tracknums}); @tracknums = keys %h; # quick unique.

# each tracking number, look it up.
foreach my $tracknum (@tracknums) {

    # suck down the data or end.
    my $data = get("$url_base$tracknum") or die $!;
    $data =~ s/ / /g; # sticky spaces.

    # and load our specific tracking table in.
    my $te = HTML::TableExtract->new(
            headers => ["Scan Activity","Date/Time"]);
    $te->parse($data); # alright, we've got everything loaded, hopefully.

    # now, get the new info.
    my $new_data_from_site;
```

```
    foreach my $ts ($te->table_states) {
        foreach my $row ($ts->rows) {
            $new_data_from_site .= " " . join(', ', @$row) . "\n";
        }
    }

    # if this is a broken tracking number,
    # move on and try the other ones we have.
    unless ($new_data_from_site) {
        print "No data found for package #$tracknum. Skipping.\n"; next;
    }

    # if this package has never been tracked
    # before, then we'll create a file to
    # hold the data. this will be used for
    # comparisons on subsequent runs.
    unless (-e "fedex_tracker_$tracknum.dat") {
        open(FILE, ">fedex_tracker_$tracknum.dat") or die $!;
        print FILE $new_data_from_site; close (FILE);
        print "Adding the following data for #$tracknum:\n";
        print $new_data_from_site;
    }

    # if the datafile does exist, load it
    # into a string, and do a simplisitic
    # comparison to see if they're equal.
    # if not, assume things have changed.
    if (-e "fedex_tracker_$tracknum.dat") {
        open(FILE, "<fedex_tracker_$tracknum.dat");
        $/ = undef; my $old_data_from_file = <FILE>; close(FILE);
        if ($old_data_from_file eq $new_data_from_site) {
            print "There have been no changes for package #$tracknum.\n";
        } else {
            print "Package #$tracknum has advanced in its journey!\n";
            print $new_data_from_site; # update the user.
            open(FILE, ">fedex_tracker_$tracknum.dat");
            print FILE $new_data_from_site; close(FILE);
            # the file is updated for next compare.
        }
    }
}
```

Running the Hack

To use the script, pass a package number on the command line. If you've
already entered one, the script will try to use those packages you've entered
previously. When you run the script with a package number, the output will
look like this:

```
% perl fedex_tracker.pl 047655634284503
Adding the following data for #047655634284503:
```

```
Departed FedEx sort facility/SACRAMENTO, CA, 08/06/2003 06:54
Scanned at FedEx sort facility/SACRAMENTO, CA, 08/06/2003 00:14
Scanned at FedEx origin location/SACRAMENTO, CA, 08/05/2003 23:57
Customer-Loaded Trailer Picked Up/SACRAMENTO, CA, 08/05/2003 00:00
There have been no changes for package #047655634284503.
```

Once you've run this search, the script will create a new file, *fedex_tracker_ PACKAGENUM.dat*, in the same directory. In the previous example, the new file is called *fedex_tracker_047655634284503.dat*. Each successive run, the script will search for and update this package's information. How do you get it to stop searching for a particular package? Simply delete its *.dat* file.

Just because you have an existing package doesn't mean you can't continue to search for other packages. Say you run the previous search and then want to run another. This will work:

```
% perl fedex_tracker.pl 123456789
No data found for package #123456789. Skipping.
There have been no changes for package #047655634284503.
```

If no data is found for a package, a *.dat* file will not be created for it.

Hacking the Hack

If you want to write something similar that grabs information from Amazon.com's order-tracking pages, there are a variety of things you could do.

First, you could run it from *cron* [Hack #90] so you'd have a daily update of where your package is. Alternatively, you could have another small script that periodically gathers up the names of the various *.dat* files you generate and sends them to you, so you could metatrack which packages you've tracked. Or, perhaps you want to export the package information into a comma-delimited file, in which case you'll need a permanent record of shipping progress.

Checking Blogs for New Comments

Tend to respond directly to weblog posts with a comment or three? Ever wonder about the reactions to your comments? This hack automates the process of keeping up with the conversation you started.

Blogs are the savior of independent publishing, and the ability of most to allow commenting creates an intimate collaboration between performer and audience: read the blog's entry and any existing comments, and then add your own thoughts and opinions. What's most annoying, however, is needing to return on a regular basis to see if anyone has added additional comments, whether to the original posting or to your own follow up.

Checking Blogs for New Comments

With the RSS syndication format, you can monitor new blog entries in a standard way with any number of popular aggregators. Unfortunately, unless the site in question has provided its comments in RSS format also, there's not really a standard way for comments to be used, repurposed, or monitored.

However, the more you read blogs and the comments themselves, you'll begin to see patterns emerge. Perhaps a comment always starts with "On *DATE*, *PERSON* said" or "posted by *PERSON* on *DATE*," or even plain old "*DATE*, *PERSON*." These *comment signatures* can be the beginning of an answer to your needs: a script that uses regular expressions to check for various types of signatures can adequately tell you when new comments have been posted.

The Code

Save this script as *chkcomments.pl*:

```perl
#!/usr/bin/perl -w
use strict;
use Getopt::Long;
use LWP::Simple;
my %opts; GetOptions(\%opts, 'v|verbose');

# where we find URLs. we'll also use this
# file to remember the number of comments.
my $urls_file = "chkcomments.dat";

# what follows is a list of regular expressions and assignment
# code that will be executed in search of matches, per site.
my @signatures = (
    { regex  => qr/On (.*?), <a href="(.*?)">(.*?)<\/a> said/,
      assign => '($date,$contact,$name) = ($1,$2,$3)'
    },
    { regex  => qr/&middot; (.*?) &middot; .*?<a href="(.*?)">(.*?)<\/a>/,
      assign => '($date,$contact,$name) = ($1,$2,$3)'
    },
    { regex  => qr/(\d{4}-\d{2}-\d{2} \d{2}:\d{2}:\d{2}) (.*)/,
      assign => '($date,$name,$contact) = ($1,$2,"none")'
    },
);

# open our URL file, and suck it in.
open(URLS_FILE, "<$urls_file") or die $!;
my %urls; while (<URLS_FILE>) { chomp;
    my ($url, $count) = split(/\|%%\|/);
    $urls{$url} = $count || undef;
} close (URLS_FILE);
```

```
# foreach URL in our dat file:
foreach my $url (keys %urls) {

    next unless $url; # no URL, no cookie.
    my $old_count = $urls{$url} || undef;

    # print a little happy message.
    print "\nSearching $url...\n";

    # suck down the data.
    my $data = get($url) or next;

    # now, begin looping through our matchers.
    # for each regular expression and assignment
    # code, we execute it in this namespace in an
    # attempt to find matches in our loaded data.
    my $new_count; foreach my $code (@signatures) {

        # with our regular expression loaded,
        # let's see if we get any matches.
        while ($data =~ /$code->{regex}/gism) {

            # since our $code contains two Perl statements
            # (one being the regex, above, and the other
            # being the assignment code), we have to eval
            # it once more so the assignments kick in.
            my ($date, $contact, $name); eval $code->{assign};
            next unless ($date && $contact && $name);
            print "  - $date: $name ($contact)\n" if $opts{v};
            $new_count++; # increase the count.
        }

        # if we've gotten a comment count, then assume
        # our regex worked properly, spit out a message,
        # and assign our comment count for later storage.
        if ($new_count) {
            print " * We saw a total of $new_count comments".
                " (old count: ". ($old_count || "unchecked") . ").\n";
            if ($new_count > ($old_count || 0)) { # joy of joys!
                print " * Woo! There are new comments to read!\n"
            } $urls{$url} = $new_count; last; # end the loop.
        }
    }
} print "\n";

# now that our comment counts are updated,
# write it back out to our datafile.
open(URLS_FILE, ">$urls_file") or die $!;
foreach my $url (keys %urls) {
    print URLS_FILE "$url|%%|$urls{$url}\n";
} close (URLS_FILE);
```

Running the Hack

This script depends on being fed a file that lists URLs you'd like to monitor. These should be the URLs of the page that holds comments on the blog entry, often the same as the blog entry's permanent link (or *permalink*). If you're reading *http://www.gamegrene.com*, for instance, and you've just commented on the "The Lazy GM" article, you'll add the following URL into a file named *chkcomments.dat*:

```
http://www.gamegrene.com/game_material/the_lazy_gm.shtml
```

A typical first run considers all comments new—new to you and your script:

```
% perl chkcomments.pl
Searching http://www.gamegrene.com/game_material/the_lazy_gm.shtml...
  * We saw a total of 5 comments (old count: unchecked).
  * Woo! There are new comments to read!
```

You can also show the name, date, and contact information of each individual comment, by passing the --verbose command-line option. This example shows the script checking for new comments on the same URL:

```
% perl chkcomments.pl --verbose
Searching http://www.gamegrene.com/game_material/the_lazy_gm.shtml...
  - July 23, 2003 01:53 AM: VMB (mailto:vesab@jippii.fi)
  - July 23, 2003 10:55 AM: Iridilate (mailto:)
  - July 29, 2003 02:46 PM: The Bebop Cow (mailto:blackcypress@yahoo.com)
  ... etc ...
  * We saw a total of 5 comments (old count: 5).
```

Since no comments were added between our first and second runs, there's nothing new.

But how did the script know how many comments there were in the first place? The answer, as I alluded to previously, is comment signatures. In HTML, every comment on Gamegrene looks like this:

```
On July 23, 2003 01:53 AM,<a href="mailto:vesab@jippii.fi">VMB</a> said:
```

In other words, it has a signature of On DATE, <a href="CONTACT">PERSON</a> said or, if you were expressing it as a regular expression, On (.*?), <a href="(.*?)">(.*?)<\/a> said. Keen observers of the script will have noticed this regular expression appear near the top of the code:

```
my @signatures = (
    { regex  => qr/On (.*?), <a href="(.*?)">(.*?)<\/a> said/,
      assign => '($date,$contact,$name) = ($1,$2,$3)'
    },
```

What about the assign line, though? Simply enough, it takes our captured bits of data from the regular expression (the bits that look like (.*?)) and assigns them to more easily understandable variables, like $date, $contact, and $name. The number of times our regular expression matches is the number of comments we've seen on the page. Likewise, the information stored in our variables is the information printed out when we ask for --verbose output.

If you refer back to the code, you'll notice two other signatures that match the comment styles on Dive Into Mark (*http://www.diveintomark.org*) and the O'Reilly Network (*http://www.oreillynet.com*) (and possibly other sites that we don't yet know about). Since their signatures already exist, we can add the following URLs to our *chkcomments.dat* file:

```
http://diveintomark.org/archives/2003/07/28/atom_news
http://www.oreillynet.com/pub/wlg/3593
http://macdevcenter.com/pub/a/mac/2003/08/01/cocoa_series.html?page=2
```

and run our script on a regular basis to check for new comments:

```
% perl chkcomments.pl
Searching http://www.gamegrene.com/game_material/the_lazy_gm.shtml...
 * We saw a total of 5 comments (old count: 5).

Searching http://diveintomark.org/archives/2003/07/28/atom_news...
 * We saw a total of 11 comments (old count: unchecked).
 * Woo! There are new comments to read!

Searching http://www.oreillynet.com/pub/wlg/3593 ...
 * We saw a total of 1 comments (old count: unchecked).
 * Woo! There are new comments to read!

Searching http://macdevcenter.com/pub/a/mac/2003/08/01/cocoa_seri...
 * We saw a total of 9 comments (old count: unchecked).
 * Woo! There are new comments to read!
```

Hacking the Hack

The obvious way of improving the script is to add new comment signatures that match up with the sites you're reading. Say we want to monitor new comments on Harvard Weblogs (*http://blogs.law.harvard.edu/*). The first thing we need is a post with comments, so that we can determine the comment signature. Once we find one, view the HTML source to see something like this:

```
<div class="date"><a href="http://scripting.com">
Dave Winer</a> &#0149; 7/18/03; 7:58:33 AM</div>
```

The comment signature for Harvard Weblogs is equivalent to `<a href="CONTACT">PERSON</a>  DATE`, which can be stated in regular expression form as `date"><a  href="(.*?)">(.*?)<\/a> &#0149;  (.*?)<\/div>`. Once we have the signature in regular expression form, we just need to assign our matches to the variable names and add the signature to our listings at the top:

```
my @signatures = (
    { regex  => qr/On (.*?), <a href="(.*?)">(.*?)<\/a> said/,
      assign => '($date,$contact,$name) = ($1,$2,$3)'
    },
    { regex  => qr/&middot; (.*?) &middot; .*?<a href="(.*?)">(.*?)<\/a>/,
      assign => '($date,$contact,$name) = ($1,$2,$3)'
    },
    { regex  => qr/(\d{4}-\d{2}-\d{2} \d{2}:\d{2}:\d{2}) (.*)/,
      assign => '($date,$name,$contact) = ($1,$2,"none")'
    },
    { regex  => qr/date"><a href="(.*)">(.*)<\/a> &#0149; (.*)<\/div>/,
      assign => '($contact,$name,$date) = ($1,$2,$3)'
    },
);
```

Now, just add the URL we want to monitor to our *chkcomments.dat* file, and run the script as usual. Here's an output of our first check, with verbosity turned on:

```
Searching http://blogs.law.harvard.edu/comments?u=homeManilaWebs...
  - 7/18/03; 1:23:14 AM: James Farmer (http://radio.weblogs.com/0120501/)
  - 7/18/03; 4:06:10 AM: Phil Wolff (http://dijest.com/aka)
  - 7/18/03; 7:58:33 AM: Dave Winer (http://scripting.com)
  - 7/18/03; 6:23:14 PM: Phil Wolff (http://dijest.com/aka)
 * We saw a total of 4 comments (old count: unchecked).
 * Woo! There are new comments to read!
```

HACK #69   Aggregating RSS and Posting Changes

With the proliferation of individual and group weblogs, it's typical for one person to post in multiple places. Thanks to RSS syndication, you can easily aggregate all your disparate posts into one weblog.

You might have heard of RSS. It's an XML format that's commonly used to syndicate headlines and content between sites. It's also used in specialty software programs called *headline aggregators* or *readers*. Many popular weblog software packages, including Movable Type (*http://www.movabletype.org*) and Blogger (*http://www.blogger.com*), offer RSS feeds. So too do some of the content management systems—Slashcode (*http://slashcode.com*), PHPNuke (*http://phpnuke.org*), Zope (*http://www.zope.org*), and the like—that run some of the more popular tech news sites.

If you produce content for various people, you might find your writing and commentary scattered all over the place. Or, say you have a group of friends and all of you want to aggregate your postings into a single place without abandoning your individual efforts. This hack is a personal spider just for you; it aggregates entries from multiple RSS feeds and posts those new entries to a Movable Type blog.

The Code

You'll need *LWP::Simple*, *Net::Blogger*, and *XML::RSS* to use this. Save the following code to a file named *myrssmerger.pl*:

```perl
#!/usr/bin/perl -w
#
# MyRSSMerger - read multiple RSS feeds, post new entries to Movable Type.
# http://disobey.com/d/code/ or contact morbus@disobey.com.
#
# This code is free software; you can redistribute it and/or
# modify it under the same terms as Perl itself.
#

use strict; $|++;
my $VERSION = "1.0";
use Getopt::Long;
my %opts;

# make sure we have the modules we need, else die peacefully.
eval("use LWP::Simple;");  die "[err] LWP::Simple not installed.\n" if $@;
eval("use Net::Blogger;"); die "[err] Net::Blogger not installed.\n" if $@;
eval("use XML::RSS;");     die "[err] XML::RSS not installed.\n" if $@;

# define our command line flags (long and short versions).
GetOptions(\%opts, 'server|s=s',      # the POP3 server to use.
                   'username|u=s',    # the POP3 username to use.
                   'password|p=s',    # the POP3 password to use.
                   'blogid|b=i',      # unique ID of your blog.
                   'catid|c=i',       # unique ID for posting category.
                   'showcategories',  # list categories for blog.
                   'filter|f=s',      # per item filter for posting?
);

# at the very least, we need our login information.
die "[err] XML-RPC URL missing, use --server or -s.\n" unless $opts{server};
die "[err] Username missing, use --username or -u.\n"
    unless $opts{username};
die "[err] Password missing, use --password or -p.\n"
    unless $opts{password};
die "[err] BlogID missing, use --blogid or -b.\n"      unless $opts{blogid};

# every request past this point requires
# a connection, so we'll go and do so.
print "-" x 76, "\n"; # visual separator.
my $mt = Net::Blogger->new(engine=>"movabletype");
$mt->Proxy($opts{server});       # the servername.
$mt->Username($opts{username});  # the username.
```

```
$mt->Password($opts{password});   # the... ok. self-
$mt->BlogId($opts{blogid});       # explanatory!

# show existing categories.
if ($opts{showcategories}) {

    # get the list of categories from the server.
    my $cats = $mt->mt()->getCategoryList()
      or die "[err] ", $mt->LastError(), "\n";

    # and print 'em.
    if (scalar(@$cats) > 0) {
        print "The following blog categories are available:\n\n";
        foreach (sort { $a->{categoryId} <=> $b->{categoryId} } @$cats) {
            print " $_->{categoryId}: $_->{categoryName}\n";
        }
    } else { print "There are no selectable categories available.\n"; }

    # done with this request, so exit.
    print "\nCategory ID's can be used for --catid or -c.\n";
    print "-" x 76, "\n"; exit; # call me again, again!

}

# now, check for passed URLs for new-item-examination.
die "[err] No RSS URLs were passed for processing.\n" unless @ARGV;

# and store today's date for comparison.
# who needs the stinkin' Date:: modules?!
my ($day, $month, $year) = ((localtime)[3, 4, 5]);
$year+=1900; $month = sprintf("%02.0d", ++$month);
$day = sprintf("%02.0d", $day);  # zero-padding.
my $today = "$year-$month-$day"; # final version.

# loop through each RSS URL.
foreach my $rss_url (@ARGV) {

    # download whatever we've got coming.
    print "Downloading RSS feed at ", substr($rss_url, 0, 40), "...\n";
    my $data = get($rss_url) or print " [err] Data not downloaded!\n";
    next unless $data; # move onto the next URL in our list, if any.

    # parse it and then
    # count the number of items.
    # move on if nothing parsed.
    my $rss = new XML::RSS; $rss->parse($data);
    my $item_count = scalar(@{$rss->{items}});
    unless ($item_count) { print " [err] No parsable items.\n"; next; }

    # sandwich our post between a preface/anteface.
    my $clink = $rss->{channel}->{"link"}; # shorter variable.
    my $ctitle = $rss->{channel}->{title}; # shorter variable.
    my $preface = "From <a href=\"$clink\">$ctitle</a>:\n\n<blockquote>";
```

```
my $anteface = "</blockquote>\n\n"; # new items as quotes.

# and look for items dated today.
foreach my $item (@{$rss->{items}}) {

    # no description or date for our item? move on.
    unless ($item->{description} or $item->{dc}->{date}) {
      print " Skipping (no description/date): '$item->{title}'.\n";
      next;
    }

    # if we have a date, is it today's?
    if ($item->{dc}->{date} =~ /^$today/) {

        # shorter variable. we're lazy.
        my $creator = $item->{dc}->{creator};

        # if there's a filter, check for goodness.
        if ($opts{filter} && $item->{description} !~ /$opts{filter}/i) {
            print " Skipping (failed filter): '$item->{title}'.\n";
            next;
        }

        # we found an item to post, so make a
        # final description from various parts.
        my $description = "$preface$item->{description} ";
        $description    .= "($creator) " if $creator;
        $description    .= "<a href=\"$item->{link}\">Read " .
                           "more from this post.</a>$anteface";

        # now, post to the passed blog info.
        print " Publishing item: '$item->{title}'.\n";
        my $id = $mt->metaWeblog()->newPost(
                        title       => $item->{title},
                        description => $description,
                        publish     => 1)
                or die "[err] ", $mt->LastError(), "\n";

        # set the category?
        if ($opts{catid}) {
            $mt->mt()->setPostCategories(
                        postid     => $id,
                        categories => [ {categoryId => $opts{catid}}])
            or die " [err] ", $mt->LastError(), "\n";

            # "edit" the post with no changes so
            # that our category change activates.
            $mt->metaWeblog()->editPost(
                        title       => $item->{title},
                        description => $description,
                        postid      => $id,
                        publish     => 1)
```

```
                          or die " [err] ", $mt->LastError( ), "\n";
                }
          } else {
              print " Skipping (failed date check): '$item->{title}'.\n";
          }
      }
      print "-" x 76, "\n"; # visual separator.
}

exit;
```

Running the Hack

To run the code, you'll need a Movable Type weblog. At the very least, you need the username, password, XML-RPC URL for Movable Type, and the blog ID (normally 1 if you have only one). Here's an example of connecting to Kevin's Movable Type installation to show a list of categories to post to (the --showcategories switch is, strangely enough, showing the categories):

```
% perl myrssmerger.pl -s http://disobey.com/cgi-bin/mt/mt-xmlrpc.cgi -u
morbus -p HAAHAHAH -b 1 --showcategories
```

The output looks like this:

```
-----------------------------------------------------------------------
The following blog categories are available:

1: Disobey Stuff
2: The Idiot Box
3: CHIApet
4: Friends O' Disobey
5: Stalkers O' Morbus
6: Morbus Shoots, Jesus Saves
7: El Casho Disappearo
8: TechnOccult
9: Potpourri
10: Collected Nonsensicals

Category ID's can be used for --catid or -c.
-----------------------------------------------------------------------
```

If you have no categories, you'll be told as such. When you're actually posting to the blog, you can choose to post into a category or not; if you want to post into Disobey Stuff, use either -c 1 or --catid 1 when you run the program. If you want no category, specify no category.

Let's take a look at a few examples of how to use the script. Say Kevin wants to aggregate all the data from all the places he publishes information. Every night he'll use *cron* [Hack #90] to run the script for various RSS feeds. Here's an example:

```
% perl myrssmerger.pl --server ⏎
http://disobey.com/cgi-bin/mt/mt-xmlrpc.cgi ⏎
```

```
--username morbus --password HAAHAHAH --blogid 1 --catid 1
http://gamegrene.com/index.xml
```

In this case, he's saying, "Every night, check the Gamegrene RSS files for entries posted today. If you see any, post them to Disobey Stuff" (which is the first category, referenced with the --catid 1 switch). He can then run the script again, only for a different RSS feed with a different category switch, and so on. Let's take a look at the output of the Gamegrene example:

```
-----------------------------------------------------------------
Downloading RSS feed at http://gamegrene.com/index.xml...
 Publishing item: 'RPG, For Me'.
 Skipping (failed date check): 'Just Say No To Powergamers'.
 Skipping (failed date check): 'Every Story Needs A Soundtrack'.
 Skipping (failed date check): 'The Demise of Local Game Shops'.
 Skipping (failed date check): 'Death Of A Gaming System'.
 Skipping (failed date check): 'What Do You Do With Six Million Elves?'.
-----------------------------------------------------------------
```

As you can see, the script checks the dates in the RSS feed to make sure they're new before the items are added to the Movable Type weblog. Dates are determined from the <dc:date> entry in the remote RSS URL; if the feed doesn't have them, the script won't function correctly.

What happens when you want to check many RSS feeds but you want to add them all to the same category? You can do that by running the script one time. Say you want to check three different RSS feeds, not necessarily all yours. Here's an example of Kevin checking three feeds (including Tara's) and adding new additions to the category:

```
% perl myrssmerger.pl --server ↵
http://disobey.com/cgi-bin/mt/mt-xmlrpc.cgi ↵
--username morbus --password HAAHAHAH --blogid 1 --catid 4 ↵
http://gamegrene.com/index.xml http://researchbuzz.com/researchbuzz.rss
http://camworld.com/index.rdf
```

The shortened output looks like this:

```
-----------------------------------------------------------------
Downloading RSS feed at http://gamegrene.com/index.xml...
 Skipping (failed date check): 'RPG, For Me'.
 Skipping (failed date check): 'Just Say No To Powergamers'.
 Skipping (failed date check): 'Every Story Needs A Soundtrack'.
-----------------------------------------------------------------
Downloading RSS feed at http://camworld.com/index.rdf...
 Publishing item: 'Trinity's Hack from Matrix Reloaded'.
 Skipping (failed date check): 'Siberian Desktop'.
 Skipping (failed date check): 'The Sweet Hereafter'.
-----------------------------------------------------------------
Downloading RSS feed at http://researchbuzz.com/researchbuzz.rss...
```

```
Skipping (no description/date): 'Northern Light Coming Back?'.
Skipping (no description/date): 'This Week in LLRX'.
----------------------------------------------------------------------
```

Note that Tara's feed fails usage by this script; that's because she's generating her RSS by hand and her feed doesn't have dates. Most program-generated feeds, like those of Movable Type, have dates and descriptions and will be just fine.

As you can see, we can choose a variety of feeds to use and we can post them to any of our Movable Type categories. Is there anything else this script can do? Well, actually, yes; it can filter incoming entries that match a specified keyword. To do that, use the --filter switch. As an example, this script posts only those entries whose descriptions include the string "perl":

```
% perl myrssmerger.pl --server ↵
http://disobey.com/cgi-bin/mt/mt-xmlrpc.cgi ↵
--username morbus --password HAAHAHAH --blogid 1 --catid 4 --filter "perl" ↵
http://camworld.com/index.rdf
```

Hacking the Hack

Actually, this is both a "hacking the hack" and "some things to consider" section. Right now, the biggest downside is that this hack works only on Movable Type. You could dive into *Net::Blogger* a bit and make it usable by Blogger (*http://www.blogger.com*), Radio Userland (*http://radio.userland.com/*), or any one of the other weblogging platforms.

This script is designed to run once a day. To that end, the script does a full download of the RSS feed every time. As it stands, you should probably run it just once a day, for two reasons:

- If you run the script more than once a day, you might have bandwidth issues running the script and downloading full RSS files too often.

- The more often you run the script, the more often you're going to post repetitive items.

All right, let's talk about a couple of actual hacks. First is error checking; as is, the script doesn't check the URLs to make sure they start with *http://*. That's easily solved; just add the code in bold:

```
# loop through each RSS URL.
foreach my $rss_url (@ARGV) {

    # not an HTTP URL.
    next unless $rss_url =~ !^http://!;

    # download whatever we've got coming.
```

Next, the preface and the anteface (i.e., the text that surrounds the posted entry) are hardcoded into the script, but we can change that via a switch on the command line. First make the preface and anteface command-line options:

```
GetOptions(\%opts, 'server|s=s',      # the POP3 server to use.
                   'username|u=s',     # the POP3 username to use.
                   'password|p=s',     # the POP3 password to use.
                   'blogid|b=i',       # unique ID of your blog.
                   'catid|c=i',        # unique ID for posting category.
                   'showcategories',   # list categories for blog.
                   'filter|f=s',       # per item filter for posting?
                   'preface|r=s',      # the preface text before a posted item
                   'anteface|a=s"      # the text included after a posted item
);
```

You'll then need to make a change to the preface line:

```
my $preface = $opts{preface} || "From <a href=\"$clink\">$ctitle</a>:\n\
n<blockquote>";
```

and a similar change to the anteface line:

```
my $anteface = $opts{anteface}
      || "</blockquote>\n\n"; # new items as quotes.
```

See Also

- For users of the Blosxom (*http://www.blosxom.com*) weblog system, there's Blagg (*http://www.raelity.org/lang/perl/blagg*), an RSS aggregator that will aggregate your disparate posts into one weblog.

H A C K **Using the Link Cosmos of Technorati**

#70 Similar to other indexing sites like Blogdex, the Link Cosmos at Technorati keeps track of an immense number of blogs, correlating popular links and topics for all to see. With the recently released API, developers can now integrate the results into their own scripts.

Technorati (*http://www.technorati.com*) walks, crawls, investigates, and generally mingles around weblog-style web sites and indexes them, gathering loads of information. I mean *loads*: it keeps track of articles on the web site, what links to it, what it links to, how popular it is, how popular the web sites that link to it are, how popular the people that read it are, and who is most likely to succeed. Well, it does *most* of those things.

Need Some REST?

The current version of the Technorati interface uses a REST (Representational State Transfer) interface. REST interfaces allow for transfer of data via the GET or POST method of a URL. We will initially use the interface to access the Technorati Cosmos data. The *Cosmos* is the set of data that keeps track of who links to whom and essentially contains who thinks who is interesting. Technorati allows queries of the following information via the REST interface:

Link Cosmos
> Who you link to, who links to who, and when.

Blog info
> General information about a specified weblog, including the weblog name, URL, RSS URL (if one exists), how many places it links to, how many places link to it, and when it was last updated. This is the same information that is returned for each weblog in the Cosmos lookup.

Outbound blogs
> A list of web sites that the specified URL links to.

We're going to focus on the Link Cosmos information, which in my bloated opinion is the most important. The following small piece of code uses the Technorati interface to grab the current weblog listing and print the resulting XML data that is returned from the Technorati interface. You'll need to become a member of the site to receive your developer's API key:

```perl
#!/usr/bin/perl -w
use strict;
use LWP::Simple;

my $key       = "your developer key";
my $searchURL = "http://www.perceive.net/";
my $restAPI   = "http://api.technorati.com/cosmos?key=$key&url=".
                "$searchURL&type=weblog&format=xml";
my $xml = get($restAPI);
print "$xml\n";
```

Dave Sifry, the developer of Technorati, has also made a small distinction between general web sites and weblogs. Notice type=weblog in the URL of the previous code. You can change this to type=link, and you'll get the last 20 web sites that link to your site, rather than just the last 20 blogs. This is a small distinction, but one that could be useful.

The returned result is a chunk of XML, which resembles this:

```xml
<item>
  <weblog>
    <name>phil ringnalda dot com</name>
    <url>http://philringnalda.com</url>
    <rssurl>http://www.philringnalda.com/index.xml</rssurl>
    <inboundblogs>339</inboundblogs>
    <inboundlinks>471</inboundlinks>
```

```
    <lastupdate>2003-07-11 21:09:28 GMT</lastupdate>
  </weblog>
</item>
```

Many REST interfaces use XML as the format for returning data to the requestor. This allows the data to be parsed easily and used in various ways, such as creating HTML for your web site:

```
use XML::Simple;
my $parsed_data = XMLin($xml);
my $items = $parsed_data->{document}->{item};

print qq{<ol>\n};
for my $item (@$items) {
    my ($weblog, $url) = ($item->{weblog}->{name}, $item->{weblog}->{url});
    print qq{<li><a href="$url">$name</a></li>};
}
print qq{</ol>};
```

First, we load the *XML::Simple* module, which will allow us to load the data into a hash. The XMLin function does this for us and returns a hash of hashes and arrays. After XMLin has loaded the data, we get an array of weblog items and iterate through it, printing some HTML with links to the web sites. We could just as easily have printed it as a comma-delimited file or anything else we could cook up in our silly little heads.

The most interesting part of all of this is the transfer and use of the information; Technorati allows us to see who has created links to our web site and use that data *for free*. Dave obviously learned how to share in kindergarten.

A Skeleton Key for Words

In addition to the lovely Cosmos API, Technorati provides us with an interface to query for weblog posts that contain a specified keyword. For instance, say you really like Perl; you can query the API periodically to get all the recent posts that contain "Perl." I can imagine some handy uses for that: if you have keywords attached to posts in your weblog, you could have a Related Posts link that queries Technorati for other posts containing those keywords and shows a list of articles similar to yours.

The API to retrieve this information is also a REST interface, following the lead made by the Cosmos API. We can alter the code for the Cosmos API to provide access to this data:

```
#!/usr/bin/perl-w
use strict;
use LWP::Simple;

my $key       = "your developer key";
my $searchTerm = "Perl";
```

```
my $restAPI    = "http://api.technorati.com/search?key=$key".
                  "&query=$searchTerm&format=xml";
my $xml = get($restAPI);
print "$xml\n";
```

Searching using the Keyword API returns more information in the XML stream, which gives some context to why it returned a match for a given item:

```
<context>
   <excerpt>
    Ben Trott has uploaded version 0.02 of XML::FOAF to CPAN.
    This is a<b>Perl</b> module designed to make it...
   </excerpt>
   <title>New version of XML::FOAF in CPAN</title>
   <link>http://rdfweb.org/mt/foaflog/archives/000033.html</link>
</context>
```

The returned data consists of an excerpt of words that appear near the keyword that was searched for (the keyword is also tagged as bold in the HTML—Perl in this example), the title of the article it was found in, and a URL to the item. The result also contains the same information about the weblog it was found in, such as inbound and outbound links.

We can slightly modify the previous code from the Cosmos API to display these related articles in a nice, concise format:

```
use XML::Simple;
my $parsed_data = XMLin($xml);
my $items = $parsed_data->{document}->{item};

print qq{<dl>\n};
for my $item (@$items) {
    my ($weblog, $context, $title, $link) =
        ($item->{weblog}->{name}, $item->{context}->{excerpt},
        $item->{context}->{title}, $item->{context}->{link});
    print qq{<dt><a href="$link">$weblog : $title</a></dt>};
    print qq{<dd>$context</dd>};
}
print qq{</dl>};
```

The Technorati API is a useful method for retrieving information about weblogs, and it can help in the aggregation of useful data. With the attention that is paid to Technorati, I'm sure that these interfaces will become even more robust and useful as the development progresses. With the information in this hack, you are capable of using and expanding on these interfaces, creating uses of the data that are even more interesting. Further information is available at the Technorati Developer Wiki (*http://developers.technorati.com/wiki/*) and mailing list (*http://developers.technorati.com/mailman/listinfo/api-discuss*).

—*Eric Vitiello*

Finding Related RSS Feeds

#71 If you're a regular reader of weblogs, you know that most syndicate their content in a format called RSS. By querying aggregated RSS databases, you can find related sites you may be interested in reading.

One of the fastest growing applications on the Web is the use of RSS feeds. Although there's some contention regarding what RSS stands for—one definition of the acronym calls it "Really Simple Syndication" and another calls it "Rich Site Summary"—RSS feeds are XML documents that provide a feed of headlines from a web site (commonly a weblog or news site) that can be processed easily by a piece of software called a *news aggregator*. News aggregators allow you to subscribe to content from a multitude of web sites, allowing the program to go out and check for new content, rather than requiring you to go out and look for it.

RSS feeds are like potato chips, though. Once you subscribe to one, you find yourself grabbing one after another. It would be nice if you could supply a list of feeds you already read to a robot and have it go out and find related feeds in which you might also be interested.

Filling Up the Toolbox

We're going to need a number of tools to get this script off the ground. Also, we'll be calling on a couple of web services, namely those at Syndic8 (*http://www.syndic8.com*) and Technorati (*http://www.technorati.com*).

Syndic8 is a catalog of feeds maintained by volunteers, and it contains quite a bit of information on each feed. It also catalogs feeds for sites created by people other than the site owners, so even if a particular site might not have a feed, Syndic8 might be able to find one anyway. Also, Syndic8 employs several categorization schemes; so, given one feed, we might be able to find others in its category. Since Syndic8 offers an XML-RPC web service, we can call upon this directory for help.

Technorati is a search engine and a spider of RSS feeds and weblogs. Among other things, it indexes links between weblogs and feeds, and it maps the relationships between sites. So, while we're looking for feeds, Technorati can tell us which sites link to each other. Since it supports a simple URL-based API that produces XML, we can integrate this into our script fairly easily.

Let's gather some tools and start the script:

```perl
#!/usr/bin/perl -w
use strict;
use POSIX;
```

Finding Related RSS Feeds

```
use Memoize;
use LWP::Simple;
use XMLRPC::Lite;
use XML::RSS;
use HTML::RSSAutodiscovery;

use constant SYNDIC8_ID => 'syndic8_id';
use constant FEED_URL   => 'feed_url';
use constant SITE_URL   => 'site_url';
```

This script starts off with some standard Perl safety features. The *Memoize* module is a useful tool we can use to cache the results of functions so that we aren't constantly rerequesting information from web services. *LWP::Simple* allows us to download content from the Web; *XMLRPC::Lite* allows us to call on XML-RPC web services; *XML::RSS* allows us to parse and extract information from RSS feeds themselves; and *HTML::RSSAutodiscovery* gives us a few tricks to locate a feed for a site when we don't know its location.

The rest of this preamble consists of a few constants we'll use later. Now, let's do some configuration:

```
our $technorati_key = "your Technorati key";
our $ta_url         = 'http://api.technorati.com';
our $ta_cosmos_url  = "$ta_url/cosmos?key=$technorati_key&url=";

our $syndic8_url = 'http://www.syndic8.com/xmlrpc.php';
our $syndic8_max_results = 10;

my @feeds =
  qw(
   http://www.macslash.com/macslash.rdf
   http://www.wired.com/news_drop/netcenter/netcenter.rdf
   http://www.cert.org/channels/certcc.rdf
  );
```

Notice that, like many web services, the Technorati API requires you to sign up for an account and be assigned a key string in order to use it (*http://www.technorati.com//members/apikey.html*). You might also want to check out the informal documentation for this service (*http://www.sifry.com/alerts/archives/000288.html*). After we set our API key, we construct the URL we'll be using to call upon the service.

Next, we set up the URL for the Syndic8 XML-RPC service, as well as a limit we'll use later for restricting the number of feeds we want the robot to look for at once.

Finally, we set up a list of favorite RSS feeds to use in digging for more feeds. With configuration out of the way, we have another trick to use:

```
map { memoize($_) }
  qw(
     get_ta_cosmos
```

```
    get_feed_info
    get_info_from_technorati
    get_info_from_rss
);
```

This little map statement sets up the *Memoize* module for us so that the mentioned function names will have their results cached. This means that, if any of the four functions in the statement are called with the same parameters throughout the program, the results will not be recomputed but will be pulled from a cache in memory. This should save a little time and use of web services as we work.

Next, here's the main driving code of the script:

```
my $feed_records = [];
for my $feed (@feeds) {
  my %feed_record = (url=>$feed);
  $feed_record{info}    = get_feed_info(FEED_URL, $feed);
  $feed_record{similar} = collect_similar_feeds($feed_record{info});
  $feed_record{related} = collect_related_feeds($feed_record{info});
  push @$feed_records, \%feed_record;
}

print html_wrapper(join("<hr />\n",
                   map { format_feed_record($_) }
                   @$feed_records));
```

This loop runs through each of our favorite RSS feeds and gathers records for each one. Each record is a hash, whose primary keys are info, similar, and related. info will contain basic information about the feed itself; similar will contain records about feeds in the same category as this feed; and related will contain records about feeds that have linked to items from the current feed.

Now, let's implement the functions that this code needs.

Getting the Dirt on Feeds

The first thing we want to do is build a way to gather information about RSS feeds, using our chosen web services and the feeds themselves:

```
sub get_feed_info {
  my ($type, $id) = @_;
  return {} if !$id;

  my ($rss, $s_info, $t_info, $feed_url, $site_url);

  if ($type eq SYNDIC8_ID) {
    $s_info = get_info_from_syndic8($id) || {};
    $feed_url = $s_info->{dataurl};
  } elsif ($type eq FEED_URL) {
```

```
      $feed_url = $id;
    } elsif ($type eq SITE_URL) {
      my $rss_finder = new HTML::RSSAutodiscovery();
      eval {
        ($feed_url) = map { $_->{href} } @{$rss_finder->locate($site_url)};
      };
    }

    $rss = get_info_from_rss($feed_url) || {};
    $s_info ||= get_info_from_syndic8($feed_url) || {};
    $site_url = $rss->{channel}{link} || $s_info->{dataurl};

    $t_info = get_info_from_technorati($site_url);

    return {url=>$feed_url, rss=>$rss, syndic8=>$s_info, technorati=>$t_info};
}
```

This function gathers basic information on a feed. It accepts several different forms of identification for a feed: the Syndic8 feed internal ID number, the URL of the RSS feed itself, and the URL of a site that might have a feed. The first parameter indicates which kind of identification the function should expect (using the constants we defined at the beginning of the script), and the second is the identification itself.

So, we must first figure out a URL to the feed from the identification given. With a Syndic8 feed ID, the function tries to grab the feed's record via the Syndic8 web service and then get the feed URL from that record. If a feed URL is given, great; use it. Otherwise, if a site URL is given, we use the *HTML::RSSAutodiscovery* module to look for a feed for this site.

Once we have the feed URL, we get and parse the feed, grab information from Syndic8 if we haven't already, and then get feed information from Technorati. All of this information is then collected into a hash and returned. You might want to check out the documentation for the Syndic8 and Technorati APIs to learn what information each service provides on a feed.

Moving on, let's see what it takes to get information from Syndic8:

```
sub get_info_from_syndic8 {
  my $feed_url = shift;
  return {} if !$feed_url;

  my $result = {};
  eval {
    $result = XMLRPC::Lite->proxy($syndic8_url)
      ->call('syndic8.GetFeedInfo', $feed_url)->result() || {};
  };
  return $result;
}
```

Here, we expect a feed URL and return empty-handed if one isn't given. If a feed URL is given, we simply call the Syndic8 web service method syndic8.GetFeedInfo with the URL to our feed and catch the results. One thing to note is that we wrap this call in an eval statement, which prevents any ostensibly fatal errors in this call or XML parsing from exiting the script. In the case of such an error, we simply return an empty record.

Grabbing information from Technorati is a little more complex, if only because we'll be parsing the XML resulting from calls without the help of a convenience package such as *XMLRPC::Lite*. But let's get on with that:

```perl
sub get_info_from_technorati {
  my $site_url = shift;
  return {} if !$site_url;

  my $xml = get_ta_cosmos($site_url);

  my $info = {};
  if ($xml =~ m{<result>(.*?)</result>}mgis) {
    my $xml2 = $1;
    $info = extract_ta_bloginfo($xml2);
  }
  return ($info->{lastupdate} =~ /1970/) ? {} : $info;
}
```

Here, we make a request to the web service's cosmos method with the site URL parameter. Using a regular expression, we look for the contents of a results tag in the response to our query and call upon a convenience function to extract the XML data into a hash. We also check to make sure the date doesn't contain 1970, a value that occurs when a record isn't found.

The implementation of our first convenience function goes like so:

```perl
sub get_ta_cosmos {
  my $url = shift;
  return get($ta_cosmos_url.$url);
}
```

This is just a simple wrapper around *LWP::Simple*'s get function, done so that we can memoize it without interfering with other modules' use of the same function. Next, here's how to extract a hash from the XML data:

```perl
sub extract_ta_bloginfo {
  my $xml = shift;
  my %info = ( );

  if ($xml =~ m{<weblog>(.*?)</weblog>}mgis) {
    my ($content) = ($1||'');
    while ($content =~ m{<(.*?)>(.*?)</\1>}mgis) {
      my ($name, $val) = ($1||'', $2||'');
      $info{$name} = $val;
    }
  }
```

```
    }

    return \%info;
}
```

With another couple of regular expressions, we look for the weblog tag in a given stream of XML and extract all of the tags it contains into a hash. Hash keys are tag names, and the values are the contents of those tags. The resulting hash contains basic information about a weblog cited in the Technorati results. We'll also use this in another function in a little bit.

We can extract information from both services, but how about feeds themselves? We can extract feeds with a simple function:

```
sub get_info_from_rss {
    my $feed_url = shift;
    return {} if !$feed_url;

    my $rss = new XML::RSS();
    eval {
        $rss->parse(get($feed_url));
    };
    return $rss;
}
```

Again, we expect a feed URL and return empty handed if one is missing. If a feed URL is given, we download the contents of that URL and use the *XML::RSS* module to parse the data. Notice that we use another eval statement to wrap this processing so that parsing errors do not exit our script. If everything goes well, we return an instance of *XML::RSS*.

Our basic feed information–gathering machinery is in place now. The next thing to tackle is gathering feeds. Let's start with employing the Technorati API to find feeds that have referred to a given feed:

```
sub collect_related_feeds {
    my $feed_info = shift;
    my $site_url = $feed_info->{rss}{channel}{link} || $feed_info->{url};
    my %feeds = ();
```

We start off by expecting a feed information record, as produced earlier by our get_info function. From this record, we get the site URL for which the feed is a summary. We try two options. First, we check the RSS feed itself for the information. Then, we check the record as a backup and treat the RSS feed URL itself as the site URL so that we at least have something to go on.

With that, we call on the Technorati API to get a list of related feeds:

```
my $xml = get_ta_cosmos($site_url);
while ($xml =~ m{<item>(.*?)</item>}mgis) {
    my $xml2 = $1;
    my $ta_info = extract_ta_bloginfo($xml2);
```

```
my $info = ($ta_info->{rssurl} ne '') ?
    get_feed_info(FEED_URL, $ta_info->{rssurl}) :
    get_feed_info(SITE_URL, $ta_info->{url});
```

With our previous call to the Technorati API, we were gathering information about a feed. This time, we're using the same call to gather information about related feeds. Thanks to *Memoize*, we should be able to reuse the results of a given API call for the same site URL over and over again, though we actually call upon the API only once.

So, we use a regular expression to iterate through item tags in the resulting data and extract weblog information from each result. Then, we check to see if a URL to this weblog's RSS feed was supplied. If so, we use it to get a feed record on this site; otherwise, we use the site URL and try to guess where the feed is.

After getting the record, we grab the rest of the information in the item tag:

```
$info->{technorati} = $ta_info;

while ($xml2 =~ m{<(.*?)>(.*?)</\1>}mgis) {
    my ($name, $val) = ($1||'', $2||'');
    next if $name eq 'weblog';
    $info->{technorati}{$name} = $val;
}
```

Once more, we use a regular expression to convert from tag names and contents to a hash. The hash contains information about the weblog's relationship to the feed we're considering, among other things.

To finish up, let's add this record to a hash (to prevent duplicate records) and return that hash when we're all done:

```
    $feeds{$info->{url}} = $info;
}

return \%feeds;
}
```

The returned hash will contain feed URLs as keys and feed records as values. Each of these feeds should be somewhat related to the original feed, if only because they linked to its content at one point.

Now, let's go on to use the Syndic8 API to find feeds in a category:

```
sub collect_similar_feeds {
    my $feed_info = shift;
    my %feeds = ();

    my $categories = $feed_info->{syndic8}->{Categories} || {};
    for my $cat_scheme (keys %{$categories}) {
        my $cat_name = $categories->{$cat_scheme};
```

The first thing we do is expect a feed information record and try to grab a list of categories from it. This will be a hash whose keys are codes that identify categorization schemes and whose values identify category titles. We'll loop through each of these pairs and gather feeds in each category:

```
my $feeds = XMLRPC::Lite->proxy($syndic8_url)
  ->call('syndic8.GetFeedsInCategory', $cat_scheme, $cat_name)
  ->result() || [];

# Limit the number of feeds handled in any one category
$feeds = [ @{$feeds}[0..$syndic8_max_results] ]
  if (scalar(@$feeds) > $syndic8_max_results);
```

Once we have a category scheme and title, we call on the Syndic8 API web service to give us a list of feeds in this category. This call returns a list of internal Syndic8 feed ID numbers, which is why we built in the ability to use them to locate feeds earlier, in our get_feed_info function. Also, we limit the number of results used, based on the configuration variable at the beginning of the script.

Next, let's gather information about the feeds we've found in this category:

```
    for my $feed (@$feeds) {
      my $feed_info = get_feed_info(SYNDIC8_ID, $feed);
      my $feed_url = $feed_info->{syndic8}{dataurl};
      next if !$feed_url;
      $feeds{"$cat_name ($cat_scheme)"}{$feed_url} = $feed_info;
    }
  }

  return \%feeds;
}
```

Using the Syndic8 feed ID returned for each feed, we get a record for each and add it to a hash whose keys are based on the category and the feed URL. This is an attempt to make sure there is a list of unique feeds for each category. Finally, we return the results of this process.

Reporting on Our Findings

At this point, we can gather information about feeds and use the Syndic8 and Technorati APIs to dig for feeds in similar categories and feeds related by linking. Now, let's produce an HTML page for what we find for each of our favorite feeds:

```
sub html_wrapper {
  my $content = shift;
  return qq^
    <html>
      <head>
        <title>Digging for RSS feeds</title>
```

```
      </head>
      <body>
         $content
      </body>
   </html>
   ^;
}
```

We just put together a simple HTML shell here to contain our results. It wraps whatever content it is given with a simple HTML skeleton. The next step, since our basic unit of results is the feed information record, is to come up with a means of formatting one:

```
sub format_feed_info {
  my $info = shift;
  my ($feed_url, $feed_title, $feed_link) =
    ($info->{url}, feed_title($info), feed_link($info));
  return qq^<a href="$feed_link">$feed_title</a>
    (<a href="$feed_url">RSS</a>)^;
}
```

This doesn't do much with the wealth of data contained in a feed information record, but for now we simply construct a link to the site and a link to the feed. We'll use this to format the results of our digging for a given feed:

```
sub format_feed_record {
  my $record = shift;
  my $out = '';
  $out .= qq^
    <div class="record">
      ^;

  $out .= qq^<h2 class="main_feed">^.
    format_feed_info($record->{info})."</h2>\n";
```

The first thing we do here is open a div tag to contain these particular record results. Then, we format the record that describes the favorite feed under investigation. Next, we format the results of looking for related feeds:

```
  my $related = $record->{related};
  if (keys %{$related}) {
    $out .= "<h3>Feeds related by links:</h3>\n<ul>\n";
    $out .= join
      ('',
       map { "<li>".format_feed_info($related->{$_})."</li>\n" }
       sort keys %{$related})."\n\n";
    $out .= "</ul>\n";
  }
```

This produces a bulleted list of feeds discovered, as related by linking to our feed. Next, we include the feeds related by category:

```
  my $similar = $record->{similar};
  if (keys %{$similar}) {
```

```
$out .= "<h3>Similar feeds by category:</h3>\n<ul>\n";
for my $cat (sort keys %{$similar}) {
  $out .= "<li>$cat\n<ul>";
  $out .= join
    ('',
     map { "<li>".format_feed_info($similar->{$cat}{$_})."</li>\n" }
     sort keys %{$similar->{$cat}})."\n\n";
    );
  $out .= "</ul>\n</li>\n";
}
$out .= "</ul>\n";
}
```

A little bit more involved, this produces a set of nested lists, with the outer bullets describing categories and the inner bullets describing feeds belonging to the categories. Finally, let's wrap up our results:

```
$out .= qq^
</div>
  ^;

return $out;
}
```

We now have just a few loose ends to tie up. Some feed titles have a bit of extra whitespace in them, so we'll need to tidy that:

```
sub trim_space {
  my $val = shift;
  $val=~s/^\s+//;
  $val=~s/\s+$//g;
  return $val;
}
```

And, since there's a lot of variability in our results as to where a feed's title is, we employ several options in grabbing it:

```
sub feed_title {
  my $feed_info = shift;
  return trim_space
    (
     $feed_info->{rss}{channel}{title} ||
     $feed_info->{syndic8}{sitename} ||
     $feed_info->{technorati}{name} ||
     $feed_info->{url} ||
     '(untitled)'
    );
}
```

As with the title, there are many places where a link to the feed can be found, so we do something similar with it:

```
sub feed_link {
  my $feed_info = shift;
  return trim_space
    (
```

```
        $feed_info->{rss}{channel}{link} ||
        $feed_info->{syndic8}{siteurl} ||
        $feed_info->{technorati}{url} ||
        $feed_info->{url} ||
        ''
    );
}
```

Figure 4-7 shows a sample of the generated HTML results.

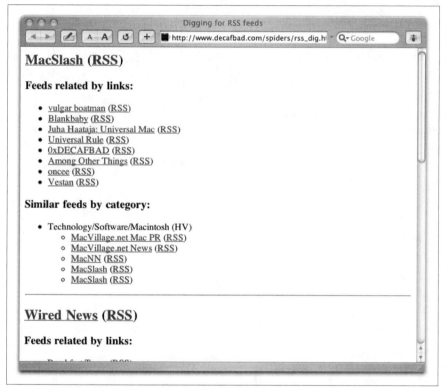

Figure 4-7. A sampling of possibly related sites

With the use of two web services, we have a pretty powerful robot with which to dig for more interesting feeds. This hack makes quite a few calls to web services, so, although you might want to run it every now and then to find updates, you might want to go easy on it.

Hacking the Hack

A few things are left as exercises for the reader. Most notably, we don't make much use of all the information gathered into a feed information record. In our report, we simply display a link to a site and a link to its feed. In fact, this record also contains all the most recent headlines for a feed, as well as the wealth of information provided by the Syndic8 and Technorati APIs. With some homework, this tool could be expanded even further to make use of all of this additional information.

—l.m.orchard

HACK Automatically Finding Blogs of Interest
#72
An easy way to find interesting new sites is to peruse an existing site's blogroll: a listing of blogs they read regularly. Let's create a spider to automate this by looking for keywords in the content of outbound links.

I enjoy reading blogs, but with the demands of the day, I find it difficult to read the dozen or so I like most, let alone discover new ones. I often have good luck when clicking through the blogrolls of writers I enjoy.

I decided to set out and automate this process, by creating a script that starts at one of my favorite sites and then visits each outbound link that site has to offer. As the script downloads each new page, it'll look through the content for keywords I've defined, in hopes of finding a new daily read that matches my own interests.

The Code

Save the following script as *blogfinder.pl*:

```perl
#!/usr/bin/perl  -w
use strict; $|++;

use LWP::UserAgent;
use HTML::LinkExtor;
use URI::URL;

# where should results go?
my $result_file   = "./result.html";
my $keywords_reg = qr/pipe-delimited search terms/;
my $starter_url   = "your favorite blog here";

# open and create the result.html file.
open(RESULT, ">$result_file") or die "Couldn't create: $!\n";
print RESULT "<html><head><title>Spider Findings</title></head><body>\n";

# our workhorse for access.
my $ua = LWP::UserAgent->new;
print "\nnow spidering: $starter_url\n";

# begin our link searching. LinkExtor takes a
# subroutine argument to handle found links,
# and then the actual data of the page.
HTML::LinkExtor->new(
```

```
sub {
      my ($tag, %attr) = @_;
      return if $tag ne 'a';

      # make any href relative link into
      # an absolute value, and add to an
      # internal list of links to check out.
      my @links = map { url($_, $starter_url)->abs() }
                      grep { defined } @attr{qw/href/};

      # make 'em all pretty...
      foreach my $link (@links) {
          print " + $link\n"; # hello!
          my $data = $ua->get($link)->content;
          if ($data =~ m/$keywords_reg/i) {
              open(RESULT, ">>$result_file");
              print RESULT "<a href=\"$link\">$link</a><br>\n";
              close(RESULT); # one match printed, yes!
          }
      }

# and now, the actual content that
# HTML::LinkExtor goes through...
})->parse(
  do {
      my $r = $ua->get($starter_url);
      $r->content_type eq "text/html" ? $r->content : "";
  }
);

print RESULT "</body></html>";
close RESULT; exit;
```

Once the *LWP::UserAgent* [Hack #10] object is created, we drop into the main workhorse loop of the spider subroutine. Here is where the script decides which link to spider. Obviously, the seed link is first, but as the spider traverses the first web page, it is on the lookout for links to extract. This is handled by the *HTML::LinkExtor* object (*http://search.cpan.org/author/ GAAS/HTML-Parser-3/lib/HTML/LinkExtor.pm*). Each link, in turn, is passed to an *HTML::LinkExtor* callback, which downloads each page, looks for the magic keywords, and makes note of any matches in a newly created *results.html* file.

When the spider has finished its run, you will be left with an HTML file that contains links that match your search criteria. There is, of course, room for refinement. However, one thing I enjoy about this script is the subtle entropy that seems to arise in it. Through this unintended randomness, I am able to discover blogs I would never have discovered by other means. More often than not, such a discovery is one I would rather not have made. But every now and then, a real gem can be seen gleaming at the bottom of the trash heap that is so often our beloved Internet.

Running the Hack

The first thing you should do is replace the two lines at the top of the script with your favorite blog URL and a pipe-delimited (|) list of values, like so:

```
my $keywords_reg = qr/foaf|perl|os x/;
my $starter_url  = "http://myfavoriteblog.com";
```

The pipe is the equivalent of *OR*, so these lines mean "Spider *myfavoriteblog.com* and search for foaf *OR* perl *OR* os x." If you know regular expressions, you can modify this even further to check for word boundaries (so that perl would not match amityperl, for instance). Once these two lines are configured, run the script, like so:

```
% perl blogfinder.pl
now spidering: http://www.myfavoriteblog.com
  + http://myfavoriteblog.com
  + http://www.luserinterface.net/index.cgi/colophon/
  + mailto:saf@luserinterface.net
  + http://jabber.org/
  + http://sourceforge.net/projects/gaim/
  + http://scottfallin.com/hacks/popBlosx.text
```

Once the script is finished spidering the outbound links, you'll have a new file in the current directory, with a list of URLs that match your keyword criteria.

Hacking the Hack

There are a few ways to modify the hack, the most interesting of which is to add another level of link crawling to begin creating "blog neighborhoods" similar to the idea of "Six Degrees of Kevin Bacon" (*http://www.wired.com/news/culture/0,1284,49343,00.html*; see also an implementation by Mark Pilgrim based on Google search results: *http://diveintomark.org/archives/2002/06/04/who_are_the_people_in_your_neighborhood*). One of the easiest additions, however, involves stopping the spider from indexing more data than necessary.

As you can see from the sample output, the spider will look at any URI that has been put into an HTML A tag, which could involve email addresses, IRC and FTP servers, and so forth. Since the spider isn't equipped to handle those protocols, telling it to skip over them is a simple modification:

```
foreach my $link (@links) {
    next unless $link =~ /^http/i;
    print " + $link\n"; # hello!
    my $data = $ua->get($link)->content;
```

Other possibilities could restrict spidering to third-party sites only (since you're not interested in spidering your favorite site, but rather the sites it links to) or add an upper limit to the number of sites spidered (i.e., "spider as much as you can, to a maximum of 200 sites").

—Scott Fallin

Scraping TV Listings

Freeing yourself from flipping through a weekly publication by visiting the TV Guide Online web site might sound like a good idea, but being forced to load heavy pages, showing only hours at a time and channels you don't care for, isn't exactly the utopia for which you were hoping.

To grab the latest TV listings from TV Guide Online (*http://www.tvguide.com*), we could write an HTML scraper from scratch using *HTML::TableExtract* [Hack #67] and similar modules, or we could go Borg on a script called *tvlisting* and assimilate it into our collective consciousness. Why reinvent the wheel if you don't have to, right? The author of *tvlisting*, Kurt V. Hindenburg, has extensively reverse-engineered TV Guide Online's dynamic site and created a script that can pull down all the TV listings for a whole day and output it in several different formats, including XML.

Grab *tvlisting* from *http://www.cherrynebula.net/projects/tvlisting/tvlisting.html* and follow the terse documentation to get it running on your platform. There are tons of options you can use when running *tvlisting*, most of which we won't cover for sake of brevity. So, snoop around in the *tvlisting* code, as well as the included *sample_rc* file, and check out the various options available. For our purposes, we'll modify the *sample_rc* file and use command-line arguments when we call the script. Open the *sample_rc* file and save it as *tvlisting_config*; then we'll get started. Let's look at a small portion of our new *tvlisting_config* file:

```
## To use this script as a
## CGI; please read CGI.txt
## Choices : $TRUE, $FALSE
$options{USE_CGI} = $FALSE;

## Choices : WGET, LYNX, CURL, LWPUSERAGENT
$options{GET_METHOD} = qw(LWPUSERAGENT);

## Choices : HTML, TEXT, LATEX, XAWTV, XML
$options{OUTPUT_FORMAT} = qw(XML);

## Choices : TVGUIDE
$options{INPUT_SOURCE} = qw(TVGUIDE);
```

```
### Attributes dealing with channels.
## Should channels be run through the filter?
## Choices : $TRUE, $FALSE
$options{FILTER_CHANNELS} = $TRUE;

## Filter by NAME and/or NUMBER?
$options{FILTER_CHANNELS_BY_NAME} = $FALSE;
$options{FILTER_CHANNELS_BY_NUMBER} = $TRUE;

## List of channels to OUTPUT
$options{FILTER_CHANNELS_BY_NAME_LIST} =
    ["WTTV", "WISH", "WTHR", "WFYI", "WXIN", "WRTV", "WNDY", "WIPX"];

$options{FILTER_CHANNELS_BY_NUMBER_LIST} =
    [qw( 2 3 4 5 6 7 9 11 12 14 15 16 18 28 29 30 31 32
        33 34 35 36 37 38 39 49 50 53 55 71 73 74 75 78)];

## Your personal Service ID, used by
## tvguide.com to localize your listings.
$options{SERVICE_ID} = 359508;
```

As you can see, there are many options available (the preceding listing is about half of what you'd see in a normal configuration file). Starting from the top, I set USE_CGI to $FALSE, GET_METHOD to LWPUSERAGENT, and OUTPUT_FORMAT to XML. You may have noticed that you can output to HTML as well, but I'm not crazy about the quality of its HTML output. The FILTER_ options allow us to choose only the channels we are interested in, rather than having to weed through hundreds of useless entries to find what we're looking for. The most important option, SERVICE_ID, is what TV Guide Online uses to specify the stations and channel numbers that are available in your area. Without this option set correctly, you'll receive channels that do not map to the channels on your TV, and that's no fun. The *Readme.txt* file has some further information on how to hunt this ID down.

After configuration, it's simply a matter of running the script to get an output of the current hour's listings for just the channels you're interested in. If you specified TEXT output, you'll see something like this (severely truncated for readability):

```
% bin/tvlisting
              6:30 PM           7:00 PM           7:30 PM
           +---------+---------+---------+---------+---------+
  76 WE     Felicity           Hollywood Wives
  77 OXYGN  Can You Tell?      Beautiful
```

An XML output format grants the following snippet, which is readily parseable:

```
% bin/tvlisting
<Channel Name="TOON" Number="53">
  <Shows Title="Dexter's Laboratory" Sequence="1" Duration="6" />
```

```
<Shows Title="Ed, Edd n Eddy" Sequence="2" Duration="6" />
<Shows Title="Courage the Cowardly Dog" Sequence="3" Duration="6" />
<Shows Title="Pokemon" Sequence="4" Duration="6" />
</Channel>
```

Even though you can filter by channels within *tvlisting*, there doesn't seem to be a way to filter by type of program, such as all "horror" movies or anything with Mister Miyagi. For that, we'd have to build our own quick scraper.

The Code

Save the following code as *tvsearch.pl*:

```perl
#!/usr/bin/perl -w
use strict;
use Getopt::Long;
use LWP::Simple;
use HTML::TableExtract;
my %opts;

# our list of tvguide.com categories.
my @search_categories = ( qw/ action+%26+adventure adult Movie
                              comedy drama horror mystery+%26+suspense
                              sci-fi+%26+paranormal western Sports
                              Newscasts+%26+newsmagazines health+%26+fitness
                              science+%26+technology education Children%27s
                              talk+%26+discussion soap+opera
                              shopping+%26+classifieds music / );

# instructions for if the user doesn't
# pass a search term or category. bah.
sub show_usage {
 print "You need to pass either a search term (--search)\n";
 print "or use one of the category numbers below (--category):\n\n";
 my $i=1; foreach my $cat (@search_categories) {
    $cat =~ s/\+/ /g; $cat =~ s/%26/&/; $cat =~ s/%27/'/;
    print "  $i) ", ucfirst($cat), "\n"; $i++;
 } exit;
}

# define our command-line flags (long and short versions).
GetOptions(\%opts, 'search|s=s',      # a search term.
                   'category|c=s',    # a search category.
); unless ($opts{search} || $opts{category}) { show_usage; }

# create some variables for use at tvguide.com.
my ($day, $month) = (localtime)[3..4]; $month++;
my $start_time = "8:00";         # this time is in military format
my $time_span  = 20;             # number of hours of TV listings you want
my $start_date = "$month\/$day"; # set the current month and day
my $service_id = 61058;          # our service id (see tvlisting readme)
```

```
my $search_phrase = undef;        # final holder of what was searched for
my $html_file = undef;            # the downloaded data from tvguide.com
my $url = 'http://www.tvguide.com/listings/search/SearchResults.asp';

# search by category.
if ($opts{category}) {
   my $id = $opts{category}; # convenience.
   die "Search category must be a number!" unless $id =~ /\d+/;
   die "Category ID was invalid" unless ($id >= 1 && $id <= 19);
   $html_file = get("$url?l=$service_id&FormCategories=".
                    "$search_categories[$id-1]");
   die "get() did not return as we expected.\n" unless $html_file;
   $search_phrase = $search_categories[$id-1];
}
elsif ($opts{search}) {
   my $term = $opts{search}; # convenience.
   $html_file = get("$url?I=$service_id&FormText=$term");
   die "get() did not return as we expected.\n" unless $html_file;
   $search_phrase = $term;
}

# now begin printing out our matches.
print "Search Results for '$search_phrase':\n\n";

# create a new table extract object and pass it the
# headers of the tvguide.com table in our data.
my $table_extract =
   HTML::TableExtract->new(
        headers => ["Date","Start Time", "Title", "Ch#"],
           keep_html => 1 );
$table_extract->parse($html_file);

# now, with our extracted table, parse.
foreach my $table ($table_extract->table_states) {
    foreach my $cols ($table->rows) {

        # this is not the best way to do this...
        if(@$cols[0] =~ /Sorry your search found no matches/i)
          { print "No matches to found for your search!\n"; exit; }

        # get the date.
        my $date = @$cols[0];
        $date =~ s/<.*>//g;        $date =~ s/\s*//g;
        $date =~ /(\w*)\D(\d*)/g; $date = "$1/$2";

        # get the time.
        my $time = @$cols[1];
        $time =~ m/(\d*:\d*\s+\w+)/;
        $time = $1;

        # get the title, detail_url, detail_number, and station.
        @$cols[2] =~ /href="(.*\('\d*','(\d*)','\d*','\d*','(.*)',.*)"/i;
        my ($detail_url, $detail_num, $channel) = ($1, $2, $3);
```

```
my $title = @$cols[2]; $title =~ s/<.*>//g;
$title =~ /(\b(.*)\b)/g; $title = $1;

# get channel number
my $channel_num = @$cols[3];
$channel_num =~ m/>\s*(\d*)\s*</;
$channel_num = $1;

# turn the evil Javascript URL into a normal one.
$detail_url =~ /javascript:cu\('(\d+)','(\d+)'/;
my $iSvcId = $1; my $iTitleId = $2;
$detail_url = "http://www.tvguide.com/listings/".
              "closerlook.asp?I=$iSvcId&Q=$iTitleId";

# now, print the results.
print " $date at $time on chan$channel_num ($channel): $title\n";
print "    $detail_url\n\n";
    }
}
```

Running the Hack

A search for *Farscape* looks something like this:

```
% perl tvsearch.pl --search  farscape
Search Results for 'farscape':

Mon/28 at 12:00 AM on chan62 (SCI-FI): Farscape: What Was Lost: Sacrifice
    http://www.tvguide.com/listings/closerlook.asp?I=61058&Q=3508575

Mon/4 at 12:00 AM on chan62 (SCI-FI): Farscape: What Was Lost: Resurrection
    http://www.tvguide.com/listings/closerlook.asp?I=61058&Q=3508576
```

—William Eastler

What's Your Visitor's Weather Like?

You have a web site, as most people do, and you're interested in getting a general idea of what you're visitor's weather is like. Want to know if you get more comments when it's raining or sunny? With the groundwork laid in this hack, that and other nonsense will be readily available.

When you're spidering, don't consider only data available on the Web. Sometimes, the data is right under your nose, perhaps on your own server or even on your own hard drive **[Hack #82]**. This hack demonstrates the large amount of information available, even when you have only a small amount of your own data to start with. In this case, we're looking at a web server's log file, taking the IP address of the last few visitors' sites, using one database to look up the geographical location of that IP address, and then using another to find the weather there. It's a trivial example, perhaps, but it's also quite nifty. For example, you could easily modify this code to greet visitors to your site with commiserations about the rain.

For the geographical data, we're going to use the Perl interface to the CAIDA project (*http://www.caida.org/tools/utilities/netgeo/NGAPI/index.xml*); for the weather data, we're using the *Weather::Underground* module, which utilizes the information at *http://www.wunderground.com*.

The Code

Copy this code, changing the emphasized line to reflect the path to your Apache installation's *access_log*. Here, mine is in the same directory as the script:

```perl
#!/usr/bin/perl -w
#
# Ben Hammersley ben@benhammersley.com
# Looks up the real-world location of visiting IPs
# and then finds out the weather at those places
#

use strict;
use CAIDA::NetGeoClient;
use Weather::Underground;
use Geography::Countries;

my $apachelogfile = "access_log";
my $numberoflines = 10;
my $lastdomain    = "";

# Open up the logfile.
open (LOG, "<$apachelogfile") or die $!;

# Place all the lines of the logfile
# into an array, but in reverse order.
my @lines = reverse <LOG>;

# Start our HTML document.
print "<h2>Where my last few visitors came from:</h2>\n<ul>\n";

# Go through each line one
# by one, setting the variables.
my $i; foreach my $line (@lines) {
    my ($domain,$rfc931,$authuser,$TimeDate,
        $Request,$Status,$Bytes,$Referrer,$Agent) =
        $line =~ /^(\S+) (\S+) (\S+) \[([^\]\[]+)\] \"([^"]*)\" (\S+) (\S+)
\"?([^"]*)\"? \"([^"]*)\"/o;

        # If this record is one we saw
        # the last time around, move on.
        next if ($domain eq $lastdomain);
```

```
    # And now get the geographical info.
    my $geo      = CAIDA::NetGeoClient->new( );
    my $record   = $geo->getRecord($domain);
    my $city     = ucfirst(lc($record->{CITY}));
    my $region   = "";

    # Check to see if there is a record returned at all.
    unless ($record->{COUNTRY}) { $lastdomain = $domain; next; }

    # If city is in the U.S., use the state as the "region".
    # Otherwise, use Geography::Countries to munge the two letter
    # code for the country into its actual name. (Thanks to
    # Aaron Straup Cope for this tip.)
    if ($record->{COUNTRY} eq "US") {
        $region = ucfirst(lc($record->{STATE}));
    } else { $region = country($record->{COUNTRY}); }

    # Now get the weather information.
    my $place    = "$city, $region";
    my $weather  = Weather::Underground->new(place => $place);
    my $data     = $weather->getweather( );
    next unless $data; $data = $data->[0];

    # And print it for our HTML.
    print " <li>$city, $region where it is $data->{conditions}.</li>\n";

    # Record the last domain name
    # for the repeat prevention check
    $lastdomain = $domain;

    # Check whether you're not at the limit, and if you are, finish.
    if ($i++ >= $numberoflines-1) { last; }
}

print "</ul>";
```

The code loads up the *access_log*, reverses it to put the last accesses at the top, and then goes through the resulting list, line by line. First, it runs the line through a regular expression:

```
my
($domain,$rfc931,$authuser,$TimeDate,$Request,$Status,$Bytes,$Referrer,$Agen
t) = $line =~ /^(\S+) (\S+) (\S+) \[([^\]\[]+)\] \"([^"]*)\" (\S+) (\S+) \
"?([^"]*)\"? \"([^"]*)\"/o;
```

This splits the line into its different sections and is based on Apache's *combined* log format. We'll be using only the first variable (the domain itself) from these results, but, because this regular expression is so useful, I include it for your cannibalistic pleasure.

Anyhow, we take the domain and pass it to the *CAIDA* module, retrieving a result and checking whether that result is useful. If it's not useful, we go to the next line in the *access_log*. This highlights an important point when using third-party databases: you must always check for a failed query. Indeed, it might even be a good idea to treat a successful query as the exception rather than the rule.

Assuming we have a good result, we need to detect if the country is the U.S. If it is, we make the $region the value of the U.S. state; otherwise, we use the two-letter code for the country. We use the country function from the *Geography::Countries* module to convert the full name of the country to the two-letter code.

Running the Hack

Here's a typical run of the script, invoked on the command line:

```
% perl weather.pl
<h2>Where my last few visitors came from:</h2>

<ul>
 <li>London, UK, where it is cloudy</li>
 <li>New York, NY, where it is sunny</li>
</ul>
```

Using and Hacking the Hack

I have this script installed on my weblog using an Apache server-side include. This is probably a bad idea, given the potential for slow server responses on behalf of *CAIDA* and Weather Underground, but it does allow for completely up-to-date information. A more sensible approach might be to change the script to produce a static file and run this from *cron* [Hack #90] every few minutes.

If you're sure of fast responses, and if you have a dynamically created page, it would be fun to customize that page based on the weather at the reader's location. Pithy comments about the rain are always appreciated. Tweaking the Weather Underground response to give you the temperature instead of a descriptive string creates the possibility of dynamically selecting CSS stylesheets, so that colors change based on the temperature. Storing the weather data over a period of time gives you the possibility of creating an "average readership temperature" or the amount of rain that has fallen on your audience this week. These would be fun statistics for some and perhaps extremely useful for others.

—Ben Hammersley

Trendspotting with Geotargeting

HACK
#75

Compare the relative popularity of a trend or fashion in different locations, using only Google and Directi search results.

One of the latest buzzwords on the Internet is *geotargeting*, which is just a fancy name for the process of matching hostnames (e.g., *www.oreilly.com*) to addresses (e.g., 208.201.239.36) to country names (e.g., USA). The whole thing works because there are people who compile such databases and make them readily available. This information must be compiled by hand or at least semiautomatically, because the DNS system that resolves hostnames to addresses does not store it in its distributed database.

While it is possible to add geographic location data to DNS records, it is highly impractical to do so. However, since we know which addresses have been assigned to which businesses, governments, organizations, or educational establishments, we can assume with a high probability that the geographic location of the institution matches that of its hosts, at least of most of them. For example, if the given address belongs to the range of addresses assigned to British Telecom, then it is highly probable that it used by a host located within the territory of the United Kingdom.

Why go to such lengths when a simple DNS lookup (e.g., `nslookup 208.201.239.36`) gives the name of the host, and in that name we can look up the top-level domain (e.g., *.pl*, *.de*, or *.uk*) to find out where this particular host is located? There are four good reasons for this:

- Not all lookups on addresses return hostnames.
- A single address might serve more than one virtual host.
- Some country domains are registered by foreigners and hosted on servers on the other side of the globe.
- *.com*, *.net*, *.org*, *.biz*, or *.info* domains tell us nothing about the geographic location of the servers they are hosted on. That's where geotargeting can help.

Geotargeting is by no means perfect. For example, if an international organization like AOL gets a large chunk of addresses that it uses not only for servers in the USA, but also in Europe, the European hosts might be reported as being based in the U.S. Fortunately, such aberrations do not constitute a large percentage of addresses.

The first users of geotargeting were advertisers, who thought it would be a neat idea to serve local advertising. In other words, if a user visits a *New York Times* site, the ads they see depend on their physical location. Those in the U.S. might see the ads for the latest Chrysler car, while those in Japan might see ads for i-mode; users from Poland might see ads for Ekstradycja (a cult Polish police TV series), and those in India might see ads for the latest Bollywood movie. While such use of geotargeting might be used to maximize the return on the invested dollar, it also goes against the idea behind the Internet, which is a global network. (In other words, if you are entering a global audience, don't try to hide from it by compartmentalizing it.) Another problem with geotargeted ads is that they follow the viewer. Advertisers must love it, but it is annoying to the user; how would you feel if you saw the same ads for your local burger bar everywhere you went in the world?

Another application of geotargeting is to serve content in the local language. The idea is really nice, but it's often poorly implemented and takes a lot of clicking to get to the pages in other languages. The local pages have a habit of returning out of nowhere, especially after you upgrade your web browser to a new version. A much more interesting application of geotargeting is analysis of trends, which is usually done in two ways: via analysis of server logs and via analysis of results of querying Google.

Server log analysis is used to determine the geographic location of your visitors. For example, you might discover that your company's site is being visited by a large number of people from Japan. Perhaps that number is so significant that it will justify the rollout of a Japanese version of your site. Or it might be a signal that your company's products are becoming popular in that country and you should spend more marketing dollars there. But if you run a server for U.S. expatriates living in Tokyo, the same information might mean that your site is growing in popularity and you need to add more information in English. This method is based on the list of addresses of hosts that connect to the server, stored in your server's access log. You could write a script that looks up their geographic location to find out where your visitors come from. It is more accurate than looking up top-level domains, although it's a little slower due to the number of DNS lookups that need to be done.

Another interesting use of geotargeting is analysis of the spread of trends. This can be done with a simple script that plugs into the Google API and the IP-to-Country database provided by Directi (*http://ip-to-country.directi.com*). The idea behind trend analysis is simple: perform repetitive queries using the same keywords, but change the language of results and top-level domains for each query. Compare the number of results returned for each language, and you will get a good idea of the spread of the analyzed trend across cultures. Then, compare the number of results returned for each top-level domain, and you will get a good idea of the spread of the analyzed trend across the globe. Finally, look up geographic locations of hosts to better approximate the geographic spread of the analyzed trend.

You might discover some interesting things this way: it could turn out that a particular *.com* domain that serves a significant number of documents and that contained the given query in Japanese is located in Germany. It might be a sign that there is a large Japanese community in Germany that uses that particular *.com* domain for their portal. Shouldn't you be trying to get in touch with them?

The *geospider.pl* script shown in this hack is a sample implementation of this idea. It queries Google and then matches the names of hosts in returned URLs against the IP-to-Country database.

The Code

You will need the *Getopt::Std* and *Net::Google* modules for this script. You'll also need a Google API key (*http://api.google.com*) and the latest *ip-to-country.csv* database, available from *http://ip-to-country.directi.com/*.

Save the following code as *geospider.pl*:

```perl
#!/usr/bin/perl-w
#
# geospider.pl
#
# Geotargeting spider -- queries Google through the Google API, extracts
# hostnames from returned URLs, looks up addresses of hosts, and matches
# addresses of hosts against the IP-to-Country database from Directi:
# ip-to-country.directi.com. For more information about this software:
# http://www.artymiak.com/software or contact jacek@artymiak.com
#
# This code is free software; you can redistribute it and/or
# modify it under the same terms as Perl itself.
#

use strict;
use Getopt::Std;
use Net::Google;
use constant GOOGLEKEY => 'Your Google API key here';
use Socket;

my $help = <<"EOH";
-------------------------------------------------------------------------
Geotargeting trend analysis spider
-------------------------------------------------------------------------
Options:

   -h    prints this help
   -q    query in utf8, e.g. 'Spidering Hacks'
   -l    language codes, e.g. 'en fr jp'
   -d    domains, e.g. '.com'
   -s    which result should be returned first (count starts from 0), e.g. 0
   -n    how many results should be returned, e.g. 700
```

```
---------------------------------------------------------------------
EOH

# define our arguments and show the
# help if asked, or if missing query.
my %args; getopts("hq:l:d:s:n:", \%args);
die $help if exists $args{h};
die $help unless $args{'q'};

# create the Google object.
my $google = Net::Google->new(key=>GOOGLEKEY);
my $search = $google->search();

# language, defaulting to English.
$search->lr(qw($args{l}) || "en");

# what search result to start at, defaulting to 0.
$search->starts_at($args{'s'} || 0);

# how many results, defaulting to 10.
$search->starts_at($args{'n'} || 10);

# input and output encoding.
$search->ie(qw(utf8)); $search->oe(qw(utf8));

my $querystr; # our final string for searching.
if ($args{d}) { $querystr = "$args{q} .site:$args{d}"; }
else { $querystr = $args{'q'} } # domain specific searching.

# load in our lookup list from
# http://ip-to-country.directi.com/
my $file = "ip-to-country.csv";
print STDERR "Trying to open $file... \n";
open (FILE, "<$file") or die "[error] Couldn't open $file: $!\n";

# now load the whole shebang into memory.
print STDERR "Database opened, loading... \n";
my (%ip_from, %ip_to, %code2, %code3, %country);
my $counter=0; while (<FILE>) {
    chomp; my $line = $_; $line =~ s/"//g; # strip all quotes.
    my ($ip_from, $ip_to, $code2, $code3, $country) = split(/,/, $line);

    # remove trailing zeros.
    $ip_from =~ s/^0{0,10}//g;
    $ip_to =~ s/^0{0,10}//g;

    # and assign to our permanents.
    $ip_from{$counter} = $ip_from;
    $ip_to{$counter}   = $ip_to;
    $code2{$counter}   = $code2;
    $code3{$counter}   = $code3;
    $country{$counter} = $country;
```

```
        $counter++; # move on to next line.
}

$search->query(qq($querystr));
print STDERR "Querying Google with $querystr... \n";
print STDERR "Processing results from Google... \n";

# for each result from Google, display
# the geographic information we've found.
foreach my $result (@{$search->response()}) {
    print "-" x 80 . "\n";
    print " Search time: " . $result->searchTime() . "s\n";
    print "       Query: $querystr\n";
    print "   Languages: " . ( $args{l} || "en" ) . "\n";
    print "      Domain: " . ( $args{d} || "" ) . "\n";
    print "    Start at: " . ( $args{'s'} || 0 ) . "\n";
    print "Return items: " . ( $args{n} || 10 ) . "\n";
    print "-" x 80 . "\n";

    map {
        print "url: " . $_->URL() . "\n";
        my @addresses = get_host($_->URL());
        if (scalar @addresses != 0) {
            match_ip(get_host($_->URL()));
        } else {
            print "address: unknown\n";
            print "country: unknown\n";
            print "code3: unknown\n";
            print "code2: unknown\n";
        } print "-" x 50 . "\n";
    } @{$result->resultElements()};
}

# get the IPs for
# matching hostnames.
sub get_host {
    my ($url) = @_;

    # chop the URL down to just the hostname.
    my $name = substr($url, 7); $name =~ m/\//g;
    $name = substr($name, 0, pos($name) - 1);
    print "host: $name\n";

    # and get the matching IPs.
    my @addresses = gethostbyname($name);
    if (scalar @addresses != 0) {
        @addresses = map { inet_ntoa($_) } @addresses[4 .. $#addresses];
    } else { return undef; }
    return "@addresses";
}
```

```perl
# check our IP in the
# Directi list in memory.
sub match_ip {
    my (@addresses) = split(/ /, "@_");
    foreach my $address (@addresses) {
        print "address: $address\n";
        my @classes = split(/\./, $address);
        my $p; foreach my $class (@classes) {
            $p .= pack("C", int($class));
        } $p  = unpack("N", $p);
        my $counter = 0;
        foreach (keys %ip_to) {
            if ($p <= int($ip_to{$counter})) {
                print "country: " . $country{$counter} . "\n";
                print "code3: "   . $code3{$counter}   . "\n";
                print "code2: "   . $code2{$counter}   . "\n";
                last;
            } else { ++$counter; }
        }
    }
}
```

Running the Hack

Here, we're querying to see how much worldly penetration AmphetaDesk, a popular news aggregator, has, according to Google's top search results:

```
% perl geospider.pl -q "amphetadesk"
Trying to open ip-to-country.csv...
Database opened, loading...
Querying Google with amphetadesk...
Processing results from Google...
--------------------------------------------------------------
 Search time: 0.081432s
       Query: amphetadesk
   Languages: en
      Domain:
    Start at: 0
Return items: 10
--------------------------------------------------------------
url: http://www.macupdate.com/info.php/id/9787
host: www.macupdate.com
host: www.macupdate.com
address: 64.5.48.152
country: UNITED STATES
code3: USA
code2: US
-------------------------------------------------
url: http://allmacintosh.forthnet.gr/preview/214706.html
host: allmacintosh.forthnet.gr
host: allmacintosh.forthnet.gr
address: 193.92.150.100
country: GREECE
```

```
code3: GRC
code2: GR
--------------------------------------------------
...etc...
```

Hacking the Hack

This script is only a simple tool. You will make it better, no doubt. The first thing you could do is implement a more efficient way to query the IP-to-Country database. Storing data from *ip-to-country.csv* on a database server would speed script startup time by several seconds. Also, the answers to address-to-country queries could be obtained much faster.

You might ask if it wouldn't be easier to write a spider that doesn't use the Google API and instead downloads page after page of results returned by Google at *http://www.google.com*. Yes, it is possible, and it is also the quickest way to get your script blacklisted for the breach of the Google's user agreement. Google is not only the best search engine, it is also one of the best-monitored sites on the Internet.

—Jacek Artymiak

Getting the Best Travel Route by Train
A web scraper can help you find faster train connections in Europe.

If you ever visit Europe and want to travel by train, you will find the PKP (Polskie Koleje Panstwowe, or Polish State Railways) server (*http://www. rozklad.pkp.pl*) a handy place to find information about European train connections.

This hack queries the timetables of the PKP site and scrapes a variety of information from the results, including the time of departure and arrival, as well as the number of changes you'll have to make along the way.

The Code

Save the following code as *broute.pl*:

```perl
#!/usr/bin/perl -w
#
# broute.pl
#
# A European train timetable hack that displays available train connections
# between two cities, with dates, times, and the number of changes. You
# can limit the number of acceptable changes with -c. If there are no
# connections, try earlier/later times/dates or search again for connections
# with intermediate stops, e.g., instead of Manchester -> Roma, choose
# Manchester -> London, London -> Paris, and Paris -> Roma.
#
```

```
# This code is free software; you can redistribute it and/or
# modify it under the same terms as Perl itself.
#

use strict;
use LWP::UserAgent;
use Net::HTTP;
use Getopt::Std;

my $help = <<"EOH";
---------------------------------------------------------------------------
Best train routes in Europe

Options: -a   depart from
         -z   arrive in
         -d   date (of departure, if -s d; arrival, if -s a)
              in dd.mm.yy format (e.g. June 1, 2004 is 01.06.04)
         -t   time (of departure, if -s d; arrival, if -s a)
              in hh:mm format (e.g. 12:45)
         -s   select time point for -d and -t options, default -s d
         -c   maximum number of changes, default 0
         -h   print this help
EOH

# set out command-line options,
# requirements, and defaults.
my %args; getopt('ha:z:d:t:s:c:', \%args);
die $help if exists $args{h};
die $help unless $args{a};
die $help unless $args{z};
die $help unless $args{t};
$args{'s'} = 'depart' unless $args{'s'};
$args{'s'} = 'depart' if $args{'s'} eq 'd';
$args{'s'} = 'arrive' if $args{'s'} eq 'a';

# our requesting agent. define our URL and POST.
my $url  = 'http://www.rozklad.pkp.pl/cgi-bin/new/query.exe/en';
my $post = "protocol=http:&from=$args{a}&to=$args{z}&datesel=custom".
           "&date=$args{d}&timesel=$args{s}&time=$args{t}";

# the headers we'll send off...
my $hdrs = HTTP::Headers->new(Accept => 'text/plain',
                'User-Agent' => 'PKPTrainTimetableLookup/1.0');

# and the final requested documents.
my $uable = HTTP::Request->new(POST, $url, $hdrs, $post);
my $ua    = LWP::UserAgent->new; my $req = $ua->request($uable);

# if a success,
# let's parse it!
die $req->message
  unless $req->is_success;
my $doc = $req->content;
```

```
$doc =~ s/[\f\t\n\r]//isg; # remove linefeeds.
while ($doc =~ m/ NAME=sel[0-9]{1,2}>/isg) {
    my $begin = pos($doc);
    $doc =~ m/<TR>/isg;
    my $end = pos($doc);
    next unless $begin;
    next unless $end;

    # munch our content into columns.
    my $content = substr($doc, $begin, ($end -= 5) - $begin);
    $doc = substr($doc, $end);
    my @columns = split(/<TD/, $content); shift @columns;
    foreach my $column (@columns) {
        $column = '<TD' . $column;
        $column =~ s/<[^>]*>//g;
        $column =~ s/<[^>]*//g;
    }

    # skip schedules that have more hops than we want.
    if ($args{c} and int $args{c} < int $columns[2]) { next; }

    # and print out our data.
    print "-" x 80 . "\n";
    print "            From: $columns[0]\n";
    print "              To: $columns[1]\n";
    print "         Changes: $columns[2]\n";
    print "Date of Departure: $columns[3]\n" if $args{'s'} eq 'depart';
    print " Date of Arrival: $columns[3]\n" if $args{'s'} eq 'arrive';
    print "  Departure Time: $columns[4]\n";
    print "    Arrival Time: $columns[5]\n";
}
```

Running the Hack

The script has several command-line options that are viewable in the code or by requesting its display with perl broute.pl –h.

Here are a couple of example runs. Let's find all connections from Berlin to Szczecin with an arrival time of 8:00 A.M. on December 15, 2004 with no changes:

```
% perl broute.pl -a Berlin -z Szczecin -s a -d 12.15.04 -t 8:00 -c 0
```

How about all connections from Manchester to Rome with departure time of 8:00 A.M. on December 15, 2004 with a maximum of four changes:

```
% perl broute.pl -a Manchester -z Roma -s d -d 12.15.04 -t 8:00 -c 4
```

A typical run looks something like this:

```
trying http://www.rozklad.pkp.pl/cgi-bin/new/query.exe/en ...
--------------------------------------------------------------------------
            From: Berlin Ostbf
              To: Szczecin G≠_wny
```

```
        Changes: 0
Date of Arrival: 05.07.03
Departure Time: 5:55
   Arrival Time: 7:41
```

Hacking the Hack

There a few things you can do to expand this hack. For example, you could add subroutines that find connections within 24 hours (12 hours before and 12 hours ahead) of the given time of departure or arrival. Another addition could be a module that displays names of the transfer stations.

—Jacek Artymiak

H A C K   Geographic Distance and Back Again
#77
When you're traveling from one place to another, it's usually handy to know exactly how many miles you're going to be on the road. One of the best ways to get the most accurate result is to use latitude and longitude.

Dr. Seuss once wrote, "From here to there, from near to far, funny things are everywhere." But just how far apart are those funny things, anyway?

Given the latitude and longitude of two terrestrial objects, and assuming the earth to be a perfect sphere with a smooth surface, the "great circle" calculation to find the shortest surface distance between those two objects is a simple bit of trigonometry. Even though the earth is neither smooth nor a perfect sphere, the calculation is surprisingly accurate. I found the position—i.e., the latitude and longitude—of my home and the home of a friend who lives a short distance away. Using a town map and a ruler, I calculated the distance at 7.49 miles. Using the positions and trigonometry, the calculated distance came out at 7.43 miles.

That was good enough for me, so I set about to create a program that would accept two addresses and return the distance between them. Initially, I thought I'd have the program done in about 30 minutes. Ultimately, it required a few hours of research and a creative hack of MapPoint. The tough part? Getting the true latitude and longitude for an address, something I mistakenly thought would be trivial on our little high-tech planet—not so!

The Latitude/Longitude Question

The difficulty associated with this hack can be demonstrated through a very simple exercise: right now, before you read any further, using any online resource that you like, go find the latitude and longitude of your house—not just of your *Zip Code*, but of your *actual house*.

Not so easy, is it? In fact, I was surprised by the difficulty this problem presented. I found several resources—the easiest to use being the U.S. Census web site (*http://www.census.gov*)—that could turn Zip Codes into positions, presumably somewhere near the center of the Zip Code's geographic region, but virtually nothing that would give me the position of an actual address. In the past, I used a mapping service called MapBlast! (*http://www.mapblast.com*), and I thought I recalled that this service would give me map positions. However, a trip to MapBlast! now lands you at Map-Point, Microsoft's mapping service, which apparently acquired MapBlast! in the not-too-distant past.

At this point, I'll spare you the details of my research and cut to the chase:

- If you want the position for a Zip Code, it's easy; there are lots of sites and even some Perl packages that will do this automatically for you.
- The major mapping services will take a position and present you with a map, but they won't give you a position if you give them an address.
- Microsoft has a nice set of web service APIs in addition to MapPoint, and they can be used to find the position of an address. Unfortunately, it's a subscription service.
- Pay services (search *http://www.geocode.com* to find a few) can turn an address into a position.
- Whether intentional or not, MapPoint does publish the position for an address in its publicly accessible web interface. It's not published on the page; it's published in the URL.

I found that last item in the list most intriguing. I discovered it quite by accident. I had mapped my address and by chance took a look at the URL. I recognized some numbers that looked suspiciously like my latitude and longitude. I played around a bit and found the behavior was consistent; MapPoint returns a latitude/longitude position in its URL whenever it maps an address. Try it. Go to *http://mappoint.msn.com/* and map an address. Then, look closely at the URL for the parameter whose name is C. It's the latitude and longitude of the address you just looked up. Now, all I needed to do was find a way to make MapPoint give that data up to a Perl script!

Hacking the Latitude Out of MapPoint

Getting MapPoint to respond to a Perl script as it would to a browser was a bit more difficult than a straightforward GET or POST. My first few quick attempts earned me return data that contained messages like "Function not allowed," "ROBOT-NOINDEX," and "The page you are looking for does not exist." In the end, I grabbed my trusty packet analyzer and monitored the traffic between IE and MapPoint, ultimately learning what it would take to make MapPoint think it was talking to a browser and not to a script. Here's what happens:

1. The first GET request to *http://mappoint.msn.com/* earns you a Location: HTTP header in return. The new location redirects to *home.aspx*, prefixed by a pathname that includes a long string of arbitrary characters, presumably a session ID or some other form of tracking information.

2. A GET on the new location retrieves the "Find a Map" form. Among the obvious fields—street, city, and so on—are some hidden ones. In particular, one hidden field named __VIEWSTATE contains about 1 KB of encoded data. It turns out that returning the exact __VIEWSTATE is important when sending the address query.

3. Next, we do a POST to send MapPoint the address we want mapped. In addition to the address information and the __VIEWSTATE field, there are a few other hidden fields to send. In the present code, we send a request specifically for an address in the United States. MapPoint supports other countries, as well as "Place" queries for the entire world, and it wouldn't be too much work to extend the program to handle these as well.

4. In response to the POST, we get another Location: HTTP header, this time redirecting to *map.aspx*. The URL contains several arguments, and among them is the latitude/longitude data that we want.

5. If you perform a GET on the new location, now you get the map. Our script doesn't do this last GET, however, because the data we want is in the URL, not on the result page.

The Code

If you take a look at the GetPosition function in the code, you'll see that it follows the five steps in the previous section exactly. The code also includes a simple routine to parse an address—to make the thing user-friendly, not because we had to—and a mainline to glue it all together and report the results. I used a nice package named *Geo::Distance* to perform the actual distance calculations. Time for some Perl!

Save the following code as *geodist.pl*:

```perl
#!/usr/bin/perl -w

# Usage: geodist.pl --from="fromaddr" --to="toaddr" [--unit="unit"]
# See ParseAddress() below for the format of addresses. Default unit is
# "mile". Other units are yard, foot, inch, kilometer, meter, centimeter.

use strict;
use Getopt::Long;
use Geo::Distance;
```

```perl
use HTTP::Request::Common;
use LWP::UserAgent;

# - - - - - - - - - - - - - - - - - - - - - - - - - - - - - - - - - - - - - -

my $_ADDRESS_REGEX = q<(((([^\,]+),\s*)?([^\,]+),\s*)?([A-Z]{2}))?> .
  q<(\s*(\d{5}(-\d{4})?))?>;

sub ParseAddress {

  # Moderately robust regex parse of an address of the form:
  #   Street Address, City, ST ZIP
  # Assumes that a city implies a state, and a street address implies a
  # city; otherwise, all fields are optional. Does a good job so long as
  # there are no commas in street address or city fields.

  my $AddrIn = shift;
  my $ComponentsOut = shift;
  $AddrIn =~ /$_ADDRESS_REGEX/;
  $ComponentsOut->{Address} = $4 if $4;
  $ComponentsOut->{City} = $5 if $5;
  $ComponentsOut->{State} = $6 if $6;
  $ComponentsOut->{Zip} = $8 if $8;
}

# - - - - - - - - - - - - - - - - - - - - - - - - - - - - - - - - - - - - - -

sub GetPosition {

  # Hack mappoint.msn.com to obtain the longitude and latitude of an
  # address. MapPoint doesn't actually return lon/lat as user data, but
  # it can be found in a Location header when a successful map request is
  # made. Testing has shown this to be a robust hack. Biggest caveat
  # presently is failure when MapPoint returns multiple address matches.

  my $AddressIn = shift;
  my $LatitudeOut = shift;
  my $LongitudeOut = shift;

  # Create a user agent for HTTP requests.
  my $ua = LWP::UserAgent->new;

  # First do a simple request to get the redirect that MapPoint sends us.
  my $req = GET( 'http://mappoint.msn.com/' );
  my $res = $ua->simple_request( $req );

  # Save the redirect URI and then grab the full page.
  my $uri = $res->headers->{location};
  my $req = GET( 'http://mappoint.msn.com' . $uri );
  my $res = $ua->request( $req );

  # Get the __VIEWSTATE hidden input from the result.
  my ( $__VIEWSTATE ) =
```

```
      $res->content =~ /name="__VIEWSTATE" value="([^\"]*)"/s;

  # Construct the form fields expected by the mapper.
  my $req = POST( 'http://mappoint.msn.com' . $uri,
    [ 'FndControl:SearchType' => 'Address',
      'FndControl:ARegionSelect' => '12',
      'FndControl:StreetText' => $AddressIn->{Address},
      'FndControl:CityText' => $AddressIn->{City},
      'FndControl:StateText' => $AddressIn->{State},
      'FndControl:ZipText' => $AddressIn->{Zip},
      'FndControl:isRegionChange' => '0',
      'FndControl:resultOffSet' => '0',
      'FndControl:BkARegion' => '12',
      'FndControl:BkPRegion' => '15',
      'FndControl:hiddenSearchType' => '',
      '__VIEWSTATE' => $__VIEWSTATE
    ] );

  # Works without referer, but we include it for good measure.
  $req->push_header( 'Referer' => 'http://mappoint.msn.com' . $uri );

  # Do a simple request because all we care about is the redirect URI.
  my $res = $ua->simple_request( $req );

  # Extract and return the latitude/longitude from the redirect URI.
  ( $$LatitudeOut, $$LongitudeOut ) = $res->headers->{location} =~
    /C=(-?[0-9]+\.[0-9]+)...(-?[0-9]+\.[0-9]+)/;
}

# - - - - - - - - - - - - - - - - - - - - - - - - - - - - - - - - -

sub main {

  # Get the command-line options.
  my ( $FromOpt, %FromAddress, $ToOpt, %ToAddress );
  my $UnitOpt = 'mile';
  GetOptions( "from=s" => \$FromOpt,
              "to=s"   => \$ToOpt,
              "unit=s" => \$UnitOpt );

  # Parse the addresses.
  ParseAddress( $FromOpt, \%FromAddress );
  ParseAddress( $ToOpt, \%ToAddress );

  # Get latitude/longitude for the addresses.
  my ( $FromLat, $FromLon, $ToLat, $ToLon );
  GetPosition( \%FromAddress, \$FromLat, \$FromLon );
  GetPosition( \%ToAddress, \$ToLat, \$ToLon );

  # If we at least got some numbers, then find the distance.
  if ( $FromLat && $FromLon && $ToLat && $ToLon ) {
    print "($FromLat,$FromLon) to ($ToLat,$ToLon) is ";
    my $geo = new Geo::Distance;
    print $geo->distance_calc( $UnitOpt, $FromLon,
```

```
                               $FromLat, $ToLon, $ToLat );
    if ( $UnitOpt eq 'inch' ) { print " inches\n"; }
    elsif ( $UnitOpt eq 'foot' ) { print " feet\n"; }
    else { print " ", $UnitOpt, "s\n"; }
  }
  else {
    print "Latitude/Longitude lookup failed for FROM address\n"
      if !( $FromLat && $FromLon );
    print "Latitude/Longitude lookup failed for TO address\n"
      if !( $ToLat && $ToLon );
  }
}

main( );
```

Running the Hack

A couple of quick examples will show how the hack *would* work:

```
% perl geodist.pl --from="Los Angeles, CA" --to="New York, NY"
(34.05466,-118.24150) to (40.71012,-74.00657) is 2448.15742500315 miles

% perl geodist.pl
    --from="14 Horseshoe Drive, Brookfield, CT"
    --to="5 Mountain Orchard, Bethel, CT"
(41.46380,-73.42021) to (41.35659,-73.41078) is 7.43209675476431 miles

% perl geodist.pl --from=06804 --to=06801
(41.47364,-73.38575) to (41.36418,-73.39262) is 7.57999735385486 miles
```

If something goes wrong with a position lookup—either because MapPoint didn't find the address or because it found multiple addresses—the script simply indicates which address had a problem:

```
% perl geodist.pl --from="Los Angeles, CA" --to="New York"
Latitude/Longitude lookup failed for TO address
```

In this case, "New York" is too general and needs to be refined further.

Hacking the Hack

The most obvious enhancement is to address the two shortcomings of the existing hack: it works only with addresses within the U.S., and it fails if MapPoint returns multiple address matches. Addressing the first issue is a matter of adding some options to the command line and then changing the fields sent in the POST query. Addressing the second issue is a bit more difficult; it's easy to parse the list that comes back, but the question is what to do with it. Do you just take the first address in the list? This may or may not be what the user wants. A true solution would probably have to present the list to the user and allow him to choose.

—*Ron Pacheco*

Super Word Lookup

#78

Working on a paper, book, or thesis and need a nerdy definition of one word, and alternatives to another?

You're writing a paper and getting sick of constantly looking up words in your dictionary and thesaurus. As most of the hacks in this book have done, you can scratch your itch with a little bit of Perl. This script uses the dict protocol (*http://www.dict.org*) and Thesaurus.com (*http://www.thesaurus.com*) to find all you need to know about a word.

By using the dict protocol, DICT.org and several other dictionary sites make our task easier, since we do not need to filter through HTML code to get what we are looking for. A quick look through CPAN (*http://www.cpan.org*) reveals that the dict protocol has already been implemented as a Perl module (*http://search.cpan.org/author/NEILB/Net-Dict/lib/Net/Dict.pod*). Reading through the documentation, you will find it is well-written and easy to implement; with just a few lines, you have more definitions than you can shake a stick at. Next problem.

Unfortunately, the thesaurus part of our program will not be as simple. However, there is a great online thesaurus (*http://www.thesaurus.com*) that we will use to get the information we need. The main page of the site offers a form to look up a word, and the results take us to exactly what we want. A quick look at the URL shows this will be an easy hurdle to overcome—using *LWP*, we can grab the page we want and need to worry only about parsing through it.

Since some words have multiple forms (noun, verb, etc.), there might be more than one entry for a word; this needs to be kept in mind. Looking at the HTML source, you can see that each row of the data is on its own line, starting with some table tags, then the header for the line (Concept, Function, etc.), followed by the content. The easiest way to handle this is to go through each section individually, grabbing from Entry to Source, and then parse out what's between. Since we want only synonyms for the exact word we searched for, we will grab only sections where the content for the entry line contains only the word we are looking for and is between the highlighting tag used by the site. Once we have this, we can strip out those highlighting tags and proceed to finding the synonym and antonym lines, which might not be available for every section. The easiest thing to do here is to throw it all in an array; this makes it easier to sort, remove duplicate words, and display it. In cases in which you are parsing through long HTML, you might find it easier to put the common HTML strings in variables and use them in the regular expressions; it makes the code easier to read. With a long list of all the words, we use the *Sort::Array* module to get an alphabetical, and unique, listing of results.

The Code

Save the following code as *dict.pl*:

```perl
#!/usr/bin/perl -w
#
# Dict - looks up definitions, synonyms and antonyms of words.
# Comments, suggestions, contempt? Email adam@bregenzer.net.
#
# This code is free software; you can redistribute it and/or
# modify it under the same terms as Perl itself.
#

use strict; $|++;
use LWP;
use Net::Dict;
use Sort::Array "Discard_Duplicates";
use URI::Escape;

my $word = $ARGV[0]; # the word to look-up
die "You didn't pass a word!\n" unless $word;
print "Definitions for word '$word':\n";

# get the dict.org results.
my $dict = Net::Dict->new('dict.org');
my $defs = $dict->define($word);
foreach my $def (@{$defs}) {
    my ($db, $definition) = @{$def};
    print $definition . "\n";
}

# base URL for thesaurus.com requests
# as well as the surrounding HTML of
# the data we want. cleaner regexps.
my $base_url      = "http://thesaurus.reference.com/search?q=";
my $middle_html   = ":</b>  </td><td>";
my $end_html      = "</td></tr>";
my $highlight_html = "<b style=\"background: #ffffaa\">";

# grab the thesaurus results.
my $ua = LWP::UserAgent->new(agent => 'Mozilla/4.76 [en] (Win98; U)');
my $data = $ua->get("$base_url" . uri_escape($word))->content;

# holders for matches.
my (@synonyms, @antonyms);

# and now loop through them all.
while ($data =~ /Entry(.*?)<b>Source:<\/b>(.*)/) {
    my $match = $1; $data = $2;

    # strip out the bold marks around the matched word.
    $match =~ s/${highlight_html}([^<]+)<\/b>/$1/;
```

```
        # push our results into our various arrays.
        if ($match =~ /Synonyms${middle_html}([^<]*)${end_html}/) {
            push @synonyms, (split /, /, $1);
        }
        elsif ($match =~ /Antonyms${middle_html}([^<]*)${end_html}/) {
            push @antonyms, (split /, /, $1);
        }
    }

    # sort them with sort::array,
    # and return unique matches.
    if ($#synonyms > 0) {
        @synonyms = Discard_Duplicates(
            sorting       => 'ascending',
            empty_fields => 'delete',
            data          => \@synonyms,
        );

        print "Synonyms for $word:\n";
        my $quotes = ''; # purtier.
        foreach my $nym (@synonyms) {
            print $quotes . $nym;
            $quotes = ', ';
        } print "\n\n";
    }

    # same thing as above.
    if ($#antonyms > 0) {
        @antonyms = Discard_Duplicates(
            sorting       => 'ascending',
            empty_fields => 'delete',
            data          => \@antonyms,
        );

        print "Antonyms for $word:\n";
        my $quotes = ''; # purtier.
        foreach my $nym (@antonyms) {
            print $quotes . $nym;
            $quotes = ', ';
        } print "\n";
    }
```

Running the Hack

Invoke the script on the command line, passing it one word at a time. As far as I know, these sites know how to work with English words only. This script has a tendency to generate a lot of output, so you might want to pipe it to *less* or redirect it to a file.

Here is an example where I look up the word "hack":

```
% perl dict.pl "hack"
Definitions for word 'hack':
```

```
<snip>
hack

    <jargon> 1. Originally, a quick job that produces what is
    needed, but not well.

    2.  An incredibly good, and perhaps very time-consuming, piece
    of work that produces exactly what is needed.

<snip>

    See also {neat hack}, {real hack}.

    [{Jargon File}]

    (1996-08-26)

Synonyms for hack:
be at, block out, bother, bug, bum, carve, chip, chisel, chop, cleave,
crack, cut, dissect, dissever, disunite, divide, divorce, dog, drudge,
engrave, etch, exasperate, fashion, form, gall, get, get to, grate, grave,
greasy grind, grind, grub, grubber, grubstreet, hack, hew, hireling, incise,
indent, insculp, irk, irritate, lackey, machine, mercenary, model, mold,
mould, nag, needle, nettle, old pro, open, part, pattern, peeve, pester,
pick on, pierce, pique, plodder, potboiler, pro, provoke, rend, rip, rive,
rough-hew, sculpt, sculpture, separate, servant, sever, shape, slash, slave,
slice, stab, stipple, sunder, tear asunder, tease, tool, trim, vex, whittle,
wig, workhorse

Antonyms for hack:
appease, aristocratic, attach, calm, cultured, gladden, high-class, humor,
join, make happy, meld, mollify, pacify, refined, sophisticated, superior,
unite
```

Hacking the Hack

There are a few ways you can improve upon this hack.

Using specific dictionaries. You can either use a different dict server or you can use only certain dictionaries within the dict server. The DICT.org server uses 13 dictionaries; you can limit it to use only the 1913 edition of *Webster's Revised Unabridged Dictionary* by changing the $dict->define line to:

```
my $defs = $dict->define($word, 'web1913');
```

The $dict->dbs method will get you a list of dictionaries available.

Clarifying the thesaurus. For brevity, the thesaurus section prints all the synonyms and antonyms for a particular word. It would be more useful if it separated them according to the function of the word and possibly the definition.

—Adam Bregenzer

Word Associations with Lexical Freenet

HACK
#79

There will come a time when you want a little more than simple word definitions, synonyms, or etymologies. Lexical Freenet takes you beyond these simple results, providing associative data, or "paths," from your word to others.

Lexical Freenet (*http://www.lexfn.com*) allows you to search for word relationships like puns, rhymes, concepts, relevant people, antonyms, and so much more. For example, a simple search for the word disease returns a long listing of word *paths*, each associated with other words by different types of connecting arrows: disease triggers both aids and cancer; comprises triggers symptoms; and bio triggers such relevant persons as janet elaine adkins, james parkinson, alois alzheimer, and so on. This is but a small sampling of the available and verbose output.

In combination with "Super Word Lookup" **[Hack #78]**, a command-line utility of the Lexical Freenet functionality would bring immense lookup capabilities to writers, librarians, and researchers. This hack shows you how to create said interface, with the ability to customize which relationships you'd like to see, as well as turn the visual connections into text.

The Code

Save the following code as *lexfn.pl*:

```perl
#!/usr/bin/perl-w
#
# Hack to query and report from www.lexfn.com
#
# This code is free software; you can redistribute it and/or
# modify it under the same terms as Perl itself.
#
# by rik - ora@rikrose.net
#


#######################
# support stage       #
#######################

use strict;
use Getopt::Std qw(getopts);
use LWP::Simple qw(get);
use URI::Escape qw(uri_escape uri_unescape);
use HTML::TokeParser;

sub usage () { print "
usage: lexfn [options] word1 [word2]
options available:
  -s Synonymous     -a Antonym        -b Birth Year
  -t Triggers       -r Rhymes         -d Death Year
```

```
 -g Generalizes    -l Sounds like    -T Bio Triggers
 -S Specialises    -A Anagram of     -k Also Known As
 -c Comprises      -o Occupation of
 -p Part of        -n Nationality

or -x for all

word1 is mandatory, but some searches require word2\n\n"
}


#######################
# parse stage         #
#######################

# grab arguments, and put them into %args hash, leaving nonarguments
# in @ARGV for us to process later (where word1 and word2 would be)
# if we don't have at least one argument, we die with our usage.
my %args; getopts('stgScparlAonbdTkx', \%args);
if (@ARGV > 2 || @ARGV == 0) { usage(); exit 0; }

# turn both our words into queries.
$ARGV[0] =~ s/ /\+/g; $ARGV[1] ||= "";
if ($ARGV[1]) { $ARGV[1] =~ s/ /\+/g; }

# begin our URL construction with the keywords.
my $URL = "http://www.lexfn.com/l/lexfn-cuff.cgi?sWord=$ARGV[0]".
          "&tWord=$ARGV[1]&query=show&maxReach=2";

# now, let's figure out our command-line arguments. each
# argument is associated with a relevant search at LexFN,
# so we'll first create a mapping to and fro.
my %keynames = (
 s => 'ASYN', t => 'ATRG', g => 'AGEN', S => 'ASPC', c => 'ACOM',
 p => 'APAR', a => 'AANT', r => 'ARHY', l => 'ASIM', A => 'AANA',
 o => 'ABOX', n => 'ABNX', b => 'ABBX', d => 'ABDX', T => 'ABTR',
 k => 'ABAK'
);

# if we want everything all matches
# then add them to our arguments hash,
# in preparation for our URL.
if (defined($args{'x'}) && $args{'x'} == 1) {
   foreach my $arg (qw/s t g l S c p a r l A o n b d T k/){
       $args{$arg} = 1; # in preparation for URL.
   } delete $args{'x'}; # x means nothing to LexFN.
}

# build the URL from the flags we want.
foreach my $arg (keys %args) { $URL .= '&' . $keynames{$arg} . '=on'; }

#######################
# request stage       #
#######################
```

```
# and download it all for parsing.
my $content = get($URL) or die $!;

#######################
# extract stage       #
#######################

# with the data sucked down, pass it off to the parser.
my $stream = HTML::TokeParser->new( \$content ) or die $!;

# skip the form on the page, then it's the first <b>
# after the form that we start extracting data from
my $tag = $stream->get_tag("/form");
while ($tag = $stream->get_tag("b")) {
    print $stream->get_trimmed_text("/b") . " ";
    $tag = $stream->get_tag("img");
    print $tag->[1]{alt} . " ";
    $tag = $stream->get_tag("a");
    print $stream->get_trimmed_text("/a") . "\n";
}

exit 0;
```

The code is split into four basic stages:

Support code
Such as includes and any subroutines you will need

The parsing stage
Where we work out what the user actually wants and build a URL to perform the request

The request stage itself
Where we retrieve the results

The extract stage
Where we recover the data

In this case, the Lexical Freenet site is basic enough that the request is a single URL. A typical Freenet URL looks something like this:

```
http://www.lexfn.com/l/lexfn-cuff.cgi?fromresub=on&
ASYN=on&ATRG=on&AGEN=on&ASPC=on&ACOM=on&APAR=on&AANT=on&
ARHY=on&ASIM=on&AANA=on&ABOX=on&ABNX=on&ABBX=on&ABDX=on&
ABTR=on&ABAK=on&sWord=lee+harvey+oswald&tWord=disobey&query=SHOW
```

The data we wish to extract is formed by repeatedly pulling the information from a standard and repetitive chunk of HTML in the search results. This allows us to use the simple *HTML::TokeParser* module **[Hack #20]** to retrieve chunks of data easily by parsing the HTML tags, allowing us to query their attributes and retrieve the surrounding text. As you can tell from the previous code, this is not too difficult.

Running the Hack

As you can see from the code, the hack has several switches available for you to decide which kind of word results you want. In this case, we'll run a search for everything related to disease:

```
% perl lexfn.pl -x disease
disease triggers aids
disease triggers cancer
disease triggers patients
disease triggers virus
disease triggers doctor
...
disease is more general than blood disorder
disease is more general than boutonneuse fever
disease is more general than cat scratch disease
...
disease rhymes with breeze
disease rhymes with briese
disease rhymes with cheese
disease rhymes with crees
...
```

Or perhaps a person's name is more to your liking:

```
% perl lexfn.pl -bdonT "lee harvey oswald"
lee harvey oswald was born in 1939
lee harvey oswald died in 1963
lee harvey oswald has the nationality american
lee harvey oswald has the occupation assassin
lee harvey oswald triggers 1956-1959
lee harvey oswald triggers 1959
lee harvey oswald triggers 1962
lee harvey oswald triggers attempted
lee harvey oswald triggers become
lee harvey oswald triggers book
lee harvey oswald triggers citizen
lee harvey oswald triggers communist
...
```

—*Richard Rose*

HACK #80 Reformatting Bugtraq Reports

Since Bugtraq is such an important part of a security administrator's watch list, it'll only be a matter of time before you'll want to integrate it more closely with your daily habits.

In this hack, we will write some code to extract the latest Bugtraq reports from *http://www.security-focus.com* and then output the simplified results for your viewing pleasure. Bugtraq, if you're not familiar with it, is a moderated discussion list devoted to security issues. Discussions are detailed accounts of new security issues and vulnerabilities, both how they're exploited and how they can be fixed. Let's start by examining the web page where the Bugtraq report is located: *http://www.security-focus.com/archive/1*.

One nice thing to notice about this page is that the data is formatted in a table, complete with column headers. We can use those headers to simplify the data-scraping process by using a handy Perl module called *HTML:: TableExtract* (*http://search.cpan.org/author/MSISK/HTML-TableExtract/*). *TableExtract* allows us to scrape the data from the web page without tying our code to a particular layout (at least, not too much). It accomplishes this feat by using those nice column headers. As long as those column headers stay the same, then the script should continue to work, even if SecurityFocus gives the page a facelift. In addition to that nice feature, *TableExtract* takes all the hard work out of parsing the HTML for the data we're after. Let's get started.

In the end, this script will use runtime options to allow the user to choose from a number of output formats and locations. I'm not a big fan of those one-letter flags sent to scripts to choose options, so we'll be using short words instead.

The Code

You'll need the *HTML::TableExtract* and *LWP::Simple* modules to grab the Bugtraq page. As we add more features, you'll also need *XML::RSS*, *Net:: AIM*, and *Net::SMTP*. You could use other modules like *URI::URL* or *HTML::Element* to simplify this hack even further.

There are a couple of things to note about this code. We start by retrieving the arguments passed to the script that will be used to determine the output formats; we'll discuss those later. Next, the data scraped from the Bugtraq page is stuck into a custom data structure to make accessing it easier for later additions to this hack. Also, a subroutine is added to format the data contained in the data structure to ensure minimal code duplication once we have to format for multiple types of output.

Save the following code to a file called *bugtraq_hack.pl*:

```perl
#!/usr/bin/perl -w
use strict;
use LWP::Simple;
use HTML::TableExtract;
use Net::SMTP;
use Net::AIM;
use XML::RSS;
```

```
# get params for later use.
my $RUN_STATE = shift(@ARGV);

# the base URL of the site we are scraping and
# the URL of the page where the bugtraq list is located.
my $base_url = "http://www.security-focus.com";
my $url      = "http://www.security-focus.com/archive/1";

# get our data.
my $html_file = get($url) or die "$!\n";

# create an iso date.
my ($day, $month, $year) = (localtime)[3..5];
$year += 1900; my $date = "$year-$month-$day";

# since the data we are interested in is contained in a table,
# and the table has headers, then we can specify the headers and
# use TableExtract to grab all the data below the headers in one
# fell swoop. We want to keep the HTML code intact so that we
# can use the links in our output formats. start the parse:
my $table_extract =
   HTML::TableExtract->new(
      headers    => [qw(Date Subject Author)],
      keep_html => 1 );
$table_extract->parse($html_file);

# parse out the desired info and
# stuff into a data structure.
my @parsed_rows; my $ctr = 0;
foreach my $table ($table_extract->table_states) {
   foreach my $cols ($table->rows) {
      @$cols[0] =~ m|(\d+/\d+/\d+)|;
      my %parsed_cols = ( "date" => $1 );

      # since the subject links are in the 2nd column, parse unwanted HTML
      # and grab the anchor tags. Also, the subject links are relative, so
      # we have to expand them. I could have used URI::URL, HTML::Element,
      # HTML::Parse, etc. to do most of this as well.
      @$cols[1] =~ s/ class="[\w\s]*"//;
      @$cols[1] =~ m|(<a href="(.*)">(.*)</a>)|;
      $parsed_cols{"subject_html"} = "<a href=\"$base_url$2\">$3</a>";
      $parsed_cols{"subject_url"}  = "$base_url$2";
      $parsed_cols{"subject"}      = $3;

      # the author links are in the 3rd
      # col, so do the same thing.
      @$cols[2] =~ s/ class="[\w\s]*"//;
      @$cols[2] =~ m|(<a href="mailto:(.*@.*)">(.*)</a>)|;
      $parsed_cols{"author_html"}  = $1;
      $parsed_cols{"author_email"} = $2;
      $parsed_cols{"author"}       = $3;
```

```
        # put all the information into an
        # array of hashes for easy access.
        $parsed_rows[$ctr++] = \%parsed_cols;
    }
}

# if no params were passed, then
# simply output to stdout.
unless ($RUN_STATE) { print &format_my_data(); }

# formats the actual
# common data, per format.
sub format_my_data() {
    my $data = "";

    foreach my $cols (@parsed_rows)  {
        unless ($RUN_STATE) { $data .= "$cols->{'date'} $cols->{'subject'}\n";
    }
    }

    return $data;
}
```

Running The Hack

Invoke the script on the command line to view the latest Bugtraq listings:

```
% perl bugtraq.pl
07/11/2003 Invision Power Board v1.1.2
07/11/2003 LeapFTP remote buffer overflow exploit
07/11/2003 TSLSA-2003-0025 - apache
07/11/2003 W-Agora 4.1.5
...etc...
```

Okay, that was easy, but what if you want it in HTML, RSS, email, or sent to your AIM account? No problem.

Hacking the Hack

Before we get to the code that handles the different outputs, let's start with the format_my_data() subroutine. This will be used to decide what format we want our data to be presented in, tweak the display based on that decision, and then return the results. We'll use the $RUN_STATE variable to decide what action format_my_data() will take. Normally, I would try to keep the code and variables used inside a subroutine as black-boxed as possible, but in this case, to keep things simple and compact, we'll be accessing the dreaded global variables directly. Here's the new code:

```
sub format_my_data() {
    my $data = "";
```

```
foreach my $cols (@parsed_rows) {
    unless ($RUN_STATE || $RUN_STATE eq 'file') {
        $data .= "$cols->{date} $cols->{subject}\n";
    }
    elsif ($RUN_STATE eq 'html') {
        $data .= "<tr>\n<td>$cols->{date}</td>\n".
                 "<td>$cols->{subject_html}</td>\n".
                 "<td>$cols->{author_html}</td>\n</tr>\n";
    }
    elsif ($RUN_STATE eq 'email') {
        $data .= "$cols->{date} $cols->{subject}\n".
                 "link: $cols->{subject_url}\n";
    }
    elsif ($RUN_STATE eq 'aim') {
        $data .= "$cols->{date} $cols->{subject} $cols->{subject_url}\n";
    }
}

return $data;
}
```

Now, let's implement the different runtime options. We'll set up similar conditional code from the format_my_data( ) function in the main body of the script so that the script can handle all of the various output tasks. Here's the code for outputting to email, file, RSS, HTML, and AIM. The AIM networking code is similar to "Creating an IM Interface" [Hack #99], so, in the interest of brevity, I've declined to show it here:

```
unless ($RUN_STATE) { print &format_my_data( ); }
elsif ($RUN_STATE eq 'html') {
    my $html .= "<html><head><title>Bugtraq $date</title></head><body>\n";
    $html    .= "<h1>Bugtraq listings for: $date</h1><table border=0>\n";
    $html    .= "<tr><th>Date</th><th>Subject</th><th>Author</th></tr>\n";
    $html    .= &format_my_data( ) . "</table></body></html>\n";
    print $html;
}

elsif ($RUN_STATE eq 'email') {
    my $mailer = Net::SMTP->new('your mail server here');
    $mailer->mail('your sending email address');
    $mailer->to('your receiving email address');
    $mailer->data( );
    $mailer->datasend("Subject: Bugtraq Report for $date\n\n");
    $mailer->datasend( format_my_data );
    $mailer->dataend( );
    $mailer->quit;
}

elsif ($RUN_STATE eq 'rss') {
    my $rss = XML::RSS->new(version => '0.91');
    $rss->channel(title            => 'SecurityFocus Bugtraq',
                  link             => $bugtraq_url,
```

```
language       => 'en',
description    => 'Latest Bugtraq listings' );

# add items to the RSS object.
foreach my $cols (@parsed_rows) {
   $rss->add_item(title       => $cols->{date},
                  link        => $cols->{subject_url},
                  description => $cols->{subject} );
} print $rss->as_string;
}

elsif ($RUN_STATE eq 'aim') {
  # AIM-related code goes here.
}
```

So what else could you do to enhance this hack? How about adding support for other instant messengers or allowing multiple command-line options at once? Alternatively, what about having the AIM bot email the Bugtraq report upon request, or make it a CGI script and output the RSS to an RSS aggregator like AmphetaDesk (*http://www.disobey.com/amphetadesk/*) or NetNewsWire (*http://ranchero.com/netnewswire*)?

—William Eastler

HACK #81 Keeping Tabs on the Web via Email

If you find yourself checking your email more than cruising the Web, you might appreciate a little Perl work to bring the Web to your mailbox.

If you're an info-junky, you have a growing list of sites that you visit daily, maybe hourly. But sometimes, no matter how many times you refresh the page, some sites just don't update soon enough. It would be better if there were a way to be notified when the site changes, so that you could spend your browsing time better.

Some sites offer a service like this, and others offer syndication feeds that programs can monitor, but there are many sites with which you're out of luck in this regard. In this case, you're going to need your own robot.

Planning for Change

For this hack, we'll choose email as the method of notification, since that seems to be the simplest yet most flexible. We can use some common Perl modules to handle email and download web pages. This just leaves us with figuring out how to determine whether a web page has changed.

Actually, it would be more useful if we could figure out *how much* a web page has changed. Many web pages change constantly, since some might display the current time, others might show updated comment counts on news stories, and others might include a random quote on the page or feature different headlines for each request. If we're just interested in major differences, such as a brand new front-page story on a news site, we'd like some relative measure.

While there are likely smarter ways of doing this, one quick way is to use the GNU *diff* utility to compare downloads of a web page across time. Further, it would be useful if we compared only the text of pages, not the HTML, since we're more interested in content than layout or markup changes. For this, we can employ the venerable text-based web browser *lynx*. *lynx* is commonly found with many Linux distributions and is easily acquired on most other Unix operating systems. This browser already works to format web pages for a plain text display and, with the use of a command-line option, it can redirect this text to a file.

So, given *lynx* and *diff*, we can boil web pages down to their text content and compare changes in content. As an added benefit, we can include the text version of web pages in emails we send as an alternative to HTML.

With all this in mind, let's start our script:

```perl
#!/usr/bin/perl -w
use strict;
use LWP::Simple;
use HTTP::Status;
use MIME::Lite;

# Locate the utility programs needed
our $lynx = '/usr/bin/lynx';
our $diff = '/usr/bin/diff';

# Define a location to store datafiles,
# and an address for notification
my $data_path = "$ENV{HOME}/.pagediff";
my $email = 'your_email@here.com';
```

So far, we've set up some safety features and loaded up our tool modules. We've also located our utility programs, given the script a place to store data, and chosen an email address for notifications. Next, let's make a list of sites to visit:

```perl
my %sites =
    (
    'slashdot'     => ['http://slashdot.org/index.html', 500],
    'penny_arcade' => ['http://www.penny-arcade.com/view.php3', 20],
    );
```

This is a hash that consists of nicknames for sites and, for each site, a list that consists of a URL and a change threshold. This number is very fuzzy and will require some tweaking to get the right frequency of notification.

Higher numbers require more changes before an email goes out. We'll see how this works in just a minute.

Next, let's handle each of our favorite sites:

```
for my $site (keys %sites) {
  my ($url, $threshold) = @{$sites{$site}};

  # Build filenames for storing the HTML content, text
  # content, as well as content from the previous notification.
  my $html_fn = "$data_path/$site.html";
  my $new_fn  = "$data_path/$site.txt";
  my $old_fn  = "$data_path/$site-old.txt";

  # Download a new copy of the HTML.
  getstore($url, $html_fn);

  # Get text content from the new HTML.
  html_to_text($html_fn, $new_fn);

  # Check out by how much the page has changed since last notification.
  my $change = measure_change($new_fn, $old_fn);

  # If the page has changed enough,
  # send off a notification.
  if ($change > $threshold) {
    send_change_notification
      ($email,
       {
         site      => $site,
         url       => $url,
         change    => $change,
         threshold => $threshold,
         html_fn   => $html_fn,
         new_fn    => $new_fn,
         old_fn    => $old_fn
       }
      );

    # Rotate the old text content for the new.
    unlink $old_fn if (-e $old_fn);
    rename $new_fn, $old_fn;
  }
}
```

The main loop of our script is quite simple. For each site, it does the following:

- Downloads a new copy of the web page.
- Saves a copy of the page's text contents.
- Measures the amount of change detected between this latest download and content saved from the last time an email was sent. If the change is

greater than the threshold for this site, it sends an email summarizing the change and rotates out the previously saved content for the new download.

Calling In Outside Help

Now that we have the backbone of the script started, let's work on the functions that the script uses. In particular, these first functions will make use of our external tools, *diff* and *lynx*:

```
sub html_to_text {
  my ($html_fn, $txt_fn) = @_;
  open(FOUT, ">$txt_fn");
  print FOUT `$lynx -dump $html_fn`;
  close(FOUT);
}
```

This function, by way of *lynx*, extracts the text content from one HTML file and writes it to another file. It just executes the *lynx* browser with the -dump command-line option and saves that output.

Next, let's use *diff* to examine changes between text files:

```
sub get_changes {
  my ($fn1, $fn2) = @_;
  return `$diff $fn1 $fn2`;
}
```

Again, this simple function executes the *diff* program on two files and returns the output of that program. Now, let's measure the amount of change between two files using this function:

```
sub measure_change {
  my ($fn1, $fn2) = @_;
  return 0 if ( (!-e $fn1) || (!-e $fn2) );
  my @lines = split(/\n/, get_changes($fn1, $fn2));
  return scalar(@lines);
}
```

If one of the files to compare doesn't exist, this function returns no change. But if the files exist, the function calls the get_changes function on two files and counts the number of lines of output returned. This is a dirty way to measure change, but it does work. The more two versions of a file differ, the more lines of output *diff* will produce. This measure says nothing about the nature of the changes themselves, but it can still be effective if you supply a little human judgment and fudging.

Keep this in mind when you adjust the change thresholds defined at the beginning of this script. You might need to adjust things a few times per site to figure out how much change is important for a particular site. Compared with the complexity of more intelligent means of change detection, this method seems best for a quick script.

Send Out the News

Now that all the tools for extracting content and measuring change are working, we need to work out the payoff for all of this: sending out change notification messages. With the *MIME::Lite* Perl module *(http://search.cpan.org/author/YVES/MIME-Lite/)*, we can send multipart email messages with both HTML and plain text sections. So, let's construct and send an email message that includes the original HTML of the updated web page, the text content, and a summary of changes found since the last update.

First, create the empty email and set up the basic headers:

```
sub send_change_notification {
  my ($email, $vars) = @_;

  # Start constructing the email message
  my $msg = MIME::Lite->new
    (
      Subject => "$vars->{site} has changed.".
        "($vars->{change} > $vars->{threshold})",
      To      => $email,
      Type    => 'multipart/alternative',
    );

  # Create a separator line of '='
  my $sep = ("=" x 75);
```

Note that we indicate how much the page has changed with respect to the threshold in the subject, and we create a separator line for formatting the text email portion of the message.

Next, let's build the text itself:

```
  # Start the text part of email
  # by dumping out the page text.
  my $out = '';
  $out .= "The page at $vars->{url} has changed. ";
  $out .= "($vars->{change} > $vars->{threshold})\n\n";
  $out .= "\n$sep\nNew page text follows:\n$sep\n";

  open(FIN, $vars->{new_fn});
  local $/; undef $/;
  $out .= <FIN>;
  close(FIN);

  # Follow with a diff summary of page changes.
  $out .= "$sep\nSummary of changes follows:\n$sep\n\n";
  $out .= get_changes($vars->{new_fn}, $vars->{old_fn})."\n";
```

Here, we dump the text contents of the changed web page, courtesy of *lynx*, followed by the output of the *diff* utility. It's a little bit of Perl obscura, but we do some finessing of Perl's file handling to simplify reading the whole text file into a variable. The variable $/ defines what Perl uses as an end-of-line character, normally set to some sort of carriage return or linefeed combination. By using undef to clear this setting, Perl considers the entire contents of the file as one long line without endings and slurps it all down into the variable.

Now that we have the text of the email, let's add it to our message:

```
# Add the text part to the email.
my $part1 = MIME::Lite->new
  (
   Type => 'text/plain',
   Data => $out
  );
$msg->attach($part1);
```

This bit of code creates a message part containing our text, gives it a header describing its contents as plain text, and adds it to the email message. Having taken care of the text, let's add the HTML part of the email:

```
# Create and add the HTML part of the email, making sure to add a
# header indicating the base URL used for relative URLs.
my $part2 = MIME::Lite->new
  (
   Type => 'text/html',
   Path => $vars->{html_fn}
  );
$part2->attr('Content-Location' => $vars->{url});
$msg->attach($part2);

# Send off the email
$msg->send( );
}
```

This code creates an HTML part for our email, including the HTML content we last downloaded and setting the appropriate header to describe it as HTML. We also define another header that lets mail readers know the base URL for the HTML in order to resolve relative URLs. We set this to the original URL of the page so that images and links resolve properly.

Finally, we send off the message.

Hacking the Hack

You'll probably want to use this script in conjunction with *cron* [Hack #90] or some other scheduler, to check for changes in pages on a periodic basis.

Just be polite and don't run it too often. Checking every hour or so should be often enough for most sites.

As for the script itself, we're cheating a little, since external tools do most of the work. But when we're writing hacks, it's best to be lazy and take advantage of other smart people's work as much as possible. In working out the amount of change between notifications, we're pretty inexact and fuzzy, but the method works. An exercise for the reader might be to find better means for measuring change, possibly methods that also can tell what kind of changes happened, to help you make better decisions on when to send notifications.

Also note that, though this hack uses both the *diff* and *lynx* programs directly, there are more cross-platform and pure Perl solutions for finding differences between files, such as the *Text::Diff* (*http://search.cpan.org/author/RBS/Text-Diff/*) or *HTML::Diff* (*http://search.cpan.org/author/EZRAKILTY/html-diff/*) modules on CPAN. And, with a bit of work, use of *lynx* could be replaced as well.

—l.m.orchard

H A C K   Publish IE's Favorites to Your Web Site
#82   You're surfing at a friend's house and think, "What is that URL? I have a link to it in my favorites. I wish I were home." How about making your favorites available no matter where you go?

You can't take them with you—your Internet Explorer bookmarks, I mean. They live on a particular machine, accessible only to you only when you're at that machine. Yes, there are some online bookmarking services, but the ones worth using have started making their users ante up or live through pop-up advertising hell. Of course, we Perl hackers don't have to settle for either.

This hack publishes the contents of your IE Favorites to any server that you can access via FTP, setting you up with a nice little navigable menu frame on the left to hold your favorites and a content area on the right to display the sites you click on. Yes, this hack is a bit Windows- and IE-specific, but before you complain too much, it's easily extendible to process any form of bookmark data that's stored in tree structure, and the output is templated. The template shown here generates just the simple HTML menu system, but templates for PHP, ASP, raw data—anything you like—should be a breeze!

IE's Favorites

Let's start by taking a quick look at IE's Favorites folder. If you use Windows, you probably know that this folder is now used by more than IE, but most people I know, myself included, still use it mainly in the context of web browsing. On Windows NT, 2000, and XP running IE4 or later, the Favorites folder is nothing more than a directory stored within your user profile tree. The easiest and most consistent method for locating the folder is through the USERPROFILE environment variable. You'll note at the top of the script that a configurable global that identifies the root of the Favorites tree uses precisely this environment variable by default.

The structure of the Favorites tree itself is simple. It's a directory tree that contains folders and links. It is possible to put things other than URL links into your Favorites; since we're interested in publishing web bookmarks, we'll ignore everything except directories and links (in this context, *links* are defined as files with a *.url* extension). A link document contains a bit of data in addition to the actual URL; fortunately, it's easy to ignore, because the one thing that every link document has is a line that starts with URL= and then specifies the location in question. In our hack, we'll simply extract this one line with a regular expression.

What It Does and How It Works

The script goes through three processes:

1. Parse the Favorites tree and load the structure.
2. Generate the output documents.
3. Upload the documents via FTP.

We'll take a quick look at each and then get right to the code.

Parsing the Favorites tree is handled by walking through the tree recursively using Perl's system-independent opendir, readdir, and closedir routines. We use *File::Spec* routines for filename handling, to make enhancing and porting to other systems easier. The structure itself is read into a hash of hashes, one of the basic Perl techniques for creating a tree. For each hash in the tree, subdirectories map to another hash and links map to a scalar with the link URL. Reading the entire Favorites tree into an internal data structure isn't strictly necessary, but it simplifies and decouples the later processes, and it also provides a great deal of flexibility for enhancements to the script.

Generating the output based on the Favorites data is done with a template so that the script doesn't lock its user into any one type of output. When you're using Perl, *Text::Template* is always an excellent choice—since Perl itself is the templating language—so we use it here. The template in this hack outputs HTML, defining a simple menu based on the folders and links and using HTML anchors to open the link targets in a named frame. It is expected that the entire set of documents, one document per Favorites directory, will be published to a single output directory, so filenames are generated using each directory's relative path from the main Favorites directory, each path component being separated by a period. The documents themselves are generated in a *temp* directory, which the script attempts to remove upon completion.

The upload code is straightforward and nonrobust. Upload is via FTP, and the published script requires that the FTP parameters be coded in the configuration globals at the top of the file. If anything other than an individual put fails, the code gives up. If a put itself fails, a warning is issued and we move to the next file.

The Code

You need three files. *PublishFavorites.pl* is the Perl code that does the work. The template for our example is *favorites.tmpl.html*. Finally, a simple *index.html*, which defines the frameset for our menus, will need to be uploaded manually just once.

First, here's *PublishFavorites.pl*:

```perl
#!/usr/bin/perl -w
use strict;
use File::Spec;
use File::Temp;
use Net::FTP;
use Text::Template;

# - - - - - - - - - - - - - - - - - - - - - - - - - - - - - - - - - - - - - - -

## Configurable Globals

## $FAV_ROOT = Location of the root of the Favorites folder
my $FAV_ROOT = File::Spec->join( $ENV{USERPROFILE}, 'Favorites' );

## $FAV_NAME = Top level name to use in favorites folder tree
my $FAV_NAME = 'Favorites';

## $FAV_TMPL = Text::Template file; output files will use same extension
my $FAV_TMPL = 'favorites.tmpl.html';

## Host data for publishing favorites via ftp
my $FAV_HOST = 'myserver.net';
my $FAV_PATH = 'favorites';
my $FAV_USER = 'username';
my $FAV_PASS = 'password';

## End of Configurable Globals
```

```perl
# - - - - - - - - - - - - - - - - - - - - - - - - - - - - - - - - - - - - - -

my $_FAV_TEMPDIR = File::Temp->tempdir( 'XXXXXXXX', CLEANUP => 1 );

# - - - - - - - - - - - - - - - - - - - - - - - - - - - - - - - - - - - - - -

sub LoadFavorites {

  # Recursively load the structure of an IE
  # Favorites directory tree into a tree of hashes.

  my $FolderIn = shift;       # Folder to process
  my $FavoritesOut = shift;   # Hashref to load with this folder's entries

  # Do a readdir into an array for a
  # quick load of the directory entries.
  opendir( FOLDER, $FolderIn ) ||
    die "Could not open favorites folder '$FolderIn'";
  my @FolderEntries = readdir( FOLDER );
  closedir( FOLDER );

  # Process each entry in the directory.
  foreach my $FolderEntry ( @FolderEntries ) {

    # Skip special names . and ..
    next if $FolderEntry eq '.' || $FolderEntry eq '..';

    # Construct the full path to the current entry.
    my $FileSpec = File::Spec->join( $FolderIn, $FolderEntry );

    # Call LoadFavorites recursively if we're processing a directory.
    if ( -d $FileSpec && !( -l $FileSpec ) ) {
      $FavoritesOut->{$FolderEntry} = {};
      LoadFavorites( $FileSpec, $FavoritesOut->{$FolderEntry} );
    }

    # If it's not a directory, check for a filename that ends with '.url'.
    # When we find a link file, extract the URL and map the favorite to it.
    elsif ( $FolderEntry =~ /^.*\.url$/i ) {
      my ( $FavoriteId ) = $FolderEntry =~ /^(.*)\.url$/i;
      next if !open( FAVORITE, $FileSpec );
      ( $FavoritesOut->{$FavoriteId} ) =
          join( '', <FAVORITE> ) =~ /^URL=([^\n]*)\n/m;
      close( FAVORITE );
    }
  }
}

# - - - - - - - - - - - - - - - - - - - - - - - - - - - - - - - - - - - - - -

sub MakeDocName {
```

```
# Quick hack to generate a safe filename for a favorites entry. Replaces
# all whitespace and special characters with underscores, concatenates
# parent spec with the new spec, and postfixes the the whole thing with
# the same file extension as the globally named template document.

my $FavoriteIn = shift;        # Label of new favorites entry
my $ParentFilenameIn = shift;  # MakeDocName of the parent level

my ( $FileType ) = $FAV_TMPL =~ /\.([^\.]+)$/;
$FavoriteIn =~ s/(\s+|\W)/_/g;
$ParentFilenameIn =~ s/$FileType$//;
return lc( $ParentFilenameIn . $FavoriteIn . '.' . $FileType );
}

# - - - - - - - - - - - - - - - - - - - - - - - - - - - - - - - - - - - - -

sub GenerateFavorites {

  # Recurse through a tree of Favorites entries and generate a document for
  # each level based on the globally named template document.

  my $FavoritesIn = shift;       # Hashref to current tree level
  my $FolderNameIn = shift;      # Name of the current folder
  my $ParentFilenameIn = shift;  # MakeDocName of the parent level

  # Create shortcut identifiers for things that get reused a lot.
  my $Folder = $FavoritesIn->{$FolderNameIn};
  my $FolderFilename = MakeDocName( $FolderNameIn, $ParentFilenameIn );

  # Separate the entries in the current folder into folders and links.
  # Folders can be identified because they are hash references, whereas
  # links are mapped to simple scalars (the URL of the link).
  my (%Folders,%Links);
  foreach my $Favorite ( keys( %{$Folder} ) ) {
    if ( ref( $Folder->{$Favorite} ) eq 'HASH' ) {
      $Folders{$Favorite} = { label => $Favorite,
        document => MakeDocName( $Favorite, $FolderFilename ) };
    }
    else {
      $Links{$Favorite}={label => $Favorite, href => $Folder->{$Favorite} };
    }
  }

  # Set up Text::Template variables, fill in the template with the folders
  # and links at this level of the favorites tree, and then output the
  # processed document to our temporary folder.
  my $Template = Text::Template->new( TYPE => 'FILE',
    DELIMITERS => [ '<{', '}>' ], SOURCE => $FAV_TMPL );
  my %Vars = (
    FAV_Name => $FAV_NAME,
    FAV_Home => MakeDocName( $FAV_NAME ),
    FAV_Folder => $FolderNameIn,
    FAV_Parent => $ParentFilenameIn,
```

```
      FAV_Folders => \%Folders,
      FAV_Links => \%Links
  );
  my $Document = $Template->fill_in( HASH => \%Vars );
  my $DocumentFile = File::Spec->join( $_FAV_TEMPDIR, $FolderFilename );
  if ( open( FAVORITES, ">$DocumentFile" ) ) {
    print( FAVORITES $Document );
    close( FAVORITES );
  }

  # Generate Favorites recursively for each of this folder's subfolders.
  foreach my $Subfolder ( keys( %Folders ) ) {
    GenerateFavorites( $Folder, $Subfolder, $FolderFilename );
  }
}

# - - - - - - - - - - - - - - - - - - - - - - - - - - - - - - - - - - - -

sub PublishFavorites {

  # Publish the generated documents via FTP. Pretty
  # much just gives up if something goes wrong.

  my $ftp = Net::FTP->new( $FAV_HOST ) ||
    die( "Cannot connect to '$FAV_HOST'" );
  $ftp->login( $FAV_USER, $FAV_PASS ) ||
    die( "Authorization for user '$FAV_USER' failed" );
  $ftp->cwd( $FAV_PATH ) ||
    die( "Could not CWD to '$FAV_PATH'" );
  opendir( FOLDER, $_FAV_TEMPDIR ) ||
    die( "Cannot open working directory '$_FAV_TEMPDIR'" );
  my @FolderEntries = readdir( FOLDER );
  closedir( FOLDER );
  foreach my $FolderEntry ( @FolderEntries ) {
    next if $FolderEntry eq '.' || $FolderEntry eq '..';
    $ftp->put( File::Spec->join( $_FAV_TEMPDIR, $FolderEntry ) ) ||
      warn( "Could not upload '$FolderEntry'...skipped" );
  }
  $ftp->quit;
}

# - - - - - - - - - - - - - - - - - - - - - - - - - - - - - - - - - - - -

sub main {
  my %Favorites;
  $Favorites{$FAV_NAME} = {};
  LoadFavorites( $FAV_ROOT, $Favorites{$FAV_NAME} );
  GenerateFavorites( \%Favorites, $FAV_NAME, '' );
  PublishFavorites();
}

main();
```

Here's our example template, *favorites.tmpl.html*:

```html
<html>
<body>
  <h1><a href="<{$FAV_Home}>"><{$FAV_Name}></a></h1>
  <select onChange="location.replace(this[this.selectedIndex].value)">
    <{
      $OUT .= '<option selected>' . $FAV_Folder . '</option>' . "\n";
      if ( $FAV_Parent ne '' ) {
        $OUT .= '<option value="' . $FAV_Parent . '">..</option>' . "\n";
      }
      foreach my $folder ( sort( keys( %FAV_Folders ) ) ) {
        $OUT .= '<option value="' . $FAV_Folders{$folder}->{document} .
          '">&gt;' . $FAV_Folders{$folder}->{label} . '</option>' . "\n";
      }
    }>
  </select>
  <table>
    <{
      foreach my $link ( sort( keys( %FAV_Links ) ) ) {
        $OUT .= '<tr><td><a target="net" href="' .
          $FAV_Links{$link}->{href} . '">' .
          $FAV_Links{$link}->{label} . '</a></td></tr>' . "\n";
      }
    }>
  </table>
</body>
</html>
```

And, finally, here's the simple *index.html*:

```html
<html>
<head>
  <title>Favorites</title>
</head>
<frameset cols="250,*">
  <frame name="nav" scrolling="yes" src="favorites.html" />
  <frame name="net" src="http://refdesk.com"/>
</frameset>
</html>
```

Running the Hack

Before you run the code, you need to take care of a few configuration items.

First, let's make sure that your Favorites directory is where the script thinks it will be. At a command prompt, execute the following:

```
dir "%USERPROFILE%"\Favorites
```

If you get a directory listing with lots of names that appear to match things in your IE Favorites, then you're good to go. If this directory doesn't exist or if its contents don't appear to be your Favorites, then you'll have to find out where on your disk your Favorites are really stored and then change the $FAV_ROOT variable at the top of the script to match.

Second, you need to define your FTP information through the $FAV_HOST, $FAV_PATH, $FAV_USER, and $FAV_PASS variables at the top of the script.

Third, just once, you need to manually upload the *index.html* document to the directory on your server where you're going to publish your Favorites. Of course, you are free to rename this document and publish your Favorites to a directory that already contains other files, but we suggest setting aside a separate directory. You are also welcome to change the default page that the *index.html* file initially shows in the net frame.

Okay, now simply run the script as follows:

```
% perl PublishFavorites.pl
```

The script runs quietly unless it encounters a problem. For most problems it might encounter, it just gives up and outputs an error message.

That's it. Suppose you publish to the Favorites directory on *http://www. myserver.net*. Just point your browser to *http://www.myserver.net/favorites*, and you should have a web-accessible menu of all your IE Favorites! An example is available at *http://www.ronpacheco.net/favorites/*.

Hacking the Hack

There's a ton of room for enhancement and modification to this hack. Most changes will probably fall into one of the hack's three major processing tasks: loading the bookmark data, generating output, and publishing.

First, you can make it read something other than the IE Favorites tree. Maybe you want to read Mozilla bookmarks, or suck links off a web site, or read your own tree or bookmarks—whatever. If you can read it into the simple tree structure that the script already uses, you'll have a plug-and-play subroutine.

Second, you can change the output. You can pretty up the existing HTML template, you can write new templates for things beyond simple HTML, or you can completely rip out the output section and replace it with something new. The framework for the code to traverse the bookmark tree is already in place. You can use the templating tools as is, or you can use the framework to build something new.

Finally, you can get more sophisticated about publishing. If someone were to ask me if, in practice, I'd really hardcode my username and password into a script and then use that script to publish stuff via an unsecured FTP session, I'd probably have to say no. I'm fairly comfortable putting the access information in the script, as long as I have good control over the system where it's located—I've been doing it for a couple decades now without any incidents—but I would be reluctant to use cleartext FTP. In fact, I use FTP to my servers all the time, including a variation of this script, but I tunnel all the connections through SSH. For more sophistication, you could add SSH support directly to the script, and you could consider methods of publication other than FTP.

Like I said, there's a ton of possibilities, limited only by the imagination of the hacker!

—Ron Pacheco

Spidering GameStop.com Game Prices

#83 Looking to get notification when "Army Men: Quest for Some Semblance of Quality" goes on sale at $5.99? With this hack, you'll be able to keep an eye on your most desired (or derisive) video game titles.

All work and no play makes Jack a dull geek. Of course, having to hunt down game prices to figure out what he can afford to play on his PlayStation 2 makes Jack even duller. It's so much better to get a spider to do it for him.

We like GameStop.com (*http://www.gamestop.com*), a retail site for console and PC video games, so we came up with a simple spider that gathers up information about a certain platform of games—the way the script is written, it gathers information on XBox games—but, as you'll see, it's easy to adapt the script to other uses.

The Code

Save the following code as *gamestop.pl*:

```perl
#!/usr/bin/perl -w
use strict;
use HTML::TokeParser;
use LWP::Simple;

# the magical URL.
my $url = "http://www.gamestop.com/search.asp?keyword=&platform=26".
          "&lookin=title&range=all&genre=0&searchtype=adv&sortby=title";

# the magical data.
my $data = get($url) or die $!;

# the magical parser.
my $p = HTML::TokeParser->new(\$data);
```

```
    # now, find every table that's 510 and 75.
    while (my $token = $p->get_tag("table")) {
        next unless defined($token->[1]{height});
        next unless defined($token->[1]{width});
        next unless $token->[1]{height} == 75;
        next unless $token->[1]{width} == 510;

        # get our title.
        $p->get_tag("font"); $p->get_tag("a");
        my $title = $p->get_trimmed_text;

        # and our price.
        $p->get_tag("font"); $p->get_tag("/b");
        my $ptoken = $p->get_token;
        my $price = $ptoken->[1];
        $price =~ s/\$//;

        # comma spliced.
        print "\"$title\",$price\n";
    }
```

Running the Hack

The hack is simple enough. It gathers information about XBox games, sorted by title, and puts that information into a comma-delimited file, as per the following output:

```
% perl gamestop.pl
"4x4 Evolution 2 - Preowned",16.99
"Aggressive Inline - Preowned",16.99
"Air Force Delta Storm - Preowned",27.99
"Alias",49.99
...etc...
```

It's very basic right now, but there's some fun stuff we can build in.

Hacking the Hack

Let's start by making the request keyword-based instead of platform-based; maybe you're interested in racing games and don't care about the platform.

GameStop by keyword. Add these two lines to the top of the script, after the use statements:

```
# get our query, else die miserably.
my $query = shift @ARGV; die unless $query;
```

Then, change your magical URL, like this:

```
# the magical URL.
  my $url = "http://www.gamestop.com/search.asp?keyword=$query&platform=".
            "&lookin=title&range=all&genre=0&searchtype=adv&sortby=title";
```

This'll give you 10 results based on your keyword. For example:

```
% perl gamestop.pl racing
"All Star Racing",7.99
"Andretti Racing - Preowned",9.99
"Andretti Racing - Preowned",7.99
"Antz Extreme Racing - Preowned",16.99
"Antz Racing",4.99
"Antz Racing - Preowned",29.99
"ATV Quad Power Racing 2 - Preowned",24.99
"ATV Quad Power Racing 2 - Preowned",17.99
"ATV Quad Power Racing 2 - Preowned",17.99
"ATV: Quad Power Racing 2",19.99
"Batman: Gotham City Racer - Preowned",27.99
"Beetle Adventure Racing - Preowned",29.99
```

Putting the results in a different format. Of course, getting the results in a comma-delimited format might not be what you want. How about sorting results by price and saving them to an RSS file, so you can have an RSS feed of the cheapest games that match a keyword? (Unabashed capitalist hackers could even add an affiliate code to the link URL.)

Here's how to do it. The first thing you want to do is add use `XML::RSS` to the use lines at the top of the script. Then, as in the first example, you can add the query word from the command line, or you can hardcode it into the query. In this example, I hardcode it into the query, with the idea that you can add this to your server and run it as a *cron* job periodically:

```
# the magical URL.
my $url = "http://www.gamestop.com/search.asp?".
          "keyword=your search keyword here&platform=".
          "&lookin=title&range=all&genre=0&searchtype=adv&sortby=title";
```

Now, you want to change the output from a comma-delimited file to an RSS feed. Remove these lines:

```
# comma spliced.
print "\"$title\",$price\n";
```

and add these lines above the magical URL line:

```
# start the RSS feed.
my $rss = XML::RSS->new(version => '0.91');
$rss->channel(
    'link'       => http://www.gamestop.com,
    title        => "Game Prices from GameStop",
    description  => "Great Games and Stuff!"
);
```

Then, add the lines that create the RSS feed itself:

```
# add this item
# to our RSS feed.
$rss->add_item(
```

```
    title      => "$title, $price...",
    'link'     => "http://www.gamestop.com/search.asp?keyword=$title".
                  "&platform=0&lookin=title&range=all&genre=0&sortby=title"
);
```

Finally, add this as the last lines of the script, to save your output as a feed:

```
# and save our RSS.
$rss->save("gamestop.rdf");
```

There are several minor hacks you can try with this script. GameStop.com offers several different search options; try experimenting with the different searches and see how they impact the result URLs. Experimenting with the URL options in the magical URL lines can get you lots of different results. Likewise, as written, the script reports on the first page of results; catering to the entire listing of search results can be done with *WWW::Mechanize* [Hack #21] or a manual loop.

HACK #84 Bargain Hunting with PHP

If you're always on the lookout for the best deals, coupons, and contests, a little bit of PHP-scraping code can help you stay up-to-date.

Scraping content is a task than can be handled by most programming languages. PHP is quickly becoming one of the most popular scripting languages, and it is particularly well-suited for scraping work. With a moderate grasp of PHP, programmers can write scrapers in a matter of minutes. In this section, we'll work through some of the basic code and concepts for scraping with PHP.

There are a handful of useful functions that most scraping tasks will need, which will make writing customized scrapers almost painless. For the sake of simplicity, we won't use regular expressions here, but the more agile programmers will quickly note where regular expressions might make these functions work better.

The first function that we want uses PHP's fopen( ) function to fetch individual pages from a web server. For more sophisticated scrapers, a direct socket connection is probably more desirable, but that's another matter. For now, we'll go the simple way:

```
function getURL( $pURL ) {
    $_data = null;
    if( $_http = fopen( $pURL, "r" ) ) {
        while( !feof( $_http ) ) {
            $_data .= fgets( $_http, 1024 );
        }
        fclose( $_http );
    }
    return( $_data );
}
```

Calling this function is done simply, like this:

```
$_rawData = getURL( "http://www.example.com/" );
```

If `$_rawData` is null, the function wasn't able to fetch the page. If `$_rawData` contains a string, we're ready for the next step.

Because every author codes her HTML slightly different, it's useful to normalize the raw HTML data that getURL( ) returns. We can do this with the cleanString( ) function. This function simply removes newline, carriage return, tab, and extra space characters. Regular expressions could simplify this function a bit, if you are comfortable with them.

```
function cleanString( $pString ) {
    $_data = str_replace( array( chr(10), chr(13), chr(9) ), chr(32), ↵
$pString );
        while( strpos( $_data, str_repeat( chr(32), 2 ), 0 ) != false ) {
            $_data = str_replace( str_repeat( chr(32), 2 ), chr(32), $_data );
        }
        return( trim( $_data ) );
}
```

We'll clean up the raw HTML source with the following code:

```
$_rawData = cleanString( $_rawData );
```

Now, we have some data that is easy to parse. Two other useful functions will parse out particular pieces of the source and get data from individual HTML tags:

```
function getBlock( $pStart, $pStop, $pSource, $pPrefix = true ) {
    $_data = null;
    $_start = strpos( strtolower( $pSource ), strtolower( $pStart ), 0 );
    $_start = ( $pPrefix == false ) ? $_start + strlen( $pStart ) : $_start;
    $_stop = strpos( strtolower( $pSource ), strtolower( $pStop ), $_start );
    if( $_start > strlen( $pElement ) && $_stop > $_start ) {
        $_data = trim( substr( $pSource, $_start, $_stop - $_start ) );
    }
    return( $_data );
}

function getElement( $pElement, $pSource ) {
    $_data = null;
    $pElement = strtolower( $pElement );
    $_start = strpos( strtolower( $pSource ), chr(60) . $pElement, 0 );
    $_start = strpos( $pSource, chr(62), $_start ) + 1;
    $_stop = strpos( strtolower( $pSource ), "</" . $pElement . ↵
chr(62), $_start );
    if( $_start > strlen( $pElement ) && $_stop > $_start ) {
        $_data = trim( substr( $pSource, $_start, $_stop - $_start ) );
    }
    return( $_data );
}
```

We can use each of these functions with the following code:

```
$_rawData = getBlock( start_string, end_string, raw_source, ⏎
include_start_string );
$_rawData = getElement( html_tag, raw_source );
```

Let's assume for a moment that we have source code that contains the string "Total of 13 results", and we want just the number of results. We can use getBlock() to get that number with this code:

```
$_count = getBlock( "Total of", "results", $_rawData, false );
```

This returns "13". If we set $pPrefix to true, $_count will be "Total of 13". Sometimes, you might want the start_string included, and other times, as in this case, you won't.

The getElement() function works basically the same way, but it is specifically designed for parsing HTML-style tags instead of dynamic strings. Let's say our example string is "Total of 13 results". In this case, it's easier to parse out the bold element:

```
$_count = getElement( "b", $_rawData );
```

This returns "13" as well.

It's handy to put the scraping functions into an includable script, because it keeps you from having to copy/paste them into all your scraping scripts. In the next example, we save the previous code into *scrape_func.php*.

Now that we have the basics covered, let's scrape a real page and see it in action. For this example, we'll scrape the latest deals list from TechDeals.net (*http://www.techdeals.net*).

The Code

Save the following code as *bargains.php*:

```
/* include the scraping functions script:  */
include( "scrape_func.php" );

/* Next, we'll get the raw source code of
   the page using our getURL() function:  */
$_rawData = getURL( "http://www.techdeals.net/" );

/* And clean up the raw source for easier parsing:  */
$_rawData = cleanString( $_rawData );

/* The next step is a little more complex. Because we've already
   looked at the HTML source, we know that the items start and
   end with two particular strings. We'll use these strings to
   get the main data portion of the page:*/
$_rawData = getBlock( "<div class=\"NewsHeader\">",
                      "</div> <div id=\"MenuContainer\">", $_rawData );
```

```
/* We now have the particular data that we want to parse into
   an itemized list. We do that by breaking the code into an
   array so we can loop through each item: */
$_rawData = explode( "<div class=\"NewsHeader\">", $_rawData );

/* While iterating through each value, we
   parse out the individual item portions:  /*
foreach( $_rawData as $_rawBlock ) {
  $_item = array( );
  $_rawBlock = trim( $_rawBlock );
  if( strlen( $_rawBlock ) > 0 ) {

    /*  The title of the item can be found in <h2> ... </h2> tags   */
    $_item[ "title" ] = strip_tags( getElement( "h2", $_rawBlock ) );

    /*  The link URL can is found between
        http://www.techdeals.net/rd/go.php?id= and "   */
    $_item[ "link" ] = getBlock( "http://www.techdeals.net/rd/go.php?id=",
                                 chr(34), $_rawBlock );

    /*  Posting info is in <span> ... </span> tags   */
    $_item[ "post" ] = strip_tags( getElement( "span", $_rawBlock ) );

    /*  The description is found between an </div> and a <img tag   */
    $_item[ "desc" ] = cleanString( strip_tags( getBlock( "</div>",
                                    "<img", $_rawBlock ) ) );

    /*  Some descriptions are slightly different,
        so we need to clean them up a bit   */
    if( strpos( $_item[ "desc" ], "Click here for the techdeal", 0 ) ↵
    > 0 ) {
       $_marker = strpos( $_item[ "desc" ], "Click here for the techdeal", ↵
       0 );
       $_item[ "desc" ] = trim( substr( $_item[ "desc" ], 0, $_marker ) );
    }

    /*  Print out the scraped data   */
    print( implode( chr(10), $_item ) . chr(10) . chr(10) );

    /*  Save the data as a string (used in the mail example below)   */
    $_text .= implode( chr(10), $_item ) . chr(10) . chr(10);
  }
}
```

Running the Hack

Invoke the script from the command line, like so:

```
% php -q bargains.php
```

```
Values on Video
http://www.techdeals.net/rd/go.php?id=28
```

```
Posted 08/06/03 by david
TigerDirect has got the eVGA Geforce FX5200 Ultra 128MB video card
with TV-Out & DVI for only $124.99+S/H after a $20 rebate.

Potent Portable
http://www.techdeals.net/rd/go.php?id=30
Posted 08/06/03 by david
Best Buy has got the VPR Matrix 220A5 2.2Ghz Notebook for just
$1049.99 with free shipping after $250 in rebates.

...etc...
```

Hacking the Hack

This output could be emailed easily, or you could even put it into an RSS
feed. If you want to email it, you can use PHP's mail( ) function:

```
mail( "me@foo.com", "Latest Tech Deals", $_text );
```

But how do you output RSS in PHP? While there are many ways to go about
it, we'll use the simplest to keep everything concise. Creating an RSS 0.91
feed is a matter of three small sections of code—the channel metadata, the
item block, and the closing channel tags:

```
<rss version="0.91">
    <channel>
        <title><?= htmlentities( $_feedTitle ) ?></title>
        <link><?= htmlentities( $_feedLink ) ?></link>
        <description><?= htmlentities( $_feedDescription ) ?></description>
        <language>en-us</language>

        <item>
            <title><?= htmlentities( $_itemTitle ) ?></title>
            <link><?= htmlentities( $_itemLink ) ?></link>
            <description><?= htmlentities( $_itemDescription ) ?></description>
        </item>

    </channel>
</rss>
```

By putting together these three simple blocks, we can quickly output a full RSS
feed. For example, let's use our scraper and output RSS instead of plain text:

```
<rss version="0.91">
    <channel>
        <title>TechDeals: Latest Deals</title>
        <link>http://www.techdeals.net/</link>
        <description>Latest deals from TechDeals.net (scraped)</description>
        <language>en-us</language>
<?
    include( "scrape_func.php" );
    $_rawData = getURL( "http://www.techdeals.net/" );
```

```
$_rawData = cleanString( $_rawData );
$_rawData = getBlock( "<div class=\"NewsHeader\">",
                      "</div> <div id=\"MenuContainer\">", $_rawData );
$_rawData = explode( "<div class=\"NewsHeader\">", $_rawData );
foreach( $_rawData as $_rawBlock ) {
    $_item = array();
    $_rawBlock = trim( $_rawBlock );
    if( strlen( $_rawBlock ) > 0 ) {
        $_item[ "title" ] = strip_tags( getElement( "h2", $_rawBlock ) );
        $_item[ "link" ]
        = getBlock( "http://www.techdeals.net/rd/go.php?id=",
        chr(34), $_rawBlock );
        $_item[ "post" ] = strip_tags( getElement( "span", $_rawBlock ) );
        $_item[ "desc" ] = cleanString( strip_tags( getBlock( "</div>",
                           "<img", $_rawBlock ) ) );
        if( strpos($_item[ "desc" ], "Click for the techdeal", 0 ) > 0 ) {
            $_marker = strpos($_item[ "desc" ], "Click for the techdeal",0 );
            $_item[ "desc" ] = trim(substr( $_item[ "desc" ], 0, $_marker) );
        }
?>
    <item>
        <title><?= $_item ["title" ] ?></title>
        <link><?= $_item[ "link" ] ?></link>
        <description>
            <?= $_item[ "desc" ] . " (" . $_item[ "post" ] . ")" ?>
        </description>
    </item>
<?
        }
    }
?>
    </channel>
</rss>
```

Keep in mind that this is the quick-and-dirty way to create RSS. If you plan on generating a lot of RSS, look into RSS 1.0 and build yourself a PHP class for the RSS-generating code.

As you can see, a few simple functions and a few lines of code are all that is needed to make a usable scraper in PHP. Customizing the script and the output are a matter of personal whim. In this particular example, you could also parse out information about the comments that are included in the items, or you could merge in other bargain sites, like AbleShoppers (*http://www.ableshopper.com*) or Ben's Bargains (*http://www.bensbargains.net*).

—James Linden

Aggregating Multiple Search Engine Results

#85 Even though Google may solve all your searching needs on a daily basis, there may come a time when you need a "super search"—something that queries multiple search engines or databases at once.

Google is still the gold standard for search engines and still arguably the most popular search spot on the Web. But after years of stagnation, the search engine wars are firing up again. AlltheWeb.com (*http://www.alltheweb.com*) in particular is working hard to offer new search syntax, a larger web index (over 3.2 billion URLs at the time of this writing), and additional interface options. If you want to keep up with searching on the Web, it behooves you to try search engines other than Google, if only to get an idea of how the other engines are evolving.

This hack builds a meta–search engine, querying several search engines in turn and displaying the aggregated results. Actually, it can query more than just search engines; it can request data from anything to which you can submit a search request. It does so by using a set of plug-ins—each of which knows the details of a particular search engine or site's search request syntax and the format of its results—that perform the search and return the results. The main script, then, does nothing more than farm out the request to these plug-ins and let them perform their magic. This is an exercise in hacking together a client/server protocol. The protocol I use is simple: each plug-in needs to return URL and text pairs. How do we delimit one from the other? By finding a character that's illegal in URLs, such as the common tab, and using that to separate our data.

The protocol runs as follows:

1. The server starts up a plug-in as an executable program, with the search terms as command-line parameters.

2. The client responds by printing one result per new line, in the format of URL, tab, then text.

3. The server receives the data, formats it a little before printing, and then moves on to the next available plug-in.

Note that because we have a simple call and response pattern, the plug-ins can query anything, including your own local databases with Perl's DBI, Python scripts that grok FTP servers, or PHP concoctions that do reverse lookups on phone numbers. As long as the plug-in returns the data in URL-tab-text format, what it does and how it's programmed don't matter.

The Code

The following short piece of code demonstrates the server portion, which searches for a *./plugins* directory and executes all the code within:

```perl
#!/usr/bin/perl -w

# aggsearch - aggregate searching engine
#
# This file is distributed under the same licence as Perl itself.
#
# by rik - ora@rikrose.net


######################
# support stage      #
######################

use strict;

# change this, if neccessary.
my $pluginDir = "plugins";

# if the user didn't enter any search terms, yell at 'em.
unless (@ARGV) { print 'usage: aggsearch "search terms"', "\n"; exit; }

# this routine actually executes the current
# plug-in, receives the tabbed data, and sticks
# it into a result array for future printing.
sub query {
    my ($plugin, $args, @results) = (shift, shift);
    my $command = $pluginDir . "/" . $plugin . " " . (join " ", @$args);
    open RESULTS, "$command |" or die "Plugin $plugin failed!\n";
    while (<RESULTS>) {
        chomp; # remove new line.
        my ($url, $name) = split /\t/;
        push @results, [$name, $url];
    } close RESULTS;

    return @results;
}


######################
# find plug-ins stage #
######################

opendir PLUGINS, $pluginDir
    or die "Plugin directory \"$pluginDir\"".
      "not found! Please create, and populate\n";
my @plugins = grep {
    stat $pluginDir . "/$_"; -x _  && ! -d _  && ! /\~$/;
} readdir PLUGINS; closedir PLUGINS;
```

```
#####################
# query stage       #
#####################

for my $plugin (@plugins){
    print "$plugin results:\n";
    my @results = query $plugin, \@ARGV;
    for my $listref (@results){
        print " $listref->[0] : $listref->[1] \n"
    } print "\n";
}

exit 0;
```

The plug-ins themselves are even smaller than the server code, since their only purpose is to return a tab-delimited set of results. Our first sample looks through the freshmeat.net (*http://freshmeat.net*) software site:

```
#!/usr/bin/perl -w

# Example freshmeat searching plug-in
#
# This file is distributed under the same licence as Perl itself.
#
# by rik - ora@rikrose.net

use strict;
use LWP::UserAgent;
use HTML::TokeParser;

# create the URL from our incoming query.
my $url = "http://freshmeat.net/search-xml?q=" . join "+", @ARGV;

# download the data.
my $ua = LWP::UserAgent->new();
$ua->agent('Mozilla/5.0');
my $response = $ua->get($url);
die $response->status_line . "\n"
  unless $response->is_success;

my $stream = HTML::TokeParser->new (\$response->content) or die "\n";
while (my $tag = $stream->get_tag("match")){
    $tag = $stream->get_tag("projectname_full");
    my $name = $stream->get_trimmed_text("/projectname_full");
    $tag = $stream->get_tag("url_homepage");
    my $url = $stream->get_trimmed_text("/url_homepage");
    print "$url\t$name\n";
}
```

Our second sample uses the Google API:

```
#!/usr/bin/perl -w

# Example Google searching plug-in
```

```perl
use strict;
use warnings;
use SOAP::Lite;

# all the Google information
my $google_key  = "your API key here";
my $google_wdsl = "GoogleSearch.wsdl";
my $gsrch       = SOAP::Lite->service("file:$google_wdsl");
my $query       = join "+", @ARGV;

# do the search...
my $result = $gsrch->doGoogleSearch($google_key, $query,
                        1, 10, "false", "",  "false",
                        "lang_en", "", "");

# and print the results.
foreach my $hit (@{$result->{'resultElements'}}){
    print "$hit->{URL}\t$hit->{title}\n";
}
```

Our last example covers AlltheWeb.com:

```perl
#!/usr/bin/perl -w

# Example alltheweb searching plug-in
#
# This file is distributed under the same licence as Perl itself.
#
# by rik - ora@rikrose.net

use strict;
use LWP::UserAgent;
use HTML::TokeParser;

# create the URL from our incoming query.
my $url = "http://www.alltheweb.com/search?cat=web&cs=iso-8859-1" .
          "&q=" . (join "+", @ARGV) . "&_sb_lang=en";

print $url;
# download the data.
my $ua = LWP::UserAgent->new();
$ua->agent('Mozilla/5.0');
my $response = $ua->get($url);
die $response->status_line . "\n"
  unless $response->is_success;

my $stream = HTML::TokeParser->new (\$response->content) or die "\n";
while (my $tag = $stream->get_tag("p")){
    $tag = $stream->get_tag("a");
    my $name = $stream->get_trimmed_text("/a");
    last if $name eq "last 10 queries";
    my $url = $tag->[1]{href};
    print "$url\t$name\n";
}
```

Running the Hack

Invoke the script from the command line, like so:

```
% perl aggsearch.pl spidering
alltheweb results:
 Google is now better at spidering dynamic sites. : [long url here]
 Submitting sites to search engines : [long url here]
 WebcamCrawler.com  : [long url here]
 ...etc...

freshmeat results:
 HouseSpider : http://freshmeat.net/redir/housespider/28546/url_homepage/
 PhpDig : http://freshmeat.net/redir/phpdig/15340/url_homepage/
 ...etc...

google results:
 What is Spidering? : http://www.1afm.com/optimization/spidering.html
 SWISH-Enhanced Manual: Spidering : http://swish-e.org/Manual/spidering.html
 ...etc...
```

The power of combining data from many sources gives you more scope for working out trends in the information, a technique commonly known as *data mining*.

—*Richard Rose*

HACK #86 Robot Karaoke

Who says people get to have all the fun? With this hack, you can let your computer do a little singing, by scraping the LyricsFreak.com web site and sending the results to a text-to-speech translator.

There are things that are text-only and things that are multimedia. Then there's this hack, which turns boring old text into multimedia—specifically, a *.wav* file.

This hack, as it stands, is actually pretty silly. It searches the lyric collections at LyricsFreak.com for the keywords you specify, then sends the matching lyrics to yet another site (*http://naturalvoices.com*) that turns them into a *.wav* file. If you're running a Win32 system, the code will then automatically play the *.wav* file ("sing" the lyrics, for some narrow definition of *sing*) via the *Win32::Sound* module (*http://search.cpan.org/author/ACALPINI/Win32-Sound/*).

Listening to your computer's rendition of the Spider-Man theme song can be detrimental to your health.

As you're playing with this code, you might want to think of more sublime and less ridiculous implementations. Do you have a site read by low-vision people? Are there short bits of text, such as a local weather forecast, that would be useful for them to have read aloud? Would it be helpful to have a button that would convert a story summary to a *.wav* file for later download?

The Code

One of the modules used with this code, *Win32::Sound*, is for Win32 machines only. Since it's used to play back the generated *.wav* file, you will not get a "singing" robot if you're on a non-Win32 machine; you'll just get a *.wav* file, suitable for playing through your preferred music player.

Save this script as *robotkaroake.pl*:

```perl
#!/usr/bin/perl -w
use strict;
use LWP::Simple;
use URI::Escape;
use Win32::Sound;
use SOAP::Lite;

# use your own Google API key here!
my $google_key  = "your Google key here";
my $google_wdsl = "GoogleSearch.wsdl";

# load in our lyrics phrase from the command line.
my $lyrics_phrase = shift or die "Usage: robot-karaoke.pl <phrase>\n";

# and perform the search on Google.
my $google_search_term = "intitle:\"$lyrics_phrase\" site:lyricsfreak.com";
my $googleSearch = SOAP::Lite->service("file:$google_wdsl");
my $result = $googleSearch->doGoogleSearch(
                    $google_key, $google_search_term,
                    0, 10, "false", "", "false",
                    "", "", "");

# if there are no matches, then say so and die.
die "No LyricsFreak matches were found for '$lyrics_phrase'.\n"
        if $result->{estimatedTotalResultsCount} == 0;

# and take the first Google result as
# the most likely location on LyricsFreak.com.
my @results       = @{$result->{'resultElements'}};
my $first_result  = $results[0];
my $lyricsfreak_url = $first_result->{'URL'};
print "Downloading lyrics from:\n $lyricsfreak_url\n";
```

```
# and download the data from LyricsFreak.com.
my $content = get($lyricsfreak_url) or die $!;
print "Connection to LyricsFreak was successful.\n";

# we have the data, so let's parse it.
# all lyrics are stored in a pre tag,
# so we delete everything before and after.
$content =~ s/.*<pre><b>.*<\/b><br>//mgis;
$content =~ s/<\/pre>.*//mgis;
my @lyrics_lines = split("\x0d", $content);

# AT&T's demo TTS service takes a maximum of 30 words,
# so we'll create a mini chunk of the lyrics to send off.
# each of these chunks will be sent to the TTS server
# then saved seperately as multiple mini-wav files.
my (@lyrics_chunks, $current_lyrics_chunk); my $line_counter = 0;
for (my $i = 0; $i <= scalar(@lyrics_lines) - 1; ++$i) {
    next if $lyrics_lines[$i] =~ /^\s*$/;
    $current_lyrics_chunk .= $lyrics_lines[$i] . "\n";

    if (($line_counter == 5) || ($i == scalar(@lyrics_lines) - 1) ) {
        push(@lyrics_chunks, $current_lyrics_chunk);
        $current_lyrics_chunk = ''; $line_counter = 0;
    } $line_counter++;
}

# now, we'll go through each chunk,
# and send it off to our TTS server.
my @temporary_wav_files;
foreach my $lyrics_chunk (@lyrics_chunks) {

    # and download the data.
    my $url = 'http://morrissey.naturalvoices.com/tts/cgi-bin/nph-talk';
    my $req = HTTP::Request->new('POST', $url); # almost there!
    $req->content('txt=' . uri_escape($lyrics_chunk) .
                  '&voice=crystal&speakButton=SPEAK');
    $req->content_type('application/x-www-form-urlencoded');
    my $res = LWP::UserAgent->new->simple_request($req);

    # incorrect server response? then die.
    unless ($res->is_success || $res->code == 301) {
       die "Error connecting to TTS server: " . $res->status_line . ".\n"; }

    # didn't get the response we wanted? die.
    if ($res->content !~ /can be found <A HREF=([^>]*)>here<\/A>/i) {
       die "Response from TTS server not understood. Odd.\n"; }

    # side effect of error checking above is to set $1 to
    # the actual wav file that was generated. this is good.
    my $wav_url  = "http://morrissey.naturalvoices.com$1";
    my $wav_file = $1; # for use in saving to disk.
```

```
    $wav_file =~ s/.*?\/(\w+.wav)/$1/;
    getstore($wav_url, "$wav_file") or
      die "Download of $wav_file failed: $!";
    push(@temporary_wav_files, $wav_file);
}

# with all our files downloaded, play them in
# order with the Win32::Sound module. else, they
# just sit there in hopes of the user playing them.
print  "Playing downloaded wav files...\n";
foreach my $temporary_wav_file (@temporary_wav_files) {
    print " Now Playing: $temporary_wav_file\n";
    Win32::Sound::Play("$temporary_wav_file");
}

}
```

Running the Hack

Invoke the script on the command line, passing it the phrase you're inter-ested in; the script will search for that phrase in the titles of pages on Lyris-Freak.com. If it doesn't find the phase, it'll just stop:

```
% perl robotkaroake.pl "fish heads"
No LyricsFreak matches were found for 'fish heads'.
```

If it does find the phrase, it'll download the lyrics and generate the .*wav* file:

```
% perl robotkaroake.pl "born never asked"
Downloading lyrics from:
 http://www.lyricsfreak.com/l/laurie-anderson/81556.html
Connection to LyricsFreak was successful.
Playing downloaded wav files...
 Now Playing: 7a0c0093f2f531ac98691152d1f74367.wav
```

The previous example shows the output of a rather short entry. Longer songs will result in more .*wav* files saved to the current directory, each repre-senting a small chunk (a single chunk representing one request to the TTS server):

```
% perl robotkaroake.pl "under the moon"
Downloading lyrics from:
 http://www.lyricsfreak.com/i/insane-clown-posse/67657.html
Connection to LyricsFreak was successful.
Playing downloaded wav files...
 Now Playing: fe34e081ab8a3abaeecdb1e50b030209.wav
 Now Playing: 80709499765f9bfe75d3c7234c435a79.wav
 Now Playing: f1ca99233f9cdc6a78f311db887914f1.wav
 Now Playing: fd6b61421f3fc56510cf4b9e0d3a0e12.wav
 Now Playing: b954f58f906d53ec312bbcc6579ebe12.wav
 Now Playing: 407415e685260754174cf45338ba4d10.wav
 Now Playing: 8a2ade6e7f8fe950ddcb58747d241694.wav
 Now Playing: 22ed038190b9ed0fb4e3077655503422.wav
```

Searching the Better Business Bureau

Is that new company offering to build your house, deliver your groceries, and walk your dog legit and free of complaint? Find out with an automated query of the Better Business Bureau's web site.

If you're a citizen of the United States, you're probably aware of the Better Business Bureau (*http://www.bbb.org*), a nonprofit organization that acts as a neutral party in resolving complaints between businesses and consumers. There are over 125 local Better Business Bureaus across the country.

The Better Business Bureau (BBB) company database is searchable by URL. This hack runs a BBB search by URL and provides information on a business if one is found. Further, the hack searches PlanetFeedback.com for any additional online feedback about that company.

Links to feedback and basic company information is provided, but a tally of customer complaints from the BBB is not. Why? Each of the 125 local bureaus provides varying amounts of data and formats that data in slightly different ways; adding the code to handle them all would be, we suspect, a monumental undertaking. So, we are not going to provide that here; instead, we'll stick to basic company information only.

The Code

Save this script as *bbbcheck.pl*:

```perl
#!/usr/bin/perl -w
use strict;
use LWP::Simple;
use URI::Escape;

# $MAX_BBB_SEARCH_RETRIES is the number of times that the
# script will attempt to look up the URL on the BBB web site.
# (Experimentally, the BBB web site appeared to give "database
# unavailable" error messages about 30% of the time.)
my $MAX_BBB_SEARCH_RETRIES = 3;

# $MAX_BBB_REFERRAL_PAGE_RETRIES is the number of times the
# script will attempt to download the company information
# from the URL provided in the search results.
my $MAX_BBB_REFERRAL_PAGE_RETRIES = 3;

# suck in our business URL, and append it to the BBB URL.
my $business_url = shift || die "You didn't pass a URL for checking!\n";
my $search_url   = "http://search.bbb.org/results.html?tabletouse=".
                   "url_search&url=" . $business_url;
my %company; # place we keep company info.

# look for the results until requested.
for (my $i = 1; $i <= $MAX_BBB_SEARCH_RETRIES; ++$i) {
```

```perl
my $data = get($search_url); # gotcha, bugaboo!

# did we have a problem? pause if so.
if ($data =~ /apologize.*delay/ or !defined($data)) {
  print "Connection to BBB failed. Waiting 5 seconds to retry.\n";
  sleep(5); next; # let's try this again, shall we?
}

# die if there's no data to yank.
die "There were no companies found for this URL.\n"
    if $data =~ /There are no companies/i;

# get the company name, address, and redirect.
if ($data =~ /<!-- n -->.*?href="(.*?)">(.*)<!-- -->.*?">(.*)<\/f/i) {
  $company{redir}   = "http://search.bbb.org/$1";
  $company{name}    = $2; $company{address} = $3;
  $company{address} =~ s/<br>/\n/g;
  print "\nCompany name and address:\n";
  print "$company{name}\n$company{address}\n\n";
}

# if there was no redirect, then we can't
# move on to the local BBB site, so we die.
unless ($company{redir}) {
  die "Unable to process the results returned. You can inspect ".
      "the results manually at the following url: $search_url\n"; }

last if $data;
}

# now that we have the redirect for the local BBB site,
# we'll try to download its contents and parse them.
for (my $i = 1; $i <= $MAX_BBB_REFERRAL_PAGE_RETRIES; ++$i) {
  my $data = get($company{redir});

  # did we have a problem? pause if so.
  unless (defined $data) {
    print "Connection to BBB failed. Waiting 5 seconds to retry.\n";
    sleep(5); next; # let's try this again, shall we?
  }

  $data =~ s/\n|\f|\r//g; # grab even more information.
  $data =~ s/\n|\f|\r//g; # grab even more information.
  if ($data=~/Date:<\/b>.*?<td.*?>(.*?)<\/td>/i){$company{start}=$1;}
  if ($data=~/Entity:<\/b>.*?<td.*?>(.*?)<\/td>/i){$company{entity}=$1;}
  if ($data=~/l ?:<\/b>.*?<td.*?>(.*?)<\/td>/i){$company{principal}=$1;}
  if ($data=~/Phone.*?:<\/b>.*?<td.*?>(.*?)<\/td>/i){$company{phone}=$1;}
  if ($data=~/Fax.*?:<\/b>.*?<td.*?>(.*?)<\/td>/){$company{fax}=$1;}
  if ($data=~/Status:<\/b>.*?<td.*?>(.*?)<\/td>/){$company{mbr}=$1;}
  if ($data=~/BBB:<\/b>.*?<td.*?>(.*?)<\/td>/){$company{joined}=$1;}
  if ($data=~/sification:<\/b>.*?<td.*?>(.*?)<\/td>/){$company{type}=$1;}
  last if $data;
}
```

```
# print out the extra data we've found.
print "Further information (if any):\n";
foreach (qw/start_date entity principal phone fax mbr joined type/) {
    next unless $company{$_}; # skip blanks.
    print " Start Date: " if $_ eq "start_date";
    print " Type of Entity: " if $_ eq "entity";
    print " Principal: " if $_ eq "principal";
    print " Phone Number: " if $_ eq "phone";
    print " Fax Number: " if $_ eq "fax";
    print " Membership Status: " if $_ eq "mbr";
    print " Date Joined BBB: " if $_ eq "joined";
    print " Business Classification: " if $_ eq "type";
    print "$company{$_}\n";
} print "\n";

# alright. we have all our magic data that we can get from the
# BBB, so let's see if there's anything on PlanetFeedback.com to display.
my $planetfeedback_url = "http://www.planetfeedback.com/sharedLetters".
                         "Results/1,2933,,00.html?frmCompany=".
                         uri_escape($company{name})."&frmFeedbackType".
                         "One=0&frmIndustry=0&frmFeedbackTypeTwo=0".
                         "&frmMaxValue=20&buttonClicked=submit1".
                         "&frmEventType=0";
my $data = get($planetfeedback_url) or # go, speed
    die "Error downloading from PlanetFeedback: $!"; # racer, go!

# did we get anything worth showing?
if ($data =~ /not posted any Shared Letters/i) {
    print "No feedback found for company '$company{name}'\n";
} else { print "Feedback available at $planetfeedback_url\n"; }
```

Running the Hack

Invoke the script on the command line with the URL of a business site you'd like to check. If there's no match at the BBB—a distinct possibility, since it doesn't contain every known business URL—the script will stop:

```
% perl bbbcheck.pl http://www.oreilly.com
There were no companies found for this URL.
```

If there is a match, it'll give you some information about the company, then check PlanetFeedback.com for additional data. If they've received any comments on the business at hand, you'll be provided a URL for further reading.

Let's do a little checking up on Microsoft, shall we?

```
% perl bbbcheck.pl http://www.microsoft.com
Company name and address:
MICROSOFT CORPORATION
9255 Towne Center Dr 4th Fl
SAN DIEGO, CA
```

```
Further information (if any):
Start Date: January 1975
Type of Entity: Corporation

Principal: Ms Shaina Houston FMS
Phone Number: January 1975
Fax Number: (858) 909-3838
Membership Status: Yes
Date Joined BBB: May 2003
Business Classification: Computer Sales & Service

Feedback available at http://www.planetfeedback.com/sharedLettersResults/
1,2933,,00.html?frmCompany=MICROSOFT%20CORPORATION&frmFeedbackTypeOne=0&
frmIndustry=0&frmFeedbackTypeTwo=0&frmMaxValue=20&buttonClicked=submit1&
frmEventType=0
```

Hacking the Hack

The script here is extensive in what it does. After all, it visits two sites and provides you with a fair amount of information. But despite that, it's still pretty bare-bones. The output is sent only to the screen, and the amount of information it scrapes is limited because of the multiple formats of the various local BBBs.

So, when you're planning on improving the script, focus on two different things. First, think about how you might scrape more information if it were presented in a more standard format. For example, say you want to search only businesses in San Francisco. The BBB search site allows for that, though you'll have to search by business name instead of URL (see the first search option at *http://search.bbb.org/search.html*). If you search for businesses only in San Francisco, you'll get results only from the Golden Gate BBB. With one data format, you can access more information, including any complaint numbers and the company's standing in the BBB.

The second thing you'll want to improve is output. Currently, this hack sends out only plain text, but, as you saw previously, the PlanetFeedback.com URL is extensive. To fix this, you might want to spit out HTML instead, allowing you to simply click a link instead of copying and pasting. For that matter, you could set up an array with several business URLs and send all their results to the same file.

HACK #88 Searching for Health Inspections

How healthy are the restaurants in your neighborhood? And when you find a good one, how do you get there? By combining databases with maps!

You don't have to scrape a site to build a URL that leads to their resources! This hack searches Seattle's King County database of restaurant inspections

(*http://www.decadeonline.com/main.phtml?agency=skc*), which can be queried with a complete restaurant name or just a single word. The script
returns a list of the restaurants found, links to the restaurant's health inspection information, and also adds a direct link to a MapQuest map of the restaurant's location.

What? Isn't scraping MapQuest against its TOS? Yes, but this program
doesn't touch the MapQuest site; instead, it builds a direct link to a relevant
MapQuest map. So, while a user might access a MapQuest page based on
this program's output, we never programmatically access the site and thus
never violate the TOS.

The Code

Save this script as *kcrestaurants.pl*:

```perl
#!/usr/bin/perl -w
use strict;
use HTML::TableExtract;
use LWP::Simple;
use URI::Escape;

# get our restaurant name from the command line.
my $name = shift || die "Usage: kcrestaurants.pl <string>\n";

# and our constructed URL to the health database.
my $url = "http://www.decadeonline.com/results.phtml?agency=skc".
        "&forceresults=1&offset=0&businessname=" . uri_escape($name) .
        "&businessstreet=&city=&zip=&soundslike=&sort=FACILITY_NAME";

# download our health data.
my $data = get($url) or die $!;
die "No restaurants matched your search query.\n"
    if $data =~ /no results were found/;

# and suck in the returned matches.
my $te = HTML::TableExtract->new(keep_html => 1, count => 1);
$te->parse($data) or die $!; # yum, yum, i love second table!

# and now loop through the data.
foreach my $ts ($te->table_states) {
  foreach my $row ($ts->rows) {
    next if $row->[1] =~ /Site Address/; # skip if this is our header.
    foreach ( qw/ 0 1 / ) { # remove googly poofs.
        $row->[$_] =~ s/^\s+|\s+|\s+$/ /g; # remove whitespace.
        $row->[$_] =~ s/\n|\f|\r/ /g; # remove newlines.
    }

    # determine name/addresses.
    my ($url, $name, $address, $mp_url);
    if ($row->[0] =~ /href="(.*?)">.*?2">(.*?)<\/font>/) {
```

```
        ($url, $name) = ($1, $2); # almost there.
    } if ($row->[1] =~ /2">(.*?)<\/font>/) { $address = $1; }

    # and the MapQuest URL.
    if ($address =~ /(.*), ([^,]*)/) {
        my $street = $1; my $city = $2;
        $mp_url = "http://www.mapquest.com/maps/map.adp?".
                    "country=US&address=" . uri_escape($street) .
                    "&city=" . $city . "&state=WA&zipcode=";
    }

    print "Company name: $name\n";
    print "Company address: $address\n";
    print "Results of past inspections:\n " .
            "http://www.decadeonline.com/$url\n";
    print "MapQuest URL: $mp_url\n\n";
    }
}
```

Running the Hack

To run the hack, just specify the restaurant name or keyword you want to
search for. If there's no restaurant found based on your query, it'll say as
much:

```
% perl kcrestaurants.pl perlfood
No restaurants matched your search query.
```

A matching search returns health inspection and MapQuest links:

```
% perl kcrestaurants.pl "restaurant le gourmand"
Company name: RESTAURANT LE GOURMAND
Company address: 425 NW MARKET ST , Seattle
Results of past inspections:
 http://www.decadeonline.com/fac.phtml?
    agency=skc&forceresults=1&facid=FA0003608
MapQuest URL: http://www.mapquest.com/maps/map.adp?country=US&address
    =425%20NW%20MARKET%20ST%20&city=Seattle&state=WA&zipcode=
```

Or, if there are a number of results, it returns a complete list:

```
% perl kcrestaurants.pl restaurant
Company name: RESTAURANT EL TAPATIO
Company address: 3720 FACTORIA BL , Bellevue
Results of past inspections:
 http://www.decadeonline.com/fac.phtml?
    agency=skc&forceresults=1&facid=FA0003259
MapQuest URL: http://www.mapquest.com/maps/map.adp?country=US&address
    =3720%20FACTORIA%20BL%20&city=Bellevue&state=WA&zipcode=

Company name: RESTAURANT ICHIBAN
Company address: 601 S MAIN ST , Seattle
Results of past inspections:
 http://www.decadeonline.com/fac.phtml?
```

```
        agency=skc&forceresults=1&facid=FA0001743
MapQuest URL: http://www.mapquest.com/maps/map.adp?country=US&address
        =601%20S%20MAIN%20ST%20&city=Seattle&state=WA&zipcode=
```

...

Hacking the Hack

If you don't live in Seattle, you might not personally have much use for this particular example. But if you live anywhere within the United States, the code can be adapted to suit you. Many counties in the United States have posted their restaurant inspection scores online. Go to your state or county's official web site (the county site is better if you know what it is) and search for restaurant inspections. From there, you should be able to find restaurant scores from which you can build a script like this. Bear in mind that different counties have different levels of information.

You don't have to use MapQuest either. If you have the name, city, and state of a restaurant, you can build a URL to get the phone number from Google. (However, you can't use the Google API to perform this search, because it does not yet support the phonebook: syntax.)

Let's take our previous example of the Restaurant Le Gourmand, located in Seattle, Washington. The Google search syntax for a phonebook query would be:

```
bphonebook:Restaurant Le Gourmand Seattle WA
```

And the URL to lead to the result would look like this:

```
http://www.google.com/search?q=bphonebook:Restaurant+Le+Gourmand+Seattle+WA
```

You might want to use that instead of, or in addition to, a link to MapQuest.

HACK #89   Filtering for the Naughties

Use search engines to construct your own parental control ratings for sites.

As we've attempted to show several times in this book, your scripts don't have to start and end with simple Perl spidering. You can also incorporate various web APIs (such as Technorati **[Hack #70]** or All Consuming **[Hack #66]**). In this hack, we're going to add some Google API magic to see if a list of domains pulled off a page contain prurient (i.e., *naughty*) content—as determined by Google's SafeSearch filtering mechanism.

As the hack is implemented, a list of domains is pulled off Fark (*http://www.fark.com*), a site known for its odd selection of daily links. Each domain has 50 of its URLs (generated by a Google search) put into an array, and each array item is checked to see if it appears in a Google search with SafeSearch enabled. If it does, it's considered to be a *good URL*. If it doesn't, it's put under suspicion of being a *not-so-good URL*. The idea is to get a sense of how much of an entire domain is being filtered, instead of just one URL.

Filtering mechanisms are not perfect. Sometimes they filter things that aren't bad at all, while sometimes they miss objectionable content. While the goal of this script is to give you a good and general idea of a domain's content on the naughtiness scale, it won't be perfect.

The Code

Save the following code as *purity.pl*:

```perl
#!/usr/bin/perl -w
use strict;
use LWP::Simple;
use SOAP::Lite;

# fill in your google.com API information here.
my $google_key  = "your Google API key here";
my $google_wdsl = "GoogleSearch.wsdl";
my $gsrch       = SOAP::Lite->service("file:$google_wdsl");

# get our data from Fark's "friends".
my $fark = get("http://www.fark.com/") or die $!;
$fark =~ m!Friends:</td></tr>(.*?)<tr><td class=\"lmhead\">Fun Games:!migs;
my $farklinks = $1; # all our relevances are in here.

# and now loop through each entry.
while ($farklinks =~ m!href="(.*?)"!gism) {
   my $farkurl = $1; next unless $farkurl;
   my @checklist; # urls to check for safety.
   print "\n\nChecking $farkurl.\n";

   # getting the full result count for this URL.
   my $count = $gsrch->doGoogleSearch($google_key, $farkurl,
                       0, 1, "false", "",  "false", "", "", "");
   my $firstresult = $count->{estimatedTotalResultsCount};
   print "$firstresult matching results were found.\n";
   if ($firstresult > 50) { $firstresult = 50; }

   # now, get a maximum of 50 results, with no safe search.
   # getting the full result count for this URL.
   my $counter = 0; while ($counter < $firstresult) {

       my $urls = $gsrch->doGoogleSearch($google_key, $farkurl,
                        $counter, 10, "false", "",  "false", "", "", "");
```

```
        foreach my $hit (@{$urls->{resultElements}}) {
            push (@checklist, $hit->{URL});
        } $counter = $counter +10;
    }

    # and now check each of the matching URLs.
    my (@goodurls, @badurls); # storage.
    foreach my $urltocheck (@checklist) {
        $urltocheck =~ s/http:\/\///;

        my $firstcheck = $gsrch->doGoogleSearch($google_key, $urltocheck,
                            0, 1, "true", "",  "true", "", "", "");

        # check our results. if no matches, it's naughty.
        my $firstnumber = $firstcheck->{estimatedTotalResultsCount} || 0;
        if ($firstnumber == 0) { push @badurls, $urltocheck; }
        else { push @goodurls, $urltocheck; }
    }

    # and spit out some results.
    my ($goodcount, $badcount) = (scalar(@goodurls), scalar(@badurls));
    print "There are $goodcount good URLs and $badcount ".
        "possibly impure URLs.\n"; # wheeEeeeEE!

    # display bad domains if there are only a few.
    unless ( $badcount >= 10 || $badcount == 0) {
        print "The bad URLs are\n";
        foreach (@badurls) {
            print " http://$_\n";
        }
     }

    # happy percentage display.
    my $percent = $goodcount * 2; my $total = $goodcount+$badcount;
    if ($total==50) { print "This URL is $percent% pure!"; }


}
```

Running the Hack

The hack requires no variables. Simply run it from the command line as you would any Perl script, and it'll return a list of domains and each domain's purity percentage (as determined by Google's SafeSearch):

```
% perl purity.pl

Checking http://www.aprilwinchell.com/.
161 matching results were found.
There are 36 good URLs and 14 possibly impure URLs.
This URL is 72% pure!

Checking http://www.badjocks.com/.
```

```
47 matching results were found.
There are 36 good URLs and 9 possibly impure URLs.
The bad URLs are
 http://www.thepunchline.com/cgi-bin/links/bad_link.cgi?ID=4052&d=1
 http://www.ilovebacon.com/020502/i.shtml
 http://www.ilovebacon.com/022803/l.shtml
...
```

Hacking the Hack

You might find something else you want to scrape, such as the links on your site's front page. Are you linking to something naughty by mistake? How about performing due diligence on a site you're thinking about linking to; will you inadvertently be leading readers to sites of a questionable nature via a seemingly innocent intermediary? Perhaps you'd like to check entries from a specific portion of the Yahoo! or DMOZ directories [Hack #47]? Anything that generates a list of links is fair game for this script.

As it stands, the script checks a maximum of 50 URLs per domain. While this makes for a pretty thorough check, it also makes for a long wait, especially if you have a fair amount of domains to check. You may decide that checking 10 domains is a far better thing to do. In that case, just change this line:

```
if ($firstresult > 10) { $firstresult = 10; }
```

When Tara originally wrote the code, she was a little concerned that it might be used to parse naughty sites and generate lists of naughty URLs for porn peddling. So, she chose not to display the list of naughty URLs generated, unless they were a significantly minor proportion of the final results (currently, the threshold is set to no more than 10 of the 50 URLs). You might want to change that, especially if you're using this script to check links from your own site and you want to get an idea of the kind of content you might be linking to. In this case you'll need to change just one line:

```
unless ( $badcount >= 50 || $badcount == 0) {
```

By increasing the count to 50, you'll be informed of all the bad sites associated with the current domain. Just be forewarned: certain domains may return nothing but the naughties, and even the individual words that make up the returned URLs can be downright disturbing.

## CHAPTER FIVE

Maintaining Your Collections
Hacks #90–93

It's rare that one script will solve all your data-grubbing needs. You might want, weekly, to know about new movies being listed on Amazon.com, grab a summary page from IMDB, find the last five movies that each actor or actress starred in, and then image-search and download pictures of them. On the other hand, you might be graphing important information and need to automatically grab the data every hour, day, or week. And what if you're downloading or mirroring data with *wget* [Hack #26]?

We have these great tools to automate our information needs, but how do we then automate the running of said tools? Where is our meta-automation?

HACK #90 Using cron to Automate Tasks
Run scripts on a repetitive basis with the cron utility.

There will come a time when you've created a script so perfect for your day-to-day life that it becomes absolutely imperative to run on a regular basis. Sure, you could run it manually during your morning routine, but if you can automate the retrieval of data with scraping, why not automate the execution too?

Meet *cron*, a Unix utility whose life revolves around running things every minute, hour, day, week, month, or year. Give it a command or script and a schedule and let it go. Each user on the system can automate his own tasks with no restrictions: hear the date spoken every minute, have a backup performed every three days at 12:15, or automatically open your email every day at 7:00 A.M. and then again at 6:00 P.M. Whatever your scheduling needs, *cron* will satisfy them.

If you're running any flavor of Unix (including Mac OS X), you already have *cron*, and it's been running ever since you turned on your computer. To begin adding automated tasks, edit your personal *crontab* file, which just keeps track of which tasks you want to run and when. Type crontab -e in your shell to begin editing your schedule. Here are a few example *crontab* entries :

```
0 7 * * Mon-Fri echo "Whoo, I rule!" > /dev/null
0 18 * * Mon-Fri echo "Ok, one more time for good luck." > /tmp/lucky
0 12 * * Sat-Sun echo "Alright, now this is superflous." >> /tmp/lucky
```

These three entries will do insatiably pointless tasks every weekday morning at 7:00 A.M., then again at 6:00 P.M. the same day, and a "worst…example …ever!" note at noon on the weekends. The order of fields will eventually become simple to remember: minute, hour, day of month, month, day of week, and the actual command to run. A * represents every possible match for that field (i.e., every minute, every hour, etc.).

For example, to mirror your web site every Wednesday morning, you could do this:

```
# back up gamegrene.com every Wednesday at 7:06 A.M.
6 7 * * 3 cd /path/to/backup  && wget -m http://gamegrene.com/
```

If you're a media file collector, you might be running some combination of the following hacks: "Saving Only POP3 Email Attachments" [Hack #40], "Downloading with curl and wget" [Hack #26], and "Downloading Images from Webshots" [Hack #36]. A *crontab* set to run these automatically on a regular basis might look something like this:

```
# download new POP3 mail. this assumes you've set up a
# POP account solely for attachments (such as a bunch of
# Yahoo! mailing lists), and have modified leechpop
# to delete email messages after they're downloaded.
# we start at 5:30 so that when I get home at 6:00,
# I'll have a nice collection downloaded and waiting.
30 17 * * Mon-Fri perl leechpop.pl -u morbus -p secret -s mail

# download 2 megs worth of the dailywav.com, weekly.
50 23 * * Sun wget -q -A.wav -Q=2m -m http://dailywav.com/

# grab any new matches for "kittens" on webshots. I
# check these once a week when I awake on Saturday.
15 7 * * Sat perl webshots.pl --max=40 "kittens"
```

On the other hand, if you're a marketing analyst, you might be running a combination of "Scattersearch with Yahoo! and Google" [Hack #48], "Related Amazon.com Products with Alexa" [Hack #57], and "Graphing Data with RRD-TOOL" [Hack #62]. The following *crontab* runs at staggered times before you get in to work, ready for your reading pleasure after you've had a chance to grab that first cup of coffee:

```
# run a search for our product name to get counts.
# we first prepend the current date for archiving.
29 8 * * Mon-Fri date >> ourproduct.txt
30 8 * * Mon-Fri perl scattersearch.pl "product name" >> ourproduct.txt
```

```
# run an Alexa report every week to see
# related products and websites for our own.
15 8 * * Mon perl alexa.pl http://oursite.com/ related.html

# graph our book's rank over at Amazon.
5 0 * * * perl grabrank.pl
```

See Also

- man cron, man crontab, and man 5 crontab. The last entry is probably most useful for learning about the available syntaxes (including ranges, step values, and more).

Scheduling Tasks Without cron

HACK #91

If you want to run any of the hacks in this book on a regular basis, your best option is to use cron, a powerful Linux-based scheduler. But what if you're on a different OS or don't have access for some other reason?

You've probably noticed that we mention *cron* often in this book. *cron* is a task scheduler for Unix that lets you set up a file of scheduled jobs (a *crontab*) that will run automatically without your supervision.

That's the good news. The bad news is that many web-hosting services do not offer access to *cron*. Alternatively, you might be using Perl on an operating system without *cron* (Windows, Mac OS 9, etc.). If you're in that boat, all is not lost. There are several alternatives to standard *cron*, from just going about the problem a different way to finding third-party services.

Do You Really Need Anything cron-Like?

Yes, nothing satisfies your mad scientist jones like the thought of dozens of little Perl scripts, waiting until exactly the right moment to be unleashed onto the world. But think about it a minute. Do you really need to use *cron* to run your scripts? Can you just run your scripts when the need arises? Make sure you actually have to use timed scheduling before you go any further with these alternatives.

Running Scripts on the Client Side

Okay, you have to schedule your scripts somehow. If you're not using your scripts in a web-hosting environment, why not try something on the client side? There are many scheduling utilities out there for Windows and Mac; just visit a software site like *http://www.download.com* and search for "scheduling utility" or "schedule utility".

Windows users already have one on board. You'll find Scheduled Tasks under My Computer or Control Panels. And it's easy as pie to get up and running. For a new entry, choose Add Scheduled Task, as shown in Figure 5-1.

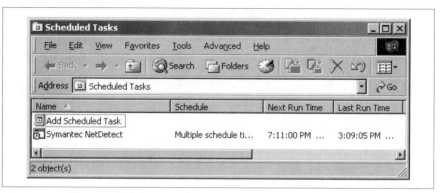

Figure 5-1. Adding a Scheduled Task

This will start the Scheduled Task Wizard. Next, choose the program you'd like to schedule (see Figure 5-2). Since you'll be setting up one of the scripts in this book, rather than using a garden-variety Windows application, choose Browse to pinpoint its location on your hard drive.

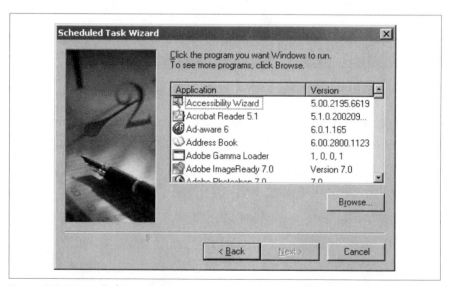

Figure 5-2. Browsing for a script to run

Give the task a name and choose a schedule for it, as shown in Figure 5-3.

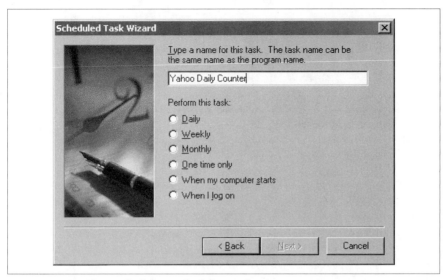

Figure 5-3. Creating a schedule on which to run the script

Your options will differ depending on your choice of frequency. In my case, I chose Daily, so my options look like those shown in Figure 5-4. You'll have a chance to tweak your settings further by choosing the Advanced Properties checkbox on the wizard's final screen, as shown in Figure 5-5.

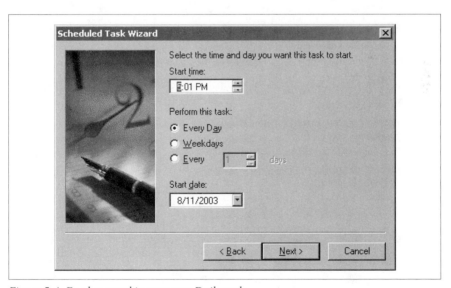

Figure 5-4. Further tweaking our new Daily task

Figure 5-5. Setting a scheduled task's Advanced Properties

After you schedule your new task, it'll be listed in the *Scheduled Tasks* folder and—so long as your computer is on at the time—will run when you've requested.

Using Perl's sleep Function

Here's a cheap and cheesy way to make sure your Perl script runs regularly: don't ever let it stop. Just jacket your Perl program with a `sleep` statement:

```
while (1) { sleep 14400;
  [your code here]
}
```

The number 14000 represents the number of seconds the program will pause.

> If you're using your scripts in a web-hosting environment, this particular way around *cron* is likely to irritate the average ISP. Be sure to ask before you start running it. This kind of workaround is really designed for those who have their own boxes and, for whatever reason, can't use *cron*.

Scheduling with Something Besides cron

Okay, so you really, really, really need to use *cron*. Or at least you need some way to run a script on a regular basis. You don't have to use *cron*; you can use fake *cron*. There are a couple of scripts available online:

Fake Cron (http://www.smarterscripts.com/cron/)
> Launches scripts based on an image loading in one of your web pages. While you don't need *cron* to get this program to work, you will need the *LWP::UserAgent* module.

Crone (http://mareksscripts.w2w.cc/txt/crone_readme.txt)
> A script scheduler that works either by loading via an image tag or via a SSI call. You can set it to run based on time or after every *x* visitors to a page. If you have *sendmail*, Crone will also send you an email upon execution.

Those just won't do, huh? Okay, you have one more option.

Using Hosted cron Services

If you just have to use *cron* and you're not willing to take the big step of moving your site to another, more *cron*-friendly host than the one you have now, there's one more option: *cron* services. Just as there are web-hosting services, there are services that will schedule *cron* jobs on your behalf. Here are two of them:

Script Schedule (http://www.script-schedule.com)
> Offers the ability to schedule jobs or run jobs when triggered by an email. Pricing ranges from free to $15 a year.

Fastcron (http://www.fastcron.com/)
> Doesn't appear from its web site to be as extensive as Script Schedule, but it has a flat rate of $9.95 a year.

HACK
#92

Mirroring Web Sites with wget and rsync

Is there a site you check frequently, or do you want a backup of your own site? Various mirroring tools are available that can ensure you're creating duplicate and complete backups on another machine.

Maybe you have a favorite picture site that you are always checking out or a music site that posts new files daily; either way, it can be cumbersome to write a script to grab new content every day for each site. And then there is the hassle of always making a backup of your own sites. Regardless, you do not always have to write some fancy *LWP* script or spend hours parsing HTML, trying to get just what you want. If you have the disk space, mirroring the site can be an effective, if somewhat lazy, solution.

There are two basic ways to go about mirroring sites: downloading the pages through the web server or accessing the content directly from the server it is hosted on. Obviously, if you don't have access to the server itself, you will have to go with the first option.

Mirroring via the Web

For downloading content directly from the web, the easiest tool to use is *wget* (*http://www.gnu.org/software/wget/wget.html*). With one command line, you can mirror an entire site, set it up in *cron*, and forget about it. The -m option to *wget* is most likely all you will need:

```
% wget -m "http://www.gnu.org/"
```

Run this and watch your screen scroll. The first time you mirror a site will likely take quite a while; remember, you are getting every image, file, and web page on a site. (There are ways to limit how far *wget* goes, which we'll get to in a minute.) Once it is finished, you will notice in the current directory a new directory with the same name as the root of the site you downloaded—for example, *www.gnu.org*. Within that directory, you will find the entire structure of the site, which you can browse with your favorite browser as if you were on the actual site. From here, all you have to do is run the same command from the same directory you ran it initially, and it will go back through the site and update files as necessary, taking as many advantages of the HTTP protocol allows in determining which files need to be updated.

When you first run a mirror, you may quickly realize that you're grabbing more content than you need. One way to help limit this is not to mirror the entire site; instead, mirror only what you really want:

```
% wget -m "http://www.gnu.org/software/wget/wget.html"
```

This is still not perfect. However, here is where some more of *wget*'s options come into play. First of all, there is the -np option. This option prevents *wget* from going into a higher directory than where you made it start. For example, the following command:

```
% wget -m -np "http://www.gnu.org/software/wget/wget.html"
```

does not download any pages in *http://www.gnu.org/software/*, nor does it go across and download anything from different web sites, which is probably a good idea. However, should you want *wget* to travel to different hosts, try adding the -H option.

Here are a few more options you may find worthwhile. The -l option limits the number of links *wget* will follow. For example, passing -l1 makes *wget* get the page you specify and all the links on that page, then stop. The -l option is useful if you want to follow only relative links. Not only does this prevent *wget* from crossing over and downloading from another site, but it also prevents it from following absolute URLs within the same site.

If you plan on browsing the HTML pages locally after mirroring, you will want to take a look at the -k and -p options. The -k option makes sure all links in the pages are made to be relative; this keeps you from crossing over into the live site if you are browsing locally and click on the link that previously was absolute. The -p option makes sure it downloads all the images and files on a page, even if they are located on a different site.

After you determine which options are best for your particular need, simply run it once in a directory and then *cron* the job with a line like this:

```
0 0 * * 6 (cd ~/mirrors; wget -m -np -k -p "http://www.gnu.org/" >/dev/null)
```

Mirroring Directly with the Server

In this case, you have access to the server. Most likely, you want to mirror your own site or perhaps some other data. For this, *rsync* (*http://rsync.samba.org/*) is the ideal tool. *rsync* is a versatile tool for mirroring or backing up data across computers. There are multiple ways of using *rsync* between machines; however, here we are going to use *ssh*. This is the easiest to configure and has the added advantage of providing good security for the files being transferred.

Obviously, you will need *ssh* installed and configured on both systems. You will also need to make sure you can log in to the system you want to mirror from. Next, you'll need to determine which directories you want to mirror and where you want them mirrored to on your system. With that in mind, you just need to run *rsync*, passing it the necessary options:

```
rsync -a -e ssh remote.machine.com:/some/directory /local/directory
```

The -a option tells *rsync* you want to mirror the directory; it sets a series of options that make *rsync* keep timestamps, permissions, user and group ownership, soft links, and so on for all the files, and it recurses through the directory. The -e option followed by ssh tells *rsync* to use *ssh* to connect to the remote server; if you are not using public key encryption, you will be prompted for the password by *ssh* when it connects to the server. The next argument is the server to connect to, followed by the directory to mirror from and, finally, the directory to mirror to. Make sure the last argument is a directory that already exists on your system, because *rsync* will create directories only inside this one.

Before getting into more options, it is a good idea to take a look at what this command just did. The mirrored directory should now appear the same as the directory on the server. Every file should be the same and should have the same timestamps, permissions, and so on. If you ran the command as *root*, the mirrored directory will also have the same usernames, assuming they exist on this system.

Now, we'll talk a bit about how *rsync* works; it was designed for exactly what we are using it for. It checks each file, comparing it to see if changes were made. If changes exist, it attempts to update the local file by sending only the parts that have changed. For new files, it sends the whole file. This is great, because not only is it better at checking for changes than *wget*'s use of the HTTP protocol, but it also tries to send only the data necessary to update the file, saving nicely on bandwidth.

Now, onto the other options. The -z option is probably one you will always want to use; it tells *rsync* to compress the data stream, decreasing bandwidth and most likely making the entire process go faster.

The -v option tells *rsync* to spit out the names of the files it is syncing; this works well when coupled with the --progress and --stats options. The former adds a progress indicator to each file as it is downloaded, and the latter details statistics about the entire mirroring operation.

The -u option tells *rsync* to only update files (it does not touch local files with a timestamp newer than the one on the server). This option is useful only if you modify the files locally and want to keep those changes. If you intend to keep a fully accurate mirror of the remote site, do not use this option; however, keep in mind that any changes you make to the files locally will be overwritten.

Finally, the --delete option deletes files that no longer exist on the server. If a file is deleted on the server, it will also be deleted on your backup. Again, this is very useful if you want to maintain an exact mirror of the files on the server.

Hacking the Hack

The way we use *rsync* here is a secure, easy way to handle it. However, if you do not have *ssh* installed, you may be looking for an alternative. There are basically two other options. One is to use *rsync* with *rsh* instead of *ssh*. This still requires setup on the server, though it is more traditional than *ssh* and considerably less secure than *ssh*. If you use *rsh*, remove the -e ssh option and make sure you have *rsh* set up correctly on your server. Another option is to run *rsync* as a service on the server. This option does not have the security of *ssh*, but it allows you to use *rsync* without having *ssh* set up. To do this, you still need *rsync* installed on both servers, but you have to create an *rsync* configuration file on the server and make sure *rsync* runs as a service.

To begin, you'll want the following command run at startup on the server:

```
rsync --daemon
```

Then, you will want to create a configuration file for *rsync*, such as the following:

```
[backup]
    path = /some/directory
```

Put this in the */etc/rsyncd.conf* file and have *rsync* start as shown previously. Now, when you connect to the *rsync* server, you will want to change the options a bit. Instead of `remote.machine.com:/some/directory`, you will want `remote.machine.com::backup`. This tells *rsync* to connect to the backup module on the *rsync* server. You will also want to omit the `-e ssh` option. There is more you can do with the *rsyncd.conf* file, including restricting access based on usernames, setting read-only access, and so on. For a complete list of options, view the manpage for *rsyncd.conf* by typing `man rsyncd.conf`.

—Adam Bregenzer

Accumulating Search Results Over Time
Graphing search results over time can lead to interesting discoveries.

If you're doing regular research over time, the quality of results might become just as interesting as the quantity. In other words, you might find it useful to track how popular certain words are getting on the Internet as events occur and time passes.

Many search engines offer varying levels of date-search capacity, including Google. With other engines, however, we'd have to use some scraping techniques to do result counts by date. With Google, we just need to use the Google API and some code. In order to use this code, you'll need the *Julian:: Date* module and a Google API key (which can be obtained for free by registering at *http://api.google.com/*).

Before we continue, there are two things of note:

- Result counts will tend to rise over time anyway, as Google adds more pages to its index. If you run this search often enough, you'll soon be able to easily recognize a regular growth curve from a spike of interest.
- Even though Google makes a date range syntax available, Google does not guarantee its results. So, don't use this application to make important decisions or draw definitive conclusions about keyword popularity.

The Code

Save the following code as *goocount.pl*:

```perl
#!/usr/bin/perl -w
# goocount.pl
# Runs the specified query for every day between the specified
# start and end dates, returning date and count as CSV. From
# Tara Calishain, Rael Dornfest, and Google Hacks.
#
# usage: goocount.pl query="{query}" start={date} end={date}
# where dates are of the format: yyyy-mm-dd, e.g. 2002-12-31
#
use strict;
use SOAP::Lite;
use Time::JulianDay;
use CGI qw/:standard/;

# Your Google API developer's key.
my $google_key = 'insert key here';

# Location of the GoogleSearch WSDL file.
my $google_wdsl = "./GoogleSearch.wsdl";

# For checking date validity.
my $date_regex = '(\d{4})-(\d{1,2})-(\d{1,2})';

# Make sure all arguments are passed correctly.
( param('query')
   and param('start') =~ /^(?:$date_regex)?$/
   and param('end') =~ /^(?:$date_regex)?$/
) or die qq{usage: goocount.pl query="{query}" start={date} end={date}\n};

# Julian date manipulation.
my $query = param('query');
my $yesterday_julian = int local_julian_day(time) - 1;
my $start_julian = (param('start') =~ /$date_regex/)
   ? julian_day($1,$2,$3) : $yesterday_julian;
my $end_julian   = (param('end') =~ /$date_regex/)
   ? julian_day($1,$2,$3) : $yesterday_julian;

# Create a new Google SOAP request.
my $google_search = SOAP::Lite->service("file:$google_wdsl");

# Start our CSV file.
print qq{"date","count"\n};

# Iterate over each of the Julian dates for your query.
foreach my $julian ($start_julian..$end_julian) {
    $full_query = "$query daterange:$julian-$julian";
    my $results = $google_search->doGoogleSearch(
                      $google_key, $full_query, 0, 10, "false",
```

```
                   "",   "false", "", "latin1", "latin1"
            );

      # Output our CSV record.
      print '"', sprintf("%04d-%02d-%02d", inverse_julian_day($julian)),
              qq{","$result->{estimatedTotalResultsCount}"\n};
   }
```

Running the Hack

Run the code from the command line, like so:

```
% perl goocount.pl query="PalmOS" start=2002-01-01 end=2002-12-31
```

This query searches for the keyword "PalmOS" over the entire year of 2002. (Since each day takes one query key, running the script with these parameters would take 365 keys.)

As output, you'll get a list of dates and numbers on the screen in this format:

```
"date", "count"
"2001-01-01", "200"
"2001-01-02", "210"
```

And so on and so on. If you want to save the results to a comma-delimited format (for easy import into Excel) append your query with a filename, like this:

```
% perl goocount.pl query="PalmOS" start=2002-01-01 end=2002-12-31 > data.csv
```

Perhaps you want to run this script under *cron* to gather information every day. Just run it without a date in the query (it'll default to today's date) and a >> to write additional information to the comma-delimited file:

```
% perl goocount.pl query="PalmOS" >>data.csv
```

Hacking the Hack

As written in this hack, the Google count script is a client-side application, but you can turn it into a web-based application with a little tweaking. Just change the program as noted in the following code (changes are shown in bold). And remember, this application can use a lot of API keys. Don't make this application publicly available unless you give users the option of using their own keys. Otherwise, you'll probably burn out your key!

```
   ...
   print
      header( ),
      start_html("GooCount: $query"),
      start_table({-border=>undef}, caption("GooCount:$query")),
      Tr([ th(['Date', 'Count']) ]);
```

```
foreach my $julian ($start_julian..$end_julian) {
    $full_query = "$query daterange:$julian-$julian";
    my $results = $google_search->doGoogleSearch(
                    $google_key, $full_query, 0, 10, "false",
                    "",  "false", "", "latin1", "latin1"
                );

print
  Tr([ td([
    sprintf("%04d-%02d-%02d", inverse_julian_day($julian)),
    $result->{estimatedTotalResultsCount}
  ]) ]);
}

print
    end_table( ),
    end_html;
```

See Also

- "Graphing Data with RRDTOOL" [Hack #62] for graphing Amazon Sales Ranks over a period of time.
- "A Quick Introduction to XPath" [Hack #25] for an example of pulling information from Junglescan.com.
- "Tracking Additions to Yahoo!" [Hack #47] to count how many new items Yahoo! has been adding to its index on a daily basis.

—Tara Calishain and Rael Dornfest

## CHAPTER SIX

Giving Back to the World
Hacks 94–100

The concept of *leeching* has been with us since day one, from the original land squatters, to rude time sharers in college computer labs, to BBS hogs who tied up the server's only phone line. The concept is strictly "the tragedy of the commons": most people just won't give back the resources they take. In this chapter, we'll discuss how we can use our scraping skills for the good of others.

The up-and-coming most popular way of providing your data to the world is through the use of application programming interfaces (APIs). Much like you can call *LWP::Simple*'s get function [Hack #9] without having to worry about creating network sockets and following HTTP protocols, an API to your data allows visitors to get the information they desire quickly and simply. In essence, you're removing the need for them to scrape and spider your site.

Arguably, Internet APIs hit the true mainstream when Google announced one for its entire database (*http://api.google.com*). After a few tentative steps, use of the API exploded and *Google Hacks*, dedicated to teaching, exploring, and exploiting the technology, became a *New York Times* best seller.

More APIs quickly followed, the second big announcement coming from Amazon.com (*http://www.amazon.com/webservices/*). There was no hesitation: Google had broken the ice, and developers flocked to the Amazon.com Web Services API, quickly creating libraries, shopping-cart builders, plug-ins for weblog software like Movable Type, and more. The proverbial ball had started rolling.

Existing APIs like O'Reilly's Meerkat (*http://www.oreillynet.com/meerkat/*), Syndic8 (*http://www.syndic8.com/services.php*), and NewsIsFree (*http://newsisfree.com/webservice.php*) received renewed interest, while never-before-seen APIs like Technorati (*http://developers.technorati.com/wiki/*) and All Consuming (*http://allconsuming.net/news/000012.html*) were welcomed with open arms.

Giving back to the world by creating a standard and well-defined interface will bring you the thanks, respect, and happiness of a great many people. Whether you create syndicated content with the RSS format [Hack #94], an interface through instant messaging software [Hack #99], or your very own API in one of three flavors, you'll make your data easier to repurpose and also make it easier to create brand new applications never dreamed of. All Consuming [Hack #66], for instance, merges data available from Weblogs.Com, Amazon.com, and Google, while Technorati [Hack #70] works by aggregating weblog information.

HACK #94 Using XML::RSS to Repurpose Data

By using the popular syndication format known as RSS, you can use your newly scraped data in dozens of different aggregators, toolkits, and more.

At its simplest, RSS is an XML format for publishing summaries of data, with links to more information. The main use of RSS is to syndicate news headlines and weblog postings with titles, summaries, and links to full stories. A reader can then comb through the story listings, reading a full story if it interests him, rather than having to hop from site to site looking for what's new. You read RSS files with *news aggregators*, such as NewsMonster (*http://www.newsmonster.com*), AmphetaDesk (*http://www.disobey.com/ amphetadesk/*), Radio UserLand (*http://radio.userland.com*), and many more. Due to the incredible popularity of RSS, folks are starting to syndicate just about anything one might be interested in following—recipes, job listings, sports scores, and TV schedules to name but a few.

Here's a simple RSS file:

```
<?xml version="1.0"?>
<rss version="0.91">

  <channel>
    <title>ResearchBuzz</title>
    <link>http://www.researchbuzz.com</link>
    <description>News and information on search engines... </description>
    <language>en-us</language>

    <item>
     <title>Survey Maps of Scotland Towns</title>
     <link>http://researchbuzz.com/news/2003/jul31aug603.shtml</link>
    </item>

    <item>
     <title>Directory of Webrings</title>
     <link>http://researchbuzz.com/news/2003/jul31aug603.shtml</link>
    </item>

  </channel>
</rss>
```

Thankfully, we don't have to worry about creating these files by hand. We can create RSS files with a simple Perl module called *XML::RSS* (*http://search.cpan.org/author/KELLAN/XML-RSS/*). Here's how:

```perl
#!/usr/bin/perl -w
use strict;
use XML::RSS;

my $rss = new XML::RSS(version => '0.91');
$rss->channel(
    title       => 'Research Buzz',
    link        => 'http://www.researchbuzz.com',
    description => 'News and information on search en...',
);

$rss->add_item(
    title       => 'Survey Maps of Scotland Towns',
    link        => 'http://researchbuzz.com/news/2003/etc/etc/etc#etc',
    description => 'An optional description can go here.'
);

$rss->add_item(
    title       => 'Directory of Webrings',
    link        => 'http://researchbuzz.com/news/2003/yadda/yadda#etc',
    description => 'Another optional description can go here.'
);

print $rss->as_string;
```

This code creates a channel to describe the ResearchBuzz web site, replete with some story entries, each created by a call to add_item. When we're done adding items, we print the final RSS to STDOUT. Alternatively, if we want to save our RSS to a file, we use the save method:

```perl
$rss->save("file.rss");
```

Saving your RSS to a file is *very* important. RSS is likely to be downloaded a lot by users checking for updates, so generating it on the fly each time will bog down your server unnecessarily. It's common for a mildly popular site to have its RSS feed downloaded six times a minute. You can automate the creation of your RSS files with a *cron* job [Hack #90].

Since the call to add_item always creates a new RSS entry with a title, link, and description, we can feed it from anything available, such as iterating over the results of a database search, matches from an HTML parser or regular expression, and so on. Or, we can do something much more interesting and hack it together with one of the existing scripts in this book.

In this example, we'll use our aggregated search engine [Hack #85] and repurpose its results into RSS instead of its normal format.

You'll need the *XML::RSS* module installed, as well as the code from "Aggregating Multiple Search Engine Results" [Hack #85]. Note that most fields within an RSS feed are optional, so this code outputs only a title and link, not a description:

```perl
#!/usr/bin/perl -w

# agg2rss - aggregated search to RSS converter
# This file distributed under the same licence as Perl itself
# by rik - ora@rikrose.net

use strict;
use XML::RSS;

# Build command line, and run the aggregated search engine.
my (@currentPlugin, @plugins, $url, $desc, $plugin, %results);
my $commandLine = "aggsearch " . join " ", @ARGV;
open INPUT, "$commandLine |" or die $!;
while (<INPUT>){ chomp;
    @currentPlugin = split / /, $_;
    push @plugins, $currentPlugin[0];

    while (<INPUT>){
        chomp;
        last if length == 0;
        s/</&lt;/; s/>/&gt;/;
        ($url, $desc) = split /: /, $_, 2;
        $url =~ s/^ //; $desc =~ s/^ //;
        $results{$currentPlugin[0]}{$url} = $desc;
    }
}
close INPUT;

# Results are now in the @plugins,
# %results pair. Put the results into RSS:
my $rss = XML::RSS->new(version => '0.91');

# Create the channel object.
$rss->channel(
        title       => 'Aggregated Search Results',
        link        => 'http://www.example.com/cgi/make-new-search',
        description => 'Using plugins: ' . join ", ", @plugins
);

# Add data.
for $plugin (@plugins){
    for $url (keys %{$results{$plugin}}){
        $rss->add_item(
                title       => $results{$plugin}{$url},
                link        => $url,
        );
    }
}
```

```
# Save it for later, in our RSS feed for our web site.
$rss->save("/rss/index.rdf");
```

Okay, we've created the RSS and placed it on our web site so that others can consume it. What now? *XML::RSS* not only generates RSS files, but it can also parse them. In this example, we'll download the RSS feed for the front page of the BBC and print a nice, readable summary to STDOUT (most likely to your screen):

```perl
#!/usr/bin/perl -w

# get-headlines - get the BBC headlines in RSS format, and print them
# This file distributed under the same licence as Perl itself
# by rik - ora@rikrose.net

use strict;
use LWP::UserAgent;
use XML::RSS;

my $url = "http://www.bbc.co.uk/syndication/feeds/".
          "news/ukfs_news/front_page/rss091.xml";

# get data
my $ua = LWP::UserAgent->new( );
my $response = $ua->get($url);
die $response->status_line . "\n"
  unless $response->is_success;

# parse it
my $rss = XML::RSS->new;
$rss->parse($response->content);

# print each item
foreach my $item (@{$rss->{'items'}}){
    print "title: $item->{'title'}\n";
    print "link: $item->{'link'}\n\n";
}
```

Save this code as *bbc.pl*. Its results look similar to this:

```
% perl bbc.pl

title: UK troops attacked in Basra
link: http://news.bbc.co.uk/go/click/rss/0.91/public/-
      /1/hi/world/middle_east/3137779.stm

title: 'More IVF' on the NHS
link: http://news.bbc.co.uk/go/click/rss/0.91/public/-
      /1/hi/health/3137191.stm

...etc...
```

See Also

- *Content Syndication with XML and RSS* (*http://www.oreilly.com/catalog/consynrss/*) by Ben Hammersley for a full explanation of the various RSS formats, as well as further information on parsing, creating, and adding your own elements via namespaces.

—Richard Rose

Placing RSS Headlines on Your Site

HACK
#95

Place other site's syndicated headlines on your own pages, periodically.

Including syndicated news feeds is a nice way of adding some compelling content to your site. The problem is that sometimes the news feed gets over-run during heavy news days, goes offline, and/or suffers a host of other connectivity issues. These problems make *your* site load slowly, because the software holds your user hostage while the feed retrieval portion of the application waits to time out.

A simple way around this problem is to use a program that periodically retrieves the feed and slices-n-dices it into an easy-to-include file on your host. Doing this achieves five goals:

- User page loads are not penalized when feeds go down.
- Failures to connect do not harm the existing include file.
- Multiple attempts to read the feed do not penalize the user.
- Feeds can be mirrored for local/private use.
- Content can be formatted to taste.

The Code

This is a little program I wrote to repurpose news from an AP Wire feed:

```perl
#!/usr/bin/perl -w
# ------------------------------------------------------------------------
# copyright Dean Peters © 2003 - all rights reserved
# http://www.HealYourChurchWebSite.org
# ------------------------------------------------------------------------
#
# getap.pl is free software. You can redistribute and modify it
# freely without any consent of the developer, Dean Peters, if and
# only if the following conditions are met:
#
# (a) The copyright info and links in the headers remains intact.
# (b) The purpose of distribution or modification is non-commercial.
#
```

```perl
# Commercial distribution of this product without a written
# permission from Dean Peters is strictly prohibited.
# This script is provided on an as-is basis, without any warranty.
# The author does not take any responsibility for any damage or
# loss of data that may occur from use of this script.
#
# You may refer to our general terms & conditions for clarification:
# http://www.healyourchurchwebsite.com/archives/000002.shtml
#
# For more info. about this code, please refer to the following article:
# http://www.healyourchurchwebsite.com/archives/000760.shtml
#
# combine this code with crontab for best results, e.g.:
# 59 * * * * /path/to/scriptname.pl > /dev/null
#
# -------------------------------------------------------------------------

use XML::RSS;
use LWP::Simple;

# get content from feed -- using 10 attempts.
# replace the URL with whatever feed you want to get.
my $content = getFeed("http://www.goupstate.com/apps/pbcs.dll/".
                      "section?Category=RSS04&mime=xml", 10);

# save off feed to a file -- make sure you
# have write access to file or directory.
saveFeed($content, "newsfeed.xml");

# create customized output.
my $output = createOutput($content, 8);

# save it to your include file.
saveFeed($output, "newsfeed.inc.php");

# download the feed in question.
# accepts two inputs, the URL, and
# the number of times you wish to loop.
sub getFeed {
    my ($url, $attempts) = @_;
    my $lc = 0; # loop count
    my $content;
    while($lc < $attempts) {
        $content = get($url);
        return $content if $content;
        $lc += 1; sleep 5;
    }

    die "Could not retreive data from $url in $attempts attempts";
}
```

```perl
# saves the converted data ($content)
# to final destination ($outfile).
sub saveFeed {
    my ($content, $outfile) = @_;
    open(OUT,">$outfile") || die("Cannot Open File $outfile");
    print OUT $content; close(OUT);
}

# parses the XML file and returns
# a string of custom content. You
# can pass the number of items you'd
# like as the second argument.
sub createOutput {
    my ($content, $feedcount) = @_;

    # new instance of XML::RSS
    my $rss = XML::RSS->new;

    # parse the RSS content into an output
    # string to be saved at end of parsing.
    $rss->parse($content);
    my $title = $rss->{channel}->{title};
    my $output  = '<div class="title">GoUpstate/AP NewsWire</div>';
       $output .= '<div class="newsfeed">\n';

    my $i = 0; # begin our item loop.
    foreach my $item (@{$rss->{items}}) {
        next unless defined($item->{title}) && defined($item->{link});
        $i += 1; next if $i > $feedcount; # skip if we're done.
        $output .= "<a href=\"$item->{link}\">$item->{title}</a><br />\n";
    }

    # if a copyright and link exists, then post it.
    my $copyright = $rss->{channel}->{copyright};
    my $link = $rss->{channel}->{link};
    my $description = $rss->{channel}->{description};
    $output .= "<a href=\"$link\" title=\"$description\" >".
               "$copyright</a>\n" if($copyright && $link);
    $output .= "</div>";
    return $output;
}
```

Running the Hack

Running this code creates two new files in the current directory: *newsfeed.xml* is the raw data we've downloaded, and *newsfeed.inc.php* is our repurposed data for use on our own site. Using the following *crontab* syntax [Hack #90], the program is executed every hour:

```
59 * * * * /path/to/scriptname.pl > /dev/null
```

The nice thing about this approach is that this particular feed does get busy from time to time and, at one point on a Friday, it went offline. My users did not notice because, in most cases, I was able to get by the "busy signal" on the second or third attempt out of 10. In the case where the entire remote site went offline, my users merely viewed an older include file without interruption or delay.

—Dean Peters and Tara Calishain

Making Your Resources Scrapable with Regular Expressions

A few tricks can make your web page data easier to parse, without needing complicated HTML libraries or convoluted logic. The benefits extend to more than just visitors; your own HTML will be more understandable too.

Scraping is an attempt to address a common problem in development: an application to which someone needs automated access was built around interfaces meant only for human use. For whatever reason, the application cannot be changed or replaced. The only apparent way to talk to the application is to be a human operator.

Well, someone surmised that something *simulating* a human operator might work as well. Back when text forms on green screens first fell out of favor, the functions of applications that produced them were still in demand. So, developers built programmable terminals as components in their new applications. These automated terminals were capable of extracting the characters displayed at known column and row locations, in order to harvest (or *scrape*) data from the screen displayed in form fields. This terminal software could also fill in form fields and send control commands, just like a human user, in order to run a formerly manual application through its paces.

Although it was often a convoluted and error-prone process, this simulation of a human operator made the impossible task of automation possible. For older applications that previously required human interaction, the process extended their usefulness just a bit longer. After creating automated terminals, access to legacy applications could be wrapped in more modern facades. Despite the scripted contortions of a simulated terminal going on in the background, an end developer would see, ideally, only a standard database API in her editor.

The Challenge of Web Scraping

Today, accessing information on the Web presents another challenge to automation and scraping. Content and applications on the Web are usually intended for human users via web browsers, so they have little or no support for automated access or control.

Depending on the site or service provider, this lack can be intentional, but for the most part it's merely something most webmasters and developers haven't considered. On the contrary, most projects on the Web have visual appearance and user experience as their top concerns, often resulting in convoluted and inconsistent HTML code to produce the desired effects in web browsers.

Unfortunately, trying to automate the use of web resources presents us with a somewhat more complicated situation than when terminals were first automated. Whereas developers scraping terminal screens mostly had to worry about the location of fields on a two-dimensional screen, developers scraping web sites have to worry about the many dimensions of HTML tag soup accepted by modern browsers, not to mention the various browser tricks used for navigation and session management.

Despite the difficulty, though, the solution in both situations remains similar: build a programmable browser that can simulate human access to web resources. Generally, this involves two intertwined tasks: navigating between web resources and extracting specific information from these resources.

Navigating between web resources. Consider a site that provides current weather conditions. Say that this particular site is a paid service, so it requires a valid user account and login before giving access to the information. In order to pull weather conditions from this site, a developer will need to have his application authenticate with the site first, then hunt for the information through the page that displays weather conditions.

With Perl, the first task can be accomplished using the *WWW::Mechanize* module [Hack #21] from CPAN. This module can be used to easily automate many of the tasks involved in grabbing web resources, filling out and submitting forms, managing session cookies, and following links. For example:

```
#!/usr/bin/perl -w
use strict;
use WWW::Mechanize;
my $agent = WWW::Mechanize->new( );

# Get the site login page.
$agent->get('http://my.weatherexample.com/login.html');

# Step to the third form on the page, which we've identified
# as the login form. Fill out account details and submit.
$agent->form_number('3');
```

```
$agent->field('user','my_name');
$agent->field('password','my_password');
$agent->submit();

# Having logged in, we should have valid session cookies or
# whatever the site requires. On the page following login,
# follow the link labeled "Current Conditions".
$agent->follow('Current Conditions');

# Grab the contents of the current weather conditions page.
my $content = $agent->content();
```

This code simulates the process of a human user logging in and navigating to the "Current Conditions" page on the site. The *WWW::Mechanize* module is capable of much more in the way of automating web browser activity, without requiring the use of a browser or human intervention. See "WWW:: Mechanize 101" **[Hack #21]** and "Scraping with WWW::Mechanize" **[Hack #22]** for more details on using *WWW::Mechanize*.

Extracting specific information. So, now that we have the HTML source of the page that displays the current weather conditions, we can work out an approach to extract the relevant data. Let's say that a peek at this HTML source looks like this:

```
<html>
<body>
<table><tr><td>
<table>
        <tr>
        <td>
<table CELLPADDING=2 BORDER=0 CELLSPACING=1 width="100%">
  <tr valign=top align=center bgcolor=#000088>
   <td colspan=2><font color=#ffffff><b>Conditions</b></font></td>
  </tr>
<tr BGCOLOR="#eeeeee">
<td COLSPAN=2>
Conditions at
<b>Ann Arbor, Michigan</b><br>
Updated: <b>4:53 PM EDT on June 22, 2003</b>
  </td></tr>
<tr BGCOLOR="#FFFFFF"><td width="35%">Temperature</td>
      <td>
      <b>
83
</b> &#176;F
    /
        <b>
28
</b> &#176;C
  </td>
      </tr>
```

```
<tr BGCOLOR="#ddeeff"><td>Humidity</td>
<td><b>
32%
</b></td></tr>
</table>
    </td>
</tr></table>
</td>
</TR></table>
</body>
</html>
```

This is some ugly tag soup, but it was generated by an application to look good in the browser. It was never meant to be seen by human eyes. Too bad for us, but don't worry; there are plenty of tricks left.

There are a few Perl packages that give us access to highly tolerant HTML tag soup processing. One of them is *HTML::Tree* (*http://search.cpan.org/ author/sburke/HTML-Tree/*), which has many modules and convenience methods for walking and searching through the structure of an HTML document for content to extract. After some head scratching and staring at the HTML of the weather conditions page, some patterns can be worked out and used to extract basic information, which we can then extract using *HTML::TreeBuilder* [Hack #19]:

```perl
#!/usr/bin/perl -w
use strict;
use HTML::TreeBuilder;

# Build a tree from the HTML.
my $tree = HTML::TreeBuilder->new( );
$tree->parse($the_weather_content);

# Drill down and find the first
# instance of 'Conditions' in bold.
my ($curr) = $tree->look_down
  (
    _tag => 'b',
    sub { $_[0]->as_text( ) eq 'Conditions' }
  );

# Step back up to the first
# containing table from 'Conditions'.
($curr) = $curr->look_up(_tag => 'table');

# Grab the containing table's rows.
my @rows = $curr->look_down(_tag => 'tr');

# Each table row after the first contains some info we want, and each
# piece of info is set in bold. So, extract our info as text from the
# bold tags in each row.
```

```
my %data = ();
($data{location}, $data{time}) =
    map { $_->as_text() } $rows[1]->look_down(_tag => 'b');
($data{$temp_f}, $data{temp_c}) =
    map { $_->as_text() } $rows[2]->look_down(_tag => 'b');
($data{humid}) =
    map { $_->as_text() } $rows[3]->look_down(_tag => 'b');
```

How to Be Nicer to Scrapers

It should be clear that, even with very clever tools, developers trying to auto-mate interaction with web resources need to jump through a few (occasion-ally flaming) hoops to do the simplest things a human user can do by hand. And, as mentioned earlier, some web site owners prefer things that way.

But what if, as a site owner, you'd actually like to encourage automated use of your site and make things easier? Just as the scraping process has two tasks, there are also two main things to be done to make the tasks easier: making resources easier to locate and acquire and making data within these resources easier to extract.

Make resources easier to locate and acquire. How can you make resources easier to find and obtain? Try to reduce the number of steps to reach a desired resource, ideally down to one step via a single URL.

Instead of having a login process that spans several pages and uses custom cookies for session management, why not try using HTTP authentication? Or, you could allow the username and password to be passed in as query parameters in the request for any resource. While this does have security implications, you should consider requiring access via secure HTTP to your site if this is a major worry. On the other hand, rethink your data: *must* it be secured? If our weather site followed this first suggestion and simplified access to the current weather conditions page, we could replace the *WWW:: Mechanize*-based code with the following:

```
#!/usr/bin/perl -w
use strict;
use LWP::Simple;

# Define the username, password,
# and URL to access current conditions.
my $user = 'my_name';
my $pass = 'my_pass';
my $url  = 'http://my.weatherexample.com/current';

# Grab the desired page.
my $content = get("$url?username=$user&password=$pass");
```

Notice how few hoops this example has. In fact, most of the code is there for the sake of clarity, rather than as a part of the process to find the desired resource. This is almost always a good thing, especially for the novice scraper.

Removing the authentication entirely would reduce the code to simply this:

```
#!/usr/bin/perl -w
use strict;
use LWP::Simple;

my $content = get('http://my.weatherexample.com/current');
```

Making data easier to extract. Now that we've made site resources more accessible to programs, how do we make the data within resources easier to extract? Ideally, we shouldn't need to do anything radical or drastic to the existing site or application.

Let's consider another extraction technique: regular expressions. Perl comes with built-in support for regular expressions, as do many other scripting languages. Where support is not built in, some external module is generally available. Although they have one of the most opaque of syntaxes, using regular expressions is a much more direct and lightweight way of plucking data from text such as HTML source.

As the name suggests, regular expressions are best at finding and extracting bits from regular patterns matched in data streams. Although the rich syntax of regular expressions can capture and describe complex patterns, simpler patterns call for simpler expressions. And, since we're trying to make it easier to get at data from our site, we should consider how to offer simpler patterns.

Here are some suggestions for simpler patterns that are easy to implement and have little or no impact on how HTML appears in the browser:

- Add context to your HTML data, such as ID attributes or CSS classes.
- Try to keep individual data items and surrounding tags on one line.
- Where data takes up multiple lines, try bracketing the data with HTML comments—for example: `<!-- start info -->`*DATA GOES HERE*`<!-- end info -->`.

For the most part, making data within HTML documents more easily extractable is a matter of reducing noise and adding easily described context around the data items. For example, with just a few tweaks, we can make the weather service's current conditions page incredibly easy to handle:

```
<html>
<body>
```

```
<table><tr><td>
<table>
        <tr>
        <td>
<table CELLPADDING=2 BORDER=0 CELLSPACING=1 width="100%">
  <tr valign=top align=center bgcolor=#000088>
   <td colspan=2><font color=#ffffff><b>Conditions</b></font></td>
  </tr>
<tr BGCOLOR="#eeeeee">
<td COLSPAN=2>
Conditions at
<b ID="location">Ann Arbor, Michigan</b><br>
Updated: <b ID="time">4:53 PM EDT on June 22, 2003</b>
 </td></tr>
<tr BGCOLOR="#FFFFFF"><td width="35%">Temperature</td>
     <td>
     <b ID="temp_f">83</b> &#176;F
     /
         <b ID="temp_c">28</b> &#176;C
  </td>
       </tr>
<tr BGCOLOR="#ddeeff"><td>Humidity</td>
<td><b ID="humid">32%</b></td></tr>
</table>
     </td>
</tr></table>
</td>
</TR></table>
</body>
</html>
```

The only changes we've made in this example to the original HTML are to remove all the line breaks around data and to add ID attributes to all the bold tags surrounding the data items. Now, the code used to extract this data can be reduced to this:

```
my %data = ();
foreach my $id qw(location time temp_f temp_c humid) {
  ( $data{$id} ) = ($content =~ m!<b ID="$id">(.+?)</b>!i);
}
```

This code loops through the name of each piece of desired data, and extracts the text of a bold tag, labeled with the corresponding ID attribute.

Hacking the Hack

Since we've saved so much time extracting data while working with regular expressions, we could go further and break up the date with another:

```
my ($h, $m, $ampm, $tz, $mm, $dd, $yyyy) =
  ( $data{time} =~ m!(\d+):(\d+) (..) (...) on (\w+) (\d+), (\d+)! );
```

This breaks up the date format into its individual parts so that we can do whatever further processing or reformatting we might want. Alternatively, if the date is in a readily understandable format, the *Date::Manip* module (*http://search.cpan.org/author/SBECK/DateManip/*) would be a smarter and infinitely more flexible choice.

With just a few simple changes, extracting data from the weather service page no longer requires any kind of HTML parser or document tree searching. Everything can be done with a single regular expression template. And, since the pattern is so simple, the regular expression needed to extract the data is also very simple.

—l.m.orchard

HACK #97 Making Your Resources Scrapable with a REST Interface

Consider offering alternative versions of site documents for a variety of human and machine visitors, based on how they present themselves.

Another way of looking at web resources is to consider them for the information they represent, rather than as applications that need automated access through scraping. Think about the two main facets of web site scraping: navigation and extraction. These facets reflect the architecture of the Web itself as a network of navigable links. Further, these navigable links point to resources from which we can acquire representations, among a few other things we can do.

This is a loose description of the Representational State Transfer (REST) architectural style (*http://conveyor.com/RESTwiki/moin.cgi*). In a way, the principles of REST seem like where we'd arrive if we took accommodating scrapers as far as we could go. Ultimately, REST is a fancy term for using URLs and HTTP GET/POST to represent ways of accessing resources.

Navigation between resources to find the resource we want is simple, because representations of resources (i.e., HTML pages, XML documents, etc.) contain clear links to other resources. And extracting data is simple too, since every resource should have multiple representations and the client can specify what it accepts in order to get what it needs. That is, even though people using browsers ask for HTML, a robot looking for something closer to its needs can ask for it using HTTP content negotiation.

There's a lot more to the REST style involving the manipulation of resources. But since we're concerned only with making existing resources easier to acquire, we'll leave the rest of REST to another book.

Navigating One URI at a Time

Part of the REST philosophy is careful and clean URI design. Since every resource on the Web should be addressable via a URI, good organization and understandable hierarchy make URIs more useful. Also, URIs should be put together in a way that tries to focus on the organization of the resources, hiding any underlying mechanisms such as CGI-BIN directories or file extensions. And since URIs are the way resources on your site are found, their structure and what they point to on your site should be well-documented, akin to a programming interface.

For example, you could establish a URI structure like this to acquire the current weather conditions in your, or any, area:

```
http://my.weatherexample.com/locations/48103/conditions/current
```

This shows a logical path from topic to topic, finally specifying current conditions in a specific Zip Code area. An application could take things a step at a time, though, first by requesting */locations* for a list of available Zip Codes:

```
<locations xmlns:xlink="http://www.w3.org/1999/xlink">
  ...
  <location xlink:href="48001/" code="48101" label="Algonac, MI" />
  <location xlink:href="48104/" code="48104" label="Ann Arbor, MI" />
  <location xlink:href="48105/" code="48105" label="Ann Arbor, MI" />
  ...
</locations>
```

One of the relative Zip Code links could be followed—*/locations/48103*, for example—to list the different categories of weather information available:

```
<reports xmlns:xlink="http://www.w3.org/1999/xlink">
  <report xlink:href="conditions/" label="Conditions" />
  <report xlink:href="forecasts/" label="Forecasts" />
  <report xlink:href="warnings/" label="Warnings" />
</reports>
```

At each step of the way, XML documents containing URI links would lead the application to discover further resources, either automatically or perhaps by selection from a GUI.

But REST simply defines the architecture and the philosophy. It doesn't specify any file formats in particular as representations of resources. We could use XML, RDF triples, or even comma-separated lines. REST simply suggests that, whatever the format is, when other resources are mentioned, they must be referred to by URI in order to form the web of navigable links.

Negotiating Better Content

So, now that we have a simple, solid philosophy toward providing an easily navigated web of resources identified by URI, how can we get at the data? Well, in the REST architecture, representations of resources are acquired from the Web. A single resource can have many representations, such as HTML and XML, both of which are different views of the same conceptual thing. So, with this in mind, wouldn't it be nice if, instead of scraping data from an HTML file intended for a browser, our application could simply ask for something more appropriate?

The Apache HTTP Server's description of content negotiation (*http://httpd.apache.org/docs/content-negotiation.html*) states:

> A resource may be available in several different representations. For example, it might be available in different languages or different media types, or a combination. One way of selecting the most appropriate choice is to give the user an index page, and let them select. However it is often possible for the server to choose automatically. This works because browsers can send, as part of each request, information about what representations they prefer.

For example, when a web browser is used to view the current weather conditions, the browser might send this as one of the headers in its request for the resource:

```
Accept: text/html; q=1.0, text/*; q=0.8, image/gif; q=0.6,
        image/jpeg; q=0.6, image/*; q=0.5, */*; q=0.1
```

On the other hand, an application sent to extract the raw weather conditions data itself should send a header like this:

```
Accept: application/weatherml+xml; q=1.0,
        application/xml; q=0.8,
        text/*; q=0.6, */*; q=0.1
```

These two headers each present the HTTP server with a priority list of content types preferred by each client. Accordingly, the web browser wants some form of HTML or text, possibly falling back to an image type. On the other hand, our application wants raw weather data, so it asks for a specific data format (presumably already well-defined), followed by generic XML, then text, and possibly whatever else is laying around.

On the server side, with the Apache HTTP Server, these preferences can be handled by first adding a content type and file extension for application/weatherml+xml in the server's *mime.types* file, like this:

```
AddType application/weatherml+xml wea
```

Then, the MultiViews option can be turned on for a directory:

```
Options +MultiViews
```

As long as Apache has the *mod_negotiation* module installed, turning on MultiViews will cause the server to try matching preferences up with resources available in the directory. Content types are identified automatically using file extensions and the *mime.types* mappings.

For example, the root folder of the weather site could contain two files: *current.html* and *current.wea*. When the web browser requests *http://my.weatherexample.com/current*, it will receive the preferred HTML representation. However, when our data-extracting client requests the same URL, it will receive the contents of *current.wea*, as per its preferences in the request.

The REST architecture is a good alternative to handling information on the Web. Resources identified by URI, representations of which can contain links to further resources, provide well for the construction of interrelated data that is far more complex than initially planned for. And using a form of transparent content negotiation allows us to serve both human and machine visitors from the same resources. It's all a bit more complicated than simple scraping, but in terms of scalability and compatibility between future applications it is worth it.

See Also

- For an example of one service that provides a REST interface, as well as code to access it, check out "Using All Consuming to Get Book Lists" [Hack #66].
- If you want to read more about the REST architectural style, an open-access wiki and list of resources is available at *http://internet.conveyor.com/RESTwiki/moin.cgi/FrontPage*.

—l.m.orchard

 ## H A C K Making Your Resources Scrapable with
#98 XML-RPC

If you want to make your site's information accessible to lots of aspiring spider builders, don't worry about regular expressions. Just add a little XML-RPC.

No matter how easy we make scraping, it's still scraping: a poorly supported hack meant to enable automation by working around the limitations of a resource meant for human consumption (whew!).

But what if, as a site owner, we have both the ability and desire to overcome the weaknesses of scraping? Then we can replace scraping as the method to access our web resources with an explicit programming interface. This is where web services come in, and they're easier than you might think. Well, in most cases, they're easier on developers than forcing them to dig through HTML tag soup with regular expressions, anyway.

Enter Web Services

Let's consider XML-RPC. XML-RPC (Extensible Markup Language with Remote Procedure Calls) is a simple way to exploit XML and HTTP to support remote procedure calls across the Web. The process uses the basic HTTP POST method to send an XML document to a web application. This XML document contains the details of a procedure to be called in a web application, along with the arguments with which to call the procedure. The web application then returns an XML document that contains the results of the procedure call.

Since XML-RPC uses nothing more exotic for communication than a form submission via the POST method, most web environments can support XML-RPC. Likewise, many web applications can easily be adapted to support a programmable interface. The most complicated part of the process is handling the XML content of the messages, but most programming environments have XML-RPC support packages available. In fact, in practical usage, you rarely even notice the XML. Perl modules are available that provide support for building clients transparently using XML-RPC calls and building servers responding to XML-RPC calls using a variety of convenience methods.

Let's put it all together. XML-RPC sends an XML document that contains procedure arguments to a web application. The web application processes the arguments and returns an XML document, which a script can parse with one of several available XML-RPC packages. Still with me? Let's look at an example.

Building the service. Let's consider providing the current weather conditions from a weather information site. For this, we'll use the *XMLRPC::Lite* Perl module. Not only is it easy to use, but the module is also a part of the larger *SOAP::Lite* package (*http://search.cpan.org/src/KULCHENKO/SOAP-Lite/*), so we can play with the more advanced SOAP protocol later. Let's step through the service one item at a time:

```
#!/usr/bin/perl -w
# Weather via XML-RPC
# Providing current weather conditions
# from a weather information site.
use strict;
use XMLRPC::Lite;
use XMLRPC::Transport::HTTP;

# Set up CGI-based XMLRPC server handler, with all
# calls dispatched to the 'weather' package.
my $server = XMLRPC::Transport::HTTP::CGI->new( )
  ->dispatch_to('weather')
  ->handle( );
```

Thanks to the handling *XMLRPC::Lite* does in the background, implementing an XML-RPC method is fairly simple, idiomatic Perl. In fact, most of the XML involved in the process is translated to and from Perl data structures automatically, so no worries there. In fact, our method to support the retrieval of current weather conditions can look something like this:

```perl
package weather;
sub getCurrentConditions {
  my $pkg = shift;
  my ($user, $pass) = @_;
  main::auth_user($user, $pass) || die("Invalid login");
  my ($location, $time, $temp_f, $temp_c, $humid) =
    main::get_current_conditions($user, $pass);
  return
    {
     location => $location,
     time     => $time,
     temp_f   => $temp_f,
     temp_c   => $temp_c,
     humid    => $humid
    };
}
```

This implements an XML-RPC method that expects two parameters: username and password. Upon successful authentication, a data structure is returned with the current weather condition data items.

Making the service useful. You'll need a few more subroutines to make this example work, namely auth_user() and get_current_conditions():

```perl
package main;

# Authenticate users.
sub auth_user {
  my ($user, $pass) = @_;
  return ( ($user eq 'my_user') && ($pass eq 'my_pass') );
}

# Look up current weather conditions.
# Use fake values, just for example.
sub get_current_conditions {
  my ($user, $pass) = @_;
  my ($location, $time) = ("Ann Arbor", "4:53 PM EDT on June 22, 2003");
  my ($temp_f, $temp_c) = ("83", "28");
  my ($humid)           = ("32%");
  return ($location, $time, $temp_f, $temp_c, $humid);
}
```

As implemented, these subroutines don't do much: a hardcoded user account named my_user with password my_pass is accepted, and canned weather data is returned. But, after testing, these two subroutines can be replaced with code that does real authentication and looks up real data.

Using the service from the client side. Here's how to use *XMLRPC::Lite* as a client:

```
use XMLRPC::Lite;
my $data = XMLRPC::Lite
   -> proxy('http://my.weatherexample.com/service.cgi')
   -> call('weather.getCurrentConditions', 'my_user', 'my_pass')
   -> result;
for my $name qw(location time temp_f temp_c humid) {
    print $name . ": " . $data->{$name} . "\n";
}
```

There are other ways to call this service, with one of the other Perl XML-RPC packages or with an XML-RPC package from another programming environment altogether. That's the beauty of providing this as a web service: easy interoperability.

Hacking a scrape together with a service. If you've already written code to successfully scrape the current conditions from the weather site via automated browsing or regular expressions, you can drop your existing code into get_current_conditions:

```
use LWP::Simple;
sub get_current_conditions {
  my ($user, $pass) = @_;

  # Grab the desired page.
  my $content = get("http://my.weatherexample.com/current?".
                    "username=$user&password=$pass");

  # Extract weather
  # conditions, bub.
  my %data = ();
  foreach my $id qw(location time temp_f temp_c humid) {
    ( $data{$id} ) = ($content =~ m!<b ID="$id">(.+?)</b>!i);
  }
  # Return the conditions data in a list.
  return map { $data{$_} } qw(location time temp_f temp_c humid);
}
```

This takes us back to scraping web resources, but using the results of scraping to feed a web service creates a sort of adapter to the weather site. In this case, you could offer your web service to others so that they don't have to scrape the site themselves.

However, this can be a tricky path to tread. Before building a web service as a gateway on top of someone else's web site, you should have permission to do so. At best, the site's owner might find you rude; at worst, you might find yourself looking for a lawyer.

Hacking the Hack

If you want to build a web service with SOAP instead of XML-RPC, the *SOAP::Lite* package makes it easy. Simply replace XMLRPC with SOAP:

```
use SOAP::Lite;
use SOAP::Transport::HTTP;

# Set up CGI-based SOAP server handler, with
# all calls dispatched to the 'weather' package.
my $server = SOAP::Transport::HTTP::CGI->new( )
  ->dispatch_to('weather')
  ->handle( );
```

There's much more to be said about SOAP as a more complicated yet more flexible cousin to XML-RPC, but an explanation of that is best left to another book.

—l.m.orchard

HACK #99 Creating an IM Interface

Add some Perl code here, an AOL Instant Messenger account there, and one of your favorite scraping scripts, and you have yourself an automated instant-messaging bot.

AOL Instant Messenger (AIM) isn't the most likely place you'll need to scrape data, but that doesn't mean the applications aren't fun to connect. With Perl and the *Net::AIM* module (*http://search.cpan.org/author/ARYEH/Net-AIM-1.22/*), you can have your own bot perform multiple scraping tasks at your behest.

First you'll need the *Net::AIM* library. It provides all the functions for logging into AIM and sending or receiving messages. To get a jump start on coding, check out Wired Bots (*http://www.wiredbots.com/tutorial.html*). They have some fully functional sample bots and lots of example code for working with *Net::AIM*. You'll also need an AIM screen name and password for your new assistant, along with a screen name for yourself if you don't already have one.

The Code

To show you how easy it is to add IM connectivity to your scripts, we'll modify one from "Reformatting Bugtraq Reports" [Hack #80].

Save this script as *bugbot.pl*:

```
#!/usr/bin/perl -w
use strict;
use LWP::Simple;
use HTML::TableExtract;
```

```perl
use Net::AIM;

my $aim_un = 'your AIM name';
my $aim_pw = 'your AIM password';

# the base URL of the site we are scraping and
# the URL of the page where the bugtraq list is located.
my $base_url = "http://www.security-focus.com";
my $url      = "http://www.security-focus.com/archive/1";

# get our data.
my $html_file = get($url) or die "$!\n";

# create an iso date.
my ($day, $month, $year) = (localtime)[3..5];
$year += 1900; my $date = "$year-$month-$day";

# since the data we are interested in is contained in a table,
# and the table has headers, then we can specify the headers and
# use TableExtract to grab all the data below the headers in one
# fell swoop. We want to keep the HTML code intact so that we
# can use the links in our output formats. start the parse:
my $table_extract =
   HTML::TableExtract->new(
      headers    => [qw(Date Subject Author)],
      keep_html => 1 );
$table_extract->parse($html_file);

# parse out the desired info and
# stuff into a data structure.
my @parsed_rows; my $ctr = 0;
foreach my $table ($table_extract->table_states) {
   foreach my $cols ($table->rows) {
      @$cols[0] =~ m|(\d+/\d+/\d+)|;
      my %parsed_cols = ( "date" => $1 );

      # since the subject links are in the 2nd column, parse unwanted
      # HTML and grab the anchor tags. Also, the subject links are relative,
      # so we have to expand them. I could have used URI::URL,
      # HTML::Element, HTML::Parse, etc. to do most of this as well.
      @$cols[1] =~ s/ class="[\w\s]*"//;
      @$cols[1] =~ m|(<a href="(.*)">(.*)</a>)|;
      $parsed_cols{"subject_html"} = "<a href=\"$base_url$2\">$3</a>";
      $parsed_cols{"subject_url"}  = "$base_url$2";
      $parsed_cols{"subject"}      = $3;

      # the author links are in the 3rd
      # col, so do the same thing.
      @$cols[2] =~ s/ class="[\w\s]*"//;
      @$cols[2] =~ m|(<a href="mailto:(.*@.*)">(.*)</a>)|;
      $parsed_cols{"author_html"}  = $1;
      $parsed_cols{"author_email"} = $2;
      $parsed_cols{"author"}       = $3;
```

```perl
        # put all the information into an
        # array of hashes for easy access.
        $parsed_rows[$ctr++] = \%parsed_cols;
    }
}

# create an AIM connection.
my $aim = Net::AIM->new;
$aim->newconn(Screenname=>$aim_un,Password=>$aim_pw)
               or die "Cannot connect to AIM.";
my $conn = $aim->getconn();

# set up a handler for messages.
$conn->set_handler('im_in', \&on_im);
$conn->set_handler('error', \&on_error);
print "Logged on to AIM!\n\n";
$aim->start;

# incoming.
sub on_im {

    my ($aim, $evt, $from, $to) = @_;
    my $args = $evt->args();
    ($from, my $friend, my $msg) = @$args;

    # cheaply remove HTML.
    $msg =~ s/<(.|\n)+?>//g;

    # if the user sends us a "bugtraq"
    # message, then send back our data.
    if( $msg =~ /bugtraq/ ) {

        # send each item one at a time.
        foreach my $cols (@parsed_rows)  {

            # format our scraped data.
            my $line = "$cols->{date} $cols->{subject} ".
                       "$cols->{subject_url}";

            # so as not to exceed the speed limit...
            sleep(2); $aim->send_im($from, $line);
        }
    } # give a warning if we don't know what they're saying.
    else { $aim->send_im($from, "I  only understand 'bugtraq'!"); }
}

# oops!
sub on_error {
    my ($self, $evt) = @_;
    my ($error, @stuff) = @{$evt->args()};

    # Translate error number into English.
    # then filter and print to STDERR.
```

```
    my $errstr = $evt->trans($error);
    $errstr =~ s/\$(\d+)/$stuff[$1]/ge;
    print "ERROR: $errstr\n";

}
```

Notice that inside the on_im subroutine, it checks the incoming message for the word bugtraq before proceeding. It's a good idea to set up rules like this for any kind of queries you allow, because bots should always send a message about success or failure. This is also a good way to set up a robot with multiple capabilities; perhaps your next version will also accept bugtraq, similar to, or word lookup, all built using code from within this book.

Running the Hack

Start up AOL Instant Messenger and add your new virtual screen name to your buddy list. When you run *bugbot.pl*, you should see the bot appear among your online buddies. Send a message that contains the word bugtraq, and you should get the latest security reports back, as shown in Figure 6-1.

Figure 6-1. Bugtraq security reports through IM

It's not exactly stimulating conversation, but expanding its vocabulary is simply a matter of adding further requests and responses to the script. Likewise, you're not limited by AIM; you can also use *Net::ICQ*, *Net::Jabber*, or similar modules.

—*Paul Bausch and William Eastler*

Going Beyond the Book

As much as we would have liked to deliver a 1,500-page tome, sooner or later you're going to have to think outside the confines of this book.

There are two very frustrating things about writing computer books. The first is knowing that it's unlikely anyone will revere your book as a classic and be studying your "Twenty Ways to Use Caps Lock" 50 years from now. The other frustrating thing is the fact that you can't cover as much as you'd like in the confines of one book. So, because we don't want to leave you without direction, here are some other places you can go to find scraping information, resources, and code. Onward!

Using Google and Other Search Engines

If you have a question about your code not working or figuring out what part of a site to scrape, you are of course welcome to visit the O'Reilly Hacks site at *http://hacks.oreilly.com* and participate in one of our discussions. But if that isn't enough, you can also search Google and see what you can see.

Say I want to find out if there's a Perl module for scraping Yahoo! Finance. This query gives you plenty of resources:

```
perl module "Yahoo Finance"
```

Or you might have a question about a regular expression that you can't get to work. In that case, using keywords that describe what you want can work, as in:

```
"remove html" Perl ( regex | "regular expressions" )
```

Mailing Lists

A search engine is the first place I go when I have a scraping/spidering question but can't think of the right community for it. But sometimes, if you want to debate the points of using a particular solution, or if you want an in-depth discussion of a certain module, single web pages don't work as well. In that case, you'll want to check out more community-oriented solutions. We'll list a few here.

Perl4Lib (*http://perl4lib.perl.org/*) focuses on Perl as used by librarians and information professionals. Why focus on that here? Because online libraries have some of the most extensive and well-organized information collections available on the Web, and they're only going to add more. This page features several Perl modules that deal with information collection and unique identifying information.

Speaking of Perl.org, there's a huge list of available mailing lists at *http:// lists.perl.org*. Other lists you should check out here include libwww (for discussing *LWP*) perl-xml (using Perl with XML) and www-search (a discussion group for the *WWW::Search* modules).

Web Sites

If we were to talk about web sites that deal with Perl and offer Perl resources, we could be here for days. Let me just focus on three that offer different things.

CPAN (http://www.cpan.org)
> CPAN (the Comprehensive Perl Archive Network) contains scripts, modules, source code, and binary distributions. There are also the aforementioned mailing lists and a pretty brief link list.

Perl Monks (http://www.perlmonks.org/index.pl)
> Perl Monks is a great community. On the front page, you'll see several ongoing conversations about various aspects of Perl, a "CB" channel (online chat; it takes up a very small part of the righthand column), and a list of who's currently browsing the site. There are several other areas you might find useful, including snippets (bits of Perl code used for various tasks), Questions and Answers (divided up into categories; there's a nice section on regular expressions here), and tutorials.

WebmasterWorld (http://www.webmasterworld.com)
> This might seem like an odd thing to include on this list. After all, its primary audience is webmasters. But it's here for several reasons: it has a Perl forum, extensive discussions about User-Agents and spidering (and you can learn a lot from the perspective of a webmaster), and some tools that will give you information about web pages from a spider's point of view.

Index

A

Aas, Gisle, 56
AbleShoppers, 330
absolute URLs, 38
acceptable use policies, 15–18
    consequences of violating, 17
Acceptable Use Policy (AUP), 15
Accept-Charset headers, 31
Accept-Encoding HTTP header, 45
Accept-Language headers, 31
accessing particular URLs, 27
ActiveState's ActivePerl, 26
advertisers and geotargeting, 281
aggregating data, 3, 16
AIM (AOL Instant
        Messenger), 385–388
Alexa, 188–192
    scraping competitive data, 193–194
All Consuming, 236–240, 363
    book metadata and weblog
        mentions, 237
    friends and recommendations, 237
    most-mentioned lists, 236
    personal book lists, 237
AlltheWeb.com, 164, 331, 334
AltaVista
    Prisma, 163
    search request to, 34
Amazon.com, 20
    Alexa, 188–192
    ASIN, 178, 240
    Associates account, 183

Associates sales statistics,
        publishing, 182–185
    combining information from FreeDB
        and, 194–203
        presenting results, 201–202
    customer advice, scraping, 180–182
    graphing Sales Rank, 210–213
        multiple, 213
    navigating, 226–228
    product reviews
        email alert for new, 178–180
        scraping, 176–178
    recommendations, sorting by
        rating, 185–188
    related products, 188–192
    searching for authors, 217
    Web Services
        searching code, 199
        XML and, 198
America at Work, America at Leisure
        project (Library of
        Congress), 111
Ampache, 136
AmphetaDesk, 286, 308, 364
Andromeda, 132, 136
AOL Instant Messenger
        (AIM), 385–388
Apache
    combined log format, 279
    Xerces for Java, 194
Apache::MP3 module, 132, 136
arbitrary classification systems, 19

We'd like to hear your suggestions for improving our indexes. Send email to *index@oreilly.com*.

Colophon

Our look is the result of reader comments, our own experimentation, and feedback from distribution channels. Distinctive covers complement our distinctive approach to technical topics, breathing personality and life into potentially dry subjects.

The tool on the cover of *Spidering Hacks* is a flex scraper. Flex scrapers are sometimes referred to as putty knives or push scrapers. These rugged tools are commonly used for light-duty construction or home projects, such as wallpapering, painting, or woodworking. Flex scrapers are usually three inches wide, with steel blades ground thinner than a typical putty knife to give maximum flexibility. Thus, they are the perfect choice for applying lighter compounds over broader areas and at a faster rate than putty knives. High-end flex scrapers have ergonomic handles designed to fit the hand and reduce fatigue. Just as a well-designed flex scraper gives improved blade control, so too does a well-designed spidering or scraping hack give greater control and and flexibility when gathering information from the Web and automating and speeding complex tasks.

Genevieve d'Entremont was the production editor for *Spidering Hacks*. Brian Sawyer was the copyeditor. Matt Hutchinson proofread the book. Derek Di Matteo, Marlowe Shaeffer, and Claire Cloutier provided quality control. Julie Hawks wrote the index.

Emma Colby designed the cover of this book, based on a series design by Edie Freedman. The cover image is an original photograph by Emma Colby. Emma Colby produced the cover layout with QuarkXPress 4.1 using Adobe's Helvetica Neue and ITC Garamond fonts.

David Futato designed the interior layout. This book was converted from Microsoft Word to FrameMaker 5.5.6 by Andrew Savikas. The text font is Linotype Birka; the heading font is Adobe Helvetica Neue Condensed; and the code font is LucasFont's TheSans Mono Condensed. The illustrations that appear in the book were produced by Robert Romano and Jessamyn Read using Macromedia FreeHand 9 and Adobe Photoshop 6. This colophon was written by Derek Di Matteo.

Related Titles Available from O'Reilly

Hacks

Amazon Hacks

eBay Hacks

Google Hacks

Linux Server Hacks

Mac OS X Hacks

TiVo Hacks

WIndows XP Hacks

Wireless Hacks

Keep in touch with O'Reilly

1. Download examples from our books

To find example files for a book, go to:

www.oreilly.com/catalog

select the book, and follow the "Examples" link.

2. Register your O'Reilly books

Register your book at *register.oreilly.com*

Why register your books? Once you've registered your O'Reilly books you can:

- Win O'Reilly books, T-shirts or discount coupons in our monthly drawing.
- Get special offers available only to registered O'Reilly customers.
- Get catalogs announcing new books (US and UK only).
- Get email notification of new editions of the O'Reilly books you own.

3. Join our email lists

Sign up to get topic-specific email announcements of new books and conferences, special offers, and O'Reilly Network technology newsletters at:

elists.oreilly.com

It's easy to customize your free elists subscription so you'll get exactly the O'Reilly news you want.

4. Get the latest news, tips, and tools

http://www.oreilly.com

- "Top 100 Sites on the Web"—PC Magazine
- CIO Magazine's Web Business 50 Awards

Our web site contains a library of comprehensive product information (including book excerpts and tables of contents), downloadable software, background articles, interviews with technology leaders, links to relevant sites, book cover art, and more.

5. Work for O'Reilly

Check out our web site for current employment opportunities:

jobs.oreilly.com

6. Contact us

O'Reilly & Associates, Inc.
1005 Gravenstein Hwy North
Sebastopol, CA 95472 USA

TEL: 707-827-7000 or 800-998-9938
(6am to 5pm PST)

FAX: 707-829-0104

order@oreilly.com
For answers to problems regarding your order or our products.
To place a book order online, visit:

www.oreilly.com/order_new

catalog@oreilly.com
To request a copy of our latest catalog.

booktech@oreilly.com
For book content technical questions or corrections.

corporate@oreilly.com
For educational, library, government, and corporate sales.

proposals@oreilly.com
To submit new book proposals to our editors and product managers.

international@oreilly.com
For information about our international distributors or translation queries. For a list of our distributors outside of North America check out:

international.oreilly.com/distributors.html

adoption@oreilly.com
For information about academic use of O'Reilly books, visit:

academic.oreilly.com

O'REILLY®

Our books are available at most retail and online bookstores.
To order direct: 1-800-998-9938 • *order@oreilly.com* • *www.oreilly.com*
Online editions of most O'Reilly titles are available by subscription at *safari.oreilly.com*